PE HIS HEAD
DU CHATEAU
MONTJOIE
ESCAPING FROM PRISON

MASSON

LEIRIS

CAILLOIS

BATAILLE

# THE
# SAC

THE INTERNAL PAPERS OF THE SECRET SOCIETY OF ACÉPHALE
AND LECTURES TO THE COLLEGE OF SOCIOLOGY

EDITED AND INTRODUCED BY
MARINA GALLETTI AND ALASTAIR BROTCHIE

TRANSLATIONS BY NATASHA LEHRER, JOHN HARMAN, MEYER BARASH

ATLAS PRESS LONDON MMXVII

# RED
# CONSPIRACY

GEORGES BATAILLE

WITH ADDITIONAL TEXTS BY ROGER CAILLOIS, PIERRE KLOSSOWSKI, MICHEL LEIRIS

AND BY GEORGES AMBROSINO, PIERRE ANDLER, MICHEL CARROUGES, JACQUES CHAVY, JEAN DAUTRY, HENRI DUBIEF, HENRI DUSSAT, IMRE KELEMEN, JEAN ROLLIN, PATRICK WALDBERG

AND WITH DRAWINGS BY ANDRÉ MASSON

# CONTENTS



---

*Translations:* The texts by the Secret Society of Acéphale, all marked with a ●, and ○29, Georges Bataille, "What we undertook a few months ago...", are translated by Natasha Lehrer. ○91, Roger Caillois, "Theory of the Festival", is translated by Meyer Barash. The remaining translations, including the texts by Marina Galletti, are by John Harman.

# I

## (1924), 1929 – March 1936



# II

## April 1936 – January 1937



# III

## February 1937 – August 1937

ACÉPHALE 3/4



THE COLLEGE OF SOCIOLOGY



## IV

September 1937 – December 1937



THE SECRET SOCIETY OF ACÉPHALE

## V

### January 1938 – August 1938



### THE SECRET SOCIETY OF ACÉPHALE



### THE COLLEGE OF SOCIOLOGY



## VI

### September 1938 – October 1938

## THE SECRET SOCIETY OF ACÉPHALE



## THE COLLEGE OF SOCIOLOGY



# VII

## October 1938 – May 1939



## THE SECRET SOCIETY OF ACÉPHALE

The texts published here under the rubric "College of Sociology" chiefly consist of lectures given to the Collège de Sociologie in Paris between November 1937 and June 1939. They were first collected together by Denis Hollier in *Le Collège de Sociologie*, published by Gallimard in 1979 and again in 1995. We are pleased to acknowledge our debt to his indispensable research.

Cross-references to the translated texts are indicated by a round bullet followed by the text number as listed in the contents. A black bullet indicates the text is from the *Acéphale* journal, grey from the Society, white from the College. Some of the texts have numbered paragraphs, and these are indicated by a §. Various abbreviations are used in the text and notes: AS = *L'Apprenti sorcier*, edited by Marina Galletti, CCD = *Cercle communiste démocratique*, CdeS = the various editions (see bibliography) of *Le Collège de Sociologie*, edited by Denis Hollier, *NRF* = the *Nouvelle revue française* and OC = the various volumes of Georges Bataille's *Œuvres complètes*. The French word *conscience*, which means both "conscience" and "consciousness", is italicised in the texts that follow when both meanings are intended, or when the meaning is ambiguous.

The publisher would like to thank the Centre National du Livre and the Burgess Programme at the Institut Français in London for grants towards the translations in this book, which would have been impossible without their assistance.

# PREFACE

This book was originally intended to be two books: a selection of the lectures given by Georges Bataille and his closest associates to the College of Sociology, edited by Alastair Brotchie, and a volume by Marina Galletti presenting the papers of the secret society of Acéphale that she had discovered. As we discussed these joint projects it gradually became inevitable that they should merge into one volume, so close were the connections between these groups — in fact Bataille himself described the College as the public face of the secret society.[1] We therefore came to the conclusion that combining the original two books would allow these connections to be appreciated for the first time, since no such volume has appeared in French.

However, Bataille was also involved in a third initiative during this period, namely the publication of the journal *Acéphale*, a project which preceded the other two, and influenced both. So we decided to include a selection of texts from this also. The finished book thus presents a selection of texts by Bataille and his closest friends that we believe accurately reflects their ideas at a particularly tumultuous and significant period, both for themselves and society in general, in the last few years before Europe was gripped by total war.

The texts included here show how Bataille was struggling towards an analysis, principally through the College, of what he saw as the essential problems of human life, and formulating an attempt to act upon this analysis through a secret "order", Acéphale. Bataille's writings grapple not only with seemingly intractable existential issues, but also gradually reveal a personal narrative of quite remarkable power and tenacity.

Our decision to combine the two books means that in the critical commentaries that follow, the texts elucidating Acéphale, both the society and the journal, have been written by Marina Galletti, and those concerning the College by Alastair Brotchie; the selection of both sets of texts have been made in the same way. The *Chronology* of events, intended to situate these texts firmly in their times, was a collaboration, although the parts relating directly to Acéphale are Marina Galletti's.[2] Both the lectures to the College and the papers of the Society were originally published in superbly comprehensive academic editions, by Denis Hollier and Marina Galletti respectively.[3] We are deeply indebted to these works, in particular to the ground-breaking scholarship of Denis Hollier, without which this book would not have been possible. It is our aim here, however, to make these texts more accessible to a general readership by extracting them from this learned matrix, because these eloquent cries of defiance confront problems that are entirely relevant to present times.

The 1930s were of course dominated by the rise of Hitler and the ideology of the Nazi Party. Fascism stalked Europe, a new World War appeared inevitable, and politics seemed powerless to avert it. The European democracies were enfeebled, no more so than when they stood by and watched the destruction of the Spanish Republic. Meanwhile, Soviet Communism was hopelessly compromised by Stalinism, the left as a whole was split and ineffectual and the French right was poised for outright collaboration. Nazism had seized the moment, propelled by a mythology of Blood, Iron, Fatherland and Volk.

The Society of Acéphale and the College of Sociology were in fact the culmination of Bataille's years of opposition to the "tricephalous monster" of Fascism, Communism and Christianity. Both were intended to embody a "moral" revolution within a community, a morality that would have three great exemplars: Sade, Kierkegaard and Nietzsche. Their creation marked the final stages on a strange itinerary, from what began as an almost conventional political opposition to Fascism in the early Thirties, and ended with torchlit ceremonies in a forest at night beneath a tree that had been struck by lightning. The texts in this book go a long way to explaining this journey of Bataille's. To many they will feel entirely relevant today, when the monolithic force of unrestrained capital is homogenising the world in its own image, fuelled by the illusory rise to power of the so-called populist right — illusory because those that have brought it to power will inevitably allow this power to be seized by an ever more limited elite.

In this way we can see, in the *Chronology* that follows, that Bataille's activism was initially concentrated in leftist politics, within the anti-Stalinist Democratic Communist Circle (CCD), whose journal *La Critique sociale* published his essay, "The Psychological Structure of Fascism". This was followed by his activities in Contre-Attaque (Counter-Attack), an organisation formed primarily by the groups around Bataille (mostly associated with the CCD), and André Breton (the Surrealists and their fellow travellers). Contre-Attaque defined itself as an anti-Communist opposition to Fascism, ●14 §5, but it was also anti-capitalist, anti-parliamentarian and anti-Christian. Its brief existence can be traced in the *Chronology* between April 1935 and September 1936. Bataille threw himself into this group whole-heartedly, despite already having serious reservations about the efficacy of political action. Its collapse in acrimony confirmed for him the impossibility of such action. The various groups he went on to form, in particular the Society and the College, were in part intended to pursue this opposition by other means, but also to align these aims with ideas Bataille had outlined in his earlier writings, explored in Marina Galletti's introduction below. *Acéphale* the journal, and Acéphale the secret society, came first, though their roots may be found in ideas dating back to the early 1920s.

*Acknowledgements.* Many people have assisted us with this book and we wish very much to offer our thanks. We especially thank Julie Bataille for permission to print Bataille's Acéphale texts, and we reiterate the assertion of our debt to the research of Denis Hollier. Likewise our thanks to Chris Allen, for extensive copy-editing and proof-reading; to Diego Masson, for his great generosity and assistance; to Jane England for the photo-booth photographs of Masson on p.99; to Philippe Blanc for his generous help and suggestions, and for rooting out the photograph of Klossowski; from the Bibliothèque Nationale: the president, Laurence Engel; Guillaume Fau, chief conservator of manuscripts; Anne Verdure-Mary of the Department of Manuscripts; Stephen Matthew of Indiana University Press; Claudine Frank; from Gallimard, for their endless patience: Nathalie Beul, Margot Miriel and Anne-Solange Noble. Finally, Véronique Ambrosino, Daniel and Martin Andler, Nicola Apicella, Michèle Boucheix Bergstrasser, Jean-Marc Chavy and Colette Peyrelevade, Antoine Chenon, Clément Chéroux, Jean-Jacques Dautry, Estelle Delvolvé, Michel Fani, Serge Fournié, Élisabeth Girard, Françoise Kite, Jean-François Louette, Cécile Moscovitz, Benoît Puttermans, Dominique Rabourdin, Jacqueline Risset, Catherine Roux Lanier, Sara Svolacchia, Emmanuel Tibloux, Eric Walbecq and Corinne Waldberg.

*Marina Galletti & Alastair Brotchie*

III

MARINA GALLETTI

# *The Secret Society of Acéphale: "A Community of the Heart"*

## THE REDISCOVERY OF ACÉPHALE

For a long time almost nothing was known of the secret society of Acéphale, even though, according to Maurice Blanchot, for Bataille it was "the only group that mattered".[1] Towards the end of the Seventies, around when Denis Hollier's book *Le Collège de Sociologie* emerged as the standard reference work for the study of the communities created by Bataille in the 1930s, my request for a telephone interview with the physicist Georges Ambrosino, an ex-member of Acéphale, came to nought, despite his initially warm reaction to my research. Pierre Klossowski had been asked to authorise the interview and must have refused to give his approval, and so Ambrosino's telephone went unanswered. As Michel Camus wrote in 1995, all those who were a part of Acéphale "have been, and remain, obstinately silent".[2]

Yet there were exceptions. Patrick Waldberg denounced the mysticism of "joy in the face of death" in 1943, and as early as 1945 Roger Caillois revealed the shocking proposal for a human sacrifice which, he said, the participants had thought would "consecrate their cause and for ever ensure their fidelity to it".[3] Michel Fardoulis-Lagrange, a friend of Bataille's in later life, even went so far as to put a name to the willing sacrificial victim, that of Michel Leiris.[4] Otherwise, those who were still alive and who had been close to Bataille never ceased to maintain that they knew nothing of the group. Leiris, meanwhile, confirmed the ritualistic aspects of Acéphale,[5] and André Masson the existence of ceremonies in the forest of Marly. Masson also clarified the distinction between the journal *Acéphale*, created by "an extremely small group, but not secret", of which he was a member, and the secret society of Acéphale, founded "some time afterwards" and in which his only involvement came after it had ended, when André Breton asked him to make a sculpture of the headless figure of the Acéphale for the Paris Surrealist Exhibition of 1947 (which he declined to do).[6]

The focal point of any study of Acéphale should have been Bataille's own "History of a Secret Society", which he announced as one of the chapters in a volume to be called

*Left:* André Masson, *The Crucified Christ*, etching from *Sacrifices*, 1936.

*L'Amitié*, part of a proposed collective work called the *Atheological Summa*. But this "History" has never been found, there is no text with this title in his *Œuvres complètes*,[7] nor among his manuscripts deposited in the Bibliothèque Nationale in Paris. All we have from him is the journal *Acéphale*, which from 1936 to 1939 partly expressed the aims of the Society, and his "Autobiographical Note", written many years after the group had broken up, which revealed the boundless ambitions he had had for it at its formation. Then he had envisaged it as pursuing "religious, but anti-Christian, essentially Nietzschean aims",[8] although in the same note Bataille acknowledged the impulsive character of this enterprise, and in a later fragment even dismissed its intentions as being purely comic. Yet although Acéphale was a community that was "short-lived of necessity, essentially unviable"[9] and hence doomed to failure, it never ceased to obsess Bataille, and he later wrote that its failure had led directly to the *Atheological Summa*. In this context, in 1959-60 — when he republished *Guilty*, a diary written just after Acéphale broke up and which was to have been a part of the *Summa* — Bataille recalled the pseudonym of "Dianus, the name of a great Roman god"[10] that he had used in 1940 for an extract from *Guilty* published in a periodical. It had been one of a number of names for a new magazine he had proposed to Caillois in July 1939, soon after the final lecture at the College, but it must especially have called to mind those night-time meditations in the ancient forest of Cruye at the foot of a great oak tree decapitated by lightning, which the sculptor Isabelle Waldberg evoked for me in her studio in the rue Larrey.[11]

These mysterious rites, only an inkling of which could be gleaned from the brief section in Bataille's complete works called "Relating to Acéphale", celebrated the sacrifice of the head in all its variant forms: from the death of God as proclaimed by Nietzsche, to the destruction of the celestial gods claimed by National Socialism. Considered specifically as a linking of religion and politics, they were also a consecration of regicide, a continuation of the celebration of Louis XVI's execution proposed by Contre-Attaque. Finally, they signified the desire to go beyond the struggle initiated by Surrealism against the triad of father, fatherland and all forms of patronage.

Decapitation, a rite whose revolutionary intentions had been signalled within Contre-Attaque by Marcel Jean's drawing of a calf's head on a plate (p.105), was transposed by Acéphale to a site of great consequence in the history of France, albeit long forgotten, where, not far from the stricken tree, these "murderers of God" pledged to bequeath their existence to the empire of death "in such a way that it makes life into a power and an eruption", ●41. Acéphale's regicidal ceremonies took place in the ruins of the ancient fortress of Montjoie, the very place of myth where the conversion of the first king of France, Clovis I, to Christianity established the meeting of military and religious might, a concentration of power that Bataille had described in his essay "The Psychological

Structure of Fascism". This then was where the battle-cry of "Montjoie", so celebrated in the *Chanson de Roland*,[12] was heard for the first time. Acéphale would lay claim to Montjoie from 1937, yet not in the name of this "pious and monarchical"[13] version of the Middle Ages. Instead Bataille championed another, more archaic, more impious and bloodier version that was personified by Gilles de Rais, the very incarnation of the feudal principle of "expenditure", but also a descendant of the first knights, the Germanic berserkers Dumézil described as initiates of the god Odin.[14] It was also the age of the "chansons de geste", the verse tales of heroic deeds which had so fascinated Bataille since his reading of Léon Gautier's *La Chevalerie* that his thesis at the École Nationale des Chartes had been written on "The Order of Knighthood, A Tale in Verse from the 13th Century". In the late Forties he commented[15] that the ritual of a knight's "dubbing", the "blow to the neck of the initiate", was a sort of "mystical decapitation" intended to bring about "a change of personality".[16] All of these elements would find their counterparts in the secret society.

For Bataille, his Dianus pseudonym above all "corresponded to the religious and paradoxical atmosphere"[17] at the time of the beginnings of Acéphale. In the late Fifities he associated its origins with his earlier studies of the history of religion as it related to secret societies in "primitive" societies, and to the theory of sacrifice put forward by Durkheim, Mauss and Hubert. Then too Bataille noted the connection with Surrealism, recalling in *Critique*[18] that according to Maurice Nadeau the group was "a sect of initiates",[19] and that Monnerot had called it a "social set, joined together by chance, without obligation or prohibitions [...] based on elective affinities".[20]

Shortly before Bataille's death, at the end of October 1960, Acéphale was still so urgent a preoccupation for him that a preliminary "meeting between a few of us" (namely Ambrosino, Leiris, Waldberg and a new adept, Jacques Pimpaneau) was proposed, prior to a more general gathering of those who had been involved with the group.[21] Such a proposal speaks volumes for the persistent validity of the sacred, and of the continuing "necessity" for what had been at stake in Acéphale, even if it was "both urgent and impossible to satisfy" owing to the "loss of any inclination for sacrifice"[22] in contemporary society.

Yet all of this, in the words of Michel Camus, "was only the visible part [of Acéphale], everything else was invisible". The situation was further complicated by the fact that some, "such as Isabelle Waldberg, Georges Ambrosino and Patrick Waldberg, participated with Georges Bataille in the elaboration of the myth of the Acéphale [...] but did not write for the journal. Whereas others, who did collaborate on the journal, did not necessarily belong to the group of initiates."[23]

The turning point in my attempts at reconstructing the history of the group came in the early Nineties when a file resurfaced containing texts written by members of the

Society which had belonged to the poet Jean Rollin, one of its adepts. Dominique Rabourdin, with whom I had come into contact through Jean-Pierre Le Bouler, a Bataille specialist, had published one of these documents, "Twenty Propositions on the Death of God" (see ●65). He put the others at my disposal, and later introduced me to Rollin. At about the same time I visited Marie Tourrès in Saint-Germain-en-Laye, and she gave me copies of Bataille's letters to Pierre Kaan, some of which had appeared in her master's thesis on the left-wing review, *La Critique sociale*.[24]

I had known André Barell since the Eighties. A chemist in the Thirties, he had formed a small group called ABC, with two other members both of the CCD and Acéphale, Ambrosino and the mathematician René Chenon. I also made contact with Jacques Chavy, a decorator, who had not only been a member of the Society but was also the legal representative for two of the issues of *Acéphale*. Meetings with Barell and Chavy resulted in a lot of material on Bataille, but strangely little on Acéphale. This was because Barell was not an initiate of the group, but also because Chavy insisted on maintaining an ironical attitude that reduced everything we spoke about to insignificance. It took me a while to understand that this was a mask that allowed him to keep a secret which was as meaningful to him then as it had been originally. Even so, for many years, I established a ritual of meeting up with Chavy and Barell at least once a year, Barell at his apartment at 84 rue Michel-Ange in the 16th *arrondissement*, and Chavy in a café, usually the Ruc, near the Bibliothèque Nationale, where Bataille had been a regular visitor. Two other members of Acéphale gave me interviews, the historian Henri Dubief, whom I went to see at Cachan in the south of Paris, and the writer Michel Koch, whom I met several times in the apartment where I stayed in the rue de la Montagne Sainte-Geneviève. Dubief was informative on the beginnings of the group, and Koch on the end period of Acéphale.

Other contacts were also established, each of which proved essential, in their own way, to reconstructing the history of the secret society, as well as what preceded and followed it: René Lefeuvre, to discuss the magazine *Masses*; Jean Lescure, André Frénaud and Pierre Prévost, in relation to the Socratic College; Flora Acker, the widow of Adolphe Acker, an old member of Contre-Attaque; Charles Ronsac, a close friend of Boris Souvarine whom I interviewed in November 1993, just before making contact with Jean-Louis Panné, the author of Souvarine's biography; and finally Michel Pastoureau, another member of Contre-Attaque, Daniel Guérin and Maurice Nadeau.

However, it was my meeting with Pierre Andler in 1993 which proved decisive for the rediscovery of Acéphale. The first time we met he said that he could not tell me everything, but what he could tell me would be faithful to what the secret society had been. On his suggestion I arranged a meeting with him and Chavy at the Closerie des Lilas (Andler then suggested we move to a less noisy café nearby, but I don't remember its name). I am unsure whether this meeting had the effect of reviving in them the excitement they had shared as fellow-conspirators in Acéphale, but this book is the result of that meeting. Both brought documents with them: Chavy's were papers relating to Contre-Attaque, while Andler's were the "Creation of the 'Internal Journal'", ●14, and also some Acéphale documents that had been entrusted to him by another adept, Imre Kelemen, before he returned to Hungary. As we left the café, Andler told me of the existence of other papers, and Chavy abandoned his reticence, revealing what he had always concealed from me, that he too had a file of Acéphale documents.

A new phase thus began: putting all these papers in order. This became the first book, entirely overseen by Andler, which was published in Rome in 1995 under the title *Georges Bataille, Contre-attaques*. It gathered together the initial documents, which illustrated Bataille's journey, in the years of the growing menace of Fascism, through the CCD and Contre-Attaque, and after the failure of this latter group, his involvement with Acéphale.

This was only a first step though. I sent my book to Michel Waldberg, who suggested that I publish it in Paris with La Différence, with the addition of papers belonging to his parents, Isabelle and Patrick Waldberg. In the mean time, Alfredo Salsano suggested bringing together the *Acéphale* texts and those of the Society under the title *La congiura sacra*. This book was published in Turin in 1997 by Bollati Boringhieri, with an introduction by the philosopher Roberto Esposito. It included the Acéphale texts already published in *Contre-attaques*, Chavy's documents, three texts by Jean Dautry found by his son Jean-Jacques, the papers from Michel Waldberg, Ambrosino's letters to Patrick Waldberg from the Librairie Jacques Doucet (which Esther Ambrosino only authorised after reading them), as well as new texts from Andler found during my visits to his home in Recloses near Fontainebleau.

In 1995, towards the end of one of these visits, Andler told me, on Fontainebleau station, that this would be the last time: he bid me a final goodbye as I got on the train back to Paris. In the brief, silent exchange of glances that followed, numerous questions rushed into my mind, but my emotions prevented me from putting them into words... This meeting, was it perhaps a last mark of friendship made under the seal of the death he felt was imminent? Again, no words. The next moment, pressed up against the hermetically sealed window of my compartment, I could only reply with a wave of the hand. Then his silhouette, motionless on the platform, grew more indistinct until it was no more than a black shape... A while afterwards, in 1999, *L'Apprenti sorcier* came out from La Différence, and this too included previously unpublished texts: those found by Lia Andler after the death of Pierre and sent to me via Claudine Frank, as well as the papers of Henri Dussat kept by his adopted daughter, Michèle Boucheix Bergstrasser, and others by Dautry.

The present edition, which in certain respects puts forward a new interpretation of these texts, does not include all the Acéphale documents from *L'Apprenti sorcier*. It does, however, contain some found since that book was published: by adepts responding to Bataille's writings, and two texts I published in journals, "The Constitution of the Self is Highly Paradoxical", ●11, by Ambrosino,[25] and one of Bataille's letters to Louis Couturier (Michel Carrouges), ●87,[26] found by his son, Jean-Louis. My reading of the correspondence between Chavy and Dussat, which Claudine Frank is preparing for publication, has also been extremely helpful for this book.

Various other documents that must have existed are still missing, however, in particular the reports of some of the sessional meetings, and the initiation documents of many of the adepts (those not among the signatories to ●41), including that for Rollin. He told me he was initiated in November 1937,[27] probably by Patrick Waldberg, in a ceremony involving the pact of blood, a dagger and a blindfold. The corresponding document is also lost for the Japanese artist Taro Okamoto, whose rite was enacted in 1937, also with a pact of blood[28] and probably preceded by the same "oath of silence" to which Waldberg had submitted, ●68, on the balcony of the building where Bataille lived at 76 *bis* rue de Rennes. This demonstration of commitment to the Society could take various forms. Michel Koch told me that he signed his pledge in a taxi at the Place de la Concorde in the presence of Bataille and Ambrosino.[29] Also missing is the "document intended for the judiciary" which Bataille, according to Caillois, had obtained from the consenting victim of their proposed human sacrifice, in order to establish the innocence of the executioner who would carry it out.[30]

## THE ORIGINS OF ACÉPHALE

The birth of the secret society of Acéphale cannot be detached from the history of Contre-Attaque, the group whose formation in 1935 marked the reconciliation of Bataille and Breton around a common goal: to make the struggle against the threat of Fascism, then led in France by the Popular Front, more effective by forming a Popular Front of the streets. This brief experiment met with a double failure. On the one hand, it showed that left-wing politics was not up to the task of impeding the rise of Fascism and, on the other, it demonstrated the inability of the groups involved — Bataille's faction within Souvarine's CCD, the October group and Breton's Surrealists — to join together. Acéphale refused to follow Contre-Attaque on the first point by turning its back on direct political action, and modified its approach to the second, by radically reinforcing the initiatory structure this "union of revolutionary intellectuals" had inherited from Surrealism.

Moreover, in light of the documents gathered here, Contre-Attaque could even be seen as something of a parenthesis, since Acéphale was also the culmination of earlier preoccupations of Bataille's. In the mid-1920s, he and Leiris, Masson and Nicolai Bakhtin, brother of Mikhail, had had the idea of founding an "Orphic and Nietzschean secret society", ●14 §10. This was the first version of the secret society, but neither Leiris nor Masson ever spoke of it, and the inaccessibility of Bakhtin's papers makes further comment impossible. Nevertheless, ●14 does tell us what Leiris had suggested calling this community: Judas. The name of the traitorous apostle often recurs in Leiris's work in different contexts,[31] and it echoes too from the very heart of Acéphale in a text of Bataille's from 1937, ●35.

As for Orphism — which made Dionysus its central divinity, or, according to another version of the myth, put this god in opposition to the Apollonian Orpheus — it provided Bataille with the model of a heterodox initiatory sect dedicated to subverting the established order, whether religious or political, from within. The idea may well have come from Leiris who, as early as 1924, had noted in his *Journal*:[32] "Study carefully all the cosmogonies of the past". If we accept Marcel Détienne's thesis, that "Dionysism makes it possible to escape the human condition from below by becoming bestial [...], while Orphism allows a similar escape from above towards the divine",[33] then it could be said that Acéphale was intended to operate specifically from the Orphic to the Dionysiac, from the celestial world to that of base matter. Dionysism was still present in contemporary religious forms, as Henri Jeanmaire[34] noted, as exemplified by the Zar of Ethiopia, a form of spirit possession studied by Leiris himself.

It was the philosophy of Nietzsche, however, which had originally brought these four conspirators together. Bakhtin first read *The Birth of Tragedy* at the age of eleven; Leiris reviewed Chestov's *The Idea of Good in Tolstoy and Nietzsche* in 1925, a work that Bataille had co-translated;[35] whilst for Masson Nietzsche was a formative encounter he described as "the Great Awakening", and as having "fallen from heaven to bring him into the world".[36] Bataille, for his part, would write *For Nietzsche* in 1945, although he had first read his works in 1917.[37] Moreover, upon reading *Beyond Good and Evil* in 1922 he concluded "I simply thought that there was nothing left for me to write".[38]

The complicity between Bataille and Masson, based upon this shared admiration for Nietzsche, was first manifested in the illustrations created by Masson for Bataille's clandestinely published early erotic fictions. It was deepened by the various affiliations which connected the writings of the one to the pictorial work of the other, and in the Thirties it became a real communion of understanding.[39] The fruits of this collaboration included the texts Bataille wrote or completed in 1935 in Tossa de Mar, the small Spanish fishing village where Masson had settled in 1934: his novel *Blue of Noon*, which he dedicated to Masson, the brief diary *Les Présages*, whose title is a tribute to the 1933 ballet of this name by Masson and Léonide Massine, and above all their joint creation, in April 1936, of the journal *Acéphale*. "What I have thought and what I have put forward, I have not thought or put forward on my own," wrote Bataille in "The Sacred Conspiracy", ●1, the first text in this journal, and which was written in Tossa de Mar.

In English, an acephal simply means a creature without a head, and such a being first appeared in Bataille's work in an article he published in 1930 in *Documents*, "Base Materialism and Gnosticism",[40] which was illustrated with a Gnostic seal depicting a headless god. The theme of the acephal, however, may be detected even earlier in Bataille's works, in texts written in the 1920s, such as this description of the pineal eye: "The [pineal] eye is located in the centre and at the top of the skull, and as it opens on to the incandescent sun so as to look at it with all its solitary strangeness [...] it is blinded, as in consumption or in a fever that devours the whole being, or more specifically, the head."[41] But around this time Masson had also depicted an acephalous man with his head burnt away by the sun in his painting *Man*, which although now lost, was described by Artaud in his first book.[42] It is not at all surprising therefore that the acephalous man, conceived by Bataille as a representation of the "leaderless crowd" and as the image of an existence in a "Universe where God is dead", ●14 §11, should come to be visualised by Masson. His drawing for the cover of *Acéphale* depicted a mythical figure fit to represent the new moral community. In Masson's many variations on this figure, the Acéphale at times assumes the guise of Zarathustra, Dionysus (p.186) or the Minotaur (p.160, the bull of Numantia, a reference explained below); it also appears as a bicephalous beast, part goat and part bull (p.190), or even, after acquiring a head made up of a hammer and sickle, finds itself launched into the struggle against Spanish Fascism (p.34). Masson first gave this figure form in an "automatic" drawing that depicted a beheaded man, standing with legs apart, with the instrument of sacrifice and self-mutilation in his left hand, and in his right "the flaming heart of the Christians, or a grenade; or even the plucked-out heart of Dionysus, a grenade born of the blood of this same god [...] there are two stars on his chest and on the stomach a spiral [...], that special example of a maze that can only be followed in one direction and which is only found in archaeological sites in ancient Babylonia, where it represents the use of the intestines for reading omens."[43] In place of the genitalia was a skull.

Certain underlying concepts of the secret society of Acéphale make their first appearance in two publications by Bataille from 1936, both in collaboration with Masson. The first was the small collection of text and images, *Montserrat*, which relates the ecstasy experienced by Masson in 1934 "during the night of the *Landscape of Wonders*" (and re-

*Right*: Gnostic seal from the 3rd/4th century: Acephalic god surmounted by two animal heads.

experienced by Bataille and Masson together in 1935, see p.100, *8 to 12 May*). This event was recalled in Masson's drawing overleaf, for the second issue of *Acéphale*. Here the headless man is delivered to the vertigo of the abyss of heaven, with his right foot planted on the summit of the mountain of Montserrat, while the left descends into a "sea of clouds". Bataille's contribution to *Montserrat*, entitled "Blue of Noon" (not the novel of the same name), introduced an even more complex perspective and one that was reminiscent of the pineal eye that signified the possibility of "vertical" as opposed to normal vision, and thus the conflicting urges of humanity: ascension towards spiritual light, or the abject descent into base matter. Bataille later added to *Montserrat* a further text, set in Mexico, which he sent to Masson in a letter. In "Calaveras", the "ecstatic hilarity brought on by the proximity to death"[44] of the local populace is brought to the boil both by the carnival of the Mexican Day of the Dead and by the potent images in Eisenstein's documentary *¡Que viva México!* The implication was that revolutionary action may proceed from the exhilaration of the festival, which was the opposite in every way to the sombre mortuary symbolism of Fascism.

The second of these two publications was *Sacrifices*, an album of five etchings begun by Masson in 1931-2 on the theme of "gods that die" (*Mithras, Orpheus, The Crucified*

André Masson, *Montserrat*, drawing from *Acéphale* 2.

*Christ*, *The Minotaur*, *Osiris*), and accompanied by Bataille's text of 1933, "Sacrifices", which was originally entitled "Death is in One Sense a Deception". While apparently unrelated to Masson's engravings, this text contrasts the reality of the logical structure of the "abstract self" with the "revelation of the *me* that dies" that "presumes the sovereignty of individual being at the moment when it is projected into the unreal time of death. [...] and consequently attains the same state of lacerating subversion as the *god* that dies."[45] Bataille's interest in the "darkest Greek myths"[46] was shared by Masson, and influenced the choice of name for the Surrealist journal *Minotaure*. Along with *The Minotaur* in *Sacrifices*, another etching depicts *The Crucified Christ* with the head of a donkey, according to the Gnostic tradition with which both Masson and Bataille were familiar. He is surrounded by "three ecstatic women. One of them, naked, crouches down and kisses his foot, another drinks the blood that flows from the wound in Christ's side, while the third, also naked, collects it in a bowl".[47] This image resembles similar meditations undertaken within Acéphale, such as ●43, and also echoes another passage in Bataille's text:

> Christian meditation before the cross was no longer rejected with ordinary hostility, but undertaken with a total hostility that called for hand-to-hand combat with the cross. As such it must, and can be lived as the death of the *me*, not in the form of respectful adoration but with a hunger for sadistic ecstasy, and the impulsiveness of a *blind* madness which alone accedes to the *passion* of a pure imperative.[48]

It appears to have been an established practice for new members of Acéphale to write an autobiographical account of how they came to the decision to join the group. At least three such accounts survive, ●15 being one of them. Dussat's account remains unpublished, but it does reveal that Bataille's "Sacrifices" (a typescript of which circulated among adepts and sympathisers) was the text whose revelatory character attached more existential concerns to Bataille's theoretical writings in *La Critique sociale*. Dussat wrote: "The clear revelation I had of what would become the very substance of our common life, the subject of our individual and collective steps, [...] came about by reading various articles signed by Georges Bataille which appeared in *La Critique sociale*. A little later I read 'Sacrifices'. All this was, without question, of the utmost importance to me. This is the moment and the place to say of Bataille that [...] it was he more than anyone who helped us to find our path."[49]

Together with the project of the first secret society and the text of "Sacrifices", the document "Creation of the 'Internal Journal'", ●14, proposed an internal diary for Acéphale, an ongoing collection of the adepts' writings. It also singled out one particular

*"In the course of the ecstatic vision the object is finally revealed…*

*as catastrophe, but neither as God nor as nothingness…*

*the object that love, incapable of freeing itself except by external means, demands in order to give voice to the cry of lacerated existence."*

*Left:* André Masson, *Mithras*, etching from *Sacrifices*, 1936, from *Acéphale* 1. The reciprocal understanding between Masson's drawings and Bataille's text was underlined by the publicity announcement in which Masson's depiction of bloody sacrifice was captioned with the extract from Bataille's text above.

text of Bataille's from *La Critique sociale* for the attention of the members of the Society, and this was the one which more than any other marked out the new direction that would preoccupy Bataille until the end of his life. It was also the text which, in the post-war period, he hoped might become the lever that could precipitate the overthrow of the capitalist economy: "The Notion of Expenditure".

Published in 1933 in the September issue of the journal, and accompanied by a preliminary note from the editorial board in which they distanced themselves from its arguments, "The Notion of Expenditure" was, as Barell told me, "the text that made Bataille known".[50] Years afterwards it remained much admired by the members of Acéphale for whom it served as both guide and compass. Dussat alluded to it in his autobiographical text; Koch reminded me of its importance in 1995; Klossowski "unreservedly agreed"[51] with it; and Ambrosino collaborated with Bataille after the war on its re-elaboration in *The Accursed Share*, a book Chenon considered to be "a contribution of the utmost importance".[52]

"The Notion of Expenditure" is primarily a theoretical text which proposes that the central function within any social structure is one of unproductive expenditure. Bataille was prompted by two studies by Marcel Mauss, *Sacrifice, Its Nature and Function*, written in collaboration with Henri Hubert, and especially *The Gift*, his study of "potlatch", which Bataille had read "around 1925", soon after it was published.[53] In this work Mauss refuted traditional ideas of the origins of economy, in particular barter, which had long been seen as the original form of exchange. Instead he identified a "system of total prestation" as the mode of exchange in archaic societies, a prestation being, according to the *OED*, "the performance of something promised". The communities (clans, tribes, families) within this system "carry on exchange, make contracts, and are bound by obligations" not exclusively concerning "economically useful things", but also gifts, "courtesies, feasts, ritual, military assistance, women, children, dances, festivals, fairs [...] in which the market is but one element and the circulation of wealth but one part of a wide and enduring contract".[54] Durkheim had already identified two distinct periods within the religious life of so-called primitive societies, the sacred and the profane, a religious dichotomy that Mauss pointed out also determined their economic activity, since exchanges tended to take place when groups gathered and acted together, during initiations, marriages, funerals and more generally at festivals, when the whole society was mobilised to take part. A more advanced form of this system was potlatch, although this was more dominated by principles of rivalry and antagonism. Bataille summarised it as "a considerable gift of wealth publicly offered with the goal of humiliating, defying and *obligating* a rival",[55] since the recipient then had to respond to the unspoken challenge by offering an even more impressive gift. "It is through the intermediary of this form that potlatch," Bataille continued, "is reunited with religious sacrifice, since what is destroyed is theoretically offered to the mythical ancestors of the gift-giver." This was therefore not a mercantile economy, and although interest was "charged" in the form of an obligation, it did not correspond to the modern notion of interest in which an individual expects a personal benefit or profit. Potlatch ensured that the economy of archaic societies was an economy of loss, and the functioning of this economy, according to Mauss, was "constant yet, so to speak, fundamental", and constituted "one of the human foundations upon which our societies are built", a foundation he hoped would provide an answer to what he called "the crisis of our economy."[56] For Bataille, potlatch was an important discovery which convinced him of the superiority of inutilious consumption compared with production and acquisition, and led him to attack the very paradigm of modernity: *Homo œconomicus*. Bataille illustrated his thesis with various examples of what an economy of loss might entail — from luxury to mourning, from wars to cults, and more specifically to the sacred, to games, eroticism and the various forms of art (literature, poetry, theatre etc.). To these, in the last section of his article, he joined the form of social expenditure which he considered the most dramatic in the modern world, the class struggle. He saw this as being inevitably present in any struggle for the wealth at stake in potlatch, which must be based upon surpluses that can only pave the way to slavery, the situation of the proletariat in modern times. Nevertheless, the workers' revolution was only a part of what would ensue from a system based upon potlatch. Once open to the non-economic core of the social, to a world beyond that of the useful as established by the bourgeoisie, it could lead to the uncontrolled explosion of forces that once freed "lose themselves in ends that cannot be subordinated to anything that can be accountable".[57]

If the notion of expenditure was a theme Bataille returned to repeatedly for the rest of his life, it is important in the context of this book to focus on one particular example of it that may be found "in daily experience" and which he discussed in his essay,[58] namely the "sacred" (in Durkheim's meaning of the word, explored below pp.64-67). Sacred things, Bataille wrote, are created by sacrifice, they are the result of an "operation of loss",[59] in other words an expenditure. As early as the Thirties Bataille had felt that the renewal of a moribund society was only possible through a revival of the sacred. This passion became his life, and he placed it at the very heart of Acéphale.

However, although the first issue of *Acéphale* appeared in June 1936, and work was soon afterwards in hand on the second issue, and in spite of Bataille writing the group's "founding" texts (for example, ●1, ●6) and the contributions of various others (such as Dussat's "Du Sang" and "Trois poèmes de la vie sanglante"[60] and Andler's "Moriar, ergo sum", ●8) which together were intended to inaugurate this "religion" of acephality,

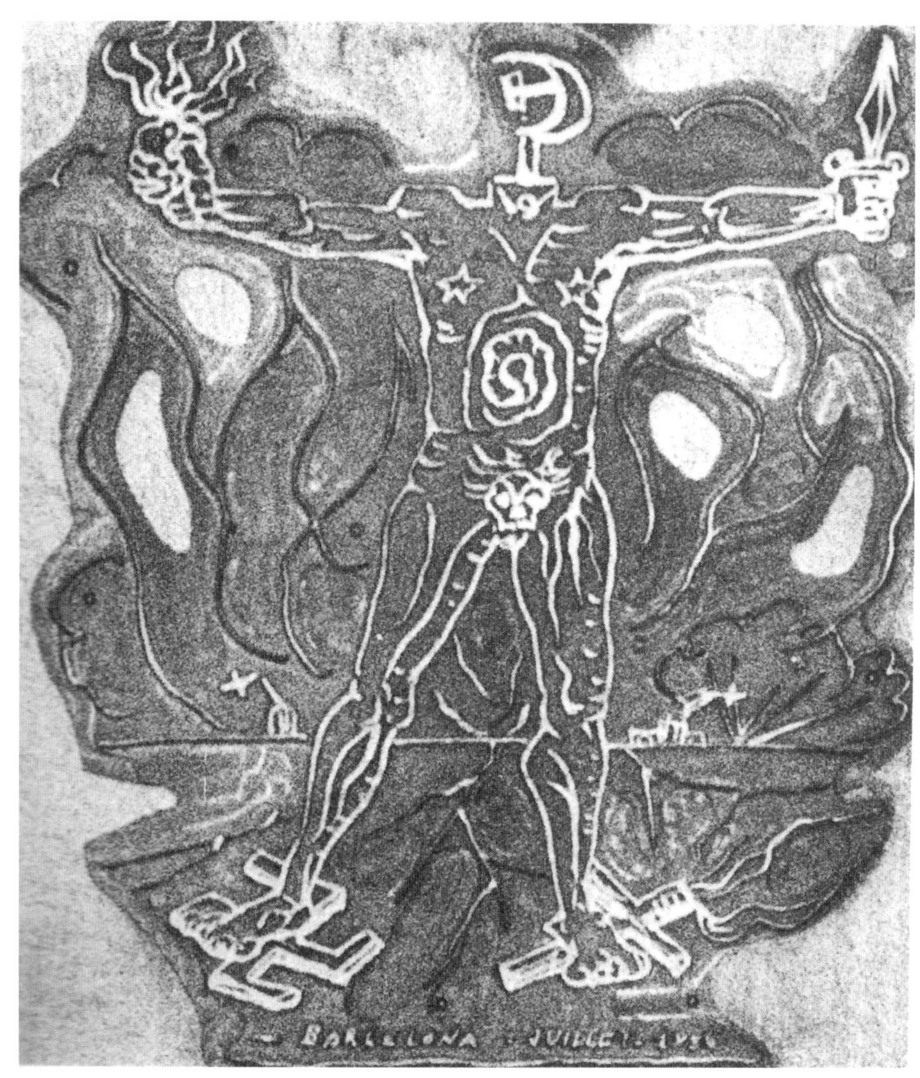


André Masson, *Barcelona, July 1936*, lithographic plate of a drawing.

progress on forming the actual Society was slow and hampered by false starts.

What seems certain is that, from 4 June 1936, the "resolution to found a moral community" (●14 §12) was merged with the idea of a "study group", still structured like a political association and with a name, the Sociological Group, that suggested both the sociological commission once proposed for Contre-Attaque[61] and a secondary community associated with one of the subjects from the masthead of *Acéphale*: Sociology (the others being Religion and Philosophy). The Group's concerns in turn related to Durkheim's sociology, which describes religion as the "administration of the sacred",[62] and opened the way to the description by Hubert and Mauss of a theory of the ambivalence of the sacred in relation to sacrifice. Yet, as Bataille later made clear from within the College,[63] the rules of the sociological method could not be followed blindly, if for no other reason than that Durkheim excluded lived experience from analysis. It was only at the meeting of 11 November that the Group turned a page and openly declared its religious character, in a final break with the political commitment of Contre-Attaque. Henceforth all militancy and even the nascent group's "deep solidarity [...] with the Spanish Revolution", ●14 §14 — as evidenced by Bataille's pained reflections upon the "merciless denouement of the tragedy of the workers' movement"[64] and by Masson's drawing of the figure of the Acéphale opposite — would be stigmatised as the expression of "an attitude whereby vital sympathy and the need for limited aggression took ideological forms".

The process of forming the Society was not without its internal crises. The first concerned the so-called "totemic" dinner scheduled for 18 December 1936, but cancelled because of Bataille's opposition. Andler, who had come up with this idea with Kelemen, perhaps also Dussat, so as to reinforce the fraternity of the group, later regretted that they had not forewarned Bataille, who presumably saw it as a profane event to be avoided when the sacred had not yet been established within the group. The eleven names on the invitation correspond to the first state of what would become the secret society and allow us to identify its original nucleus of members. Besides Bataille, it lists Georges Ambrosino, Jacques Chavy, René Chenon, Pierre Dugan (i.e. Pierre Andler), Henri Dussat, Imre Kelemen, Pierre Klossowski and Jean Rollin. Missing from this list was Henri Dubief, who joined later on but who was only a member for a brief period, while it includes Jean Dautry and Pierre Kaan, who took little part in the actual secret society.

The second, more serious crisis was caused by the arrival of Roger Caillois and Jules Monnerot. Both had been close to Bataille at the time Contre-Attaque was formed but after their split from this group the previous November (p.103, *1 November*) they had played an active role in founding the magazine *Inquisitions*, intended as the platform for the "Study Group for Human Phenomenology". The journal only ran to a single issue because of the inevitable disagreement between these two and the other co-founders,

Louis Aragon and Tristan Tzara, both members of the Communist Party. Even so, the ideas promoted by Caillois and Monnerot in *Inquisitions* were essentially in accord with Bataille's. Caillois proposed an intellectual and moral reform he called "militant orthodoxy", supposedly "applicable to all fields of human activity", through the implementation of a "totality of being",[65] while Monnerot proposed an investigation of poetry viewed not as a form of literature, but "as a means of overcoming contradictions."[66] The failure of *Inquisitions* brought them closer to Bataille, and their reconciliation, initiated by a letter from Bataille to Caillois,[67] unleashed a certain amount of disquiet among the others and endangered the very existence of the group. Traces of this discord can be seen in Ambrosino's reaction, in a letter to Kelemen, about Bataille being supposedly "under the influence of Caillois. Pffui—".[68] Not long afterwards, at the meeting of 29 December at the Grand Véfour, this dissatisfaction was openly voiced within the group. The immediate cause was that the ambiguity of Monnerot's proposals were thought to be compromised by "opportunistic considerations", ●14 §16. The matter of this disagreement was laid out in January 1937 in critical reflections by Ambrosino, ●11, and Dubief, the latter in political terms.[69] The consequences were twofold: the process of creating the society of Acéphale was speeded up, and it also led directly to the creation of the College, as described on pp.80-83.

## FORMATION OF THE SECRET SOCIETY

The Society's brief existence resembled that of a meteor whose brilliance illuminates the night sky for only a moment. Aside from the year of preparatory work which, according to Masson, was undertaken by a group that was "extremely small, but not secret", Acéphale lasted less than three years. Founded around the beginning of February 1937, it came to an end in October 1939. Nevertheless, the intensity of its existence seems to have had a profound effect and Bataille himself, years later, wrote that some of those involved "retained an impression of 'a voyage out of the world'."[70]

When Patrick Waldberg was sent information about the Society, outlining its "ceremony of initiation, rites and the acceptance of a way of life which, while not outwardly visible, was destined to separate its adepts from a world that from now on is to be considered profane",[71] he was sufficiently persuaded to return to France from the USA to take part in it. In his later account of this period he stressed its romanticism and recalled that Bataille had compared it to Balzac's *History of the Thirteen*,[72] which describes a secret society called the Devorants (literally, the devourers) modelled on Freemasonry and the Order of Jesuits. Caillois noted that Baudelaire as well as Balzac had "indulged in imagining an association of mysterious and powerful conspirators, sophisticated and pitiless, who formed a secret network of servants, spies and judges that operated in the capitals and administrations of all the greatest states of the world".[73] Such reveries, which Caillois interpreted as a sign of social discomfort, fuelled the overheated atmosphere at the beginning of 1937, when the documents appeared which mark the actual birth of Acéphale.

First was the "Memento", ●16. Its central tenet, that "in war is truth", allies it with the philosophy of Heraclitus who elevated conflict to a cosmic principle that imposed its rule upon humanity. This text is also a sort of recollection of Bataille and Masson's unforgettable "conversations of April" in Tossa de Mar in 1936, and thus of the second issue of *Acéphale*, "whose pages were like symbols of fire"[74] at the Nietzschean festival where this pre-Socratic philosopher presided over the death of God. Included with the "Memento", in a canvas folder for each member, was a map of the forest of Marly, ●17, which revealed the two sacred sites of Acéphale. The first of these was the stricken oak of Acéphale, which was probably the oak of Joyenval, at the edge of the "Étoile Mourante" (the Dying "Star"), as described in more detail in "Marly, Montjoie..." following.[75] The second was the ruins of Montjoie, connected by the Gate of Joyenval to the abbey of the same name. Beyond that was the wall surrounding the 'Désert de Retz', an estate presided over by a chateau built in the form of "a truncated column" and with various other unusual buildings, including a pyramid and a small temple, which Bataille and his partner, Colette Peignot (Laure), found conducive to their nocturnal rituals.[76]

Other early documents laid out the rules, prescriptions, oaths and rites, ●19 and 20, which would form "a body around a soul" for the Society and place "both of them under the protection of secrecy",[77] so as to strengthen the Society's cohesion and, according to Caillois's notes read by Bataille at the College in 1938, make of it "a centre of learning that partakes of the prestige of power".[78]

In these notes Caillois also specified that "A brotherhood is not 'secret' in the true sense of the term: its manifestations are public and its members are known. Yet it still draws its vital force from an *undisclosable* religious element that is associated with it." This element within the Society is revealed in the texts that evoke the myth of the "stricken oak" in which it is "possible to recognise [...] the silent presence of that which has taken the name of Acéphale, and which is expressed by these arms without a head", ●19. This new myth was related to an older myth of the sacred tree guarded by the King of the Woods, also known as Dianus (the origin of Bataille's pseudonym), the priest-king of the goddess Diana in the Alban Hills, south-east of Rome. Dianus was an escaped slave who became king by murdering the incumbent and was destined in his turn to be put to death by his successor (see "Frazer and the Death of God", pp.67-70). This idea of ritual killing was then re-connected by Bataille to the notion of power in the lecture of this name he gave to the College in place of Caillois. Here it played a central role in revealing the sacrificial character of sovereignty, considered in its religious aspect, and thus of power itself (see p.258). Frazer's study "of the prerogatives of primitive kings and the taboos imposed on them"[79] was likewise central to another essential source for the ideas underlying Acéphale, Georges Dumézil's *Ouranos-Varuna*. Dumézil found similarities between two deposed gods, Uranus from Greek mythology and Váruna from the Vedic, and interpreted their castrated sovereignty as an attenuated version of the death of the king described by Frazer. Thus the legend of the tyrannical reign of Uranus, the first father and the first king who was dethroned and emasculated by his son Cronus, is compared to the myth of the magic reign of the god-king Váruna, who loses "his virility" at his coronation ceremony.[80] In the same lecture, Bataille added to this mythological framework another version of sovereignty, the one pre-eminent in Western civilisation as elaborated by Christianity: "the ignominious killing of Jesus on the cross",[81] which is "endlessly repeated by priests identifying themselves with the victim".[82] This was precisely the version of sovereignty that Fascism and Nazism both opposed (see p.258).

However, it was not the Christian myth of the killing of the king, when man was supposed to identify with the victim, that persuaded the members of Acéphale, in their war against all forms of totalitarianism, to take the train from the Gare Saint-Lazare to Saint-Nom-la-Bretèche on the night of Good Friday 1937, and then follow the itinerary indicated on their map and walk to the "encounter with the great decapitated existence of an oak tree". Rather they did so in "the dark hope of the crime", ●21, weighed down with dread, but without complaint and without remorse, in order to reactivate the "act of tragedy" which Bataille showed when he spoke on "Power" at the College was at the heart of all social structures.

The rite of meditation was followed by a communal rite of sulphurous fire,[83] which related to "the chthonic character of the mythical reality" the group was seeking, ●19. Repeated "every month on the night of the new moon", these rites were accompanied by a radical change in the adept's way of life. His time was now divided into two distinct periods, either "tension" or "licence". Such periods correspond to the Durkheimian distinction between sacred and profane, between the sacred right, noble and auspicious, and the sacred left, ignoble and inauspicious, which express a "sacred linked to social cohesion, guaranteeing rules and taboos" or a "sacred that consists in outbursts of violation of the rules of life".[84] In the first period, "which preceded and followed the ceremony in the forest [...] silence was maintained not only between ourselves, but also with the profane world as a whole. On the other hand, as soon as we entered the licentious phase [...] of promiscuity, disorder and debauch, it was nothing less than a revival of the festivals of Dionysus".[85]

*Acéphale* 3/4, published in July 1937 in the charged atmosphere of approaching war, was devoted to the virtues of Dionysus. The fact of his double birth and partial humanity made him a god of tragic contradiction who, through embracing his own death by dismemberment, celebrated both life and death simultaneously. Unlike the God on the cross who, in Karl Jaspers's words, was "a malediction on life", Dionysus was "a conjuring-up of life".[86] This issue included an appreciation by Bataille of Jean-Louis Barrault's production in April of Cervantes's *The Siege of Numantia*. In this play the besieged and leaderless inhabitants of the city vow to die a communal death rather than submit to the Romans, and Bataille associated their ecstatic martyrdom with the "conjuration" of the Dionysian mysteries. Barrault, with Masson as his designer, had imbued this drama with a new mythical meaning, interpreted by Bataille as a "community of the heart",[87] which he believed was the only sort capable of opposing the anti-Fascist farce of the Soviet Caesar while at the same time pursuing the struggle against the Fascist German Caesar. In the same issue, Caillois called for a "force of *super-socialisation*" in order to participate in the "ecstatic rites and the communal understanding of the sacred" that was proper to the ancient mysteries of Dionysus, as well as for "the spread of cults associated with the underworld, at the expense of the Uranian religion [...] brought about by the victory of the populace over the traditional aristocracies", ●28. Monnerot's text referenced Frazer's *The Magical Origin of Kings* to announce the appearance of a new race of philosophers, endowed with the "grace" of power and drawing from the experience of "*Catilinarian existence*"[88] the right to be called seducers; meanwhile Klossowski took Mozart's Don Giovanni to be the "incarnation of the Dionysian phenomenon of erotic immediacy" at the point where Kierkegaard and Nietzsche overlapped, "the Janus head of modern consciousness".[89]

From the outset, the mythical theme of the labyrinth, as drawn by Masson for the covers of *Acéphale*, both on the figure's stomach and as a graphic symbol beside the title, had evoked the mazes to which Nietzsche "never ceased to return".[90] It also referred to the place with no exit where man, having become lost, isolates himself before becoming his own labyrinth, formed out of the composite structure of his being and "mediated by words, which means he is an 'autonomous being' only arbitrarily, but is profoundly a 'being in relation'". Man therefore finds it easy to join with a whole that transcends him (a social group, for example), and hence discovers the "impossibility of fixing existence within any given *ipse* [self]", as Bataille wrote in his essay "The Labyrinth".[91] In fact, he says that our feeling for being is so uncertain that there is a principle of insufficiency underlying human life which calls it into question to such a degree that "it was an easy ploy for an ailing malice to discover it to be divine, and situated at the summit of a pyramid made of the multitude of beings formed out of a vast amount of simple matter".[92] Otherwise, this social structure is maintained by emptying "elements of the greater part of their being for the benefit of the centre",[93] such as when a child gives its self-sufficiency to its parents, or an adult delegates to those at the core of a group of people the responsibility for realising its being. Nevertheless, certain historic forms, such as carnivals, Saturnalia and the festival of fools, testify to the fact that the presumptions of those at the core can be destroyed. So it is that Bataille comes to suppose that beyond the "minor" form of laughter, which shores up the values of society, there is a "major" form of laughter which is the complete negation of the foundation of all social structures and which he embodies in this essay as a sort of Minotaur, "the monster in the night of the labyrinth" that throws itself into "the necessity of engaging in a struggle [...] with nothingness [...] so as to tear it apart and light up its darkness for a moment with an enormous laugh."[94]

This notion of the social structure as a pyramid and its decomposition within the labyrinthine experience[95] is a central motif not only of *Acéphale*, but also within the Society. It can be found for instance in the text that Bataille wrote for the meeting of 22 July 1937. Here, within the labyrinth, "the contemplation of death leads to violent joy", which shatters "the gangue of Christian piety", ●22, and the question of being is confronted with what Simmel calls the "being for itself"[96] of elective communities, whose "chance of existence" is made possible by the isolation of its adepts.

The creation of the society of Acéphale, however, brought about the end of the journal. Apart from the June 1939 issue of *Acéphale* — written by Bataille alone and in a much smaller format and without a publisher — issue no. 3/4 was the last. Two further issues were envisaged, but never appeared. The first, announced for November 1937 and with illustrations by Masson, was to have explored eroticism as a gateway to the sacred. With this in mind, Bataille's erotic writings were circulated among the members, including *The Story of the Eye*, which Andler passed on to Koch in 1938, and a typescript of *The Blue of Noon*. The second projected issue, scheduled for early in 1938, was to be devoted to "Nietzschean Politics" (see ●39). No doubt Bataille's "Notes pour une politique nietzschéenne" was written for this, even though the text is dated 1939. The "Collection Acéphale" suffered a similar fate, and its "only publication was Leiris's *Mirror of Tauromachy*, in 1938,"[97] a small book that was nevertheless an essential contribution to the study of the sacred.[98] The two other volumes considered for the collection, Maurice Heine's *Le Tableau de l'amour macabre*, and a volume of William Blake, *The Proverbs of Hell and A Song of Liberty*, with five drawings by Masson, did not appear.

As a forum for discussion of the topics that interested the group, *Acéphale* was effectively replaced by the College of Sociology, whose founding was announced in issue 3/4 of the journal in a "Note", ○31, dated March 1937. Three of its signatories, Bataille,

Caillois and Monnerot, spoke the same month at the Salle de la Maison de la Mutualité at the launch of *Acéphale* 2 (p.149, *21 March*). Here, differences arose between Bataille and Caillois on one side and Monnerot on the other, concerning how the College should be put into practice. Monnerot duly ended his involvement, although many years afterwards he claimed the College had originally been his idea, and that he had proposed the name in opposition to Bataille's preference for the more academic "Institute". Another perhaps determining factor was the involvement of Monnerot's brother, Marcel, in the violent Stalinist repression of the POUM (Workers' Party of Marxist Unification) in Spain, a campaign strongly opposed by Bataille.[99]

Consequently it fell to Bataille and Caillois alone to organise the first meeting, at the café Grand Véfour in the spring of 1937, of what would become the College of Sociology, with Bataille ensuring that his chief preoccupation since Hitler had come to power, the struggle against totalitarianism, would be central to the new group. Caillois read an early version of "The Winter Wind", ○30, which is lost, but the text of Bataille's speech, an early draft for "The Sorcerer's Apprentice", ○61, has survived (○29). In this he introduced Freud's essay "The Church and the Army" as being an essential component of the new science that must be created, namely "sacred sociology". This essay should be considered vital both for the analysis of Fascism[100] and for the understanding of social structures of all kinds, "whether Church or religious order, army or militia, secret society or political party".

The "Creation of the 'Internal Journal'", ●14, reveals that at another early meeting, also likely connected to the future College, Caillois suggested some preliminary principles for the formation of a group, and Bataille read his text "What I have to say...", ●13, in which he saw a "*romantic church* [...] composed of the genuine contagion of the most boldly desperate voices", as a possible model for an elective community that would be opp-osed to the reductive tendencies of both Christianity and socialism. Therefore, if Acéphale could be regarded, in Klossowski's words, as "the culmination of an old conspiracy initiated in the past by isolated individuals who had passed on its watchword while apparently remaining unknown to each other"[101] — by whom he meant Sade, Lautréamont, Hegel, Baudelaire, Rimbaud and Nietzsche — then the College too was formed around the question of what might constitute a secret society. This would define its activities to some extent, but would also be the cause of a disagreement in July 1939 with Leiris, even though Leiris's experiences in Gondar were central to the College's attempt to redefine the sacred.[102]

Later still there was an even more serious dispute with Caillois.[103] However, when, after the war, Bataille looked back on the influence of Durkheim's sociology and the "remarkable" courses given by Mauss, he noted that he had shared, with Caillois,

Monnerot and Leiris, a yearning for a secondary community (which one chose to join), as opposed to the primary community "of blood" into which one was born. Moreover, this desire for a "mother cell for a new totality" offset their common feelings of a "shortfall" or a "nostalgia, linked to the present state of social life" in which the notion of the sacred, far from establishing social cohesion as in archaic societies, could no longer be anything but "antisocial" and a "subversion" of social bonds based then (as now) on self-interest. "If it is true that the social bond brings into play our deepest aspirations — which emerge under the name of religion — and that we can only respond to these aspirations by forming a social bond (which would mean that the individual alone is not whole, that an individual only becomes whole when he ceases to distinguish himself from others, his fellows), then the possibility of secondary communities is necessarily, for each of us, the decisive question."[104]

## A BICEPHALOUS COMMUNITY, RELIGION AND POLITICS

The College was not only an institution for teaching and research but was also intended to be a "moral community, somewhat different from the one that typically unites researchers" because of the "infectious nature of the field to be studied", ○31. In November 1937 it began its "theoretical teaching in the form of weekly lectures" on "social existence in all its manifestations in which the active presence of the sacred is clearly to be found".[105] What remained carefully hidden, and was revealed only in the Society's "Annual Summation" of 24 September 1937, ●39, was that the College was, in Klossowski's phrase, the "exoterising emanation of the closed and secret group of Acéphale",[106] in other words, its public manifestation. As such it intended to bring to the Society "a theoretical basis that is underpinned by a perfectly mastered understanding" while being to some extent "outwardly aggressive" (both from ●39). This remodelling of a secret society into a dual structure was not dissimilar to the arrangement found in pre-modern societies studied by French sociologists. Eliade wrote many years later that "secret societies, especially in Africa and Oceania, do not limit themselves to a religious function [...] they actually intervene in the social and political life of the community".[107] Although the College invested such initiatory groups with a radically new content, represented by the "existential secret society" whose aim, as opposed to the "conspiracy societies" described by Mauss, was simply to "exist", it did not necessarily follow that the College had to assume an apolitical or anti-political position. I have shown elsewhere[108] that the words "secret" and "secret society", while referring primarily to the religious domain, are not unconnected with the body politic and that Bataille — while studying through the College how secret societies are created in theory, and how they may be a way of rejuvenating a moribund society "at any stage of its historical development" — was forced to concede, when faced with the impossibility of establishing an unequivocal definition of these structures, that "a purely *existential* secret society" might conspire, and that "a conspiracy society" might become "existential".[109] Caillois, on the other hand, emphasised the central role of the "society of men" in archaic societies, "with its brotherhoods, at once public and secret",[110] which Mauss had compared to the organisation of modern-day revolutionary parties, while pointing out within the society of men the more specifically political role of the society of the young. Thus, in the Roman world, for example, the initiation of the youthful Luperci during the feast of Lupercalia was shown by Dumézil to be closely connected to a celebration of royalty.[111]

The relation between secret societies and the "'men's house' on some South Sea island" was likewise discussed in Leiris's "The Sacred in Everyday Life", ○60, which was a response to a part of the College's programme that concerned the establishing of "points of coincidence between the fundamental obsessive tendencies of individual psychology and the guiding structures which govern social organisation and drive its revolutions", ○31. Leiris's lecture coincided with the thesis he was writing for the École Pratique des Hautes Études on *The Secret Language of the Dogon of Sangha* in which the society of men is shown to be a closed and hierarchical organisation "which plays a leading role both in the secular and sacred life of the population."[112]

The form taken by the society of men at this particular moment in the modern world was considered in two lectures at the College that showed how it was implicated in the very beginnings of Nazism, through the Ordensburgen (elite military schools) and the extreme nationalism of political associations in "Germany during the Romantic period".[113] In light of this debate, as developed within the College, the Society — charged with rejuvenating an enfeebled society, and thereby changing "the face of the world" — intended to be a more effective subversive force than political parties, whose actions get lost in "the quicksand of contradictory words", ○61 §XIV. Hollier,[114] for his part, pointed out the connection here with Bataille's remarks in the lecture on "Brotherhoods..." (see pp.259-260) whereby the Society must be anti-Fascist, and yet oppose monocephalous totalitarianism with "the empire to which the man of tragedy belongs", and also, from Caillois's perspective, be anti-democratic and so repudiate the "emptiness" and "static meaninglessness"[115] of democratic regimes.

Not long after the College had entered the political debate with its critique of the Munich Agreement, the "Declaration on the International Crisis", ○75, Bataille announced, in "The Tricephalous Monster", ●80, the necessity for Acéphale to take a further step and join a new struggle. Heroic "works" must be undertaken "as an infection" in the battle against the "three hostile heads: Christianity, Socialism and Fascism [...] on the monster's own ground". This turning point is likewise reflected in one of the fragments of the *Anti-Christian's Manual* — a text Bataille sketched out between 1938 and 1940 before abandoning it — with a similar call for "an armour of dynamic aggression". The *Manual* also included a list of "Eleven Aggressions" which had in fact been proposed within Acéphale in 1938. The first of these formulates the terms of this new undertaking, which Patrick Waldberg saw as confirming the move from "Marx to Nietzsche", and was to have been the motto of the group itself: "Chance against the mass",[116] ●69. In September 1937, the group also felt the need to reinforce its secrecy by means of a "permanent formal covenant between each of us", ●39, as if — with Klossowski leaving the group, and Dautry and Dubief distancing themselves from it — the reduction in the number of members triggered the desire for a stricter observance in those who remained; an internal withdrawal that coincided with actions directed towards the outside.

At this time (1937, see ●39) meetings were reorganised into four sessions according to the rhythm of the seasons described in the "works of Mauss, Granet and Dumézil often referred to by Caillois in his lecture at the College [...] on the festival".[117] The rite of "interviews" conducted with individual members also dates from September 1937. These were supposed to have a therapeutic purpose and were usually suggested when a member suffered from some form of depression. They took place, as Andler told me, "without any preliminary greetings, in a café or at a fellow member's apartment". By the end of December 1937, a further set of rules had been adopted, ●45, which defined a new form of membership, that of partial initiates or "participants" who were "a sort of buffer between the Society and the uninitiated",[118] and were admitted to the group's internal meetings only after signing a declaration of commitment. This had to be followed, within a week of all the existing members agreeing to admit the new candidate, by a first meditation before the tree in the forest of Marly in the presence of Ambrosino and Bataille. They, in turn, informed each of the existing members "either verbally or in a letter simply containing the name of the new participant preceded by the sign of the labyrinth". Just such a notification letter accompanied the announcement of Waldberg's adeption in 1938, ●63.

Bataille's "Propositions on the Death of God", ●65, and "Degrees", ●66, marked the culmination of his two-pronged strategy (see ●40), directed both outwards while also strengthening "inner existence". The first of these texts opposed the Fascist revolution that was based on the authority of the God-Chief with the Acéphalian revolution of the murderers of God, as "the final historical incarnation of the figure of the dying god".[119]

The second text instituted a hierarchy of three degrees of initiation, corresponding to stages in the subversive strategy of the Society. The first degree had the secret name of larva, which "refers, etymologically, to phantom skeletons and masks", ●66, and harks back to Nietzsche, speaking through Zarathustra: "You 'pure' men who put before you the mask of a god, your hideous creeping larva is hidden behind the mask of a god".[120] Masks, of course, have other meanings too, whether in primitive secret societies whose rites are enacted almost exclusively by masked participants, or in the old rural festivals of northern Europe which Frazer showed often involved the wearing of masks, so too those worn during carnival. For Bataille, the Dionysian carnival was the bulwark of democracy, as he affirmed in his lecture on Mardi Gras at the College on 21 February 1939; here, while evoking his childhood memories of masks, he outlined their role in a possible progression from the effervescence of carnival to that of revolution. His remarks were recalled by Jean Paulhan in a letter to Édith Boissonnas, whose notes on Bataille's lecture in her diary include this progression: "Saturnalia, carnivals, revolutions".[121]

Adepts of the second and third degree were given the secret names of "mute" and "prodigal" respectively. "Muteness", according to "The Tricephalous Monster", ●80, was a characteristic of "the man who has attained the fullness of power and virility", while "prodigal" denoted the "self-giving" man who "does not live by bread alone", but "by every open wound that puts human existence at stake".[122] This rewriting by Bataille of the Gospel of St. Luke (4, 4), in a version of the *Manual* from 1939, combines it with Nietzsche's notion of "the sexual function as a wound"[123] so as to assert the decisive role of "those who accede to the necessity to be prodigal with their life without restraint" whenever "established forms of existence are at stake."[124]

This notion of the prodigal enabled Bataille to formulate, as the foundation of both individual life and history as well, a general "law of coincidence" concerning expenditure and the avidity for being, whereby expenditure is facilitated by *"a connected and simultaneous satisfaction of avidity"*[125] which is likewise *"facilitated"* by an expenditure. However, this exchange belongs to the "heterogeneous sphere", since it lies outside even an extended idea of economic transactions, where what is exchanged and what is expended cannot be correlated. "It is impossible for lovers to evaluate what they give and what they take [...] Still more so, the partisan who is so uncalculating as to prefer death to not proclaiming his devotion to his party and so wills life to it [... by] making a gift of his own life. He represents at once the hunger for being and for the flourishing of his party (sooner or later) to be granted victory."[126]

At the same time, in "The New Defenestration of Prague", a text which was not announced in the College's programme (and is also lost) but which was written soon after Hitler's invasion of Czechoslovakia on 15 March 1939, Bataille redefined the College by putting forward the *political principles* of a sacred sociology that were aimed at renewing existence by means of an organisation that formed an "irreducible core".[127]

The tenor of the indissoluble link between such subversive aims and the discipline called for in Nietzsche's text on the "hard school", ●66, is clarified by Bataille's question — almost a cry of rage and despair — at the end of the "Note", ●71, which he sent to adepts on 8 October 1938. Observing the state of inertia within Acéphale, he wrote: "how can we bear the humiliation, the wounds we suffer when we compare ourselves with those who have put themselves in service to God or to some Germany?"

This was the first sign of a general inadequacy that would only become more obvious. When a disagreement occurred with Kelemen in November 1938, Bataille quickly attempted to "get to the bottom of things" by proposing that "the will to celebrate is a profound will for death" and that "life can only consist of a contradictory alternation between action and celebration", in this way he sought to underline how the festival was profoundly connected with tragedy, in other words with failure, which then appears as "the fiery halo of success".[128]

## JOY IN THE FACE OF DEATH

The resolutions contained in "Propositions", ●85, a text whose date is uncertain and may be from the end of 1938 or the beginning of 1939, abruptly precipitated the Society into a new and decisive phase. This text determined the "attitudes which conform to the spirit that inspires" the organisation, so as to transform it into a "community of the heart", according to the formula put forward by Bataille in June 1939 at the College, but already introduced in reference to the voluntary death of the Numantians in their struggle against Rome. However, if grafting the conspiracy of Acéphale on to Barrault and Masson's *The Siege of Numantia*, made newly relevant by the Spanish Civil War, was to have been the means by which the group would embody the struggle against the totalitarian Caesars of Fascism and Nazism, now it was to be a question of binding the "power the group resolved to exercise" to its "fundamental principle [...] Joy in the Face of Death." (●85 §2). It was this principle, according to Bataille, that ensured that struggle emptied of all ideology could become "the same thing" as life, and so affirm that there was no contradiction between "existing and opposing a closed system of servitude", ●93. In June 1939 Bataille indicated to Caillois that joy in the face of death was available only to "those who are lucid", and could form the basis for an "economy of sacrifice" inspired by the model of potlatch.[129] This would be the opposite of utilitarian economies of "salvation" and would reactivate the essential values of primitive festivals by placing man once more "at the point of death"[130] but with a "*conscious* will to expenditure"[131] and freed from any concern for the afterlife. Once war had begun, only "a straightforward virile attitude, seeking neither escape nor risk" was possible for the adepts involved in it, the opposite of military courage which implies a death "that would be a condemnation of life", ●100.

When his text "Propositions" rejected "the moral bonds that claim to join the soldier to his flag, as the fundamental condition of any participation in a military operation", ●85, it was returning to a question that had already arisen at the sessional meeting of 29 September 1938, namely what position Acéphale would take in the event of war, and also with regard to the recent manifesto *For an Independent Revolutionary Art*. Written by Breton and Trotsky (but signed by Breton and Diego Rivera for tactical reasons), it was distributed in July as the founding document for an International Federation of Independent Revolutionary Art (FIARI) aimed at combating the Communist AEAR (Association of Revolutionary Writers and Artists) and with the intention of clearly defining the relationship between art and revolution. As hostile to Stalinism as it was to Fascism, the FIARI combined a "socialist policy of a central plan" with an "anarchist policy of individual freedom". The differences between the positions of Acéphale and the FIARI emerged in the agenda of the same meeting, ●69, and can be summarised in four points, the second of which was later taken up by the College's "Declaration on the International Crisis", ○75:

(1) the denunciation of "all present-day undertakings, positions and programmes, whether they are revolutionary, democratic or national";

(2) the putting forward of the notion of virility, which, deriving from the Latin word *vir*, conveys the sense of firmness, of refusing to yield either to fear or "in the face of necessity";

(3) the subordination of the principle of utility in the capitalist economy — and of the enslaving morality of labour which proceeds from it — to the notion of expenditure;

(4) the creation of an order capable of exercising, by means of a "tragic gift of the self" and a discipline modelled on that of Freemasonry or the Jesuits soon after their order had been formed, a "religious *power* that is both more real and more intangible than any that have gone before".

It now became necessary to take into account the immediate political consequences of the Sudeten crisis that resulted in the partial mobilisation of the French army between 23 September and 6 October, and a general alert. While the alert quickly became superfluous when the Munich Agreement brought a restoration of peace, the prospect of war was considered in texts by two of the group's members: Andler's "The War", ●62, and Dussat's "Debate on the Problem of War" (not included here). The first, written before the mobilisation, accepted the possibility of an armed conflict, and denounced its possible "appeal"; the second, dating from October, contrasted death in war, in which it is no more than an end, pure and simple, with the "apprehension of death as the supreme object [...] of the joy of existing." Meanwhile the very core of the group was threatened. Dussat, who had returned from a long journey to Italy, Greece and

Switzerland on 11 September, was among the first to be mobilised. He had to leave almost immediately for his former military service regiment at Metz, from where he returned to Paris on 8 October.[132] While the letters he received from Bataille, Andler, Chavy and Kelemen in the course of the various movements of his regiment were like "lights in tormented darkness" to him, his "ordeal was all too real". On 3 October he wrote from Villers-Laquenexy that the experience had forced him into "a kind of profound silence from which [...] it will be very difficult to escape from."[133]

The meditation texts Bataille produced in the summer of 1939 reflected his desire to make the "struggle" undertaken by the secret society more consequential by means of what Jean Bruno has called "techniques of illumination". These were mystical exercises, unrelated either to Christianity or Buddhism, which had their beginnings in a series of ecstatic experiences whose development Bataille later traced in his book of 1945, *Inner Experience*. Following his reading of Bergson's *Le Rire* in 1920, Bataille was struck by the importance of laughter as a "revelation", which "opened up the depth of things".[134]

It was the influence of this mysticism of Bataille's which, according to Patrick Waldberg, inaugurated a "second phase"[135] in the activities of Acéphale, and perhaps coincided with Bataille's letter to the group of 31 May 1939, in which members were urged to "put an end to all half measures," ●90. In his study of Bataille's mystical practices, Bruno distinguished two stages. The first (the only one that interests us here), consisted of various moments, during which Bataille, using silence and dramatisation, pictured to himself "themes of barely tolerable emotional acuteness, [...] a world in flames, exploding or in the process of being destroyed",[136] as in "The Star Alcohol" and "Heraclitean Meditation", ●97 and 99, both proposed as subjects of meditation for the group's members.

"These were 'sacrifices'" which "not only annihilated other beings or God, but in which he was also the principal victim."[137] They culminated in "The Practice of Joy in the Face of Death" in the final issue of *Acéphale*, an "apotheosis of the flesh and of alcohol as well as the trance states of mysticism", ●94, whose "eruptive violence" recalled "André Masson's illustrations to texts on Heraclitus and Dionysus in earlier issues of the journal".[138] At the same time, Bataille's more theoretical lecture to the College on 6 June 1939, also called "Joy in the Face of Death", ○95, aimed "to emphasise that the problem of death is the essential problem of man".[139] At this point Caillois, Jean Paulhan and Jean Wahl were unable to suppress their reservations, and the break-up of the College became inevitable. As for the secret society, the scattering of its sympathisers by the war meant that it survived the end of the College by only a few months. Ambrosino was mobilised immediately at the end of his military service and stationed at Valdahon army camp, but maintained a presence within Acéphale by joining the group reading of Nietzsche begun in July by Chavy, Farner and Waldberg. Dussat left for Belgium and then embarked from Lisbon on 29 August 1939 for Brazil, while Koch was called up at the end of August. The other adepts too were "absorbed by the immediate concerns of war",[140] and this was the beginning of a withdrawal that would unite them in unanimous disagreement with Bataille, thus preventing the extreme act he envisaged to ensure the survival of the community from being carried out, ●101. Bataille dissolved Acéphale on 20 October 1939, while noting that he did not think "it would be impossible for us to keep on good terms at a distance", ●104. France's entry into World War II was the final blow. Chenon was again called up, Kelemen left for the front[141] and Leiris was sent to an artillery unit in the southern Sahara. As for Andler and Patrick Waldberg, they both enlisted in the French army before leaving for the USA where they later worked for the Office of War Information along with Rollin. In 1940, Okamoto returned to Japan, and in 1941, Masson found himself exiled to the USA where he met up with Andler, Duthuit, Rollin and Waldberg.

The adepts were precipitated from their meditation exercises, intended to renew "that type of tragic jubilation that man 'is'", ●94, into the brutal reality of war and, for two of them (Chenon and Koch), captivity. Bataille meanwhile continued to advance his inner experience in "absolute solitude",[142] and, "like Nietzsche, entrusted to his writing the essence of what he wanted to communicate".[143]

There would be no question of Acéphale after the war, despite the brief adventure of the *Da Costa Encyclopædia*,[144] which for a while reunited Bataille and a few of the former adepts. It was more by way of a second putting-to-death of Acéphale that a new community came into being, both as "a direct successor to the College of Sociology",[145] and as a rejection of Bataille:[146] the "Saturdays". The meetings of this discussion group would also transcend the friendships of its members, and result in new ruptures.[147] Influenced by the philosophy of Eric Weil and "headed" by Ambrosino, their weekly rhythm between 1955 and 1972 marked a return to the tradition of Western philosophical study (Plato, Hegel, Spinoza, Locke etc.), although with a modernist approach that opened it up to other disciplines, including literature, music, ethnology, sociology and neurology.

André Masson, *Georges Bataille*, 1937.

ALASTAIR BROTCHIE

# *Marly, Montjoie and the Oak Tree Struck by Lightning*

The rituals of Acéphale were conducted in the Forest of Marly, which lies a mile or so to the west of Saint-Germain-en-Laye, on the western edge of Paris. Once part of the ancient forest of Cruye that covered a vast area in ancient times, it was renamed by Louis XIV in the eighteenth century when he enclosed it with a wall, breached by elegant monumental gateways, for use as a royal hunting-ground at his retreat from Versailles, the Château de Marly. The forest extends for several miles over a mixed terrain, parts of which are situated on a plateau, but there are also steep gullies and valleys. Even on the plateau, however, the ground underfoot is muddy, and extensive drainage works were undertaken in Louis's day, with ditches, bridges and ponds being constructed to facilitate hunting wild boar and deer. The most notable feature of the forest, evident from the map overleaf, is that it is criss-crossed with long, absolutely straight paths and tracks that allowed horses to gallop in pursuit of game. The junctions of these paths were called "*étoiles*" (stars) and they were given names,[1] poetic, mythological, topographical, or merely fanciful. The naming of the *étoiles* allowed a hunt to be planned, and they have retained their names to this day, with most having a sign affixed to a nearby tree.

Page 52 shows a portion of the map given to members of Acéphale on joining the Society, ●17, which enabled them to locate its two sacred sites: the ruins of the fortress of Montjoie, here marked at (M), and the famous tree struck by lightning; this has not been located hitherto, but was probably situated at (J).

Some of the Acéphale documents allow us to trace the adepts' path through the forest with a fair amount of certainty, and are here illustrated by postcards from the period. The ground immediately to the west and north of the station is exceptionally boggy, seemingly all year round, and almost impassable even in the daytime. Since meetings or "encounters" took place at night, it is almost certain that, having left the train at Saint-Nom (A), members took the track up from the station to the Route Royale (B) and followed this wide track to the Place Royale (C) and on to the Étoile des Princesses (D). In ●19, members took a road, a path and then another road. From (D) the direct route was the path to the Étoile Adonis (I) and then the road or track to (J). On this occasion they returned the same way. The letter to Couturier, ●87, describes a somewhat different route, presumably via the Étoile Parfaite

A section of the map given to members on joining Acéphale, see ●17.

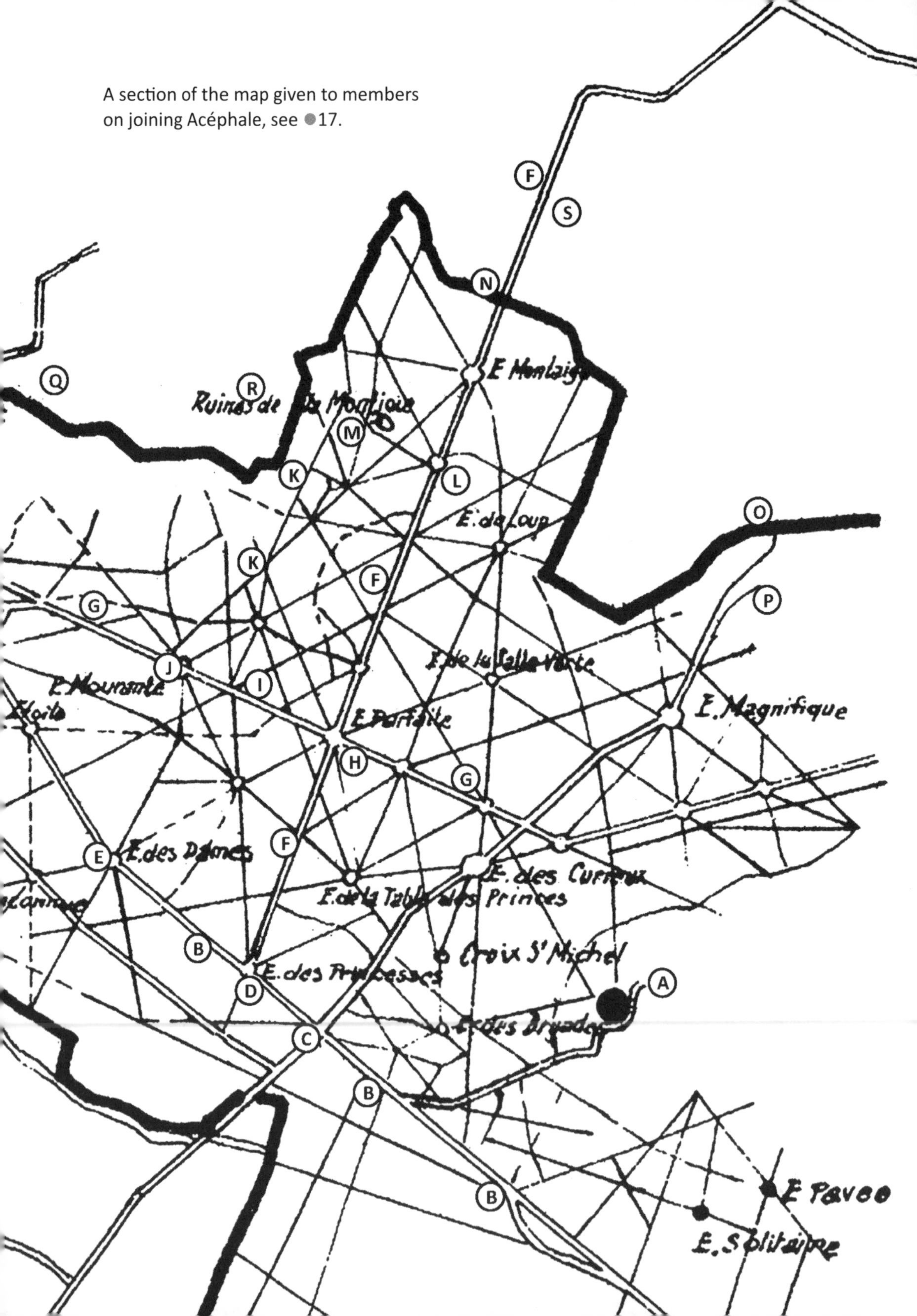

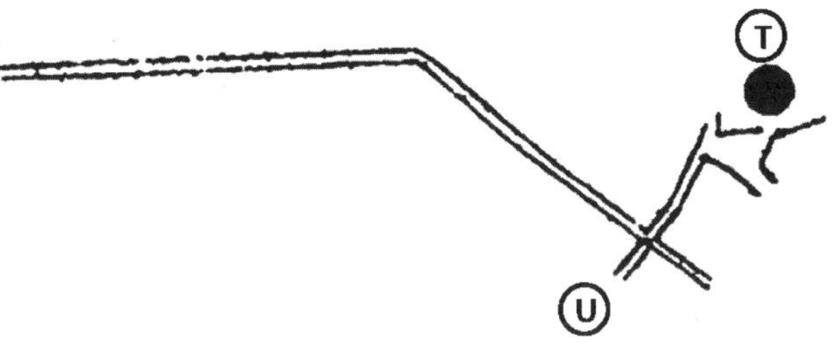

**KEY**

A. Saint-Nom-la-Bretèche railway station: above, with the track leading up to (B).
B. The Route Royale.
C. The Place Royale.
D. The Étoile des Princesses.
E. The Étoile des Dames.
F. The Route des Princesses.
G. The Route Dauphine.
H. The Étoile Parfaite.
I. The Étoile d'Adonis.
J. The Étoile Mourante (usually known as the Étoile de Joyenval).
K. Direct route between the Étoile Mourante and the ruins of Montjoie.
L. The Étoile de la Taupière.
M. Ruins of the Fortress of Montjoie.
N. Porte Dauphine.
O. Porte de Fourqueux.
P. Approximate site of the "Châtaignier Tordu".
Q. The Désert de Retz.
R. Site of the Abbey of Joyenval.
S. Plain of Montaigu.
T. Saint-Germain-en-Laye railway station.
U. Bataille's house in Saint-Germain.

16 — Saint-Nom-la-Bretèche (S.-et-O.) - Forêt de Marly - Place Royale — B. F., PARIS

18 — Saint-Nom-la-Bretèche (S.-et-O.) - Forêt de Marly - L'Etoile parfaite

Saint-Nom-la-Bretèche (S.-et-O.) - Forêt de Marly - L'Etoile d'Adonis

(H). The track between (D) and (I) is often muddy (it appears on the cover of this book), and the alternative route from (D) would be along the Route des Princesses (F), one of the main thoroughfares in the forest, to (H), the Étoile Parfaite (the Perfect Star), and along the Route Dauphine (G), then a track just about negotiable by car, to (I) and then (J).

Bataille did not make it easy for his adepts, as ●87 confirms; the walk to the site of the tree took at least 40 minutes, Montjoie was a further 20 minutes away, and the route back either to the station at Saint-Nom or at Saint-Germain amounted to about an hour. The direct route to Montjoie would be similar to that taken to (J), except that from (H), they would have continued along the Route des Princesses, as it rises up and down in a long a straight track to (L), the Étoile de la Taupière, the Star of the Mole Trap. From there to Montjoie, however, was no simple matter, since the paths were narrow, extremely muddy and it was easy to get lost, as noted in ●42 (when it seems the group failed to find the site in the dark). This is unsurprising as Montjoie is, and was, totally invisible from any of the paths that surround it, and the history of this fortress and the Abbey of Joyenval with which it was connected is likewise obscured by legend. Both places were associated with some of the most mythical figures in French history, notably Clovis I (*c.*466 – 511), the first king of the Franks and founder of the Merovingian dynasty, and his wife Clotilde.[2]

The castle of Montjoie reputedly had its origins as a hunting lodge for Clovis who, amidst the collapse of the Roman Empire, conquered most of the territory of modern France. Clotilde was a Christian, and apparently engineered a miracle from God involving three lilies (there are numerous variants of the story) to celebrate his military prowess. This duly persuaded Clovis to convert to the faith and he adopted the fleur-de-lis as the royal arms of France. Clotilde sewed him a banner emblazoned with the three lilies and had it blessed by a hermit who lived nearby, beside a spring (in one version of the tale); the banner was thenceforth kept at the castle, and "Montjoie!" became the battle cry of France, as Bataille records in ●42. The castle was in the hands of various kings and nobles for many centuries, becoming ever more fortified in the process. Its walls abutted those around the grounds of the Abbey of Joyenval, founded in 1224 on the site of the hermit's chapel beside the "fountain of the three lilies", and which housed the relics of Clotilde, who by then had been sanctified.

The origin of the name of Montjoie is generally supposed to derive from the Roman name for the prominence on which the fortress was built, Mons Jovis, the Mount of

*Left top:* On the left is the stone table of the Place Royale (C). The track to the right is the Route Royale (B) looking south-east, towards the station. The path in the middle leads eventually to the Porte de Fourqueux (O). *Middle:* The Étoile Parfaite (H); the path into the distance is almost certainly the Route Dauphine (G) going north-west towards the Étoile d'Adonis (I). *Bottom:* The Étoile d'Adonis (I); the track off to the right leads back to the Étoile Parfaite (H).

64. - MARLY-le-ROI. - Ruines du Château-fort de la Montjoie, détruit en 1431

2 — Forêt de Marly - Ruines de l'Abbaye de la Grande Eglise Ogivale de l'Abbaye de Joyenval

Jupiter. Beneath the hill was the valley where the hermit lived beside his spring. Its name of Joyenval is presumed to have a similarly homophonic derivation, from Val de Joie, the Vale of Jupiter (or Joy), and it was here that Clovis and Clotilde resided. Thus the fortress on the mount protected the abbey in the valley, and both were named after Jupiter, the god of thunder and, significantly, lightning. By the time of the Hundred Years' War, the fortress consisted principally of a huge square keep, and this was put to the flames by the Black Prince in 1346. Rebuilt and expanded, both the abbey and the fortress were then destroyed by the English in 1431. Louis XIV completed the castle's ruination almost three centuries later because deer and boar were using it as a refuge from the hunt, and the Revolution later favoured the abbey with the same treatment (*bottom left*).

Little remained of Montjoie in the 1930s but a large hollow some 25 metres across and 15 deep, a perfect secret amphitheatre, with at the bottom some low, half-buried walls and stone slabs from the foundations of the dungeons. Here, according to the *Chronicle of the Monks of Saint-Denis*, the Duke of Burgundy instructed an apostate priest, a knight, a squire and a valet to undertake rituals involving the invocation of the demons Herman and Astramon and the corpse of a thief strung up on a gibbet. These rites were intended to "hasten the death of the king", and Bataille refers to the incident in ●42.[3] The mythical meanings of the acephalised oak tree struck by lightning, like the tree that was central to Frazer's *Golden Bough*, are expanded upon below (pp.67-70), and these meanings were only made more potent by the intertwined histories of Montjoie and Joyenval. The castle ruins are close to the Étoile de Montjoie, but for some reason the Étoile de Joyenval is not to the west, near the abbey, but to the south. It is marked (J) on the map on p.52, and was renamed by Bataille the "Étoile Mourante", the Dying Star.

Julie Bataille has a very rare small paperback (even the Bibliothèque Nationale lacks a copy), once owned by her father, called *Les Arbres historiques de Saint-Germain-en-Laye et de ses forêts*. The text of a lecture by Léon Silvestre de Sacy, it was published by "Les Amis du Vieux Saint-Germain" in 1932. Bataille's copy falls open at pages 24/25 which chiefly deals with an oak tree called the "Chêne de Joyenval" (the Oak of Joyenval), and other non-oak trees such as the ancient chestnuts near Mareil. This tree had already seemed a strong candidate for the "oak tree struck by lightning" precisely because this *étoile* was the only one to have been renamed on Bataille's map. Given the ancient links that existed between Joyenval and Montjoie, we can imagine that Bataille must have been delighted to discover this stricken oak at the Étoile de Joyenval.

We know that the oak of Acéphale was a large tree from various accounts ("a dried-up tree, which must have been struck by lightning a long time ago, the largest tree I saw in the whole forest", ●88), some 45 minutes' walk from Saint-Nom station, ●87, situated at the edge of a clearing at an *étoile*, ●68 and 87, on marshy ground, ●19, and accessible

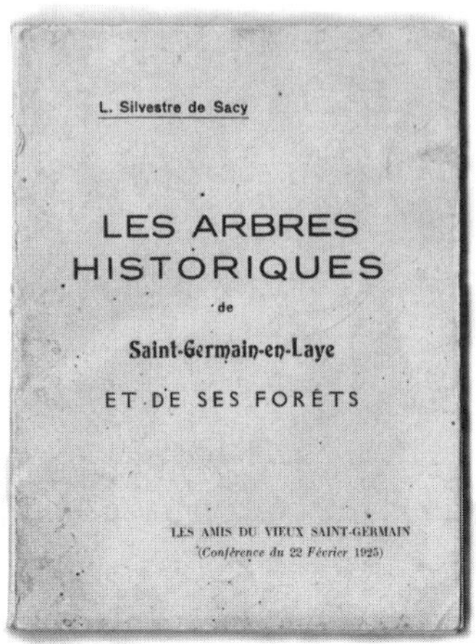


by car (p.252, *End of August*). The Étoile de Joyenval and its oak have all these attributes. The oak that once stood here was a well-known tree in the forest and there are numerous photographs of it in books[4] and on postcards. The rather poor photographs in de Sacy's book show it as it was in the 1930s, and the best representation of it in this state is the postcard opposite. Many of its branches were dead (as de Sacy noted), and there was a major loss of branches on the left side of the tree where the stump of a large branch is visible just below the main branchings from the trunk. Judging from earlier postcards, this trauma had occurred some decades previously, and the tree, some three to four hundred years old, was indeed slowly dying. It wasn't until 2007[5] that it completely perished and was felled, however, and nothing of it now remains because of the drainage works that have been undertaken at this *étoile* which remains very "marshy". Finally, we see that in ●67, the path to the Étoile Mourante is specifically incorporated into the ceremony of Waldberg's "adeption" at Montjoie. A symbolic connection between the two sites is surely being made (although in the next document, written over fifty years later, Waldberg recalled the whole of this ceremony taking place at the tree.)

This argument would be all the more convincing were it not for the inconvenient fact

*Right:* The Oak of Joyenval, and probably Acéphale's "oak tree struck by lightning". The path to the left of the tree is marked (K) on the map, and is the direct route to Montjoie.

that a photograph exists, entitled something like "*l'arbre acéphale*" on the back, and taken by Jacques-André Boiffard, apparently at Bataille's request (Boiffard had been the main photographer for *Documents*). Neither I nor my fellow editor have been allowed to see this photograph, which is now in a private collection. An intermediary who has seen it identified it as another tree mentioned on pages 25 and 26 of de Sacy's book, known as the "Châtaignier Tordu" (the Twisted Chestnut), which is one of the *bois noirs* near Mareil. The chestnut too appears on postcards (*right*), but apart from it being the wrong species of tree, it seems impossible that this could be Acéphale's oak struck by lightning. It is situated in a part of the forest that is not even on Bataille's map (P); it is not a particularly large tree, not at an *étoile*, nor at a clearing, nor on marshy ground, and it is inaccessible by car; furthermore, if it had been this tree then the adepts would have used the Porte de Fourqueux (O) to reach the station at Saint-Germain, and not the Porte Dauphine (N), as indicated on the map. Presumably Bataille and Boiffard visited the forest together, and Boiffard may well have taken a number of photographs. No doubt he photographed the oak struck by lightning, but would Bataille have revealed its significance, when Boiffard was not an initiate? If the writing on the back of the photograph is Boiffard's, it may not be accurate.

There is, lastly, a third piece of evidence,[6] from "X", an unnamed member of Acéphale, who told Claudine Frank that the tree was at the Étoile Parfaite (H on the map, and also on p.54, centre). This is a few minutes from the Étoile Mourante, and on the route to it that was probably most often taken by members. However, the Étoile Parfaite was a major crossroads in the forest, which in those days was inhabited by woodcutters in their makeshift huts — it would have been a rather public place to hold these ceremonies, even at night. The tree is described as situated at its *étoile* on the edge of a clearing, but no such clearing appears in photographs of the Étoile Parfaite, unlike at the Étoile Mourante. "X" also said that the tree was "in the star's centre", but again no significant tree is visible. "X's" statement does, however, cast further doubt on the "Châtaignier Tordu" being the tree of Acéphale, since this was not close to the Étoile Parfaite.

Certainty appears impossible, and a verifiable photograph may well turn up, showing an oak tree that resembles the chestnut, but situated near the Étoile Parfaite. Alternatively, might not this informant, after some fifty years, have forgotten the tree's exact location, or even have decided to conceal this, the final secret of Acéphale? More to the point, the Étoile Parfaite is never mentioned in Acéphale's texts, and why give the Étoile de Joyenval a secret name known only to members unless it was the Society's other sacred site, that of a dying tree at which to celebrate the agonies of a dying god?

Saint-Nom-la-Bretèche (S.-et-O.). — Forêt de Marly. — Étoile parfaite.


*Top:* The "Châtaignier Tordu", and *bottom*: a second view of the Étoile Parfaite. This photograph was probably taken from where the man is sitting in the central picture on page 54.

IV.

ALASTAIR BROTCHIE

# *The College of Sociology: a Paradoxical Institution*

The choice of name, "The College of Sociology" — circumspect to the point of evasiveness — was not unconsidered. Its prosaic, or even "profane" meaning, indicative of an educational or scientific institution, conveyed a seriousness of purpose intended, in part, to separate it from the various coteries of avant-garde culture with which its founders had been previously associated. In the late 1930s the College gathered together a rather brilliant group of intellectuals, whose self-appointed task was to discuss and attempt to comprehend the currents underlying the most pressing problems of a world obviously on the brink of catastrophe. If sociology could be seen as a sort of psychoanalysis of society, then what were its unconscious motives at this critical moment? And in this context, what were the aims of this College?

An initial, and somewhat unexpected answer might be that it was a religious organisation aiming to reactivate the sacred in society. The Catholic Church might claim the same, but for Bataille these words, society, the sacred and religion, had very different meanings from those in use in common parlance, and it is these meanings that are key to the texts that follow. Many of them derived originally from the writings of Durkheim, before acquiring slightly differing inflections in the thought of Bataille and the other participants.

## DURKHEIM AND HIS VOCABULARY

The undisputed founder of French sociology is Émile Durkheim (1858-1917), whose work was continued after his death by his nephew Marcel Mauss. The latter's courses in Paris were attended by Caillois and Leiris, and these two, along with Bataille, often employ Durkheim's vocabulary in their texts, while the College as a whole acknowledged Durkheim's ideas as formative.

*Social facts*. The basic "unit" of Durkheim's science of sociology is the "social fact", something which is the creation and attribute of a social group, not an individual, although all individuals are deeply influenced by them. According to Durkheim, social

*Left:* André Masson, *The Minotaur*, etching from *Sacrifices*, 1936.

facts are the unintended consequence of past human behaviour, and in whatever society we find ourselves, they constitute the given context for all thinking and action. Almost wholly the result of unconscious collective activity, they constrain individuals by beliefs and prohibitions of which they are largely unaware and which they cannot easily comprehend. Durkheim instances social conventions such as kinship or marriage, values, beliefs and codes, as well as political, economic, religious or social institutions and organisations.

*Collective representations*. Social facts can coalesce into a collective representation around specific totems or symbols (i.e. material objects), or narratives and allegories. Representations, "the product of a vast collective effort, the accumulation of generations of experience and knowledge",[1] allow individuals to imagine the society they are a part of, and to picture aspects of their relations with it. They acquire, Durkheim believed, a certain autonomy (rather like a meme), hence "the luxuriant growth of myths and legends, theogenic and cosmological systems etc."[2] As with all social facts, they are not consciously constructed, they are an epiphenomenon of social groups.

*Religion and the sacred*. It would be somewhat glib to observe that Durkheim took an almost religious approach to sociology, or at least to its object of study: society and what binds it together. Yet this is also something of an understatement, since for him, religion and society were nearly synonymous: "the idea of society is the soul of religion".[3] Thus the nature of religion is the subject of perhaps his most important work, *The Elementary Forms of Religious Life* (1912).

In this work, Durkheim starts off by establishing that religion is not a "system of misleading fictions".[4] On the contrary, it has a solid basis in reality. However, "it does not in the least follow that the reality that grounds it must objectively conform to the idea that believers have of it".[5] Indeed the very fact of its multiplicity of belief systems and innumerable deities is proof enough that its rites and beliefs are secondary to its real function. Consequently, it has nothing to do with the supernatural, or with spiritual beings such as God. Religion, in fact, "is a unified system of beliefs and practices relative to sacred things, that is to say, things set apart and surrounded by prohibitions [...] that unite its adherents in a single moral community."[6] This describes its function, but it does not describe the attributes of any one particular religion, which its adherents mistake for both its content and its meaning.

For Durkheim, it is humanity that populates religion with the gods it then worships, having forgotten that their existence depends on its belief in them, but also unaware that it is through them that humanity itself endures.[7] God is a social fact (a god with a single worshipper would be no more than a symptom), and the beliefs and rites of religion constitute a representation which in many societies is the most dominant representation of all. For Durkheim, the various beliefs of different religions have no bearing on what is actually being worshipped. However, "the worshipper," he wrote, "is not deluding himself when he believes in the existence of a higher moral power from which he derives his best self: that power exists, and it is society."[8] Here resides the true duality of human existence (rather than that of body and soul), since we are all both social and individual beings, and humanity as a whole depends on society for its very existence. Religion represents the individual's relationship with this society, or even more than that, it *is* society itself, hypostatised (it is the representation that finally makes the social group real to the individuals of which it is composed) and transfigured.[9] This transfiguration is accomplished by means of representations embodied in religious symbols, which Durkheim later described in *The Elementary Forms of Religious Life* as an attempt "to show that sacred things are simply collective ideals [moral beliefs] that have fixed themselves on material objects [as representations]".[10] Essentially, for Durkheim the sacred is indistinguishable from a simple hub of obligations and prohibitions, and is manifested for us in the simultaneous attraction and repulsion provoked by these prohibitions, which in turn represent the rules that guarantee social cohesion. This forms the core of the religious representation of society and its regulations.

The ritual life of religions follows a seasonal path whose cycles represent the reciprocal relation between the individual and the society that has given him or her all the beneficial products of past collective action: tools, culture, language. The individual depends on society, but society in its turn depends on the collective of individuals; it is comprised wholly of them, and so, just as humanity needs its gods, no less do they need humanity.[11] The recurring seasonal rites of religions also represent the cult as something that is as permanent as the universe, and provide those occasions when the individuals of the social group personify the group itself by gathering together as one, in festivals, "moments of collective ferment" and other *effervescent* (to use Durkheim's term) assemblies, where the participants may be transported outside of themselves, and become de-individualised. These events, separated from profane everyday life, specifically celebrate the sacred, and the notion of "the festival" will weave its way through the thought of Caillois, O91, and Bataille; as too, especially for the latter, will "effervescence".

Durkheim's notions concerning religion would find few defenders among the pious, since they are guaranteed to offend the believer in any particular cult. Yet he had a wholly positive view of the function of religion: "In all its forms its purpose is to raise man above himself and make him live a life superior to the one he would lead if he were only to obey his individual impulses. Beliefs express this life in terms of representations; rites organise it and regulate its functioning."[12] Temperamentally of the left and a believer in social progress, Durkheim was criticised for being politically conservative because his ideas seemed to support the existing structure of any particular society. He attempted to circumvent this criticism on a number of occasions, maintaining, for example, that representations could depict the society that was desired rather than the one that existed, and suggesting that common opinion might lag behind "the real condition of society".[13] However, inconveniently for Bataille and his fellow conspirators, such suppositions gave no clue as to how it might be possible to alter the prevailing relations between a society and its members, nor, more importantly, how the established representations of these relations might be deliberately modified. We shall see how both Bataille and Caillois envisaged this might be done.

*Morality and conscience*. Religion has traditionally considered itself to be the basis for morality, but following Durkheim's analysis, it could only fulfil this function in a very particular way. Morality could only be considered as a set of rules that, in essence, obliges the individual to act in the collective interest: a moral act is by definition one that strengthens society. However, Durkheim's writings on morality came some time after an essay he wrote at the time of the Dreyfus trial. Here he argued that the principal religion of western civilisation (which furthermore demonstrated the possibility of social progress) was a reverence for humanity itself, in which "man has become a god for man and he can no longer create other gods without lying to himself".[14] This religion "takes man as its object, and man is an individual by definition".[15] By this argument, the society and the individual could be one, and to persecute an individual unjustly could never, as many of Dreyfus's opponents claimed, be excused as a benefit to society as a whole, since it would be both self-contradictory and immoral in a society whose religion was that of the individual. In this society too, the implication was that the rules of morality must be a freely accepted obligation, "an enlightened acceptance".[16]

*Society.* Durkheim's ideas about what constitutes a valid society largely derive from these predicates; it is not the sum of the individuals that comprise it, for the whole is greater than its parts and has an individuality of its own. It is not based upon relations of exchange or contracts, but upon the sacred, a network of obligations, prohibitions and benefits which are expressed by representations. Comprised of human individuals, it is also a separate entity from them, with characteristics that individuals do not have, and can even be considered superior to them. Bataille and Caillois reassert these ideas in various ways in the texts below, but Bataille also went a little further.[17] He speculated whether, in contemporary society — which appeared based almost solely upon relations of exchange, indeed upon an extreme version of such relations in which one class exploited another — the sacred might acquire a subversive value. In a homogenising society, it might provide the heterogeneous elements that could perform the opposite of the sacred's usual function and disrupt the existing social structure, a spark to light the conflagration. Caillois, for his part, hoped that something he called "super-socialisation" would play this role, as he outlined in ●28 and ○30.

The meaning of religion for Durkheim was independent of its content, its actual beliefs. These beliefs might shape or decorate the representation, but the representation will always carry the same meaning: it is an allegorical depiction of the society that created it and which it worships at one remove. Here too Bataille's thought would part company with Durkheim's. The sacred for Bataille had other, more potent, meanings that projected it outside the realm of the "functional", and he likewise attributed other values to the content of religion. Yet he did agree with Durkheim in one respect: it did not in the least follow that these values or meanings must conform to the idea their believers had of them. For Bataille, the content of religion could indeed be a representation of the individual's situation in the universe, and it was largely in James George Frazer's *The Golden Bough* that he found this content. From this, might it be possible to create a new representation, one that might become the desired "spark" or "germ"?

## FRAZER AND THE DEATH OF GOD

Nowadays, *The Golden Bough* has the reputation of being little more than a repository of folklore. This was partly the author's own fault, since over some twenty-five years it grew well beyond its optimum extent, from a second edition of three volumes to a third of thirteen, and in this final incarnation its unspoken argument became so well concealed as to be almost lost. Frazer does not propose totalising theories, and although he was an "anthropological collector" like Durkheim, he used his vast quantities of data to explain, so he says, a rather obscure religious practice that took place at Nemi, south of Rome, from the early days of Antiquity until the 2nd century AD. This "strange and recurring tragedy" was associated with the cult of Diana:

> Within the sanctuary [of Diana] at Nemi grew a certain tree of which no branch might be broken. Only a runaway slave was allowed to break off, if he could, one of its boughs. Success in the attempt entitled him to fight the priest in single combat, and if he slew him he reigned in his stead with the title King of the Woods (Rex Nemorensis). According to the public opinion of the ancients the fateful branch was the Golden Bough which, at the Sibyl's bidding, Aeneas plucked before he essayed the perilous journey to the world of the dead.[18]

Why such a literally *magnum opus* to explore a topic of such apparently specialised

"... the little woodland lake of Nemi — 'Diana's Mirror' as it was called by the ancients. No one who has seen that calm water, lapped in a green hollow of the Alban hills, can ever forget it. The two characteristic Italian villages which slumber on its banks, and the equally Italian palace whose terraced gardens descend steeply to the lake, hardly break the stillness and even solitariness of the scene. Dian herself might still linger by this lonely shore, still haunt these woodlands wild. In antiquity this sylvan landscape was the scene of a strange and recurring tragedy." (*The Golden Bough*, ch. 1)

interest as the death of this king, Dianus? Whereas "the plot" (as Frazer called it himself) of this work is as he describes it — solving the meaning of this riddle — its underlying purpose appears quite different. It seems as if he saw in this story something upon which to hang a work whose actual purpose was to demonstrate that every element of the New Testament account of Christ, the Passion and resurrection, along with the church's ritual representations of them (the Eucharist etc.), were simply variants of earlier myths and rites.

This aim goes unstated, but the reader cannot help noticing, for example, that of all the various beliefs that come under consideration, the author's barbs are only ever directed at Christianity and its practitioners. In one particularly captivating example (highlighted by Robert Fraser in his introduction to the OUP edition), he discusses the fact that, in the 4th century, worshippers of Attis claimed that the resurrection of Christ was a simple imitation of their own god's rebirth, and then tells us:

> In these unseemly bickerings the heathen took what to a superficial observer might seem strong ground by arguing that their god was older and therefore presumably the original [...] This feeble argument the Christians easily rebutted. They admitted, indeed, that in point of time, Christ was the junior deity, but they triumphantly demonstrated his real seniority by falling back on the subtlety of Satan, who on so important an occasion had surpassed himself by inverting the usual order of nature.[19]

*The Golden Bough* was in fact a deeply subversive work, and along with the works of Darwin *et al.*, one that contributed much to the undermining of the foundations of Christianity. The most pointedly anti-Christian version of it was the second edition, of 1900, which was the one Bataille appears to have begun reading in 1931, and then parts of the third edition in both French and English the following year.[20] Unlike Durkheim, Frazer is not concerned with the function of religion, but with its content. The "plot" requires an immense investigation which gradually reveals a myth central to nearly all religious traditions, namely the putting to death of the God, or King (symbolically the same thing), followed by his resurrection.

This was the myth incarnated in the beheaded figure of the Acéphale, albeit with no resurrection. Once that was discarded, along with its attendant allegories, all that remained was a "religion" of confrontation with the power of death itself. Frazer's central myth was taken as a given by Bataille in various of his College lectures, and in Frazer he would also have found much that related both to Durkheim's thought and his own: ideas of the left and right sacred in relation to taboo, taboos associated with bodily expenditure, the festival as a period of licence, and also ideas of sacrifice and sovereignty.

Finally, the culmination of the entire book, and of its "plot", appears most significant. Frazer's final summation begins with a description of the death of the son of Odin, Balder, "a deity whose life might in a sense be said to be neither in heaven nor on earth but between the two".[21] Balder is slain by an arrow made from a branch of mistletoe, which grows on the most sacred of trees, the oak. The mistletoe, itself a sacred plant, as Frazer tells us, was the Golden Bough which must be plucked from the tree before the attempt is made on the life of the King of the Woods, because it was seen as the emanation of the celestial fire of an oak tree that had been struck by lightning. Like the tree around which Acéphale conducted its ceremonies, Frazer's oak constituted a meeting of heaven and earth, high and low, pure and impure, and resembled "a powerful god that has been torn apart by his own anger", ●21. This was the sacrificial arena where the slave was licensed to kill the master, the serf the king; a place where man may murder God.

"WE ARE FEROCIOUSLY RELIGIOUS", Bataille pronounced emphatically in "The Sacred Conspiracy", ●1, despite the ambiguities this last word held for him. It signified, in accord with Durkheim, the creative engine of social cohesion, but also had another, perhaps more individual meaning, in which it confirmed Nietzsche's famous proclamation. For Bataille, it was nothing less than a glorious affirmation of the death of God (that "ridiculous syllable").[22] In his essay "The Sacred", Bataille concluded: "God represented the only limits to human will, and freed from God [... man], *alone*, suddenly has at his disposal all the possible human convulsions, and cannot avoid this heritage of divine power, which belongs to him."[23] Bataille's religion was an anti-religion and yet, he would surely maintain, it was at once a real religion and a representation, one that was grounded in objective reality. The suspicion must be that Bataille's real aim was to replace religion with the sacred, with the latter seen as a sort of ultimate effervescence. When Masson, one of his closest allies, was questioned about this pronouncement of Bataille's, he underlined the distinction: "The sacred is not necessarily divine".[24]

## SACRIFICE AND EXPENDITURE

The two great texts by Bataille with respect to Acéphale and the College, effectively their overlapping manifestos, are "The Sacred Conspiracy" and "The Sorcerer's Apprentice", ●1 and ○61. These in their turn are part of the continuum of his thought, and just as Bataille's activities at this time can be seen partially as a combination or reconciliation of Durkheim's method with Frazer's content, so too they can also be seen as an attempted reconciliation of two texts of his from 1933: "The Notion of Expenditure" and "Sacrifices". Both of these are available in English translation[25] and so are not included here, but I will add a few observations — about ideas of the sacred and the inutilious — to those of

Marina Galletti in the previous introduction (pp.29-33).

"Sacrifices" is an ecstatic existential text which severely resists summary, so I shall consider only the argument that is immediately relevant. Bataille begins with the vast improbability of his own existence which, being entirely the result of countless chance encounters, is thus a representation of total heterogeneity. Awareness of this state situates his "me" outside of the void of things (in a text from 1936, "The Labyrinth", being, and thus self-awareness, is identified as a rupture in the homogeneous continuum of organisms, from biological cell to society). However, the world of things exists, with each one dependent on all the others, and all of them developing in time according to necessity and probability. The fall into this world of things and of contingency causes the *me* a loss of self which can only be restored by "tears, anxiety and painful erotic choices".[26] Christianity appears to offer the *me* an ecstatic form of being, but in fact acts only for itself, by transforming the revelation of the *me* at the point of death into "dying like a dog" for others, rather than for existence itself alone. God, proposed as "the supreme object of a rapturous escape from the self",[27] has been betrayed by political expediency and the *me* is thrown back into the platitudes of a daily life of function and accommodation. Imminent death can indeed create a new *me*, but requires "imperative completion and sovereignty of being at the moment it is projected into the unreal time of death".[28] The creation and maintenance of this state of being within the domain of proximate death was to be the main aim of Acéphale's meditations and "encounters" in the forest. The final paragraph of "Sacrifices" offers Bataille's own summary of this text:

> The being whose human name is *me* and whose coming into the world — across a space peopled with stars — was infinitely improbable, nevertheless encloses the world of the totality of things because of this fundamental improbability (which is counter to the structure of the real as it is). The death that delivers me from the world that kills me has enclosed this real world within the unreality of the *me* who dies.

In "The Notion of Expenditure", Bataille sets up an opposition between the useful and the inutilious. He associates the first with acquisition (production) and conservation (in individual terms, reproduction and the preservation of the body from illness), these being the usual concerns of political systems. The inutilious, which is privileged by Bataille, is associated with "expenditure", which here has strong echoes of Durkheim's "effervescence". Bataille points out that once the basic human requirements of subsistence are attended to, then real, more profound human needs come into play, and that what these have in common are the intense desire for expenditure and loss. Everything of value in social interaction belongs to this category of unproductive forms, which Bataille would later call "the accursed share"; priceless because it is valued least. Examples, as we have seen, include "luxury, mourning, war, cults, the construction of sumptuary monuments, games, performances, arts and perverse sexual activity",[29] but this list may be expanded — debauch, drunkenness, pleasure, bodily excretion, eroticism, death etc. — everything, essentially, that Bataille associated with "the sacred" and its "conspiracy".

Bataille then outlined the consequences of bringing expenditure into the economic, religious and political realms. In the economic realm, his interpretation relies on potlatch and its combative gift-giving (described above, p.33). Here it is worth noting that Bataille's theory of economics was built not on scarcity, the basic foundation of all other economic theories, but on abundance and surplus, namely who controls it and what is done with it (a question with enormous relevance today). In modern times, he wrote, it is *used* by the wealthy to distinguish themselves from the homogenised and degraded poor, whose lives they have ensured are limited to subsistence and production, and who are thus excluded from all inutilious social activity (something of an exaggeration, since even the most downtrodden human social group has its cultural riches). The bourgeois, in the mean time, squirrel away their material wealth, and even seem ashamed of their prudence: "The hatred of expenditure is the *raison d'être* and justification of the bourgeoisie: it is also the very principle of their appalling hypocrisy," since they exhibit a face "so fearfully small that all human life, on seeing it, seems degraded."[30]

The solution was class struggle. The ignoble poor would re-enter the circle of power by accomplishing the revolutionary destruction of the property-conserving classes "in an act of bloody social expenditure that would be limitless".[31] Here then is how two differing views of society — that of sociology, in which it is founded on cohesion, and of Marxism, in which it is the theatre of conflict and class war — might be reconciled. It is possible to see much of Bataille's future efforts as an attempt at this reconciliation, and even the separation of the Society and the College as due in part to the difficulty of it.

As for religion, or rather Christianity, originally it did at least oppose existing power relations, by "associating social ignominy and the cadaveric degradation of the torture victim with divine splendour".[32] However, Christianity's taste for submission and humiliation on the one hand, and for accumulation and power on the other, meant that the Church's chief concern became its own conservation rather than the struggle it had initially seemed to want to undertake by extolling the sovereignty of the wretched.

Bataille ends "The Notion of Expenditure" by reiterating that, since human exuberance

"Cadaveric degradation and divine splendour": a plate from Duthuit's "Representations of Death", *Cahiers d'art* 1-4, 1939, which also contained texts by Bataille and Caillois.

is limitless and uncontainable, then human life cannot be "limited to the closed systems that are assigned to it by reasonable conceptions". This is a long way from a Communism that *reasoned* that a *limited* expenditure would be *used* to create a dictatorship of the proletariat. Bataille's ideas concerning the sacred and wasteful expenditure, which gradually appear to become synonymous, expand Durkheim's concept of "effervescence" to fill the whole of life, if not the whole universe, a tendency which the College was to a large degree intended to defend, and Acéphale perhaps to actualise.

Bataille attempted to unify his ideas under these themes, and eventually codified them as an overall Heterology, "the theory of that which theory expels",[33] according to Hollier, which could encompass the whole of the accursed share in all of its inutility. But inutility could also occasion contradiction. Bataille's objection to what Mauss called a "conspiracy society", the usual sort of secret society set up with specific, often political aims in mind, was because of its utilious nature. (Here it is worth noting that the text from which we have taken the title of this book is called "La Conjuration sacrée", whereas Bataille himself avoided the word *conspiration*). Bataille insisted that a valid secret society must be "existential", and exist for existence alone, since the sacred must be inutilious and allied to expenditure, waste and exuberance, with at its pinnacle, death. From this, Acéphale derived the content of its "religion": the absence of God in a universe ruled by chance and death. Yet Durkheim had gone to great lengths to describe the utility of the sacred and of religion, and Bataille likewise proposed that the College be a community, even though this was somewhat at odds with its "project", which was undoubtedly useful, probably conspiratorial and even scientific, all of which were attributes of the homogeneous world.

## SACRED SOCIOLOGY

In retrospect, Bataille's attempts to unify these two approaches can be seen to have contributed to tensions within the College that would eventually prove impossible to reconcile: this was its "paradox", the necessity of an unscientific science. This necessity was also reinforced by the nature of the object of study, the sacred. Science is inherently profane since it abstracts objects from the totality in order to study them. But the sacred cannot be studied in this way since it is "a world of communication or contagion, where nothing is separated, where every effort is necessary precisely to prevent its indefinite fusion".[34]

Furthermore, both of the documents announcing the foundation of the College ("Note" and "Introduction", ○31 and ○59), proposed something that was beyond a sociological study of society, or even a study of the sacred in society. These parts of the "Note", later incorporated into the "Introduction" by Caillois, seem to bear Bataille's seal, but Caillois at this point was still in agreement with him. Both documents speak of going well beyond analysis to action, and the second concludes (no doubt in Caillois's words) with the hope that they will exceed their initial scheme, "moving from the will to knowledge to the will to power, and become the nucleus of a much larger conspiracy — the deliberate calculation that this body should find a soul" (○59). Hence in the "Note" of March 1937, and before its work had begun, Bataille and Caillois were imagining the College in terms that might seem rather more appropriate to the recently formed Society. Yet the "Introduction" of July 1938, following a year of the College's lectures, retained this perspective, and Caillois even accentuated it.

In 1936, in "The Sacred Conspiracy", ●1, Bataille had written "What we are starting is a war" ("we" signifying the authors associated with *Acéphale*). It was a war against the army, the church, the bourgeoisie, the current conceptions of political struggle, and ultimately, the notion of God itself. It was a war against everything — in particular "the tricephalous monster"— that had colonised the communal and emptied it of the sacred, including even the condition of man, who was a stranger in the world since "the causeless and aimless universe that gave him life has not necessarily granted him an acceptable destiny", ○61 §II. Bataille and Caillois therefore clearly intended this College of Sociology to provide a theoretical underpinning for an attack upon almost everything that is commonly meant by the word "society", sociology's traditional object of study.

Caillois later recalled "We wanted to conduct philosophical research, but philosophy was only a front, or a form. The real project was to re-establish the *sacred* in a society that tended to reject it. We were taking on the role of *sorcerers' apprentices*. We wanted to unleash some dangerous currents, while being well aware that we would probably be among their first victims."[35] Direct political action had proved itself incapable of diverting the social undercurrents that threatened Europe. According to Caillois, he and Bataille believed that sociology could "provoke a contagious activity [...] an epidemic of the sacred,"[36] that could infect society as covertly as the tuberculosis Bataille later evoked in "The Sorcerer's Apprentice" ○61 §I. Such hopes were not entirely new, for had not Durkheim and Frazer both fatally compromised several of society's most cherished representations of itself? And if, in ○61 §XIV, Bataille denied that Acéphale, although secret, was a "conspiracy society", can the same thing be said of the College? It appears instead to be both a semi-secret society *and* a conspiracy society, albeit of a particular sort, one whose "secret" was known only to its founders. Many members were seemingly unaware of its true aims, which indeed are barely hinted at in the lectures (probably the first time was in the lecture on "Brotherhoods"). The College fell between two camps, that of the "active" Society and the analytical research group implied by its name. The separation between the experiential Society and the theoretical College was imperfect, and this was perhaps inevitable because Bataille made no secret of his dislike for the limits imposed by the strictly scientific approach to sociology espoused by Durkheim (see ○61 §III, for example); nor any other limits for that matter.

This too then was "Sacred Sociology", a distancing of the College from Durkheim to a certain degree, because Bataille believed that scientific analysis could only go so far, and also an ambition to alter the society being studied. Sociologists had hitherto only *interpreted* the world; the point was to *change* it, to paraphrase Marx.[37] The blurring of analysis and, for want of a better word, action, was anyway inevitable owing to the nature of sociology, which proposed a total theory of society, while its theorists were themselves a part of the society they studied, so that objectivity was compromised from the outset. Monnerot put it well (while inexplicably citing this as part of his disagreement with Bataille):

> If, I said, the programme of the College of Sociology involves examining "burning questions" we ourselves must expect to be burnt by such inflammable matter. A truthful and pertinent description of politics "in the making" would already be an intervention in it...[38]

So it was that the "Note" and the "Introduction", ○31 and ○59, declare that "to start with" the College will be concerned with theoretical instruction, at the same time as they affirmed that the difficulty of understanding "the vital elements of society" was because of "the necessarily infectious and *activist* character of the representations" involved. In other words, the College was open to the necessity of involvement with what it studied. These announcements were the result of many, often "tumultuous"[39] discussions, and these continued long after the "Note" had appeared. One senses them behind a letter to Caillois from Bataille in August 1937, which cautions him that they must first lay down a firm scientific foundation for their endeavour before proceeding to "action itself".[40] Here it was Bataille showing some caution. These disagreements must surely also have encompassed what a sacred, or active sociology could actually mean in practice. Kojève found it factitious, Raymond Queneau later made a similar argument, that representations could not be manufactured (p.349, *February*),[41] and later still Sartre objected that a sociologist cannot integrate himself into his study however much he wishes to, since he is bound to remain outside by the very fact of being a sociologist.[42]

## FORMATION OF THE COLLEGE

There are, essentially, three first-hand accounts of the formation of the College and what it set out to do, by Bataille, Caillois and Monnerot, all written some years later. They are rather different from each other, and this is perhaps inevitable for a project that was by its nature based upon incompletion, and launched with the conviction that a certain vagueness of purpose was essential to its achieving an outcome that was anyway unpredictable. What conclusions could be envisaged, let alone reached? It was enough perhaps to set forth on the journey.

Monnerot's account is distorted by the personal animosity he felt towards Bataille after their falling out, which he appears to have nurtured for many years, and he seems too unreliable to consider here, especially when he played no actual part in the College.

Caillois's account is to be found in the texts which comprise "The Paradox of Active Sociology" (which barely touch upon the paradox of the title), and in his interviews. However, it is also necessary to address certain tendencies in Caillois's thought and writing which are evident even in the "Introduction", ○59. Its conclusion, already quoted, in which Caillois hoped for a shift "from the will to knowledge to the will to power", seems at the least unfortunately expressed in the context of Nazi aggression at the time. In fact, from as early as 1937, Theodor Adorno and Walter Benjamin had voiced serious reservations about the political implications of Caillois's writing. Adorno criticised his text "The Praying Mantis" (1937) for being "crypto-Fascist" by proposing an a-historical nature that was resistant to social analysis. He accused Caillois of attempting to "reframe myths and what they represent in the individual's psychic life as fundamental experiences akin to those of biology", something which, as Muriel Pic pointed out, was close to the collective unconscious of Jung, who in 1936 had been appointed vice-president of the Göring Institute for Psychological Research and Psychotherapy, which was the official mouthpiece of the Third Reich on these topics until 1940.[43] Caillois pursued this "biologism" within the College, refusing to distinguish between animal and human social structures, and this was the source of early disagreements between him and Bataille.[44]

Nor did Caillois much help himself. In a text written in 1945 and first published in French in 1974, he gives a rather disturbing version of the impulses that led to the formation of the College, recalled while re-reading a book by Alphonse de Châteaubriant, *La Gerbe des forces*:

> This writer, when invited to visit the Third Reich [...] was completely seduced by the various attempts then being actively pursued to reconstitute the old orders of chivalry. At that time, in various fortresses lying deep in the heart of the Black Forest and in Courland, they were endeavouring to prepare an elite body of stern and pure young leaders to assume the supreme role of directing the nation, and then the world they would go on to conquer. [...] this undertaking fired more than one imagination. Such was the case in particular amongst those of us who had

> founded the College of Sociology, dedicated exclusively to the study of closed groups, societies of men...[45]

It would be unduly charitable to categorise such a statement as naïve, especially given its date of composition, and the conclusion from it must be that divisions between Caillois and Bataille meant they were bound to fall out: was it not precisely to combat such co-options of myth by Fascism that Bataille had formed the College in the first place? Caillois continued his account:

> We were fascinated by the decisiveness of those men who, from time to time through the course of history, sought to give firm laws to an undisciplined society that was incapable of satisfying their desire for rigour. [...] But some amongst us, so full of enthusiasm, did not choose to resign ourselves to interpretation alone, but were impatient to act for ourselves.[46]

The myth of the strong leader... in Bataille's mind, precisely what the College was opposed to, and with an exactly contrary meaning to the headless figure of Acéphale. Elsewhere in the same book, Caillois maintained that it was he who had insisted that the College should be "for interpretation only", and remain a research group, against the wishes of Bataille, "who did little to conceal his intention of creating a potent and devastating sacred that would be so contagious the epidemic would overwhelm and glorify the one who had seeded the first germ."[47] Caillois's account becomes a little hard to follow at this point,[48] since he appears to confuse the College with the Society and maintains he refused to join Acéphale because he was convinced by the argument put forward by Kojève (who was surely uninvolved with Acéphale), that Bataille and he could no more be possessed by a sacred that they had knowingly unleashed than a magician could convince himself of the reality of magic by means of his own tricks. His decision, Caillois said, was only reinforced by Bataille's desire to found the Society upon an "irreparable" ritual crime, and to create "an initial focus for the irresistible expansion of the sacred" — namely a willing human sacrifice.[49] Caillois repeated his assertions about human sacrifice almost every time he mentioned Acéphale, and also claimed that Bataille asked him to be the executioner, but since he was not a member of Acéphale this request would only have made sense if the act was connected to the College too, which is difficult to envisage. At all events, such a sacrifice goes unmentioned in any of the documents here, although Claudine Frank's anonymous informant told her that the initiation procedure for Acéphale involved the *possibility* of such an event (see pp.219-20, *1 October*).[50]

For Bataille, the College was the logical extension of another aspect of his activities since *Documents* (and Acéphale was perhaps its *illogical* extension). In *Documents* he and his colleagues had employed ethnology as a method of critique, and as a bitter satire of contemporary society. It provided a new perspective on social structures, while the study of other societies, especially so-called "primitive" cultures, demonstrated that the norms of western culture were simply constructs and thus malleable and open to change. The move towards the sociology that would study such constructs was a natural progression. Even before Contre-Attaque, Bataille had written to Pierre Kaan (14 February 1934) suggesting a new approach was necessary:

> I have no doubt as to the level on which we ought to place ourselves: it can only be the same as that of Fascism itself, that is to say on the mythological plane. It is therefore a matter of proposing values that may participate in a living nihilism, fully commensurate with Fascist imperatives. These values have not yet been put forward and although it is possible to do so, it is not yet possible to know how it should be done.[51]

Bataille then suggested that in a society in which the sacred has been largely replaced by a false community based upon "the exploitation of man by man", the necessary destruction of the existing social order required that everyone must "sacrifice their individual desires to the necessities of revolution. The revolution quickly revealed its true nature, that it must be a collective movement, having as its aim the establishment of a new society, which could not demand less than the old one — which must in fact demand even more — of the individuals it unites."[52] Bataille recalled that:

> These young writers felt, more or less clearly, that society had lost the secret of its cohesion, and that this was what the obscure, difficult yet sterile efforts of poetic fever had been aiming to address. [...] They were not interested in launching a new experiment that would only prolong Surrealism, but in scientific research. They felt a certain aversion to their past links to literary effervescence, and what they excluded most vehemently was the possibility of compromise, of science put to superficial use towards some dubious undertaking. Doubtless they wondered whether the impotence of art might not be followed by the sterility of pure knowledge, but their need for rigour and intellectual honesty opposed what was for others a stronger demand, that thought should lead to action.[53]

This account differs markedly from what Caillois had written, despite the shared emphasis on rigour. Nevertheless, while the College was being formed, Bataille and Caillois persuaded themselves that they were largely in agreement, and their collaboration appears to have been what allowed them to envisage some sort of action on "the mythological plane".

Bataille later wrote that the College of Sociology "was in some way the public face" of Acéphale,[54] and it did indeed have a public presence, its lectures being advertised in the *NRF*, for example. Acéphale, on the contrary, was a secret society, and as we see from Marina Galletti's account of how she found the papers which are published here, for fifty years its members mostly kept that secret, and so nothing much could be known about its relationship to the College. The result is that the College, formed in March 1937, has been treated far more thoroughly than the Society (formed shortly before). Out of everything, this is perhaps the only solid fact, that the Society preceded the College.

In an interview for the film series Archives du XX$^{e}$ Siècle, Caillois spoke of how the College came into being. Here he said that it took a whole year after the "founding" of the College to "give it content", and since the first lecture took place in November 1937, this work would have to have begun in November 1936. This was when Bataille and Caillois made up after their disagreement over Contre-Attaque (p.113, *4 November*), and when a meeting of the Sociological Group took place (on the 11th) at which Bataille denounced the fact that politics "has drained all our emotional powers like a plague".[55] The Group had been formed immediately after the collapse of Contre-Attaque, as described in ●14 §12:

> On 4 June 1936, the resolution to found a moral community had its first result, but, deriving from the way political groups tend to be organised, it appeared to be impossible to go beyond the format of a 'study group', and so was given the name — which was never, in fact, actually used — of the 'Sociological Group'.

The formation of the Group, therefore, coincided not only with the end of Contre-Attaque, but with the publication of the first issue of *Acéphale*, while Bataille also associated it with the beginnings of the secret society, when he wrote: "Originally we were satisfied with a name appropriate to a study group", ●14 §1. So the Sociological Group seems to have provided an initial context for the formation of both the College and the Society, even though the meetings that actually led to the creation of the College took place outside of it. The members of the Group presumably included the writers involved with *Acéphale*, excluding Caillois and Monnerot: Ambrosino, Bataille, Klossowski, Rollin and Jean Wahl, along with the earliest members of the future Society from the CCD and/or Contre-Attaque (Andler, Chavy, Chenon, Dautry, Dussat, Kaan and Kelemen).

Leiris appears to have refused to take part, but Kojève may have done.[56]

While the Group may well have provided a context, Bataille was disappointed with its meetings, ●14 §13-16, until the November meeting when he announced that he was "turning his back on politics". His reconciliation with Caillois then allowed them to consider reviving their old project of a sociological commission that had been proposed for Contre-Attaque, but which had been abandoned when they fell out. The field was clear for a new approach and, as with *Acéphale* and Masson, Bataille sought a collaborator; on this occasion it was to be Caillois, and the two of them began the separate discussions which would lead to the establishment of the College. Monnerot too may have been at these meetings, and Caillois recalled Kojève being present "at all the early discussions" and that he objected to their central theme, which at this time they referred to as the *"sacré actif"*,[57] the active sacred. Kojève's objection came to a head at a meeting at Bataille's flat which is difficult to date and when, as stated earlier, he told them that they were putting themselves in the position of a conjurer who expected his own tricks to make him believe in magic.[58]

After November 1936, Bataille's letters and other writings only refer to meetings for *Acéphale*, and it was not long before Caillois's reappearance, confirmed by Bataille in a letter to Dautry on 23 December,[59] brought about dissension among those participating, with Ambrosino commenting on Caillois's supposed influence over Bataille. A general meeting for *Acéphale* was called for 29 December, when Bataille probably hoped for some sort of accord between Caillois and the *Acéphale* group and/or the Sociological Group. Caillois could not attend, however, and his position was represented by Monnerot, who himself aroused a certain amount of hostility. This was probably because those involved with *Acéphale* were now made aware of the substance of the private discussions between Bataille, Caillois and Monnerot. Indeed, this attempt at a reconciliation appears instead to have confirmed the split between the members of the Group on one hand, and Caillois and Monnerot on the other. The fact that Bataille appeared to be setting up a new association seems to have catalysed the formation of the Society as, if not exactly an opposition, then at least as a group that would exclude Caillois and Monnerot.

Even so, Bataille and Caillois pursued their plans, and the discussions about the formation of the College that took place after this meeting may also have involved others such as Leiris, Klossowski and, as we have seen, Kojève. Another general meeting was scheduled for 6 January, but was postponed until 7 February. On this occasion Bataille read "What I have to say...", ●13, and Caillois a version of "The Winter Wind", ○30, texts that make proposals relevant to the founding of either the College or the Society.

In early February 1937, Acéphale had been constituted as a secret society.[60] The College acquired its name around the end of January, and by this time Claude Chevalley had become involved (p.147, *25 February*). It came into being formally in March at a meeting at the Véfour; here Caillois read another early draft of "The Winter Wind", ○30, while Bataille read "What we undertook a few months ago...", ○29. In this text he proposed that a Freudian interpretation of social structure allowed for the transition "from knowledge to action" that seemed to be missing from Durkheim. Assisting such a transition could not be the immediate concern of an existential society such as Acéphale, so the College, which had been chiefly formed to develop a theoretical basis for the Society, was also perhaps intended to maintain Acéphale's existential "purity", while leaving the way open to political initiatives on the part of the College. However, Marina Galletti has shown in her introduction that this purity proved impossible to sustain, and that the Society too came to acknowledge an implicit political engagement.

Leiris had declined to join Acéphale, although he remained on good terms with its members. Caillois, on the contrary, maintained his distance and a mutual distrust arose between him and the group, so that even early on it was likely that Bataille anticipated a similar rejection from him. It is uncertain when he asked Caillois to join, but it must have been between mid-July and 16 October 1937. It is not known what Caillois's response was on discovering that "a moral community" had already been established without his knowledge. The fact that the College was an association which required less commitment than the Society, which Bataille was thus able to persuade these old collaborators of his to take part in, was doubtless another motive behind its creation. Walter Benjamin later wrote that the only secret of the secret society was that it was intended to bind together its founders, Caillois and Bataille (Benjamin did not usually make much of a distinction between the College and the Society in his correspondence).[61] He was not far wrong, since Bataille went out of his way to maintain his alliance with Caillois, but this did not preclude "furious slanging-matches" between the two.[62]

Benjamin and Caillois often referred to the College in their correspondence as "the College of Sacred Sociology" and this may have been a sort of private name for its inner circle of members. At the start of this introduction I referred to the "profane" meaning of its name, which implied that there was also another. Caillois explained:

> ... the College, that is the sacred college, not a college like a school but like the superior authority of the Church [...] when we said College of Sociology it implied the College of the Sacred and the Sacred College [of Cardinals], so to speak... The word "college" was chosen because of its connotations and for what it called to mind; in today's parlance it would be considered religious and not at all academic.[63]

Caillois stressed that the College was not only a "community" but an "Order", and that it had its habitual practices, even if these did not quite qualify as "rites". Bataille suggested an annual celebration of the guillotining of Louis XVI at the Place de la Concorde. This was never put into practice, but a second rite was observed by both College and Society: a refusal to shake hands with anti-Semites.

From the first, however, the College carried with it the idea of the "active sacred", later "active sociology" and finally redefined as "sacred sociology", and this was probably the reason for Leiris's second thoughts, since in Durkheimian terms, it was an inadmissible conjunction. Although he took part in the enterprise, he is not among the six who finally signed the "Note": Ambrosino, Bataille, Caillois, Klossowski, Pierre Libra and Monnerot. Only four of these would be involved in its work, however. Almost nothing is known of Libra, who was probably excluded when his anti-Semitic attitudes were exposed,[64] and Monnerot fell out with Bataille before the College began its lectures.

## OPERATION OF THE COLLEGE

The College gave lectures between November 1937 and July 1939, equivalent to two academic years. The outbreak of war brought its activities to a definitive end, although whether it could have continued anyway is rather doubtful. Membership of the College was both elective and selective. One elected, or agreed, to be a part of it, but according to its first programme (p.225), one had to be invited to join by an existing member. Masson even suggested it was a college of "initiates";[65] it was certainly a place where initiates for Acéphale were recruited, and the connection between the two groups was known to some of its members, at least (Benjamin was aware of the "secret" group, for example). Another indispensable rite of membership was the payment of a monthly or annual subscription.

The College was mostly directed by Bataille alone, because Caillois suffered long bouts of illness during this period and was also often away teaching outside Paris; Leiris was not much involved after giving his lecture in January 1938. Bataille called meetings as required with various members involved in its organisation, Ambrosino and Waldberg apparently, perhaps Chevalley and it seems Klossowski and Benjamin as well, although with the latter as something of an observer (Klossowski recalled "he was sometimes present at our secret meetings").[66] We know, for example, that just before lectures started, Bataille met Chevalley and Denis de Rougemont, who requested that abstracts of the lectures be made available beforehand so that responses could be prepared (it seems unlikely this ever happened).[67] Apart from the infrequent correspondence between Bataille and Caillois no records of these meetings or any administration have survived, but this correspondence does show that it was Bataille who decided on the

VEFOUR
TÉLÉPHONE
GALERIE DE VALOIS (PALAIS-ROYAL) RESTAURANT VÉFOUR

4745. PARIS – Rue Gay-Lussac

programme of lectures and suggested who outside of the founding group might be invited to speak, although he sought Caillois's advice on these matters.

The College went through a number of crises. Until the final collapse of its activities, the most urgent upset seems to have coincided with the invasion of Czechoslovakia in March 1939, which prompted the statement "The New Defenestration of Prague", already mentioned (for a summary, see pp.360-1).

The lectures to the College of Sociology were given in a large, book-lined room behind a bookshop called the Salle des Galeries du Livre at 15 rue Gay-Lussac, near the top of the Boulevard Saint-Michel, and not far from the gates of the Jardin du Luxembourg. Lectures were followed by comments from Bataille and Caillois, if present, then by a more general discussion.[68] Not many who attended have left an account of them (is it a coincidence that both Leiris's and Queneau's published journals omit the dates when College lectures occurred?). Duthuit, who evoked the formation of the College in terms very similar to Bataille's,[69] remembered audiences of between thirty and sixty people. This was quite an impressive figure, given that Patrick Waldberg recalled that when he and Okamoto attended the lectures given by Mauss, the audience would often number fewer than a dozen, including a few tramps sheltering from the cold, and that Kojève's lectures could be barely more popular.[70] The lack of any register means it is only possible to establish a very inadequate list of those who attended (speakers are given in italics): Jean Atlan, *Georges Bataille*, Julien Benda, Walter Benjamin, Georges Blin, Bracke-Desrousseaux, *Roger Caillois*, Georgette Camille, Michel Carrouges, André Chastel, Claude Chevalley, Pierre Drieu la Rochelle, Édouard Dujardin, *Georges Duthuit*, Isabelle Farner, David Gascoyne, *René M. Guastalla*, Maurice Heine, Pierre Kaan, *Pierre Klossowski*, *Alexandre Kojève*, Jacques Lacan,[71] Paul-Louis Landsberg, Laure, *Michel Leiris*, *Anatole Lewitsky*, Georges Limbour, André Masson, *Hans Mayer*, Victoria Ocampo, Taro Okamoto, Germaine Pascal, Jean Paulhan, Raymond Queneau, *Denis de Rougemont*, Jean-Paul Sartre, Jean Wahl, Patrick Waldberg and Eric Weil. No doubt the members of Acéphale also attended.

Our best eye-witness was the young poet Édith Boissonnas, invited by Paulhan, who attended lectures between February and June 1939. Her diary for 21 February records Paulhan introducing her to Limbour, Caillois and finally Bataille, who then took the floor:

> The talk was rather impenetrable to start with — or was I too overjoyed to listen?

---

*Left top:* The College of Sociology was founded in the upstairs room of the Grand Véfour, "then rather dilapidated". *Bottom:* Its lectures were held in the rue Gay-Lussac, in a room behind the Salle des Galeries du Livre, which was on the ground floor of the white building on the right just beyond the car.

> I liked the looks of those around me and the room was charming, completely lined with books. At the back, on the shelves where the rarer volumes were kept, there were many beautiful bindings. I was up to my elbows in books. People smoked if they liked, and leafed through the books — then captivating. Bataille described a childhood Mardi Gras, his feeling of voluptuous fear, the eyes of the masks, the masquerades and a girl getting crushed, her body.[72]

The lectures presented here are but a small selection from those in Hollier's book, the most recent edition of which is 900 pages long. Only those lectures for which a complete and finished text exists were chosen (with one exception), not least because these were also the works of writers, and some of these essays are also literary works, however much their authors would protest the irrelevance of such an observation (see, for example, ●61 §IV). Lectures given by those outside the group of College founders were excluded, since they were unfamiliar with how Acéphale and the College came into being, and the point here is to present a narrative and a continuity of thought between the two groups. Lastly, among the lectures remaining, there were some that did not contribute much that was new to this narrative, such as Caillois's "The Ambiguity of the Sacred", and others that lay somewhat outside of it, for example, Klossowski's on "The Marquis de Sade and the Revolution" (see summaries on pp.355 and 357-8 respectively). In the commentary to the texts I have provided (often rather absurdly brief) summaries of those aspects of the omitted lectures by the founders of the College that are an aid to comprehension of the ongoing argument, of the "course" followed by those attending this most unusual institution.

Finally, it should be remembered that almost none of these texts were intended for, or revised for publication. They were designed to be read, or read out, at the Society or the College, a situation in which any obscurities could be questioned and explained.

# THE SACRED CONSPIRACY

# I

(1924), 1929 – March 1936

# CHRONOLOGY

**(1924)**

Michel Leiris described his first meeting with Bataille at a café near the Élysée: "I quickly became close to Georges Bataille, who was only a little older than me. I admired not only the breadth and variety of his culture, but also his non-conformist spirit which was expressed in what we had not yet come to call 'black humour'. His appearance was striking, although he was rather thin, and he had a charm that was at once entirely modern but also had something of the romantic about it; he already possessed that elegance (albeit, of course, in a younger, less discreet form) that would never leave him [...] His eyes were deep-set and quite close together, of a brilliant noon blue, and his teeth, which strangely resembled those of some small woodland creature, were often visible when he laughed, and when I (probably wrongly) assumed he was being sarcastic."[1]

*Note:* an asterisk following the first appearance of a name in the *Chronology* indicates a biography in the *Appendices*.

## 1929

**January.** Bataille and his wife, the actress Sylvia Maklès (1908-1993), whom he had married in March 1928, move from their Paris apartment to Boulogne-sur-Seine, just to the west of the capital. Sylvia, from a family with Romanian Jewish roots, has three sisters. Bianca is married to Théodore Fraenkel, ex-Dadaist and doctor to both Bataille and Leiris; Rose is the future wife of the painter André Masson; and Simone the future wife of Jean Piel, who succeeded Bataille as editor of *Critique*, the review he founded in 1946.

**19 February.** Leiris ends his collaboration with the Surrealist group.[2] Over the year, he reads the works of the ethnographer Lucien Lévy-Bruhl, which prompt him to attend the classes of Marcel Mauss, probably in the autumn.[3]

**March.** Bataille ceases writing for *Aréthuse*, an art and archaeology journal edited by colleagues of his at the Bibliothèque Nationale.

**April.** Publication of the first issue of *Documents*, co-edited by Bataille. Its contributors include various young intellectuals, some connected to Surrealism: Jacques-André Boiffard, Robert Desnos, Leiris, Georges Limbour and Raymond Queneau; and others connected to art or ethnography: Carl Einstein, Mauss and Georges Henri Rivière (these last two are attached to the ethnographical museum in Paris, the future Musée de l'Homme). In *Documents*, a veritable "war machine directed against received ideas",[4] Bataille makes plain his distaste for the Surrealists' devotion to the "marvellous", and publishes a series of aggressively anti-idealist articles which cause serious tensions within the editorial committee. Bataille's involvement with the journal ended in 1930 and it folded the following year.[5]

**June.** Roger Caillois, aged 16, passes the first part of his baccalaureate.

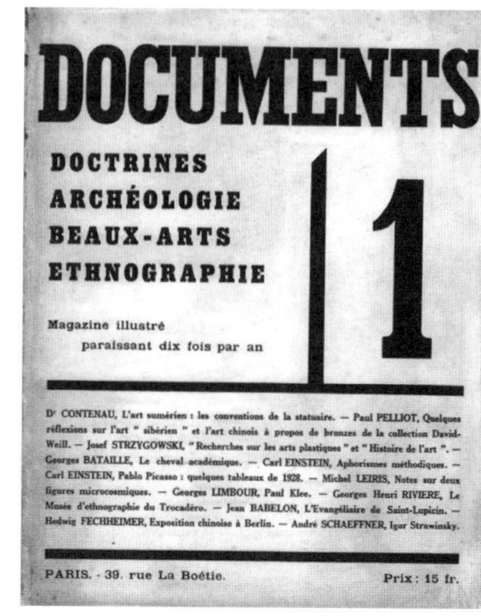

DOCUMENTS

DOCTRINES
ARCHÉOLOGIE
BEAUX-ARTS
ETHNOGRAPHIE

1

Magazine illustré
paraissant dix fois par an

Dr CONTENAU, L'art sumérien : les conventions de la statuaire. — Paul PELLIOT, Quelques réflexions sur l'art " sibérien " et l'art chinois à propos de bronzes de la collection David-Weill. — Josef STRZYGOWSKI, " Recherches sur les arts plastiques " et " Histoire de l'art ". — Georges BATAILLE, Le cheval académique. — Carl EINSTEIN, Aphorismes méthodiques. — Carl EINSTEIN, Pablo Picasso : quelques tableaux de 1928. — Michel LEIRIS, Notes sur deux figures microcosmiques. — Georges LIMBOUR, Paul Klee. — Georges Henri RIVIERE, Le Musée d'ethnographie du Trocadéro. — Jean BABELON, L'Evangéliaire de Saint-Lupicin. — Hedwig FECHHEIMER, Exposition chinoise à Berlin. — André SCHAEFFNER, Igor Strawinsky.

PARIS. - 39. rue La Boétie. Prix : 15 fr.

**1 August.** Leiris's *Journal* records long nights of drinking: "I've been out with Bataille two evenings in a row."

**September.** Leiris begins psychoanalysis under Dr. Adrien Borel, a founding member of the Paris Psychoanalytic Society. He had been Bataille's analyst during 1926-27 and would be Leiris's again in 1934.

**October.** The Wall Street Crash; the effects of the depression that follows are felt for most of the next decade.

**December/January.** Bataille is the subject of a lengthy attack by André Breton in the final section of his *Second Manifesto of Surrealism*, first published in issue 12 of *La Révolution surréaliste*. Bataille responds to Breton on 15 January 1930 with a virulent pamphlet entitled *A Corpse*, a collective publication with contributions from a number of dissident Surrealists who were attacked in the manifesto, including Desnos, Leiris and Limbour. In later years Bataille came to regret his response: "I hate that pamphlet (*A Corpse*) as I hate the polemical parts of the *Second Manifesto*. These

UN CADAVRE

*Il ne faut plus que mort cet homme fasse de la poussière.*
André BRETON (*Un Cadavre*, 1924.)

PAPOLOGIE D'ANDRÉ BRETON

MORT D'UN MONSIEUR

AUTO-PROPHÉTIE

impetuous accusations, which are impossible to retract, arise from an anger that is all too easy and premature; how much better would it have been if both sides had remained silent."[6]

## 1930

**Early 1930.** Transformation of the veterans' association Les Croix-de-Feu into a paramilitary neo-Fascist organisation by Colonel de la Rocque.

**15 January.** Death of Bataille's mother. While sleeping in an adjoining room in her apartment that night, he recalls an orgy in which he had taken part two years previously in the room in which her body is now laid out: "the extreme voluptuousness of my memories prompted me to return to this orgiastic chamber and to masturbate while looking at the corpse".[7]

**10 June.** Birth of Laurence, Bataille's daughter with Sylvia. After the war, with his second wife Diane Kotchoubey de Beauharnois (or Beauharnais), he had a second daughter, Julie.

**At the end of 1930,** Leiris finishes *Lucretia, Judith and Holofernes*, the first version of *Manhood*, originally intended for an erotic "almanac" edited by Bataille, and illustrated by Masson, which did not appear because of the "tedious attentions of the police".[8] Bataille's "The Use Value of D.A.F. de Sade" was written for this collection, and introduced for the first time the idea of Heterology as a science of what is outside of science, and linked to a "reversal of the established order".[9]

## 1931

**March.** First issue of the journal *La Critique sociale*, founded by Boris Souvarine* with the aim of creating an updated Marxism more aligned with sociology, psychoanalysis, philosophy, economics and history. Colette Peignot,* Souvarine's partner, subsidises the magazine and, from December, writes reviews for it, at first signed with her initials, and then as Claude Araxe (combining an androgynous forename with the French form of the Araxes river in the Caucasus, known since Antiquity for its turbulent and destructive torrent).

**April/May.** Final issue of *Documents*. Leiris leaves France as part of the two-year ethnographic expedition across Africa, the Dakar-Djibouti Mission, led by Marcel Griaule and organised by the Institut d'Éthnologie de l'Université de Paris and the Muséum National d'Histoire Naturelle.

**14 April.** Proclamation of the Republic in Spain.

**July.** In the first issue of the new Surrealist journal, *Le Surréalisme au service de la révolution*, Breton launches a diatribe against Souvarine.[10]

**October.** Bataille's first contribution to *La Critique sociale* is a review of Krafft-Ebing's *Psychopathia Sexualis* which immediately causes a dispute with Jean Bernier.* Bataille responds to Bernier in the March 1932 issue of the magazine.

The October issue features texts from

two former Surrealists and contributors to *Documents*, who had written for Souvarine's journal since it was founded: Jacques Baron, its editorial secretary, and Queneau.

**In November,** Bataille begins following Alexandre Koyré's course in the thought of Nicholas of Cusa, where he meets Alexandre Kojève.[11]

**27 November.** In Paris, the final session of the International Disarmament Conference is broken up by Rocque's paramilitaries in alliance with royalist and anti-Semitic groups such as the Camelots du Roi.

**November/December.** At the Brasserie Lipp, Bataille, accompanied by Sylvia, meets Colette Peignot (Laure), who is with Souvarine, for the first time. He later writes: "From the first day, I felt a complete clarity between us."[12]

**At the end of the year,** or perhaps at the beginning of 1932, and probably at the suggestion of Queneau, Bataille attends meetings of the CCD, an anti-Stalinist Communist association founded by Souvarine in 1930 (based upon a previous group that had been exclusively for ex-members of the Party). Here he meets André Barell,* Pierre Kaan,* Esther Tabacman, Simone Weil and various future members of Acéphale: Pierre Aimery (Imre Kelemen*), Georges Ambrosino,* Jacques Chavy,* René Chenon,* Jean Dautry,* Henri Dussat,* Harrick Obstfeld (alias Pierre Dugan, who later takes the name of Pierre Andler*) and Patrick Waldberg.*

## 1932

**March.** In *La Critique sociale*, Bataille publishes "Critique of the Foundations of the Hegelian Dialectic", written in collaboration with Queneau.

**14 April.** Caillois makes contact with Breton and joins the Surrealist group. He remains involved with the Grand Jeu group (having known Roger Gilbert-Lecomte in Reims since the mid-Twenties).

**3 June.** A Radical-Socialist government is formed in France, with the Socialists as the second largest party.

**12 July.** As always, and despite his position at the Bibliothèque Nationale, Bataille has financial problems and today his furniture is seized by bailiffs and sold off to pay his rent arrears.[13]

**November.** Bataille continues with Koyré's course and also his seminars on the religious philosophy of Hegel.

## 1933

**During 1933,** rightist groups become more organised in France and launch their own daily newspaper, *L'Ami du peuple*.

**January.** In *La Critique sociale*, Bataille publishes "The Notion of Expenditure", which later played a central role in Acéphale.

Caillois, with other Surrealists, joins the AEAR, the Association of Revolutionary Writers and Artists, a Communist organisation.

**30 January.** Adolf Hitler becomes Chancellor of the German Reich.

**February.** Leiris returns from Africa and joins the Musée d'Ethnographie at the Trocadéro. He returns to his studies under Mauss, but is disorientated by his return to European life and later resumes psychoanalysis with Borel in June 1934.

**27 February.** The burning of the Reichstag is used as a pretext by Hitler to suppress political opposition, especially the Communists.

*Opposite, left to right, top to bottom:* Six who joined the Society: Georges Ambrosino, Pierre Andler, Jacques Chavy, Henri Dussat, Jean Rollin and Patrick Waldberg; and three who did not: Pierre Kaan, Alexandre Kojève and Raymond Queneau.

**5 March.** The Communist Third International calls for a joint opposition against Fascism and begins negotiations with the Socialist party that will eventually lead to the formation of the Popular Front.

**April.** Bataille, with Souvarine, signs an "Appeal for Victor Serge" in *La Critique sociale*. Serge had been sentenced to three years' imprisonment in the Urals for anti-Stalinist agitation.

**June.** The second issue (which is published simultaneously with the first) of the chiefly Surrealist journal *Minotaure* is entirely devoted to the Dakar-Djibouti Mission, assembled by Leiris and with texts by him.

**7 July.** Leiris signs a contract with Gallimard for a book on the Dakar-Djibouti Mission to be called *Phantom Africa*. It is banned under the German Occupation for its anti-colonial stance, among other reasons. Leiris is appointed head of the African department at the Trocadéro.

**September.** In *La Critique sociale*, Bataille publishes "The Problem of the State" in which he proposes that the failure of Marxist theory before the spectre of the totalitarian state (Stalinism, Fascism, Nazism) can only be corrected by the violence of despair, the sole dynamic element capable of leading to successful revolutionary action.

**October.** Bataille approaches the study groups associated with the journal *Masses* and organised by René Lefeuvre, and which are close to the thought of Rosa Luxemburg. With Kaan, Leiris and Aimé Patri he plans a sociology study course on modern political and social myths: the College of Sociology in embryonic form.[14] He meets the photographer Dora Maar, who becomes his mistress (before her relationship with Picasso).

**November.** Publication in *La Critique sociale* of the first section of Bataille's "The Psychological Structure of Fascism", part of a book-length study in preparation, perhaps to be called *Fascism in France* (only a part of which was later drafted in 1934), or *Essay To Define Fascism*; both projects were abandoned. The second section of the text appears in March 1934 in the final issue of *La Critique sociale.*

**7 December.** Caillois becomes a student at the École Pratique des Hautes Études so as to take the course taught by Georges Dumézil, the philologist and mythographer.

## 1934

**1934.** Bataille meets Pierre Klossowski at some point in this year.

**January.** Kojève begins lecturing on Hegel, a course that continues until 1939 and which is attended by Bataille, Caillois, Jacques Lacan, Henri Lefebvre, Merleau-Ponty, Queneau and Eric Weil, among others. These lectures later come to be seen as a pivotal moment in modern French philosophical thought. In the early months of 1934, at an evening discussion at Lacan's house, Caillois recalls first meeting Bataille,[15] whose essay "The Notion of Expenditure" he had found "revelatory".

Leiris's *Phantom Africa* is published and he is criticised by Griaule, the mission leader, for using the expedition's journal without removing its denunciations of colonial administrators. Their split is confirmed by a lecture Griaule gives in London on Leiris's special interest, the Dogon, which does not mention his research.[16]

Caillois attends Mauss's lectures on sociology.

**January/February.** Bataille is often confined to his bed with a rheumatic illness and liver complaints[17] that have affected him since the year before. (Bataille's military service was prematurely ended by pleurisy in 1917, and he was forced to leave his job at the Bibliothèque Nationale in 1942 because of pulmonary tuberculosis.[18]) On one or two occasions Laure visits him at his home at Issy-les-Moulineaux on the outskirts of Paris.[19]

**February.** The Stavisky Affair leads to the resignation of the moderate leftist prime minister. He is replaced by Daladier from the same Radical-Socialist Party, whose dismissal of the notoriously right-wing Prefect of Police, Jean Chiappe, sparks rightist riots from La Rocque and similar groups on 6 February. They come close to overthrowing the government and the Third Republic.

Bataille is a signatory to the manifesto *Peuple, Travailleur, Alerte*, issued by the CCD and the Fédération Communiste Indépendante de l'Est in response to the crisis.

Masson concludes that the Fascists are likely to take power in France and decides to leave for Spain.[20]

**9 February.** Leftist counter-demonstrations in Paris leave hundreds injured.

**10 February.** The Surrealists issue the manifesto *Appel à la lutte* (*Call to Struggle*), which outlines a strategy for the working-class movement to combat the "immediate Fascist danger"; it calls for unity of action and support for the general strike. Caillois, Maurice Heine, Leiris and Maar are among the 90 signatories, most of whom are from the Surrealists but the list also includes a number of intellectuals unattached to Breton's group, among them Alain, Jean-Richard Bloch and André Malraux.

**12 February.** General strike and leftist anti-Fascist demonstrations across France (in which Bataille and Leiris participate); huge joint demonstrations seal the alliance of Communists and Socialists. An account of these events occurs in Bataille's *Awaiting the General Strike*, which was written immediately afterwards, when he was still gripped by the emotion of witnessing the procession of workers singing the Internationale and advancing across the Place de la Nation "IN THEIR WRETCHED MAJESTY".[21] This text introduces ideas that when elaborated form the basis of the revolutionary strategy adopted by Contre-Attaque.

**March.** Bataille suffers a "serious crisis" but does not modify his way of life; he "assiduously visits the brothels" and "drinks more than his health permits".[22] Leiris too resumes the life of heavy drinking that pre-dated his marriage; he is violently opposed to having children and his wife is pregnant. They will remain childless.

Bataille makes a trip to Italy, intended to restore his health, but he is still unwell on the 14th, according to a letter to Leiris, and is almost crippled with rheumatism.[23] In Rome he visits the Mostra della Rivoluzione Fascista (Exhibition of the Fascist Revolution), from which he retains in particular the way it dramatised the symbology of death as a means of hypnotising the masses by representing a truth unfamiliar to those from industrial civilisations, here recast as the soldier's self-sacrifice on the battlefield. He writes later: "human hearts never beat as hard for anything as they do for death".[24] While in Rome he also undertakes research at the Biblioteca Nazionale for a "universal history". This is a project that he continued to work on throughout his life, and he outlines its principles in a letter to Queneau, also written on the 14th.[25] He travels on to Albano and almost certainly visits the nearby lake of Nemi where, according to Frazer's *The Golden Bough*, the rites of the priesthood of Diana took place. Bataille's rheumatism, however, is making walking so difficult that he returns to Paris after a brief stop at Stresa, where sunshine follows downpours of rain and "afternoons spent lying on hotel beds"; on the shores of Lake Maggiore he is suddenly transfixed by the chorus of a Mass being sung and broadcast through loudspeakers.[26]

**May.** With Sylvia, Souvarine and Laure, Bataille spends two or three days in the country house of a friend at Rueil, outside Paris. It is during this stay that he realises that relations between Laure and Souvarine "were poisonous".[27] He has now fully recovered from his rheumatic illness.[28]

**26 June.** Masson and Rose Maklès move to Tossa de Mar on the coast north of Barcelona, where their sons, Diego and Luis, are born.[29]

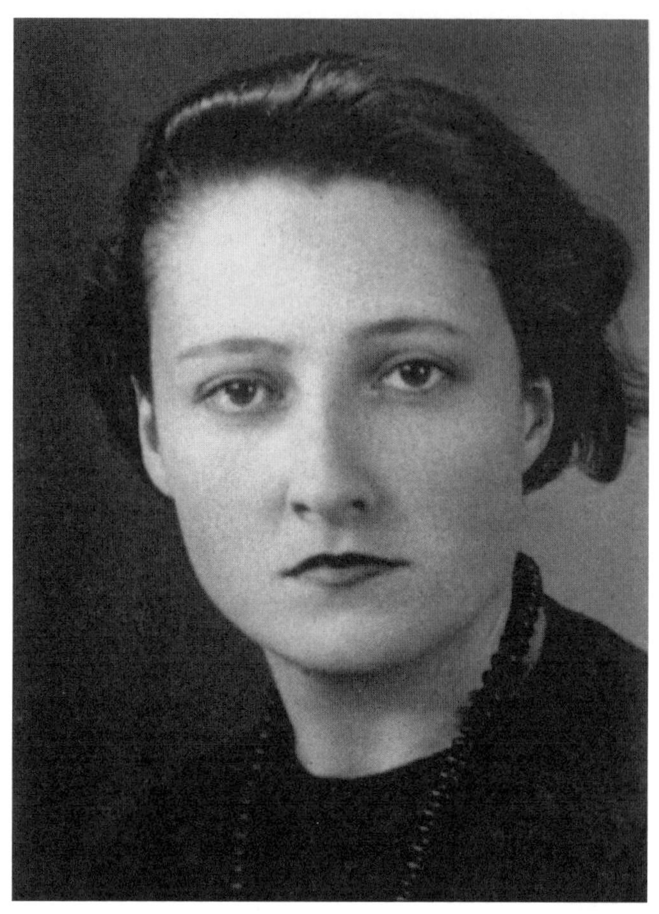

Laure (Colette Peignot).

**29 June.** Beginning of Bataille's relationship with Laure.

**30 June.** Night of the Long Knives: Hitler consolidates his power with a purge in which his most prominent opponents in the Nazi Party are murdered.

**4 July.** Laure leaves with Souvarine and some friends for Austria and Italy, having started a correspondence with Bataille. She writes to him from Innsbruck around this date: "Your love has entered my life, it will not leave. I could almost say it envelops me – I am afraid – yes terrified of saying anything at all, of uttering a single word."[30]

**16 July.** Leiris records in his *Journal*: "Meeting with Bataille: conversation about Beauty (I'm the one who uses this word). Of course, no agreement!"[31]

**18 or 19 July.** Having decided not to go to the Pyrenees with his daughter Laurence, Bataille departs for Austria to find .[32] He recounted the subsequent pursuit of her through Italy in his diary *La Rosace*, and later wrote: "although this was 'like a madman', chasing from place to place, I lived like a god (flagons of black wine, lightning, portents)."[33]

**20 (or 19) July.** Bataille and Laure meet at the Hotel Victoria, Innsbruck.[34] Afterwards she leaves with Souvarine for Steinach am Brenner, then Bolzano, from where, on the 21st, she writes: "I want to spend some time absolutely *alone*. It is during this time that I will see you."[35]

**22 July.** Laure and Souvarine arrive in Riva. The same day she leaves alone for Molveno having arranged to rejoin Souvarine in Verona on 25 July. The letters she sends him during this time apart bear witness to the crisis in their relationship and cause Souvarine much distress.

**24 July.** Laure joins Bataille at Mezzocorona and then travels with him to Trento, where the orgy evoked in his novel *Blue of Noon*, and more explicitly in *On Nietzsche*, takes place.[36]

**25 July.** The Austrian Chancellor Engelbert Dollfuss is assassinated in Vienna by Nazi agents (although he was the Fascist dictator of Austria — having closed down its parliament — he was opposed to German territorial claims). Bataille writes in *La Rosace* that he "convinces L[aure] to stay". Meanwhile Souvarine is waiting for her in Verona, having received only a couple of telegrams from her since they parted. Bataille and  travel from Molveno to Andalo in the Dolomites. On 31 July they are in Innsbruck, a town they find dominated by "black pennants". They leave for Zurich on 4 August.

**5 August.** Laure arrives in Paris,[37] and is met at the Gare de l'Est by Simone Weil, with whom she stays the night, intending to return the next day to her home in Neuilly. On the 6th, Souvarine writes, in the diary he had begun on 25 June, that Laure makes a "half-confession",[38] after which she succumbs to a depressive crisis which induces Simone's father, Dr. Weil, to have her hospitalised the same evening at the Clinique Jeanne-d'Arc in Saint-Mandé.

**25-27 August.** Bataille travels to Biarritz to join Laurence and his wife, from whom he separates shortly afterwards. He returns to Paris on the 28th, Sylvia and Laurence go to stay with the Massons.

**August/September.** Leiris and his wife Zette are in Spain, going to see bullfights and staying with Masson in Tossa de Mar,[39] along with Sylvia and Laurence. A series of letters from Bataille traces the end of their marriage: "Sylvia, don't say you're a monster, you are the most pure and charming individual I have ever met. I wish I could be a different man."[40]

**6 September.** Laure is entrusted to the care of Dr. Borel.

**Early September.** Bataille frequents brothels in Paris, the Tabarin, the Sphinx, and has various other liaisons.

**13 September.** Bataille also decides he needs to see Borel, perhaps in order to begin analysis again. He writes to Leiris: "I'm not joking but I am leaving for Privas to see Dr. Adrien Borel. Don't breathe a word to anyone about this piece of foolishness but I am on my last legs: all hell is raging in my head."[41]

**6 October.** After a leftist insurrection against the right-wing government in Madrid, which seemed on the verge of a Fascist takeover, the Catalan Republic is proclaimed, and then brutally suppressed on the 17th.

**1-3 November.** Bataille travels in Germany, to Trier, Koblenz and Frankfurt with "Edith", as he writes in *La Rosace*.

**November.** Bataille begins regular attendance of Kojève's course, which he follows in 1934-35 and 1935-36.[42] He later recalls: "How many times did Queneau and I feel overwhelmed in that little room — overwhelmed, and stunned. [...] Kojève's course broke me, crushed me, killed me ten times over."[43]

**26 December.** Caillois breaks from the Surrealist Group with an open letter to Breton, the immediate cause being the "affair of the Mexican jumping beans" which supposedly revealed incompatible attitudes to "the Marvellous". At a meeting of the Surrealists in a café someone had placed a few jumping beans on the table and a dispute arose over whether one of them should be cut open to discover how it worked; Caillois was for, Breton against. Caillois later said it catalysed his disappointment with Surrealism, which now seemed to be "literature as an end in itself rather than the end of literature".[44]

Meetings begin that will lead to the founding of Contre-Attaque.[45]

**29 December.** The so-called "soirée de Saint-Cloud" occurs in a summer-house owned by Barell's grandparents. Bataille, along with Ambrosino, Chavy, Chenon, Dussat, Kelemen and others meet for a dinner that degenerates into some sort of orgy after too much drinking. The police are called by neighbours and break into the house. This was the beginning of a brief affair between Bataille and Pauline, Chenon's sister, who later married the painter Gaston-Louis Roux, a friend of Leiris.

## 1935

**In 1935** Bataille, now separated from Sylvia (they divorce in 1946), moves to 76 *bis* rue de Rennes, a few metres from no. 85, where he had lived between 1919 and 1928 with his mother, Marie Antoinette Tournadre, and his older brother Martial, a journalist.

Also in this year, he discovers the works of William Blake.

**20 January.** Bataille addresses a long letter of clinically detailed reproach to Leiris: "The project we envisaged recently makes it clear, and this is somewhat comical, or bitter, that on a certain level, there is no more than the ghost of a friendship between us. [...] Where there might once have been some understanding in you of what really matters to me, there is now a void. And when I say a void, I also know what it covers up."[46] The reason for Bataille's belligerence is that Leiris has refused to commit himself to the political meetings in which they have been engaged, and instead is planning a new literary journal, *La Bête noire*, with Marcel Moré,* when for Bataille the time for such activity was definitively past.

**16 March.** Germany renounces the arms restrictions of the Treaty of Versailles and introduces conscription. The League of Nations condemns this violation of the treaty but takes no action.

**1 April.** Entry in *La Rosace* for this date: "meeting with Laure. At the [Café] Flore, then at Fred P[ayne]'s, then rue de Rennes." It is around this date that Laure ends her treatment with Dr. Borel (having left the sanatorium the previous October).[47]

**15 April.** Meeting at the Café du Bel-Air, 32 Avenue du Maine (along with the Café Augé, 6 rue des Archives, one of the meeting-places of the CCD), to discuss the leaflet *Que faire?* (cited in full in ● 14 §5). Bataille, Dautry and Kaan are the signatories. This is the founding meeting of

André Masson (right) in a photo-booth with
an unidentified friend, early 1930s.

what will become Contre-Attaque, in which Bataille and Breton collaborate. When Bataille sends this flyer to Leiris he writes: "... all that counts is to see whether it is possible to make people aware of their existence and prevent them, if possible, from sleepwalking through it."[48]

**18 April.** Because of the increased Fascist threat the Surrealists issue the leaflet *Enquête sur l'unité d'action* (*Survey on United Action*), a follow-up to *Appel à la lutte* which is signed by a number of Surrealists who will later be involved with Contre-Attaque.

**21 April.** Caillois publishes "Procès intellectuel de l'art", in which he settles scores both with Surrealism (guilty in his eyes of being a purely literary enterprise that is incapable of a rigorous exploration of the imagination and is also ineffective politically), and with the Grand Jeu group, whose passion for metaphysics, although legitimate, had shown only disappointing results.

**"After" 23 April.** Queneau, who often refers to himself in the third person in his diary, writes this phrase in inverted commas: "Bataille went mad and started shouting at L[eiris] and Q[ueneau]". Queneau also opts for *La Bête noire* in preference to Contre-Attaque, and he and Bataille break with each other until October 1939,[49] when Bataille recalls in his diary: "Queneau was the first to abandon me."[50]

**24 April.** Caillois signs the Surrealist tract *La Planète sans visa* (*Visaless Planet*), denouncing the decree expelling Trotsky from France by its "government of appeasement".

**End of April.** Bataille leaves with his daughter for Spain from where he returns at the end of May. It is perhaps during this stay (or in March 1936 in Tossa de Mar) that he asks Dora Maar to come and join him, and to whom, in his reply to her refusal, he wrote: "We play at a sort of bargaining. But I don't want to play any longer. [...] I belong to you completely [...] I'm sure that all in all your life is hard. Mine is as hard as rock."[51]

**2 May.** Signing of the Franco-Soviet pact by Laval and Stalin, which implies rearmament directed against Germany.

**8 to 12 May.** Bataille and Masson frequent the brothels in Barcelona. On the 10th they go together to Montserrat. This ascent of the mountain, previously climbed by Masson and his wife in 1934, becomes for Bataille a real initiatory journey and an overwhelming cosmic and religious experience which orientates him towards the "inner experience" he later examines in his book of that name. Bataille and Masson explore this event in a joint work, *Montserrat*, which appears in the Surrealist journal *Minotaure*,[52] consisting of Bataille's text "Le Bleu du Ciel" (not to be confused with the novel of the same name) and two paintings by Masson, *Aube à Montserrat* and *Paysage aux prodiges*, and his poem "Du haut de Montserrat". The manuscript includes a preface that called for "the shattering recognition of a reality that has nothing to do with the one that is commonly recognised. It changes life."[53] Montserrat reappears in the drawing by Masson at the start of issue two of *Acéphale* (p.28) which thus identifies it as a sacred place for the Society soon to be formed.

**11 and 12 May.** Bataille attends bullfights in Barcelona.

**13 May.** Bataille rejoins Laurence in Tossa, where the philosopher Paul-Louis Landsberg and his wife Madeleine are also staying. Bataille and Landsberg later become friends and he regularly attends the College of Sociology lectures. According to Michel Surya, Bataille and Madeleine have a brief affair.[54]

**16 May.** Signing of the Soviet-Czechoslovakian pact, valid only if France supports both parties.

**29 May.** Bataille finishes his novel *Blue of Noon*, which is not published until 1957.

**May and June.** On several occasions Masson writes to Leiris with a similar message: "Michel, I fear for our long friendship, wake up and do not be afraid to acknowledge that you have taken the wrong track."[55]

**June.** Souvarine's highly critical biography of

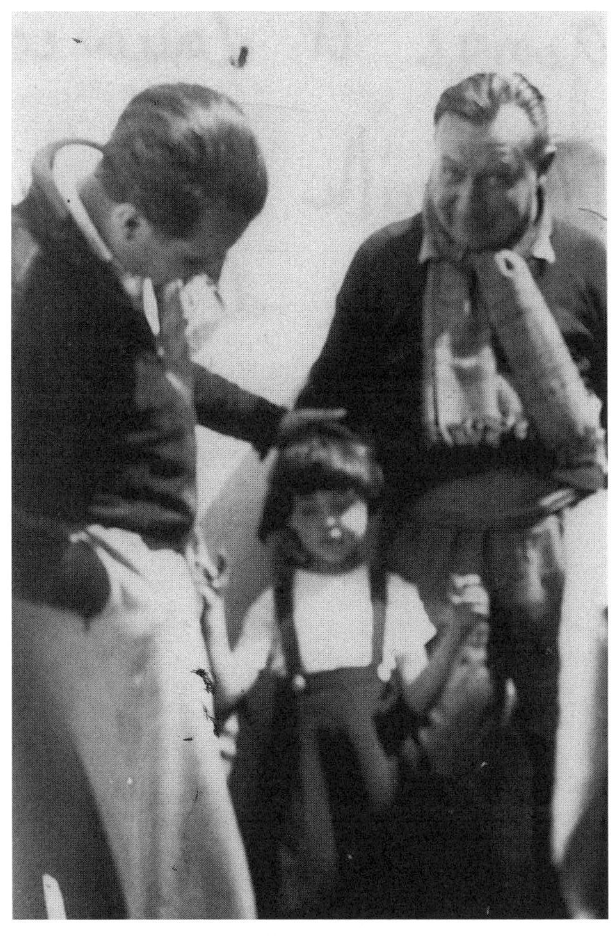

Georges and Laurence Bataille with André Masson,
Tossa de Mar, August 1935.

Boris Souvarine and Laure, August 1935.

Stalin, rejected by Gallimard despite recommendations from Bataille and Malraux, is published by Plon. The Congrès International pour la Défense de la Culture takes place, organised by the French Communist Party. Breton is prevented from speaking.

**7 June.** The leftist parties remain split, and Laval forms a centre-left government. The Socialists and Communists renew negotiations for a common front.

**13 June.** In *La Rosace*, Bataille records: "Laure at the Flo[re]. Then rue de Rennes".

**July.** Bataille and Caillois plan the formation of "an association of revolutionary intellectuals". At one of their meetings this month Bataille first introduces "the Nietzschean theme of the death of God [...] as it dominates our shared mythical existence and thus our actual existence today", ●14 §6.

**August.** Publication of the Surrealists' leaflet *On the Time When the Surrealists Were Right* denouncing the Stalinists for having silenced them in June. Laure and Souvarine leave for Spain.

**August/September.** As in the previous year, Leiris and Zette stay with André and Rose Masson in Tossa de Mar.

**September.** The events in June and August allow Bataille and Breton to bring their animosity to an end.

**15 September.** The Nuremberg racial laws are promulgated.

**18 September.** Meeting to form Contre-Attaque in the Café de la Mairie, Place Saint-Sulpice, which Caillois does not attend.[56] Other similar meetings take place during this month according to Claude Cahun, one at the Café de la Régence near the Palais Royal, which Caillois does attend; others at Cahun's studio and at Marcel Jean's.[57]

**3 October.** Mussolini invades Ethiopia.

**7 October.** Dissemination of the manifesto *Contre-Attaque* (*Counter-Attack*), see ●14 §7.[58] It begins with these words:

*We, who are violently opposed to any attempts, whatever form they may take, to appropriate the Revolution for the benefit of ideas of nation or patriotism, address ourselves to all those who, by all means possible and without reservation, are determined to bring down all capitalist authority along with its political institutions.*

Active members, along with Bataille and Breton, include Aimery (Kelemen), Ambrosino, Roger Blin, Boiffard, Cahun, Chavy, Dautry, Jean Delmas, Paul Eluard, Heine, Klossowski and Benjamin Péret. The second appearance of the manifesto has 39 signatories and, along with some of those above, includes others who later play a part in the secret society: Chenon and Henri Dubief,* and among the female signatories: Reya Garbarg and Dora Maar.

**27 October.** Leiris begins typing up the MS. of *Manhood*.[59]

**November.** Publication of Breton's *Political Position of Surrealism*, with the *Contre-Attaque* manifesto as an appendix.

**1 November.** At a meeting of Contre-Attaque Bataille breaks with Caillois and Jules Monnerot.* The split with Caillois appears to be over his refusal to sign the Contre-Attaque manifesto, despite having a role in its instigation. Caillois must have found the reconciliation between Breton and Bataille somewhat disconcerting. However, his main objection, according to a letter to Jean Paulhan of 30 October, was that he did not approve of the direction being taken by this project, in particular the way it assumed the pose of a political party with a definite programme before certain ideological questions had been properly addressed.[60] Monnerot, in a letter to Caillois that evening, protests at how vociferous Bataille was during arguments, and that he remains unconvinced by them.[61]

**21 November.** Meeting of Contre-Attaque members and sympathisers at the Café de La Mairie.

**24 November.** Joint communication from

Bataille and Breton to a general meeting of Contre-Attaque on the subject of the Popular Front at the attic studio of Jean-Louis Barrault, 7 rue des Grands-Augustins.

**27 November.** The political committee of Contre-Attaque decides to organise a public showing of *L'Age d'or*, the film by Luis Buñuel and Salvador Dalí which has been banned since December 1930, so as to provoke an *"excitation générale"*.[62]

**November 28.** Dissension between the Bataille faction and the Surrealists results from the publication of an article by Georges Blond in *Candide* which attributes the formation of Contre-Attaque solely to Breton. The group is also attacked in the Communist press.[63]

**December.** Various meetings of Contre-Attaque, including one on 8 December at Barrault's studio, which is open to non-members, during which Bataille and Breton speak on "Affective Exaltation and Political Movements".

**21 December.** In an interview in *Le Figaro*, Breton takes credit for founding the group, and this exacerbates tensions further with the Bataille faction.

**29 December.** Dussat, who has been doing his military service in Metz since 21 October, writes a first draft of his text "Du Sang" while on leave in Paris. The final version of February 1936[64] coincides with the first meetings of the future members of Acéphale.

**End of December.** Leiris sends the typescript of *Manhood* to Gallimard, but there are delays in publishing the series in which it is to be published, and it does not appear until June 1939.

## 1936

**Throughout January and February.** Several meetings of Contre-Attaque.[65]

**5 January.** Meeting of Contre-Attaque at Barrault's studio on the subject of "Fatherland and Family" to oppose abandoning the revolutionary position. The speakers are Bataille, Breton, Heine and Péret.

**7 January.** Entry from Leiris's *Journal*: "Saw Bataille yesterday, with Dora Maar, who is likable and attractive. Bataille is certainly wrong about Contre-Attaque, its value is above all literary etc. But it is precisely this will to go beyond himself, this refusal to allow himself to be fenced in by literary boundaries which is the sign of his poetic worth. Making literature while telling yourself that *it is only* literature: a way of not being duped, but still another vicious circle. Yet this determination to go beyond oneself need not necessarily take a political form."

**20 January.** Meeting to form the first of two cells within Contre-Attaque based upon geographical boundaries. "Marat", the cell for the Left Bank, has Trigonis (Nicolas Calas) as its secretary, with Jean Rollin* as his deputy. On the 25th, the "Sade" cell for the Right Bank is formed, in which Bataille and Breton participate. Its secretary is Dubief, with Jacques Brunius as deputy. This division of the movement into cells gives it something of the structure of a secret society.[66]

**21 January.** At Barrault's studio, Bataille, Breton and Heine speak on the "200 Families", a phrase coined by the Radical-Socialist leader Daladier to identify those at the core of the establishment who should face the justice of the people. Distribution of the prospectus for *Les Cahiers de Contre-Attaque*, ● 14 §8. It is the anniversary of the beheading of Louis XVI and Bataille proposes establishing an annual festival in celebration of this event.[67]

**13 February.** Léon Blum, the Jewish leader of the French Socialist Party, is dragged from his car and beaten almost to death by members of the Camelots du Roi.

**16 February.** During a young royalists' demonstration against Blum, Contre-Attaque distributes a leaflet written by Péret, *Comrades, the Fascists are Lynching Léon Blum*. Around this time Contre-Attaque issues *Appel à l'action* (*Call to Action*), a pamphlet written by Bataille.

CONTRE-ATTAQUE
21 JANVIER 1793 - 21 JANVIER 1936
ANNIVERSAIRE DE L'EXÉCUTION CAPITALE DE LOUIS XVI
Le MARDI 21 JANVIER 1936, à 21 heures,
réunion ouverte au Grenier des Augustins,
7, rue des Grands-Augustins. Métro: St Michel
Objet de la réunion:
LES 200 FAMILLES
qui relèvent de la justice du peuple
Prendront la parole: Georges BATAILLE, André BRETON, Maurice HEINE.


**26 February.** Dussat, away from Paris doing military service, replies to Chavy's letter of the 23rd which announced that a secret society is in the process of being formed, "I find the society based on ties of blood [...] to be very compelling".[68]

**February/March.** Bataille writes "The Labyrinth" for *Recherches philosophiques* 5.

**7 March.** Germany begins to remilitarise the Rhineland, in contravention of the Treaty of Versailles. The League of Nations protests but the Western democracies take no action.

**8 March.** In a radio address the French prime minister Albert Sarraut declares: "We are unwilling for Strasbourg to be within the range of German guns". Dautry is given the task of writing a leaflet for Contre-Attaque in response, and this is distributed without Breton's approval. He signs a second version with certain changes, including a new title: "Under Fire from French Guns... and Those of Our Allies".

Meeting of the members of Contre-Attaque who are close to Bataille at the Café Aux Armes de la Ville. On the agenda, a discussion of Dussat's "Du Sang", and the formation of a secret society.[69]

**14 March.** Bataille convenes a meeting of Contre-Attaque at the Café Augé. On the agenda is the leaflet *Workers, You Have Been Betrayed!* written by Bataille with Bernier and Lucie Colliard, in which, following the hawkish rhetoric of Sarraut, they urge the left not to support "a war declared by Western capitalism against the Fascist nations".[70] Other signatures were added to the leaflet, including those of Breton, Eluard and Heine without their being consulted, and Bataille's group soon afterwards issues a further tract announcing the formation, without a general vote, of a "Committee against the Sacred Union" which is to be composed only of those close to Bataille: Bernier, Colliard, Dautry, Gaston Ferdière and Georges Michon. This precipitates a new break with the Surrealists.

**16 March.** Bataille and Masson sign the contract for *Sacrifices* with the publisher Guy Lévis Mano.

**29 March.** Dussat writes to Chavy: "There must have been a meeting one or two days ago when Bataille was probably told of our clandestine activity". The reference is to the secret society which is in the process of being formed.[71]

Olga Tabakman and her sister Esther Tabacman,
with Georges Ambrosino, Grenoble, early 1930s.

# THE SACRED CONSPIRACY

# II

................................

April 1936 – January 1937

# CHRONOLOGY

## 1936

**2 April.** A general meeting of Contre-Attaque is held at which Bataille resigns as general secretary. Dautry is appointed in his place. Gilet (i.e. Nicolas Calas) resigns his position in turn, and is replaced by Rollin. Bataille applies himself to the creation of the secret society "that would turn its back on politics and have only a religious purpose (but anti-Christian and essentially Nietzschean)".[1]

**4 April.** Bataille writes "Programme", ●6, a text that proposes the formation of an "order" and which is given to the participants in Contre-Attaque who have sided with him.[2]

**7 April.** Bataille joins Masson in Tossa de Mar. They have the idea to start a journal, *Acéphale*, the first issue of which, entitled "The Sacred Conspiracy", would propose a new reading of Nietzsche. Masson, who had not joined Contre-Attaque, makes the drawing of a man without a head for its cover as directed by Bataille, who later wrote: "Man will escape his head like a condemned man escaping from prison".

**9 April.** Meeting of Contre-Attaque to discuss the prospect of war; Bataille does not attend.

**14 April.** In Tossa de Mar, Bataille finishes writing "To my eyes, my own personal existence...", ●7, in which he first distances himself from political action.

**17 April.** Andler's "Notes on Fascism" introduces the neologism "surfascism" (invented by Dautry, according to Dubief), meaning the overcoming of Fascism, as a summation of the revolutionary strategy of Contre-Attaque. Instead it prompts the group's final disbandment after it is applied with malicious intent by the Surrealists to Bataille's faction.[3]

**21 April.** Laure is in Madrid where she remains until the end of June.[4] During this stay she writes her "Fragments and plans for erotic texts", intended as a fictionalised account using the pseudonym "Laure" (the name of Petrarch's muse and of Sade's grandmother), and which she "considered [as] representing herself".[5]

**29 April.** Bataille finishes writing "The Sacred Conspiracy", ●1, the introductory text to the first issue of *Acéphale*.

**May.** Masson sends Bataille his poem "Du haut de Montserrat", intended for the first issue of *Acéphale* but which, in the event, is published in *Minotaure*.[6]

Although Contre-Attaque has been disbanded, Bataille nevertheless publishes the first of the *Cahiers de Contre-Attaque*: *The Popular Front in the Streets*. It is disowned by the Surrealists in a statement released on the 24th, and no further issues appear.

**6 May.** The Popular Front, the union of the French Communist and Socialist parties (and other smaller groupings), wins the general election. Léon Blum becomes the first Jewish prime minister of France at the beginning of June.

**End of May/beginning of June.** Bataille, Sylvia and D.-H. Kahnweiler see Eisenstein's *Thunder Over Mexico*.[7]

*Foreground, left to right:* Georges Bataille, costumed as a priest, with Sylvia Bataille and a third actor, during the filming of *Une Partie de campagne* in July-August 1936. The photograph is probably by Eli Lotar.

**Beginning of June.** Caillois publishes an article in *Inquisitions* (the magazine he founds and edits with Monnerot, Louis Aragon and Tristan Tzara), "For a Militant Orthodoxy: the Immediate Tasks of Modern Thought", which impresses Bataille. Later Caillois recalled that he had envisioned "a form of revolutionary thought that would not be limited to the intellectual sphere but would burst into real life".[8]

**4 June.** Bataille *et al.* create a study group, called the Sociological Group, which will play a part in the creation of the secret society of Acéphale, once it relinquishes politics. The brief account in ●14 §12 does not name any of the participants, perhaps suggesting that attendance was sporadic and that the meetings held between June and October were more or less informal, so informal in fact that the group's name was never actually used by participants.

**13 June.** Dussat sends Chavy his *Trois poèmes de la vie sanglante*, for one of which, "Glaive", Chavy draws an illustration.[9]

**24 June.** The first issue of the journal *Acéphale* appears, published by Guy Lévis Mano, and although it is in "clear contradiction with [...] a 'study group'", according to ●14 §13, in part it reflects the intentions of the future secret society. The contributors are Bataille, Klossowski and Masson. The issue of *Minotaure* which includes *Montserrat* by Bataille and Masson is also published this month.

**July.** At some point this month Leiris decides not to join the tentative project taking shape around Masson and Bataille in terms that the latter takes as a personal rebuff. Bataille speaks about this in a letter to Leiris's wife which, in the event, he never sends: "Michel does not realise the hurt he does me. [...] Even if what I am doing is ridiculous, Michel *knows* that I am crazy enough to stake my life on it. How could his attitude be anything but unbearable to me? I couldn't care less about the 'nobodies' who will mistake what I'm doing for something else, but Michel is wrong, and knows it since he is one of the few people in the world who understands what lies behind such an apparently infantile initiative as the one Masson and I are engaged in. [...] I hate this because I hate the fact that the limitation imposed on existence today has the same face as Michel's."[10]

Two early texts related to the society of Acéphale are written this month: Dussat's "Cosmogony" and Andler's "Moriar, ergo sum", ●8, which is dated 25 July.

**18 July.** Beginning of the Spanish Civil War.

Leiris, Zette, Queneau and his wife, who have been in Ibiza since the 9th, are repatriated following the uprising of the militias in Barcelona.[11]

**31 July.** Internal meeting for *Acéphale* (for contributors only), to work on the second issue of the journal in the basement of the Café "A la Bonne Étoile" at 80 rue de Rivoli.

**15 July-25 August.** Filming of Jean Renoir's *Une Partie de campagne* (released in 1946), on the banks of the Essonne south of Paris. Sylvia Bataille plays the main female lead, while Georges has a three-second bit-part as a novice priest (*opposite*).

**19 to 26 August.** Stalin's Bolshevik purges reach their height with the beginning of the Moscow show trials. Kamenev, Zinoviev and fourteen others are condemned to death and shot. Soon afterwards, Bataille signs the leaflet *Appel aux Hommes*, denouncing the trials.

**30 September.** Bataille is arrested with Laure and other members of Contre-Attaque for disrupting a performance of the play *Les Innocentes* at the Théâtre des Arts. The protest is aimed at one of the actresses, Marcelle Géniat, who is also the director of a reform school in Boulogne from which a dozen young girls escaped with cries of "*A nous le Front populaire!*".

**October.** Laure finally leaves Souvarine and joins Bataille in Tossa de Mar; not long afterwards she moves in with him to his apartment in the rue de Rennes. It is probably during this month too that the "unnamed"

Tossa de Mar. Masson's house is just visible outside the walls of the old town, to the left of the leftmost tower.

Sociological Group meets to express its solidarity with the Spanish Revolution.

**25 October.** Signing of the Axis treaty between Italy and Germany.

**29 October.** On returning from Spain, Bataille writes to Kaan: "... everything that I saw has affected me as I have seldom been affected before".[12]

**4 November.** Bataille reconnects with Caillois by sending him a warm letter of reconciliation.[13]

**11 November.** The first of a series of what become regular meetings of the Group is held at the Musée Social, at which Bataille denounces the general political impasse, ●14 §15. The content of what he was intending to say had been summarised in a letter to Kaan on 4 November: "politics has drained all our emotional powers like a plague".[14]

**25 November.** The Anti-Comintern Pact is signed between Germany and Japan, which Italy joins a year later.

**3 December.** *Sacrifices* is published by GLM with Masson's etchings.

**4 December.** Bataille sends a note to Ambrosino, Chavy, Chenon, Dautry, Pierre Dugan (Andler), Dussat, Kaan, Kelemen, Klossowski and Rollin, cancelling plans for a "totemic" dinner they had proposed for 18 December, but confirming their meeting the next day at 6 pm in the Brasserie Lumina, 76 rue de Rennes, ●9 and 10.

**23 December.** Bataille reconnects with Dautry (see ●12), and discusses the reconciliation under way with Caillois and Monnerot.

**28 December.** An internal meeting is held for *Acéphale* in the basement of the Brasserie Lumina. This is almost certainly to decide upon a new publication date for the second issue of the journal, which had initially been planned for September this year, and to prepare an outline of contents for issue 3/4, in the expectation that Caillois and Monnerot would contribute.

**29 December.** An external meeting for *Acéphale* (guests permitted) takes place at 9 pm, on the first floor of the Grand Véfour, rue de Beaujolais, which is attended by Monnerot, although Caillois is absent. The position Monnerot puts forward on his and Caillois's behalf is probably the one published in *Inquisitions*: a "militant orthodoxy" based on the "unitary" character of human beings which would thus be capable of binding together discipline and revolution "in all domains".[15] In January, two texts are drafted in reponse that suggest "acute unease":[16] the first is Dubief's "Critique of Caillois's Position", and the second, Ambrosino's "The Constitution of the Self is Highly Paradoxical", ●11[17] (see also ●14 §16 and 17, and p.119).

**1936.** During this year an unrealised project is proposed, to pour a large pool of blood at the base of the Obelisk in the Place de la Concorde (the site of the execution of Louis XVI). A communiqué to the press, signed by "the Marquis de Sade", was to guide journalists to the site "where the victim was buried". A similar project to leave the supposed skull of Louis XVI at the same spot was likewise never carried out.[18]

## 1937

..............................................

**In January** Leiris writes the poems that are published as *Tauromachies* by GLM in August, with an illustration by Masson. Bataille sends a copy of the first issue of *Acéphale* to Patrick Waldberg in Los Angeles, inviting him to return to Paris and participate in the secret society, which he accepts.[19]

**16 January.** A meeting for *Acéphale* in the basement of the Brasserie Lumina,[20] probably to proof issue 2 of the journal, and to work on no. 3/4, which is to be dedicated to Dionysus and is due to appear the following month.[21]

**21 January.** Publication on this date, exactly one year after the suggested celebration of the beheading of Louis XVI by Contre-Attaque, of the second issue of *Acéphale* entitled:

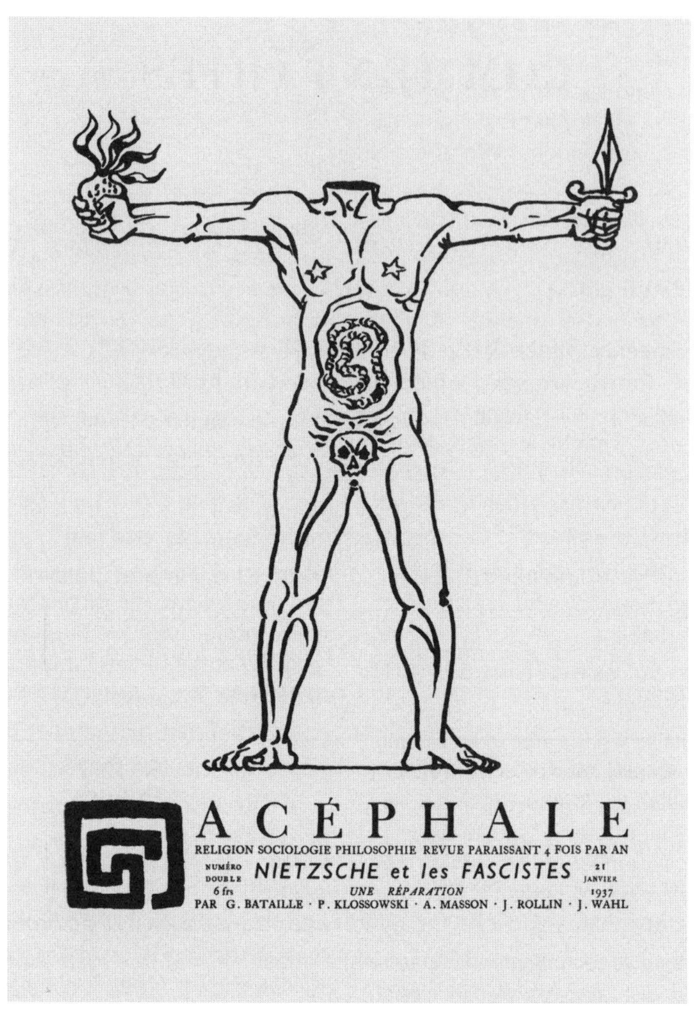


"Nietzsche and the Fascists" (*cover above*). This issue was intended to defend Nietzsche from appropriation by both Nazism and Socialism, with texts by Bataille, Klossowski, Masson, Rollin and Jean Wahl.

**30 January.** Date of the meeting during which the decision was probably taken to found the secret society of Acéphale[22] (see also ●15).

# COMMENTARIES

## ACÉPHALE [MG]

The texts in this first section situate the creation of the secret society of Acéphale within the history of Contre-Attaque, which disbanded in April 1936 "following internal disagreements", ●14 §9, as the Surrealists formally announced in the leftist newspaper *L'Œuvre* on 24 May. They show the beginnings of a new direction in Bataille's thought, and can be seen too as a response to the "rather more religious than political" spirit, ●14 §10, of those members of Contre-Attaque who were close to him.

Whilst Rollin later recalled Bataille speaking to a general political meeting in Argenteuil, north-west of Paris, in support of the central policy of Contre-Attaque ("militant action against the weak politics of the French Communist Party inaugurated by the Laval-Stalin pact"[1]), the principal concern of Acéphale was altogether different: it was a "withdrawal from politics", yet the connection made by Bataille[2] between the nucleus of the sacred and the seat of power within social structures meant that it retained a political aspect. For Rollin, the best example of this was the conspirators in Balzac's *History of the Thirteen*, whose position he characterised as being based not upon metaphysical foundations but on a solidarity that aimed for power. More specifically, he suggested that Acéphale should be thought of as a "transposition of politics into religion, a religion without a god". Koch likewise, while affirming that Acéphale was "absolutely not situated on the plane of action", defined it as "ideological rather than political."[3]

This "collusion between the political and the religious"[4] is most evident in "The Sacred Conspiracy", ●1, the first text in *Acéphale* 1. The authors of its three epigraphs were to be the inspiration behind the new enterprise: Sade, Kierkegaard and especially Nietzsche. Its announcement of a community that was "ferociously religious" was a declaration of war no less compelling than the one which had guided the fanaticism of Contre-Attaque, although its weapons were no longer deployed in support of what Bataille now saw as the "false values" of political action, but instead for the simple value of existence. This radical change can be read as a moving away from action into non-action,[5] and this non-action was a "*désœuvrement*" (disavowal) associated with a "political" initiative intended to ensure that the ideas of Nietzsche could not be put to the service of any sort of doctrine, by reformulating them into a "thought that remains comically unemployable, open only to those inspired by the void".[6] This was an extension of the "moral revolution" predicted by Nietzsche (and described in one of the unpublished *Cahiers de Contre-Attaque*), which declared the imminence of a new world that would conform to the programme outlined at the beginning of "The Sacred Conspiracy" — the necessity to "become completely different, or else to cease to be", and the condemning of "everything that is known today".

Following Bataille and Masson's revelatory experience of an "unrecognised reality" on Montserrat (p.100, *8 to 12 May*), a new time had begun, the time of "preaching", which required that "the world of civilised people and its light" should be abandoned and that its followers should "go forward without looking back over [their] shoulders and without making any allowances for those who lack the strength to forget their immediate reality", ●1. It demanded too that man escape his reason so that he can say of his existence that it "opens me up to a rapture beyond myself", and that he assume the sovereign defiance of Don Giovanni, who is "certain that Hell will engulf him yet does not bend", as Bataille wrote after the war, when he compared the libertine's rejection of prohibition with the Nietzschean cry of the death of God.[7]

For his part, Klossowski, in "The Monster", the second and only other text in the first issue of *Acéphale*, proposed the denial of the immortality of the soul as a way of accessing the "integral man". Klossowski took his inspiration from Sade, to whom he had already devoted three studies, one of which, "Time and Aggression", had appeared in the same issue of *Recherches philosophiques* as Bataille's "The Labyrinth". Klossowski's text relates both to the publication he had proposed for Contre-Attaque, on Charles Fourier's "economy of abundance" based on a "free play of passions", and on the lecture "The Marquis de Sade and the Revolution" he gave on 7 February 1939 at the College. It links too to "The Sorcerer's Apprentice", ○61 §I, in which the "whole man" comes forth, having "escaped his head" and refusing to reduce his "existence to the condition of a servile organ."

The declaration of war announced by "The Sacred Conspiracy" sought out its first targets in *Acéphale* 2. This issue, titled "Restitution for Nietzsche", contains many lengthy texts that we were unable to include here, but which are worth briefly summarising. The introductory text, "Nietzsche and the Fascists", marked a turning point in the interpretation of Nietzsche's thought at this time. In it, Bataille unmasked the various Judases who were guilty of betraying the philosopher, from the initial lie of anti-Semitism fabricated by Nietzsche's own family, to the use he was put to by parties on the left, who based their actions on so-called "rational principles",[8] and even more so by those on the right with their attachment to the values of the past. Lukacs made Nietzsche into "one of the main ancestors of Fascism", whereas for Bataille, "Fascism and Nietzscheism are mutually exclusive, even violently mutually exclusive, when considered in their totality: in the one case, life is tied down and stabilised within an endless servitude; in the other, there is not only a circulation of free air, but the blast of a tempest".[9] The ideologists of Nazism had gone beyond applying Nietzschean maxims to Fascist ends by systematically manipulating his thought. Even before Alfred Rosenberg rejected the gods of the underworld so often evoked by Nietzsche, Jakob Wilhelm Hauer and Ernst Bergmann had created German nationalist anti-Christian religious ceremonies that incorporated passages from *Thus Spake Zarathustra*. Likewise, Alfred Bäumler, whose philosophy strongly influenced the Nazi party, had transformed the will to power into a political doctrine. Bataille, however, opposed the will to power, which implied political action, by stressing Nietzsche's attitude to sovereignty: "sovereignty perhaps requires power, but the quest for power reduces man to action, which is a *means*, and thus the opposite of sovereignty".[10]

Against the backdrop of this twin political betrayal Bataille then contrasted the more recent interpretation by Jaspers, who showed that by shattering "the pre-established frameworks through which Nietzsche's politics have come to be mutilated", Nietzsche, far from providing a "complete system like Hegel's" or "a practical politics like Machiavelli", in fact "proceeds from a concern to embrace the actual condition of man... without methodically immersing himself in the specificities of political action."[11] But the condition of man — as Jean Wahl showed in his reading of Jaspers in the same issue — depends on the death of God, which offers him "the enormous gift of perfect solitude, and at the same time a possibility for greatness and creation".[12] Even so, Wahl continued, Nietzsche saw the negation of God as a tear, a wound or a passion, and thus associated it with Ixion and Prometheus, the two mythological heroes who rebelled against the authority of Zeus. Klossowski's "Creation of the World" describes Nietzsche's definitive separation from society: "He who nursed the Creator in his last moments, who saw the divine limbs feasted on by vermin, who himself felt the posthumous sufferings of God and who placed God in the tomb, has lost the world, and no longer has to be accountable to society."[13]

This issue of *Acéphale* completed its review of contemporary readings of Nietzsche with one by Karl Löwith, commented upon by Klossowski, who traced the voyage of this Columbus of the philosophy of faith in the Christian God all the way back to the will to nothingness and thence to the affirmation of being in the "eternal return". In this way it was because of Nietzsche that Rollin, in his "The Realisation of Man", ●4, was able to write: "the circle is broken of which God was the perfect expression", and connect

Nietzsche to Marx and Freud in the interests of a single goal: "this fulfilment of man [...] a fulfilment that goes *from pain and anguish, and through pain and anguish*, to joy, 'the eternal joy of becoming, the joy that carries within itself the joy of annihilation'".

Having deployed Jaspers and Löwith in cleansing the temple of the falsifiers of Nietzsche, the Holy War of "The Sacred Conspiracy" could finally preach his teachings, here expressed in Nietzsche's appreciation of his *alter ego*, the philosopher Heraclitus. He it was who "'has raised the curtain on this greatest of all stage-plays' — the play of time the destroyer", ●5. This gospel is not received passively, however. The teaching of Nietzsche-Heraclitus is transformed and renewed and then re-presented by Masson's Acéphale figure depicted (p.134) flying above the solitude of the "wildest barren mountains" into the infinite space of the cosmos, like a "star without an atmosphere" that has been expelled by a great earthquake from Earth's gravity and is destined for the pure expenditure of a dizzying journey towards the unknown. Finally, in this issue Bataille establishes the Tablets of the New Commandments, his "Propositions", in which the nine precepts of the "Propositions on the Death of God" follow the five "Propositions on Fascism". These will be later revised within Acéphale, notably in ●65.

As regards the texts of the secret society, which has not yet been formed, this section contains two foundational texts, both by Bataille. The first is his "Programme", ●6, written on 4 April 1936, two days after his resignation from Contre-Attaque and distributed, according to Dubief, "to a number of the participants in Contre-Attaque who had taken his side, with the aim of elaborating the secret society that was to be embodied by Acéphale".[14] A copy of this text was among Dubief's papers, in Kaan's, and in those of four other adepts: Andler, Chavy, Chenon[15] and Dussat. While the notion of a secret society was not yet explicit at this time, it is nevertheless present as a "community for the creation of values, values for the creation of cohesion" that opposes other communities "including national, socialist and communist communities and churches", ●6.

The second foundational text, "To my eyes, my own personal existence...", ●7, dated 14 April, was drafted in Tossa de Mar. Here Bataille opposes *"the laziness of mind that gets called action"* with chance, which, as he wrote in 1938, binds together "the structure of everything" and constitutes the very meaning of existence.[16] And it is existence which Bataille makes central in the first point of the "Creation of the 'Internal Journal'", ●14, of 9 February 1937, and thus to the history of this existential secret society which will manifest "the pure and simple will to be, independent of any particular purpose" that Bataille discussed in the lecture on "Brotherhoods" at the College on 19 March 1938. Consequently, the society, "purposeless" and devoted to non-action, while at the same time being an affirmation of the will to expenditure and effervescence, would be the opposite of Mauss's "conspiracy societies"[17] (see also p.74).

From this period too dates a small number of other texts by adherents of the future secret society. The first of these, "Du Sang" by Dussat, was discussed at a meeting of the group (p.105, *8 March*), but is not included here. The next, "Moriar, ergo sum", ●9, by Andler, marks the end of his political militancy with Contre-Attaque and follows a text by him called "Notes on Fascism" of 17 April 1936[18] which played a part in the break between the Surrealists and the faction around Bataille.[19] Both of these texts were written under the pseudonym of Pierre Dugan, with "Moriar, ergo sum" being dated 25 July 1936, and hence after the formation of the "Sociological Group" and the publication of the first issue of *Acéphale*. This text extols an ecstatic and conscious death, free of any idea of redemption or the beyond, as the sole possible "good". It can be compared to an unpublished text of 30 March 1937, "I was a demanding child...", in which Andler went over the reasons that led him to become "a socialist, a Marxist", and those that persuaded him to engage with Acéphale. "I had come to understand that the men in whose company I lived lacked any taste for chance, that they refused all that went beyond them, and they would remain for ever dead in the presence of the most vivid things — a naked woman, for example [...] my death had appeared to me, and I recognised that it belonged to me, in the same way as love, unconditionally."[20]

This section closes with texts related to disputes within the Sociological Group, ●9, 10, 11 and 12, the last of which concerns the break with Dautry. These disputes are covered in my introduction (p.36); the first was in fact only a brief misunderstanding, but the second, ●11, which followed soon after the reconciliation between Bataille and Caillois, called into question the very attempt to create a secret society. This text by Ambrosino, in which he pointed out that Caillois's "desire for totality" was simply a search for "lucid totality", reveals a difficulty that resulted from the fundamental incompatibility between Caillois and the rest of the group, and its meaning is amplified in an unpublished text by Dubief of January 1937, "Critique of Roger Caillois's Position". Here Dubief accepted Bataille's "taste for struggle and overcoming" as a vital necessity for the group in the search for "the greatest emotional tension", but indicated the confusion introduced by Bataille himself in his desire to associate himself with Caillois's approach. Whilst this mental state had a "profound meaning" for Bataille and his followers and answers the need for an "anguish to overcome", it had only a negligible meaning for Caillois who did not acknowledge this anguish within himself. As a result, his "delight in conquest" is no more than a "consequence of the joy of living, a joyous euphoria equivalent to an athlete's leap, or four of a kind to a poker player."

André Masson, *The Blade is a Bridge*, from *Acéphale* 1.

# TEXTS

## April 1936 – January 1937

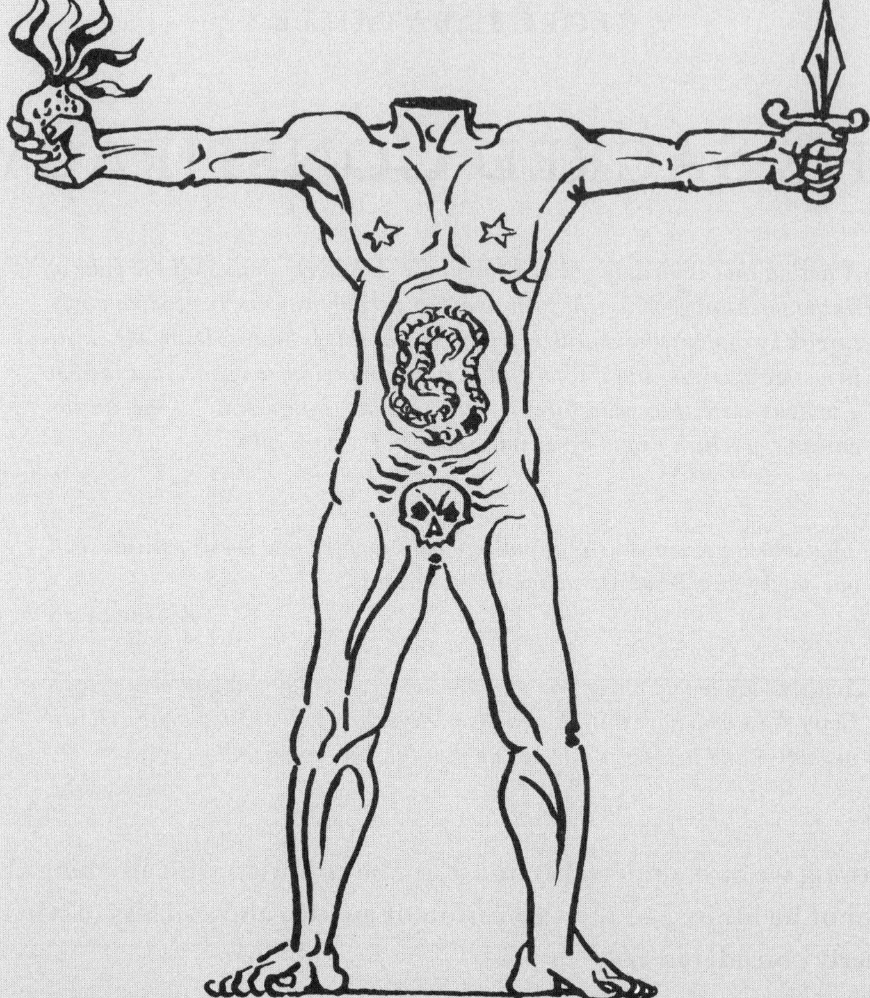

# ACEPHALE

RELIGION · SOCIOLOGIE · PHILOSOPHIE - REVUE PARAISSANT 4 FOIS PAR AN

1e année LA CONJURATION SACRÉE 24 juin 1936

PAR GEORGES BATAILLE PIERRE KLOSSOWSKI ET ANDRÉ MASSON

GEORGES BATAILLE

# THE SACRED CONSPIRACY ❶

*A nation that is already old and corrupt, that bravely shakes off the yoke of its monarchical government so as to adopt a republican one instead, can only survive by committing countless criminal acts; this is because it already exists in a state of crime, and if it wished to pass from crime to virtue, that is from a violent state to a peaceful one, it would fall into a state of inertia the outcome of which would be its imminent and certain ruin.*

**Sade**

*That which presented itself as politics and supposed that it was politics, shall one day be unmasked as a religious movement.*

**Kierkegaard**

*You that are lonely today, you who live apart, one day you will be a people. From those who have thus chosen themselves there will one day come a chosen people — and it is from this people that the Superman will be born.*

**Nietzsche**

**The thing we have undertaken must not be confused with anything else; it cannot be limited to the expression of an idea and still less to what is properly considered art.**

**It is necessary to produce and to eat: many things are necessary but also count for nothing, and so it is with political agitation.**

**Who, before he has struggled right to the end of his task, would dream of stepping aside for men it is impossible to look at without feeling the urge to destroy them? But if nothing can be found beyond the range of political activity, human avidity will encounter only the void.**

**WE ARE FEROCIOUSLY RELIGIOUS and, in so far as our existence amounts to the condemnation of everything that is known today, an inner necessity demands that we be equally unyielding.**

**What we are starting is a war.**

It is time to abandon the world of civilised people and its light. The time has passed for being reasonable and cultured — this has only led to a life lacking in any attraction. Whether secretly or not, it is necessary to become completely different, or else to cease to be.

The world of which we have been a part offers nothing that deserves our love outside each of our individual shortcomings: its existence is limited to its convenience. A world that cannot be loved to the point where it is worth dying for — in the same way that a man loves a woman — represents only financial interest and the obligation to work. If we compare it to worlds long past, this world is hideous and appears as the most failed of all.

In those past worlds it was possible to lose oneself in ecstasy, something which is impossible in our world of cultivated vulgarity. The advantages of civilisation are offset by the ways in which men profit from them: the men of today profit so as to become the most degrading of all beings that have ever existed.

Life has always proceeded in a tumult with no apparent sense of cohesion, but finds its splendour and its reality only in ecstasy and in ecstatic love. Whoever tries to ignore or disregard ecstasy is an incomplete individual whose thinking is thereby reduced to mere analytical processing. Existence is not only a restless void — it is a dance that compels us to dance like fanatics. Thought that does not revolve around dead fragments may have an inner existence in the same way as flames do.

What is required is for us to become sufficiently firm and unmovable that the existence of the world of civilisation will at last be called into question.

It is useless to respond to those who are still capable of believing in the existence of this world, and who manage to derive their authority from it; when they speak, it is quite possible to look at them without hearing what they are saying and, even while looking at them, to 'see' only what exists far behind them. We must reject all tedium and live only for what holds our fascination.

Whilst following this path, there is no point in getting worked up or trying to interest those who indulge such trivial impulses as passing the time, laughing or becoming individually eccentric. We must go forward without looking back over our shoulders and without making any allowances for those who lack the strength to forget their immediate reality.

Too long has human life served as head and reason for the universe. In so far as it becomes this head and this reason, and in so far as it becomes necessary to the universe, it accepts servitude. If it is not free, existence becomes empty and neutered, whereas if it is free, it remains in play. For as long as the Earth produced only cataclysms, trees and birds, it represented a free universe; the fascination of freedom was tarnished when the Earth produced a being who insisted that necessity was a law that was greater than the universe. Man, however, has always been free not to respond to any necessity; he is free to be like anything in the universe that is not him. He can also dispense with the idea that it is either he or God who prevents all the other things from being absurd.

Man has escaped his head like a condemned man escaping from prison.

What he has found beyond himself is not God, who is the prohibition of all crime, but a being who knows no prohibition. Beyond what I am, I encounter a being who makes me laugh because he has no head, and who fills me with anguish because he is formed of innocence and crime; he holds an iron weapon in his left hand, with flames like those of a Sacred Heart in his right. In a single outburst he unites Birth and Death. He is not a man. Neither is he a god. He is not me, but he is more me than I am: his stomach is the labyrinth in which he himself has become lost, and I along with him, and there I rediscover myself as him, in other words the monster.

What I have thought and what I have put forward, I have not thought or put forward on my own. I am writing this in a cold little house in a fishing village; a dog has just barked in the night. My room is next to the kitchen where André Masson is happily moving about and singing; at the very moment when I am writing this, he has just put a record on the phonograph of the overture to *Don*

*Giovanni*; more than anything else, the overture to *Don Giovanni* connects what has been allotted to me by existence with a sense of defiance that opens me up to a rapture beyond myself. At this precise instant, I look upon this acephalic being, an intruder composed of two equally fervent obsessions, as it becomes the "Tomb of Don Giovanni". A few days ago, I was with Masson in this same kitchen, sitting with a glass of wine in my hand, when suddenly he foresaw his own death and the death of his family; with his eyes wide in suffering, he was almost screaming that death must become tender and passionate, screaming his hatred for a world in which the worker's hand is gripped fast even until death, so that I could no longer doubt that the fate and infinite upheavals of human life were open to those who could not exist any more like sightless eyes, but as seers swept away by an overwhelming dream that can never belong to them.

Tossa, 29 April 1936

PIERRE KLOSSOWSKI

# THE MONSTER

2

*We continued on our way into the dry and scorched little plain where this phenomenon can be observed. The ground around it is sandy, uncultivated and filled with stones. As we proceeded further we perceived an extreme heat, and breathed in the smell of copper and coal exhaled by the volcano; at last we spied the flame, which had been made to blaze more brightly by a soft rain that happened to fall at that moment; the crater must be thirty or forty feet all the way round, and if the earth is dug up in this area then small fires start right away beneath the tool that has broken the surface...*

Sade (*Juliette*)

*An express letter shall be sent to Monsieur Lenormand, a timber merchant [...] requesting that he come in person, with a cart, to fetch my body so that it may be conveyed [...] to the forest on my estate at Malmaison [...] where I wish it to be placed, without ceremony of any kind, in the first thick copse to be found on the right in the aforementioned forest [...] My grave is to be dug in this copse by the farmer at Malmaison, under the supervision of M. Lenormand, who will not leave my body until it has been placed in the said grave [...] Once the grave is covered over it is to be sown with acorns, in order that, in due course, as the ground around the said grave produces new growth and the copse becomes as dense as it was before, all traces of my burial shall disappear from the face of the Earth, as I trust that my memory will be effaced from the minds of men.*

*Testament of the* Marquis de Sade

**The different types of anticipation that destroy the present are expressed in Sade's works by the mental operations which govern the different varieties of**

'experimental' debauchery. Happiness consists not in enjoyment but in the *desire to break free from what restrains desire*; things are not enjoyed for their being *present*, but *in the anticipation of these things while they are still absent* — in other words these things are to be enjoyed *by destroying their actual presence* — (murders committed during debaucheries) — or if they disappoint — and seem to be rejecting their presence (through resistance to what we should like to do to them) they will be *treated badly so as to make them at once present and destroyed* (which in moral sadism is expressed, for example, in the sacrilege addressed to God in his absence). For some of Sade's characters, disappointed anticipation ends up becoming an erogenous fiction: the object does not disappoint, but *is treated as if it did disappoint*. Furthermore, one of these overly favoured characters admits that, having only to wish for something in order to have it, his enjoyment was never motivated by the objects around him, "but by those that were not". "Is it possible to commit crimes as we conceive them and as you say here? For my part *I confess that my imagination has always exceeded my abilities, I have always conceived in my head a thousand times more than the number of deeds I have actually carried out, and I have always protested that nature, which furnished me with the desire to violate it, has always deprived me of the means to do so.*"

Here again, Nature is experienced as a presence that calls anticipation into being, but a presence that shies away from aggressive anticipation: the Sadean *conscience* sees itself face to face with its own eternity, which it has disowned and can no longer recognise in the guise of wily Nature; on the one hand, in terms of the individual's organic functions, Nature experiences his aggression; on the other hand, as regards the workings of the imagination, Nature gains some sense of the infinite; but instead of finding its eternal condition there and experiencing itself as part of the universal unity, Nature discerns — as in a mirror — only the infinite reflection of the diverse and multiple possibilities that are lost to the individual. The ultimate violation of Nature would be to cease to be an individual, and instead to assume in totality, immediately and simultaneously, everything that can be found in Nature: this would result in achieving a pseudo-eternity, or rather a temporal existence, that of polymorphous perversity. Having rejected the immortality of the soul, Sade's characters instead put themselves forward as candidates for complete monstrosity, thus denying the temporal elaboration of their own self, while their anticipation then paradoxically places them in a state of possessing all the possibilities for potential development, as expressed by their sense of uninhibited power. The erotic imagination which develops as the individual is formed, counterbalancing at times a perversion and at other times the instinct to reproduce, and which chooses an individual's moments of solitude or anticipation — moments when the world and people are absent — to invade the self, would thus correspond to an unconscious attempt to retrieve everything possible which has been made impossible because of the hold exerted by the self's *conscience* — a formation that has enabled the development of the alter ego — and which leads in turn to aggressive behaviour, to the detriment of external reality, aimed at regaining the individual's original integrity or wholeness. In this way, for the individual living in a state of permanent anticipation, the imagination must make one more effort to escape the object he is anticipating, so as to return to the atemporal condition in which the possession of everything possible nevertheless excluded the possibility of the experience of loss. Through the mouths of his characters, Sade himself confessed: "I invented horrors, and put them on paper quite deliberately: with an attitude of ruling nothing out, however costly my planned debaucheries might prove to be, I carried them out right away." Indeed Sade, the solitary prisoner, deprived of all means of action, effectively had the same power as the omnipotent hero of whom he dreamed: the uninhibited power which knows no resistance, which knows no obstacles, neither outside nor within the self, and which only has the sense of its own unseeing discharge. "I carried them out right away." Such haste, however, cannot really manage to exhaust the movement of "this type of inconstancy, the scourge of the soul and the all too fatal attribute of our sad humanity." Thus the soul, aspiring to deliverance, is prey to a contradictory hope; it hopes to escape the painful experience of loss by refusing the object its presence, while at the very same moment dying from the desire to see the object reintegrated into the present, and shattered there by the passage of time the destroyer.[1]

GEORGES BATAILLE

3

# ACÉPHALE

**[From the back cover of *Acéphale* 1]**

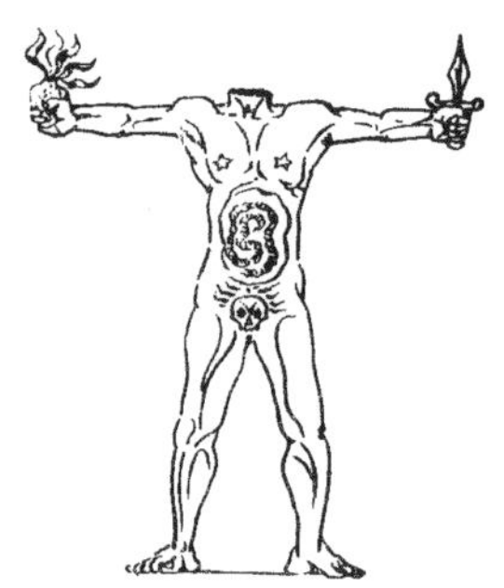

ACÉPHALE

EST LA TERRE

LA TERRE SOUS LA CROUTE DU SOL EST FEU INCANDESCENT
L'HOMME QUI SE REPRÉSENTE SOUS LES PIEDS
L'INCANDESCENCE DE LA TERRE
S'EMBRASE
UN INCENDIE EXTATIQUE DÉTRUIRA LES PATRIES
QUAND LE CŒUR HUMAIN DEVIENDRA FEU
ET FER

L'HOMME ÉCHAPPERA A SA TÊTE COMME LE CONDAMNÉ A LA PRISON

**ACÉPHALE**

**IS THE EARTH**

**THE EARTH BENEATH THE SOIL'S CRUST IS INCANDESCENT FIRE**
**THE MAN WHO CAN PICTURE BENEATH HIS FEET**
**THE EARTH'S INCANDESCENCE WILL BE**
**SET ABLAZE**
**AN ECSTATIC FIRE WILL DESTROY OUR FATHERLANDS**
**WHEN THE HUMAN HEART BECOMES FIRE**
**AND IRON**

**MAN WILL ESCAPE HIS HEAD LIKE A CONDEMNED MAN ESCAPING FROM PRISON**

JEAN ROLLIN

# THE REALISATION OF MAN 4

In a world in a state of decomposition, gradually congealing into nothing but the contemplation and foresight of its own end, whose actions, the moment they come about, destroy everything they had extracted that was conducive to living, the voice of Nietzsche rises up, full of incitement and provocation, heavy with all the pain and all the joy that Zarathustra bears within him. For us, everything that is condemned to die a miserable death, our whole civilisation, thus seems to offer certain new possibilities — the human and cosmic wave that carries us along withdraws, like the sea, so that it may return. Nietzsche's presence is sufficient to change this difficult demise into the dawn of a new birth.

By peeling back the padded layers one at a time from the wound he suffered in his being to the point of madness, Nietzsche snatched from existence the mask which made it unworthy. "Our greatest grievance against existence was the existence of God." A necessary pessimism finds its outlet in this discovery. It becomes a tragic affirmation of life.

For Nietzsche, the death of God was not so much a discovery of the mind as a revelation and an affirmation of life stripped bare, of the chaotic, glacial and irritating world with which he was in contact. If the consequences are extreme, they are so for man, the locus for metamorphoses also known as a world in flux. At last the circle is broken of which God was the perfect expression. There is no need now to seek the reasons why this circle was ineluctably closed around existence. "It cannot amount to a perfect adequacy but only a useful one". It is no longer a matter of interpretation, nor explanation, or contemplation.

*The question Nietzsche asked with increasing insistence concerns the realisation of man.*

Living is all about discovery! Accepting, that is, that existence — as assumed at birth amidst the play of forces that make, unmake and remake the world during every moment of time — is neither a redemption nor a humanisation, but, in relation to the world which forms it and only in so far as it resists it, a painful childbirth, a creation. The life we strive in vain to enclose in explanatory formulas or to paralyse with doctrines bursts out, and we must find our place right in the heart of its ceaseless and incoherent boiling so as to extract its power and be done with having to *believe* or *hope*.

Only Marx before Nietzsche and Freud afterwards have helped (by other means) this fulfilment of man which, although we cannot allow ourselves to see it as inevitable, nevertheless vindicates the monstrous gestations of the world around us — a fulfilment that goes *from pain and anguish, and through pain and anguish*, to joy, "the eternal joy of becoming, the joy that carries within itself the joy of annihilation" — but no other human voice has ever spoken to us "as clearly" as Nietzsche's. Just as with vision, where the object becomes defined and stands out until it ends up being completely integrated and lost, the superman brings us closer to ourselves and our demise. The void of existence is not filled, but we are at least given the option of the act that simultaneously kills it and creates it.

# HERACLITUS

5

## A TEXT BY NIETZSCHE

*This portrait of Heraclitus is taken from* **Philosophy in the Tragic Age of the Greeks,** *one of Nietzsche's earliest works, written in 1873, but only published after his death. Because Heraclitus saw the law in terms of a conflict between different elements, and in fire the innocent play of the universe, Nietzsche was bound to see him as his double, as someone to whom he himself had been as a shadow. If Heraclitus "has raised the curtain on this greatest of all stage-plays" — the play of time the destroyer — it was the stage-play itself which became the object of contemplation and passion for Nietzsche, and this must be what he was engaged with when the vision appeared to him, in all its frightful terror, of the eternal return. "Each moment will exist only in so far as it has exterminated the present moment, its father." "The total inconstancy of all reality is a terrible and overwhelming image. What it represents is analogous to the sensations of someone caught in an earthquake who loses their trust in solid ground." The greatest of all stage-plays, and the greatest of all festivals, is the death of God. "Are we not continually falling? And backwards, sidewards, forwards, in all directions?" Thus would Nietzsche cry out later when he experienced the rapture he called the "death of God" (***The Gay Science,*** *§125). This is a long way from the Fascist barracks…*

*Things themselves, in terms of the fixed solidity which the limited intellects of men and animals believe them to possess, have no intrinsic existence. They are the flash and dash of a brandished sword, the sparkle of victory in the battle of contrary qualities... Total consumption by fire is satiety... Satiety leads to crime (hubris)... Is the whole history of the world no more than the punishment of hubris? The aggregate, the result of one crime?... Fire... plays... turning into water and into earth... like a child building sandcastles... raising them up, destroying them and... starting the game again from the beginning. A moment of satiety. And then, it is seized again by necessity... This is not the criminal instinct, but the impulse for play, for ever awakened anew, and calling into life new worlds...*

**Nietzsche, from *Philosophy in the Tragic Age of the Greeks***

Heraclitus was a proud man, and pride in a philosopher means it is a great pride. His work was never addressed to a 'public', to the applause of the masses or the hailing chorus of his contemporaries. Indeed, it is in the nature of philosophers to wander lonely along their path. His talents were the most rare, in a certain sense the most unnatural, and at the same time exclusive and even hostile towards kindred talents. The wall of his self-sufficiency must surely have been made of diamond, if it were not to be demolished and broken down, for everything was in motion against him. His journey to immortality was more awkward and impeded than that of anyone else and yet nobody can believe more firmly than the philosopher that he will attain his goal by that journey — because if it is not on the widely spread wings of all time then he does not know where he is to stand, for it is in the essence of the great philosophic nature to disregard everything present and momentary. He nevertheless has truth, and while the wheel of time may roll wheresoever it pleases, it can never escape from truth. It is important to hear that such men have lived. Never, for example, could the pride of Heraclitus be imagined as merely an idle possibility. Considered on its own merits, every search for knowledge seems by its nature to be eternally unsatisfied and unsatisfactory. As such, unless they are required to do so by history, no one will choose to believe in such a royal self-esteem and let their conviction in their own being be the only seeker of truth. Such men live in their own solar system — and that is where they must be sought. A Pythagoras, or an Empedocles, also regarded themselves with a superhuman esteem, indeed were almost surrounded by a sense of religious awe; but nagging reminders of sympathy, united with the general belief in metempsychosis and the unity of all living things, led them back to other men, for their welfare and their salvation. As for that feeling of solitude, however, which permeated the Ephesian recluse of the Temple of Artemis,[1] only a little of it can be discerned, growing there in its numbness in the wildest barren mountains. No overriding feeling of compassionate agitation, no desire to help, heal or save emanates from him. He is a star without an atmosphere. His eye, directed inwards with all its blazing intensity, looks outward, for appearance's sake only, as something long dead and icy. All around him, and right against the citadel of his pride, beat the waves of folly and perversity: filled with loathing he turns away. But any man with a feeling heart would also shun such a Gorgon monster, as if it were some fearsome brass effigy; tucked away within a quiet sanctuary, among statues of the gods and near the cold, composedly sublime architecture, such a being may appear more comprehensible. As a man among men Heraclitus was incredible; and although he was at times seen watching noisy children at play, even then he was reflecting upon what had never been thought of by any other man on such an occasion: the playing of the great world-child, Zeus. He had no need of mankind, not even for the purposes of what he strove to discern. He had no interest in any of the things that might perhaps be ascertained from people, nor in what other sages before him had been endeavouring to ascertain. He spoke with disdain of such courses of enquiry, or the collecting, in short, of "historic" men. "I sought and examined myself," he said, using a word which denotes the examination of an oracle, thereby implying that he and no one else was the true fulfiller and achiever of the Delphic precept: "Know thyself."

What he learned from this oracle he deemed immortal wisdom, and eternally worthy of explanation, so too of unlimited effect even at a distance, after the model of the prophetic speeches of the Sibyl. That is sufficient for latent mankind, and let it be expounded to them as oracular sayings, which he, like the Delphic god, "neither enunciates nor conceals". Although it was proclaimed by him, "without smiles, finery or the scent of ointments", but rather with a "foaming mouth", it *had to* force its way through the millennia of the future. For the world needs truth eternally, and therefore it also needs Heraclitus eternally; even though he has no need of it. What does his fame matter to *him*? — fame amongst "mortals ever flowing on!" as he exclaimed scornfully. His fame is something for other men, not for himself; the immortality of mankind needs him, he does not need the immortality of the man Heraclitus. That which he beheld, *the doctrine of the Law in the Becoming, and of the Play in the Necessity*, must henceforth be looked on eternally, since he has raised the curtain on this greatest of stage-plays.

GEORGES BATAILLE *Programme* 6

*1. To establish a community for the creation of values, values for the creation of cohesion.*

*2. To lift the curse, the feeling of guilt that afflicts men and forces them into wars they do not want, and which binds them to work whose benefits elude them.*

*3. To take on the function of destruction and decomposition, but as an achievement, not as a negation of being.*

*4. To achieve the personal fulfilment of being and its tension by means of concentration, through a positive asceticism and positive personal discipline.*

*5. To achieve the universal fulfilment of being within the irony of the animal world and through the revelation of an acephalic universe, playful rather than one of status or duty.*

*6. To take upon oneself both perversion and crime not as exclusive values but as something that must be integrated into the human totality.*

*7. To fight for the break-up and abolition of all communities, including national, socialist and communist communities and churches, apart from this universal community.*

*8. To affirm the reality of these values and the human inequality which results, and to recognise the organic nature of society.*

*9. To take part in the destruction of the world as it presently exists, with eyes wide open to the world that will follow.*

*10. To consider the world that will follow in the sense of the reality it contains now and not in the sense of some ultimate happiness which is not only inaccessible but also repellent.*

*11. To affirm the value of violence and the will for aggression as the cornerstone of the all-powerful.* 4-4-[19]36

1.- Former une communauté créatrice de valeurs, valeurs créatrices de cohésion.

2.- Lever la malédiction, le sentiment de culpabilité qui frappent les hommes, les obligent à des guerres qu'ils ne veulent pas, les vouant à un travail dont le fruit leur échappe.

3.- Assumer la fonction de destruction et de décomposition mais comme achèvement et non comme négation de l'être.

4. -Réaliser l'accomplissement personnel de l'être et sa tension par la concentration, par une ascèse positive et par une discipline individuelle positive.

5.- Réaliser l'accomplissement universel de l'être personnel dans l'ironie du monde des animaux et par la révélation d'un univers acéphale, jeu et non état ou devoir.

6.- Prendre sur soi la perversion et le crime non comme valeurs exclusives mais comme devant être intégrées dans la totalité humaine.

7.- Lutter pour décomposer et exclure toute communauté autre que cette communauté universelle, telles que les communautés nationales, socialiste et communiste ou les églises.

8.- Affirmer la réalité des valeurs, l'inégalité humaine qui en résulte et reconnaitre le caractére organique de la société.

9.- Participer à la destruction du monde qui existe, les yeux ouverts sur le monde qui sera.

10.- Considérer le monde qui sera dans le sens de la réalité contenue dès maintenant et non dans le sens d'un bonheur définitif qui n'est pas seulement inaccessible mais haïssable.

11. Affirmer la valeur de la violence et de la volonté d'agression en tant qu'elles sont la base de toute puissance.

G.B. 4-4-36

6. Georges Bataille, *Programme*.

*To my eyes, my own personal existence could only ever be lost, only truly lost, in circumstances that are rather less than likely… But then I have never known how to look upon existence with the disaffected scorn of the man who is truly* alone. *I have always opened a thousand eyes upon this troubling world and its existence, opened thousands of eyes on my own existence; thousands of greedy gazes, fixing on to even those reflections of thought I would have preferred to keep concealed at all costs.*

*My egotist's eyes, unless they are simply the eyes of someone distracted, could have tolerated anything at all. I could have accommodated myself to leading an unbearable existence; eyes such as these would also have had the calm curiosity to uncover something unbearable or deficient; I should have made everything sink into a stupor of denial, but my greed was not the deliberately crude impulse I had thought it to be. It was like the greed of a dog that cannot be separated from the hunter's greed as he follows behind it, always at the same distance. All human existence was there in the oppression that so troubled me, that thousand-eyed existence, a thousand eyes so greedy to spy some prey beyond the scraps that are boredom's daily fare.*

*Perhaps I am brave, perhaps cowardly, or even brave and cowardly in turn. I live: I have access just like anyone else, sometimes more so, to light, food, meaningless conversations and thoughts made consoling by vanity; I would not want to stop having access to any of these weaknesses and that is why I speak of them with such a calm concern for accuracy. I realise — these sentences, as they fall into place, form a curtain of fog, albeit a curtain which is at times transparent — that thanks to such futile justifications a greedy man can bear the sight of the sky, the earth, or other men, without bursting into tears: so why is it impossible for me to love, to love what will in the end no longer be me — that which will demand, in exchange for the love that will eventually consume me, the gift of life,* and the whole of my life?

*No doubt this is a poor response to certain expectations. But expectations should be left unfulfilled at first.* The search for living prey is not the hurried search for the shadow that satisfies the laziness of mind that gets called action. *I distance myself from those who expect chance, or a dream or trouble-making to offer them the possibility of escape from inadequacy.*[1] *Such people resemble too closely those who, in times past, turned to God in the hope of saving their pointless existence. But I am also afraid of the opposite expectation, which presumes that everything is at the mercy of circumstance.*

*The few marvels the impoverished humanity of today takes to be the remnants of a* grand and imposing past, and the evidence of an irreversible decline, are clung to less out of any explosive desire than through a slow and primitive discipline which gradually resolves every weakness and every lapse of memory into a rhythm that beats like an endless incantation. I am frightened — I must express myself more childishly than I have ever been able to before — I get a feeling of physical distress when faced with temptations that rise up as insubstantially as ghosts — how can we avoid, in the great absence and emptiness where we are consigned to oblivion, becoming the plaything of such ghosts? — and yet these ghostlike images are themselves merely shadows cast by that absence and emptiness. That which can be loved sees itself in love, in hopeless intoxication, in cruel and lasting demands, rather than in nocturnal arousal or the deception which follows the terrors associated with the presence of death.

I am not in the position of having to see in what I write anything other, or anything more, than what life offers me: it would seem pointless to conceal anything that might contradict the advent of the "endless incantation", whether that resulted from times of solitude, hardship, suffering, or even tortures endured gladly. The tight-lipped approach that plucks and then hardens the nerves, or the meditation practised so slowly it becomes merely a sob, both forsake, perhaps more than is apparent, the desire for incoherent and unforeseeable betrayals. The route followed beyond these established paths requires not so much a furious energy as an insistence on overcoming the worst type of obstinacy: the hidden obstinacy of all those men who want to be both the bearers and the victim of a destitute existence. I am not thinking so much here of those who, having failed to find something consuming and irremediable in their lives, then take sides simply out of inadequacy with those whom life has left destitute.[2] But who can be certain, with all the quirks of fate, that some tumultuous instinct is not clumsily searching for what will one day prove to be the fulfilment of a starving dog's curse against life itself — or, even more humiliating, the blessing of a lame existence?

Chance — as sought in the happy but muffled persistence of the incantation — can here be the only response to an irony filled with anguish. Chance, that so reliably keeps away the one who wishes only to find within himself the extent, all too obviously finite, of his destitute existence.

Tossa, 14.IV.[19]36

## 8 PIERRE ANDLER Moriar, ergo sum[3]

I exist, and if the certainty of my existence has for me the lacerating value of an act of faith, that is because it springs from the continuous presence of my death, the only thing *capable of revealing my existence to itself since it is the only thing capable of bringing it to an end. I, who at the time of my birth could control neither my head nor my body, and even less the world around me, with its sympathy that right from the beginning seemed even more repellent than hostility, I who will never be able to control how long I live, who will never in the end be able to control love as I would wish — all that I can control is my death. Only death belongs to me unconditionally, and only death gives meaning to my existence and is thereby — and only thereby — rendered both fascinating and appalling.*

*In no sense do I feel the need to reduce the idea of my chosen death to a* redemption. *My ecstatic and conscious death, ecstatic because conscious, will not be the desperate cry intended to wipe away, in blood's convenient glory, the listlessness of a broken life. My death makes imperious demands for an existence that is worthy of it, overwhelmed and overwhelming,* other.

*Nor will my death be a* sacrifice, *because I have no God to give thanks to. The object of gratitude can only be gratitude itself. If my death is all I own, it is my* life, *not my death, which must be the sacrifice. Out of the whole of my life, what I should be giving thanks for is the right to choose my death.*

*Therefore it is my life, and not my death, that is the* loss. *When I die, I am not lost: I* spend *my only possession. From beginning to end, my existence is thus a greedy, frantic race, entranced by the prospect of loss. When I reach the empire, I arrive, no doubt ironically, at the very depths of the abyss. This is when, all requirements having been met, the empire reached and the loss accomplished, I enter my domain while seizing hold of death ecstatically.*

Pierre Dugan[4] 25.VII.[19]36

## ANONYMOUS *Invitation to a Totemic Dinner* 9

*On Friday, 18 December 1936, at 8.45 pm, a dinner will take place at 4 Place du Tertre, Paris, to which Georges AMBROSINO, Georges BATAILLE, Jacques CHAVY, René CHENON, Jean DAUTRY, Pierre DUGAN, Henri DUSSAT, Pierre KAAN, Imre KELEMEN, Pierre KLOSSOWSKI and Jean ROLLIN are invited.*

*The eleven guests may rest assured that they will be the only persons present.*

10 GEORGES BATAILLE *Re Totemic Dinner*

4-XII-[19]36

*I am obliged to communicate the same message to each one of those whose names appear on an anonymous invitation.*

*The fact that such a meal could be contemplated proves the existence of a profound misunderstanding as regards the objective of a collective action.*

*Georges Bataille*
*Until 6 pm tomorrow*
*Saturday*
*The Lumina*

11 GEORGES AMBROSINO *The Constitution of the Self is Highly Paradoxical*

*The sole quality that we care to recognise in the self with any degree of constancy is its divided nature, that is, within itself and against itself. And this revelation can only dawn upon us because we possess the inner conviction that the self, every self, contains a totality. When our gaze is fixed on this split, following it like a sightline tracking its target, it will only cause it to become more divided, and discover that it is intact in all these rival 'parts' which the clarifying spirit has sought to assemble. There are no gaps or blocks, just the endless cracking of fault lines, and hope left feeling giddy. Moreover, this image is exactly like the image we have of time. Participating in time, something we have also sought in political action, became apparent to me in a primitive way in the continual mirage of every being and its tiniest 'parts' as they conferred on every emotion a suspect and worrying appearance, making the impulse behind every action into something vague and illusory.*

*The desire for totality, in the way Caillois has expressed it, can only mean the search for a lucid totality, or to put it another way, making clear the totality that every self contains, by way of scientific experimentation. The nature of this search places it squarely within the domain of knowledge, and an area of knowledge that is of particular interest to us. Yet we must not hide the fact that the individuals who might successfully carry out this research will be those who [ ]* and who will be able to sacrifice their blood and nerves to Objectivity. The magnificence together with the sordidness of the human self have been* *clearly revealed to me, and however much I admire those whose intention is to reveal (which can certainly be done, and in a way that is unflinching) the phosphorescent putrefaction that is man, I can only resolve to sit back and wait until the proof has been established of what I consider to be obvious.*

## JEAN DAUTRY *Letter to Georges Bataille* 12

[January–February 1937?]

*For certain reasons and following on from experiences which concern no one but me, I feel no desire to be associated with an undertaking whose more or less unconscious aim is to abdicate all power in the name of power, to flee reality in the name of reality.*

*For these cheap mythical trappings, for the tawdriness of gods who are dead before they are born, I feel utter indifference.*

*Above all, I refuse to project the pale shadow of fear on to a universe which is alive, bloody and tortured.*

*Let others take pleasure in seeing henceforth their corpses decaying into dust.*

*Jean Dautry*

* Word missing in text.

A Georges Bataille, à propos d'Acéphale

Pour des raisons et à la suite d'expériences qui ne regardent que moi, je ne ressens aucun désir de m'associer à une entreprise dont la fin plus ou moins inconsciente est d'abdiquer toute puissance au nom de la puissance, de fuir la réalité au nom de la réalité.

J'éprouve pour les oripeaux mythiques, pour le clinquant des dieux morts avant de naître, une totale indifférence.

Surtout, je me refuse à projeter sur l'univers vivant, sanglant, torturé, l'ombre falotte de la peur.

Plaise à d'autres de regarder dès maintenant leur cadavre tomber en poussière.

Jean Dautry.

12. Jean Dautry, *Letter to Georges Bataille.*

# THE SACRED CONSPIRACY

# III

February 1937 – August 1937

# CHRONOLOGY

## 1937

**6 February.** An internal meeting of Acéphale is held at which a refusal of opportunism leads to the decision to found the "Internal Journal", ●14 §17.

**7 February.** An external (general) meeting of Acéphale is held at the Grand Véfour (Bataille calls it a "very general" meeting in a letter to Chavy[1]), at which Caillois and Bataille speak, the first to state "what he considered to be the guiding principles for the establishment of a group", the second to show "how man caught in the grip of aggression should live in the wake of attempts by Christianity and Socialism to diminish it," ●14 §18. The text delivered by Caillois appears to be lost, but it was probably a very early draft of "The Winter Wind", ○30; Bataille reads "What I have to say...", ●13.

It is during this meeting, originally planned as early as 29 December, that the project envisaged by Bataille, Caillois and Monnerot — to establish a community devoted to the study and restoration of the sacred in the modern world, the future College of Sociology — begins to come into being. As the aims of this group become clearer, certain of its members drop away. Kojève[2] opposed some of their ideas, and it was probably around this date, or possibly after the meeting at the Grand Véfour in March, that he withdrew for reasons already outlined (p.78). Kojève's name was never attached to the College, but he does speak there on Hegel, and attended its lectures.

**9 February.** The creation of an "internal journal" for Acéphale is formalised. The group now assumes its name, and abandons that of the "Sociological Group", being no longer "satisfied with a name appropriate to a study group (that is to say a function)", ●14 §1. It has its first members: Ambrosino, Bataille, Chavy, Chenon, Dubief, Dugan (Andler), Dussat, Kelemen and Klossowski. They are joined successively by Rollin, Isabelle Farner,* Patrick Waldberg,* Michel Koch,* Taro Okamoto* and, for a brief period, Dautry. The role of others, among them Louis Couturier (better known as Michel Carrouges*), Leiris, Masson, and Colette Peignot remains unclear. However, the initials of the last three all appear in the "List of Names", ●48, of March 1938, which means Bataille was at least still hoping for a deeper involvement from them at that time.

**25 February.** In a letter to Dautry, Dubief writes that Bataille met Caillois and Claude Chevalley at the offices of *L'Ordre nouveau*, the magazine of the political movement of the same name. Chevalley, a co-founder of the mathematical group Bourbaki in 1934, was an editor of the magazine. L'Ordre Nouveau, whose most prominent members were Robert Aron, Arnaud Dandieu and Denis de Rougemont, was one of the so-called Non-conformist groups of the 1930s; neither capitalist, socialist nor parliamentarian, philosophically they espoused the personalism of Emmanuel Mounier, the editor of the journal *Esprit*, and politically a sort of federalism. (This group is not to be confused

with the Fascist organisation of the same name from the late '60s and early '70s.) Dubief writes of this meeting that "their College of Sociology is on track".[3]

**February, or more likely March.** Bataille sets out the rules that will govern the Society's "encounters", which indicates that it has embarked upon its activities. "Prohibitions Regarding the Forest of Acéphale", ●18, is one of its two foundational documents (the other being ●41). Two further documents of the Society, presented to members in a canvas wallet, ●16 and 17, date from the same period. The map shows the forest of Marly, and allows the adepts to find the two sacred places of Acéphale: the oak tree struck by lightning that will be the ritual meeting-place at every new moon; and the ruins of Montjoie, near those of the Abbey of Joyenval, which will be the site for initiation rituals.

**21 March.** A public meeting on Nietzsche is held at the Maison de la Mutualité in conjunction with *Acéphale* 2. Bataille's presentation is followed by speeches from Caillois and Monnerot. Bataille is unhappy with the latter.

**25 March.** Bataille's "Instructions for the 'Encounter' in the Forest", ●19, concerns the first meditation in the forest of Marly by Acéphale members at the foot of the oak struck by lightning. "On an area of marshy ground...", ●20, which is undated, may relate to this encounter as well. The event is repeated on the 26th, Good Friday, as is revealed in the text "For the second time today...", ●21, with its meditation on the tragic theme of killing, to which Bataille returns later in the College of Sociology.

**30 March.** Dugan (i.e. Andler) writes a text (unpublished) intended for the Society, "I was a demanding child...".

**In March** also, once again above the Grand Véfour, there is another external meeting. According to Caillois,[4] he reads "The Winter Wind", ○30, presumably further revised since the reading of 7 February, and Bataille reads "The Sorcerer's Apprentice", ○61. However, this too can only have been an early draft of this text, probably "What we undertook a few months ago...", ○29, which overlaps with the final part of "The Sorcerer's Apprentice".

Whether this was the actual text read by Bataille or not, this meeting, according to Caillois, marks the birth of the College of Sociology. Envisaged by Bataille as the public face of the secret society, its aim, as he defined it to the members of Acéphale (but presumably not to Caillois), was to provide the Society with "a theoretical basis that is underpinned by a perfectly mastered understanding", ●39.

The "Note on the Foundation of a College of Sociology", ○31, is drafted by Caillois in March, but does not appear until July in issue 3/4 of *Acéphale*, with Ambrosino, Bataille, Caillois, Klossowski, Pierre Libra* and Monnerot as signatories.

**Spring of 1937.** Beginning of Leiris's relationship with Pauline Chenon, the wife of Gaston-Louis Roux. After some interruption the relationship resumes between 1939 and 1940.[5]

**April.** Bataille and Leiris are among the founders of the Société de Psychologie Collective (Society of Group Psychology, presumably named after the work by Freud translated into French in 1924), along with René Allendy, Adrien Borel and Paul Schiff. Pierre Janet is its president and Bataille the vice-president. Its aim is to "study the role played by psychological, and in particular unconscious factors in social facts".[6]

**15 April.** Caillois publishes "The Praying Mantis" in *Mesures*. This and his publications

*Opposite, left to right, top to bottom:* Walter Benjamin, *involved with the College, but not the Society. Five involved with Acéphale:* Isabelle Farner (later Waldberg), Alain Girard,* Michel Koch, Taro Okamoto and Michel Carrouges.

in May and June are criticised by Theodor Adorno and Walter Benjamin.[7]

**26 April.** The first aerial bombing by the German Luftwaffe in support of the nationalists in Spain; 16,000 civilians are killed at Guernica.

**May.** In the *NRF* Caillois publishes his essay "Paris, a Modern Myth".

**June.** In *L'Ordre nouveau* Caillois publishes "Aggressiveness as a Value", in which he defines aggression as the attribute of communities or orders that are "the collaborative result of a mutual choice, dictated by a common will and the representation of a desired aim".[8]

**22 June.** Blum resigns as prime minister, in part following conflicts in the Popular Front over practical support for the Spanish Republic (Blum being in favour). This marks the end of the Popular Front government.

**9 July.** Bataille writes to Caillois[9] to say that he is relocating a meeting originally intended for the Café "A la Bonne Étoile" to Andler and Dussat's apartment at 17 rue Séguier. Since this was where the meeting for *Acéphale* 2 took place on 31 July the previous year, it can be assumed this meeting was to decide upon the final contributions to *Acéphale* 3/4.

**Mid-July.** Bataille departs for Italy with Laure. After Genoa they stay in Rome[10] where Bataille writes "If we are truly united...", ●22, dated 17 July, which he sends to Kelemen. This text indicates that he is still hoping Caillois may join the Society but also that he has not yet been invited, nor knows of its existence. A letter to Rollin[11] in October confirms that Caillois has, after some prevarication, declined to join.

Publication of *Acéphale* 3/4, dedicated to Dionysus, with as contributors: Bataille, Caillois, Klossowski, Masson and Monnerot.

Around this time, or possibly in the following year, Bataille works on a theatrical production for Jean-Louis Barrault, *La Méduse*, in which the god of Acéphale was to appear on stage.

**20 July.** Bataille, back in Paris, announces that he and Ambrosino are preparing a manifesto for Acéphale.

**July (after the 21st).** Bataille rejoins Laure in Italy and travels with her to Naples, then to Taormina where they climb Mount Etna, an extreme experience that he evokes in his diary and which inspires Masson to produce "a painting of ash and flames" representing Empedocles. Laure cannot bear to be separated from this painting and, in *Guilty*, Bataille recalled that it was close to her when she died.[12]

**22 July.** Meeting of Acéphale at 17 rue Séguier. During the session, Ambrosino, Chenon and Dussat each read a text and Kelemen reads Bataille's "If we are truly united...", ●22. However, according to an unpublished letter from Dussat to Chavy, of 24 July 1937,[13] most of the meeting was taken up by a disagreement with Klossowski concerning the texts "Fragment on Nietzsche", ●23, and "On Nietzsche and the Moment", ●24.

**7 August.** Bataille and Laure are now in Siena. Her "Fragment from a notebook of 1937" dates from this trip.[14] Bataille sends Jean Paulhan the finished version of his text "The Obelisk" (see p.249, *15 April*).

**16 August.** Chavy writes "On Authority", ●26, first published in this book.

**21 August.** A letter from Bataille requests a meeting at his apartment on the 29th with Caillois and Chevalley. The same letter also indicates that discussions on plans for the College are taking place, and that they are often heated.[15]

**End of August.** "Attempted suicide" by Leiris "by allowing himself to be grazed by a car" in imitation of the toreador's "pass".[16] This act is in part precipitated by difficulties in his affair with Pauline Chenon.

# COMMENTARIES

## ACÉPHALE [MG]

This section begins with documents relating to the creation of the secret society in February 1937, when the members definitively adopted the name of Acéphale and relinquished that of the "Sociological Group".

Even so, Acéphale's "religious" inclinations can be traced back to the first of the regular meetings of the Group on 11 November 1936, when Bataille denounced politics for being powerless to respond to the essential aspirations of man. His text "What I have to say...", which he read at the meeting on 7 February, expands upon this topic while developing a new viewpoint in which he shows that the attraction exercised by politics is no more than a means of escaping from the "fragmented existence of ordinary life", ●13. At the same time he underlines the widespread desire, on the left at least, to nullify the aggression inherent in man and the universe, an attitude that was shared by Christianity. But whereas Christianity "made allowances for violence" by asserting that it was "the fact of mankind itself", Socialism's desire to abolish violence goes so far as to imagine individual aggression as "no more than a simple consequence of the irrational violence that operates within the economic structure". Hence the necessity of opposing "the deep-rooted moral unity" of Christianity and Socialism, in an organisation or "order" which, taking as its model the innovative nature of the early orders of the Christian Church, would seek to revivify society through a closer community "commensurate with the failure of the real world" which is marked by "the ridiculous disproportion [...] between the emptiest political action and the already much more profound reality of physical violence" of the coming war.

The texts that follow are among the most important in this book. "Creation of the 'Internal Journal' ", ●14, describes Acéphale's immediate prehistory. Dubief's "Principles", ●15, retraces the steps that led to his joining Acéphale, from political engagement to an apolitical position while nevertheless maintaining an anti-Fascist stance, and the decisive "interview" with Caillois that showed him that a community could be a way in which "the present influences the future". Bataille's "Memento", ●16, is the first of the series of texts, described in my introduction (p.37), which inaugurate the religion of acephality and the celebration of it in the forest of Marly. However, "Memento" deserves further comment here. Its affirmation that "In War is Truth" allies it with the philosophy of Heraclitus, who was closely associated with Nietzsche in *Acéphale* 2, and was further evoked in a letter from Masson to Bataille as "the one who endorses all aspects of struggle and questioning whilst laying down an absolute challenge to everything associated with the idea of Being."[1] Heraclitus reappears in the later issues of the magazine as a cosmic principle that imposes his laws on everything else. In issue 3/4 he presides over the mythical opposition between the Caesarean sky and the Dionysian earth in Bataille's "Nietzschean Chronicle", while in issue 5, the "Heraclitean Meditation", ●94, brings to a close the mystical and initiatory exercises of joy in the face of death. Heraclitus reappears again in an aphorism in Bataille's *Anti-Christian's Manual*: "Heraclitism is the sensation of the earth trembling and the fall into empty space as felt in the Nietzschean experience of the death of God".[2]

The final texts here all date from the summer of 1937, three being intended for the meeting of Acéphale on 22 July, the topic for which was chosen by Ambrosino, "How can we advance in our own way?" The first of these texts, "If we are truly united...", ●22, is by Bataille, and was written while he was in Rome; it develops a theme central to his philosophy, that of the labyrinth, which I describe in my introduction (p.40). This text is also important for the history of the secret society, since it informs us, on the one hand, of Caillois's outsider status with regard to this group, and on the other, gives us our first glimpse of what Caillois called "the tortuous founding of the College of Sociology",[3] when he referred to it at the beginning of the first draft of "The Winter Wind" (○30). Are these the first words of the text Caillois read at the Grand Véfour on 7 February when he outlined "the guiding principles for the establishment of a group", ●14 §18? Or are they from the version that was read at the actual foundation of the College, in March?

The three fragments by Klossowski were found by me among Dussat and Andler's papers. The first two, ●23 and 24, date from July 1937, and simultaneously evoke the death of God as the fall into a nihilism associated with Bataille and as an elevation, by way of the eternal return, to a sense of plenitude in Nietzsche. The third text, ●25, is neither dated nor signed, but when we met at his studio in the rue Vergniaud, in 1996 or 1997, Klossowski admitted it was his, but then disowned its contents. It does in fact constitute the starting point for the lecture he gave at the College of Sociology on 7 February 1939, on "The Marquis de Sade and the Revolution".

Klossowski read the first two of these fragments at the meeting of 22 July, and they caused some controversy. According to Dussat, the disagreements were provoked by Klossowski's views "on the subject of the death of God, and on God in general".[4] Was it his use of the term "nihilism" in relation to Bataille, and his contrasting him with Nietzsche, that triggered the controversy? Should we re-read these two texts of Klossowski's in the context of his leaving the Society? Bataille reported his defection in the "Annual Summation" of 24 September 1937: "Klossowski has gone so far as to interpose God between himself and us", ●39.

In any case, Klossowski, mentioned again during Acéphale's sessional meeting of 25 July 1938, ●52, would later return to this opposition between Nietzsche and Bataille in a lecture given in 1941 at the end of a retreat in a Dominican monastery, "Le Corps du néant", later printed in the first edition of his book *Sade My Neighbour* (1947) and which Bataille later told him he "does not like".[5] Here Klossowski recapitulated the two stages in the evolution of Nietzsche's thought outlined in Löwith's essay "Nietzsche and the Doctrine of the Eternal Return", which he had reviewed in *Acéphale* 2:

1. Liberation from the Christian YOU MUST to achieve the I WANT of supra-nihilism;
2. Liberation from the I WANT to attain the I AM of superhumanity in the eternal return."[6]

It is precisely in this "cyclical movement", according to Klossowski, that "man takes on the immeasurable responsibility of the death of God".[7] Furthermore, he associates Bataille's negation of God with the negation of utility upon which the notion of expenditure was founded, and hence the source of his "absolute political nihilism".[8] His conclusion, however, was a little more ambiguous: "In his desire to relive the Nietzschean experience of the death of God [...] he did not have the *privilege* [...] of suffering Nietzsche's punishment: *the delirium that transfigures the executioner* into a victim [...] *To be guilty or not to be*, that is his dilemma. His acephality expresses only the unease of a guilt in which *conscience* has become alienated because he has put faith to sleep: and this is to *experience God in the manner of demons*, as St. Augustine said".[9] Unlike Nietzsche, who "accused himself" of causing the death of God "in the name of all men" and paid for his guilt with madness, unlike Kirillov, the nihilist in Dostoyevsky's *Demons* who chose to commit suicide so as to kill men's fear of death and thus kill God himself, "Bataille shows us this frightful torment of not being able to make his guilt real and so attain that state of responsibility that gives knowledge of the path to absolution."[10]

The last text in this section, "On Authority", ●26, dated 16 August 1937, is the only known piece by Chavy. Again beginning with the Nietzschean experience of the death of God, Chavy poses the political question of authority as expressed in the exercise of power. If, in all successful governments, authority has always been granted by God or by the sovereign people or else, as in the case of Nazism, by God and by a "more religious form of the sovereign people", what form does it take within an initiatory society, which must

Pierre Klossowski, 1930s.

be hierarchical, but lacks a head? In other words, in a secret society based on the revelation of the death of God, "Does God only exist in that moment when he dies?" This question, following Chavy's affirmation that leaders fear the responsibility of authority, is expanded in order to add a corollary: "is God also afraid of his omnipotence?"

A reciprocal understanding was now established between the Society and the *Acéphale* journal — with both becoming a part of the "shared life", ●14 §2, of the new community — and the College. Issue 3/4 of the journal, in July 1937, included the "Note", ○31, announcing the foundation of the College and its "course of theoretical instruction in the form of weekly lectures" beginning in October (or in November as it turned out).

Otherwise, this issue continued the "restitution" of Nietzsche from issue 2, by situating the religion of Acéphale within the context of Dionysus, beginning with extracts from Walter Otto's book *Dionysus*, and followed by extracts from Nietzsche himself and from Jaspers's and Löwith's books on him (the extracts from Jaspers are omitted in "Dionysus", ●27). Otto called Dionysus "the god of joyful drunkenness and ecstatic love", but also "the Persecuted, the Suffering and the Dying", and drew attention to his divine and earthly birth. "He was the son of Zeus" who had disguised himself as a mortal, and of Semele, the daughter of Cadmus, the founder and king of Thebes, who, "even before she gave birth was consumed by the lightning-fire of her celestial bridegroom"; however, Hermes saved the child and sewed him into his father's thigh where he remained until his second birth. His dual nature explains why Dionysus is at once the god who brings joy and the god of tragic contradiction. "The inner conflict of this dual nature was so great," wrote Otto, "that like a violent storm he appeared amongst men right in their midst and terrified them, beating down all resistance with the scourge of madness." But according to another myth, Dionysus embodied within himself the Dionysian and Apollonian cults that were presided over by the Orphic sect. For Nietzsche, Dionysus was "essentially something other than what he appears to be in ancient myth, something which becomes but without ever taking solid shape".[11] According to Löwith, Dionysus combines with Zarathustra, "the most pious of atheists",[12] to become Zarathustra-Dionysus, while according to Jaspers, he is the opposite of Christ and substitutes for "the Christian conception" of suffering a "tragic idea" of it. "The God on the cross is a curse on life [...] Dionysus cut into pieces is a conjuring-up of life: reborn eternally and eternally returning from destruction".[13] Furthermore, Dionysus is also "the god who philosophises", the "coming new philosopher anticipated by Nietzsche who feels that it is he himself", a "self-identification" that "he actually fulfils within himself at the beginning of his madness".[14]

The Nietzschean Dionysus, "the original polymorphy of the self", according to a later article by Klossowski,[15] has its visual equivalent in Masson's variants of the Acéphale which reflect the Dionysian figures that spring forth from the texts: Monnerot's philosopher-seducer, the "intercessor between power and order";[16] and that of Don Juan, who was destined to become, in Mozart's version, the personification of "all the power of sensuality that is engendered in anguish"[17] and according to Kierkegaard's *Either/Or*, "an individual who never ceases coming into being". In this way, Don Giovanni, like Dionysus, is an expression of the "infinite melody into which the soul of Nietzsche wished to melt".[18]

In the texts by Caillois and Bataille, Acéphale-Dionysus determines the actual form of the community. For Caillois, in ●28, the excluding of all affiliations based on "locality, history, race or language", is envisaged as a form of resistance against established power on the model of the Dionysian mysteries which were "universal and open" and brought together popular collective energies through the "spread of cults associated with the underworld, at the expense of the Uranian religion". For Bataille, the ancient myth of Dionysus born of the "blasted belly" of Semele joins Nietzsche-Dionysus to oppose the celestial gods of National Socialism evoked in the "Restitution for Nietzsche" with the earth gods of the besieged Numantians, so as to found the communal unity of mankind upon a truly Dionysian sense of tragedy, namely "the kind of ecstatic tension spread by death"[19] which also underpins Sade's "doctrine of blood".

## THE COLLEGE OF SOCIOLOGY [AB]

The first two of the three texts in this section are what we presume were read, more or less, at "that dusty café in the Palais Royal (it was the Grand Véfour, half abandoned in those days)." [20] By the end of the meeting in March 1937, the College of Sociology had acquired its name and had been founded, at least in the eyes of those who signed the third document here, the "Note", ○31.

What is immediately apparent in all three documents is their differences both in tone and in content. Bataille's text, "What we undertook a few months ago...", ○29, appears to address the aspirations of the Society, which had already been formed, while acknowledging other aims that fall outside its remit, and which would eventually become the concerns of the College. The meeting at which it was read comprised members of Acéphale and others who were ignorant of the Society's existence, such as Caillois, and the text seems to have been designed for this dual audience. Its first sentence could have been interpreted as referring to the founding of the Society, or to the discussions held within the Sociological Group; both parties would also of course have been aware of the "only publication which up until now has served as an indicator of our activity", namely the first issue of *Acéphale*, and in particular, Bataille's "The Sacred Conspiracy", ●1.

One of the themes developed in "What we undertook..." is the necessity of continuing the scientific investigation of the forms of authority that had been proposed in the inaugural manifesto of Contre-Attaque. Bataille refers to this future work of the College when he remarks that "no one has dared to make today's society, the society in which we 'exist', the object of a structural analysis." The text continues by considering the recent political turmoil throughout Europe, and then to the proposal that a combination of Freud's Group Psychology and the methods of sociology (Durkheim is not mentioned specifically) might be tasked with this analysis. Such is the science, "the sole authority we rely on", upon which the College will be founded (a very different formulation for the basis of a community is made in "The Winter Wind", ○30). The College's field of investigation is to be "mythological sociology", which in the "Note" is recast as sacred sociology. Bataille then asserts that this field is not inimical to scientific investigation, while the last three paragraphs appear addressed more to the members of Acéphale present.

If in Bataille's text the College, or something similar to it, already makes its appearance in a rudimentary form, Caillois's consideration of the motives and precepts of a moral community lie at some distance from both the Society and the College. It even seems surprising that this essay would later represent the College when it was published in July 1938 in the *NRF*. According to the note that appeared there, this text was essentially the one Caillois read in various versions at meetings before the founding of the College, most notably at the Grand Véfour in March 1937, although it may have undergone some cursory revision for publication (which perhaps explains some of its internal contradictions). Even so, it remains unaligned with Bataille's ideas on a number of important points.

Whereas Bataille appeals to science as a founding principle, Caillois calls upon the "virtues" of honesty, contempt, courtesy and love of power. The first part of his text is an attack on individualism, with targets ranging from Romanticism as a whole to Surrealism (implicitly) and anarchism, in particular that form of it espoused by Max Stirner. For Caillois these individual efforts, and the moral values they defended, must no longer be what is cast out of society but must form the basis of a new orthodoxy, the "militant orthodoxy" he had proposed in *Inquisitions* the previous year. Unfortunately, in the last two sections of his text, it appears that the means he envisaged to bring about this orthodoxy depend on the notion of a community based upon the exclusion of an "other", and what is more an "other" defined for seemingly capricious reasons — someone who happens to fall on the wrong side of an "ideal demarcation". Caillois's decision to couch his argument *in general terms* has a disastrous effect, particularly when it is realised that this text was read out only 18 months after the promulgation of the overtly racist Nuremberg Laws in Nazi Germany. And when it was published in July 1938, this was only five months before Kristallnacht would make it all too obvious what could happen to those on the wrong side of a line of "ideal demarcation". Caillois's political allegiances lay with the left, but the least worst thing that can be said of this proposition was that it promulgated an avoidable misunderstanding, and one that surely played a part in his alienation from those involved in Acéphale and from Leiris. We have already shown that Adorno and Benjamin were extremely uneasy with regard to Caillois, and Benjamin's verdict on "The Winter Wind" in a letter to Max Horkheimer of January 1940 is moderate compared to some of his earlier criticisms:

> Caillois [...] always delights in ambiguities. His contribution "The Winter Wind" celebrates "the harsh wind" whose icy breath destroys all that is weak and makes it possible to recognise by their red cheeks — not shame, that's for certain — those who are fit for service and ready to form a caste of overlords. Not one word situates these speculations in reality. A silence far more eloquent than saying something more explicitly.[21]

In this paper Caillois essentially calls for an association of "masters", a community of the elite — not so much acephalous, in fact, as hydra-headed. This appears at odds with the celebration of the base and wretched to be found in Bataille's thought. Caillois expresses ideas common among certain of the French anarchists of the 1890s and which were, ironically, primarily derived from Stirner. Kropotkin's critique of Stirner's individualist anarchism could be as easily applied to Caillois, since the elite he envisaged would only be composed of the contemptuous egotists he criticised. In Kropotkin's words: "It is thus a return towards the most common individualism, advocated by all the would-be superior minorities, to which indeed man owes in his history precisely the state and the rest".[22] If the ideas in this text are difficult to detect within the Society, they are even more absent from the College; they can perhaps best be seen as a part of the discussions that took place, as a part of the process of the formation of these groups, and a part that went largely unused.

The "Note on the Foundation of a College of Sociology", ○31, later appeared under Caillois's name as a part of ○59. When it first appeared in *Acéphale* 3/4, however, it can be seen as combining aspects of the two preceding texts, although Bataille's thought appears predominant. Part 1 calls for an equivalent of the "structural analysis" that "no one has dared to make" he had proposed in ○29, while the inevitability of infection and activism situates the sociology that is to be pursued beyond the boundaries prescribed by Durkheim. Part 2 outlines a moral community that has none of the rigours supported by Caillois; now a simple interest in the topic would suffice. The ideas of Bataille again dominate in part 3, and the final sentence no doubt embodies a foregone conclusion, that it is forms of expenditure that will provide the "points of coincidence" to be established.

# TEXTS

February 1937 — August 1937

André Masson, *The Bull of Numantia*, from *Acéphale* 3/4.

## GEORGES BATAILLE *What I have to say…* 13

*What I have to say concerns existence as a whole. That is why right from the outset I encounter a double difficulty.*

*The existence we represent here together — by that I mean the different people gathered in this room — is in my view about the most opposite there could be to existence as revealed in its entirety. What we represent can be compared to an attic filled with abandoned objects. And this is not only true of the various individuals we embody: it would be just as true if instead of the twenty gathered here there were twenty others.*

*It is only by fighting to the death or being overcome by violent and contagious physical emotions that human beings can escape from the confused malformation of their concerns, which, seen as a whole, are no more than an accumulation of meaningless junk. If a precise expression could be given for what is going on in each of our minds right now as I am trying to speak, the resulting list would not be very entertaining; in fact it would be undeniably dull.*

*But this situation is not only saddening in itself, it also constitutes the greatest obstacle to contemplating existence in its entirety, in other words the exact vital concern I would like to introduce to my listeners. Even amidst the peaks of the highest mountains, a haze of personal concerns, as involved as they are contemptible, will frequently come between a man and the view reflected in his eyes.*

*This protective haze rarely clears, and indeed, even if it does, what connection can there be between the one who is looking and what he is looking at? As a rule, aimless everyday activities shield life from what is all around: if this incontestable reality were to enter into our common existence even once — this incontestable naked reality must of course be the thing life is seeking and for which it would even risk death — and it be present in this way, how could there be any further possibility of surrendering to those concerns that belong only in the attic with its abandoned objects?*

*A little more than two months ago I spoke in this very room about the futility, daily becoming more obvious, of all political agitation. Even so, violent forms of political unrest present themselves from the outset as one means available to isolated individuals to escape the immediate horizon of their tools of work and streets controlled by the police. It is the whole of existence, or at least the whole formed by the atmosphere, frozen or not, the greedy earth and its human parasites, that the most pedantic politics has in its sights, and there is no doubt that this wholeness, compared to the fragmented existence of ordinary life, is what gives politics its general level of attraction.*

*I will not attempt today, as I did two months ago, to define the particular impasse in which present-day politics finds itself. The question is not only whether politics has the capability to fulfil the objectives it sets itself. These objectives, which have met the needs experienced by mankind to varying degrees throughout history, are not themselves the only way to meet those needs. We must therefore ask [ourselves] again if the ambition of politics, assuming too that it is not completely powerless, truly represents the best way of responding to these needs, to the fundamental aspirations of man.*

*In truth, it seems that the authorised spokesmen for political activity have taken care in advance to discharge themselves of the preoccupations I am speaking about here: their specific ambition is openly acknowledged as being both immediate and limited. But that is only the way it appears. Man's political existence, whatever it might seem to be, stands opposed to the naked reality I referred to previously. But whereas other types of behaviour admit, between this reality external to man and man himself, complex affinities which simultaneously involve inferiority and superiority, or even equality in human existence, politics, at least in its developed form, does all it can to reduce that complexity, in order to render even the reality of the Earth and the rest of the universe equivalent to nothing. Everything that is represented obscurely in the form of dialectical materialism, so as to deprive it of any philosophical significance, is nevertheless loaded with serious meaning and even, to be exact, with dramatic meaning: that is, a desire for annihilation.*

*Such arguments are so far from the usual way of thinking that it is difficult to communicate a nuanced description of what has thus been annihilated; in this context, the political activity whose appeal has an effect well beyond those who support it, hence the political activity that can be held in large measure to have succeeded. The annihilation has, in fact, been so successful today that it has become difficult to articulate what its original objectives were.*

*The way to resolve this is to imagine man's disposition through successive periods of history; this disposition is that of a being living in dread of everything that surrounds him, present in external reality just as in the presence of the danger of death. These presences, with the one corresponding to the man facing that of the other, his externality, appear at first like the presences of two enemies locked in combat. What has ceased to be apparent to us — perhaps through various acts of subterfuge, or a shift in values — is the amount of blind aggression that permeates external reality. It appears that one of the fundamental achievements of Christianity has been precisely to unburden the universe of taking any responsibility for its avarice and its continual aggressions against man. Aggression has been defined by Christianity as the fact of mankind itself and as an evil that is specific to mankind. Even in the most general understanding, everything that human existence endures, because of the conditions in which it exists, has been attributed to man's sinfulness. Mankind's sense of responsibility ever since has been so great, even in our semi-de-Christianised world of today, that the emotion which takes hold of groups of people attacked by others is not the same as if they had been caught in the eruption of a volcano, because the volcano is innocent, whereas men are guilty.*

*Such a situation provides evidence of man's fundamental processes when in the grip of aggression, and external aggression as much as his own. It would also seem necessary to uphold as a fundamental proposition the fact that all types of man's behaviour that are connected to existence as a whole, as opposed to those fragments which occur during useful activity, are reactions expressed in the presence of aggression.*

*The aggression of both man and the external world — the sum total of outbursts of violence — was originally treated in primitive religious belief as a terrible but natural danger. In such conditions, violence was not separate from the man who lived with it, and did not challenge him with a single reaction but with all the complexity of its affective fluidity.*

*The dance of human life at times moved in close and at other times fearfully away from violence, as if these movements came about with a view to forming a compromise with violence itself.*

*It is the prevalence of this feeling of terror that characterises Christianity. Through Christianity man forbade himself, or tried to forbid himself, from allowing violence to take possession of him. Violence was considered to be evil, as something that must be cast out of human existence. All repulsion had to make way for attraction. Hatred was banished — it was stated that men had to love one another. But since repulsion and the aggression which is its consequence together constitute a natural necessity, seeing that the immediate world and probably the far distant universe too are throughout their extent gripped by violence, and without there being any serious likelihood that human nature might be excepted, Christian belief made allowances for violence, but directed individual violence entirely against the individual himself. External violence was even shifted so that it took on a value within the context of love: it was accepted in so far as it destroyed the individual desire to live physically, desire being considered evil, because if it were freely expressed it would be violence. Aggression suffered, in all its forms, whether as a fact within the individual himself or a fact of the external world, but was nevertheless preserved within Christianity. The crucifixion sets the outburst of aggression on the part of man and the elements at the summit of existence, in the absolute darkness of a night that suddenly blocks the light of day. God himself seems at that moment to have abandoned the world. With Christ exhaling his final lamentation, reproaching his father for having abandoned him, the empire of violence seems to have established on Earth injustice without end and overwhelming physical torture. Yet the crucifixion in Christian tradition is merely the image of the victory man must achieve over himself.*

*At least this is the way Christianity is represented, bringing seduction in its wake, in response to the anguish of existence torn asunder by aggression in every direction. But what seduction thereby introduces is nothing more than insipidity and platitudes. Christian violence has yoked itself to the impoverishment of existence with worldly obstinacy. According to William Blake, "As the caterpillar chooses the fairest leaves to lay her eggs on, so the priest lays his curse on the fairest joys."*[1] *Christian education aims to curtail everything in existence that is ready to burst forth, transforming even physical love into aggressive spite, the better to shatter it. And if sometimes it partakes in this desire to burst out, this is only so as to gain more authority and power in its business of seduction.*

*Socialist politics do not represent a change in direction after Christianity. Socialism is the worthy heir to Christianity, worthy in the sense of a slow decline. It is decked out, in truth, like Christianity in the bright colours of violence, but as is the case in Christianity this is an outfit of seductive nudity, whose purpose is to conceal a body from which every obscenity has been carefully excised. Socialism is an even more accomplished negation of violence than Christianity, because it either does not know or refuses to acknowledge that the aggression it exploits for its own purposes exists as a constituent element in both the universe and in man. And where Christianity made it a constant element in its mythology and practice, socialism presumes it can be reduced, and even has no other purpose than the desire to purge it from the social apparatus of production and so from the whole of humanity. Does not socialist doctrine go so far as to interpret individual aggression as no more than a simple consequence of the irrational violence that operates within the economic structure? Once such violence is eliminated, socialism claims, crime will have no reason to exist.*

*In all likelihood human existence has never before had to face the sharply lacerating and dominant reality of aggression as much as it is now forced to do in the world we live in today. Indeed today almost everywhere there is more law and order and more policing than there has ever been, but this situation has come about as though inside a mortar shell whose explosive force, and explosive contents, are in direct proportion to the increasing thickness of its casing. One day, just a few hours will be all it will take to separate our relatively risk-free existence, as neatly arranged as the workings of a clock, from an empire of stifling death. The coming change in level will be greater than any human history has ever seen, and it should be remembered when talking of this that existence depends more on such differences in level than on realities considered purely on their own terms. In other words, any situation is experienced differently according to the specific situation that preceded it.*

*Consequently it is only natural that most men follow their regular habits, habits whose paths are already established and on which the greater number of them place such special value. Only this large number offers a margin of security in the face of grave danger. Large numbers also calm anxiety, even if there is no worse path to follow than the one that has been chosen. A very large number of human beings will endure the anguish of violence by taking a Christian or a socialist position.*

*Christian and socialist positions are, however, simply two sides of the same coin, perhaps more precisely, two complementary sides of a patriotic position, which is itself an aggressive position. For a long time the former and more and more clearly the latter too have seemed suited to this role of the appeasing and incoherent counterpart. After a relatively brief period these different possible positions are each likely to be seen as mere complements to stupid behaviour. What seems at the beginning to take the form of different possible responses turns out to be a deep-rooted moral unity.*

*By rejecting this dross I mean to explain in a few words the only exit available to existence in the face of impending violence. Violence must be faced head on and without hope. The tearing apart of human beings by one another can be experienced in the same way that each individual experiences himself being torn apart. In that way, and only in that way, shall man no longer be asked to destroy his own aggression, in other words his life, still less be asked to subordinate it, to enslave it to something as limited as his fatherland. Aggression can be neither limited nor enslaved.*

*Such a position goes back to everything Christianity has destroyed of the primitive religious complexity that gave way in turn to all possible types of response, from fear to defiance, and from ecstasy to hilarity. It corresponds almost exactly to what was excised from an existence that could originally only have been whole. However, before I continue, I want to make clear that this is no gospel, which is to say, a list of instructions for overturning values by describing them in different terms. I am not trying to deliver any fully fledged moral doctrine based on my own experience. The position I have described has existed in society for as long as romantic despair has been expressed. It doesn't matter that the revelation that occurred, occurred not just on one occasion but on several occasions. Nor does it matter that those who experienced this revelation had only a dim awareness of what it might mean for humanity as a whole. There may even be some significance in the fact that everything occurred in a diffuse manner, most often without asserting the meaning we now understand was being declared. This happened when Hölderlin, Gérard de Nerval and Nietzsche went mad... But neither Sade nor even Nietzsche can be considered a guiding light that shines once and for all. And it is not strictly necessary to bear in mind the fact that both Blake and Kierkegaard were technically Christians, when they, perhaps more than any others, lent their voices to the demands of a reality that had been torn apart. The inconsistencies of Blake and Kierkegaard, when examined by those who are able to glimpse what we can see, are no more important than Rimbaud's alleged renunciation or the total obscurity that surrounds everything concerning Lautréamont.*

*What is more relevant for us is that 'romantic despair' does not exactly express what the word despair usually refers to on its own, but rather a resolution that is incompatible with a transaction. Despair signifies here that aggression can be neither limited nor enslaved. Human existence is thus free to become domination.*

*The path is opened up by romantic despair to lead as far beyond contingent circumstances as beyond the restrictions of the world today. But if a* romantic church *exists — and it exists for us, if not in any formal manner then at least in a profound sense — then it is composed of the genuine contagion of the most boldly desperate voices, and it would be futile to deny that such a church has not been defiled by the challenges of the society in which it was situated. Confusion has arisen between cries that are unquestionably savage and their echoing by the highly civilised professionals of tragedy. Yet perhaps it is one of the laws of shared existence that defilement also brings forth new concentration. So it is that in the Christian Church, as the mystical connection with the faithful was emptied of the largest part of its original meaning, monastic orders formed, which offered to restore life to the community of which they were a part by creating a community that was more strict and thus far more vigorous. They were not opposed to the Church itself, on the contrary, they were endeavouring to realise the Church more fully than the Church was able to do itself. It gives me no joy to be referring to a form of Christian existence and I cannot but see in it the birth of a confusion which is more odious to me than any other. But there is hardly any other example that can be intelligibly put forward to the dregs of Christian culture we see today. It is true that I am not thinking of a Christian order any more than the order of Freemasons, but it is understandable that I should find no more pleasure in speaking of the latter than of the former. When I speak of what belongs to the past, I must emphasise that I am speaking only about an entirely external form. But we place our reliance on rigour and rationality, and have no other purpose than to demand both of ourselves and of others the same rigour and rationality. That is why I have chosen to compare our potential situation to that of the monastic orders of the Church, in order to underline our desire not to deny in any way what might already exist outside us: we believe only that a shared and rigorous affirmation is commensurate with the failure of the real world, especially if we think of the ridiculous disproportion apparent between the emptiest political action and the already much more profound reality of physical violence, which is poised, even as I speak, to tear us all apart.* [7 February 1937]

## GEORGES BATAILLE *Creation of the 'Internal Journal'* 14

*1. We are starting this* internal journal *on the day we have resolved to assert ourselves as* existence, *and not as the function of a defined undertaking. Up until now we have been meeting without having felt any need to identify — even in our own eyes — such a 'paradox'.*

*Originally we were satisfied with a name appropriate to a study group (that is to say a function).*

*Even the title of this* journal *signifies that our shared existence may now be given a name that is as independent from servitude as is a person or a country.*

*2. The texts that will appear in this* journal *will be testimony to the efforts that will engage us in the shared life of Acéphale and will set forth what we believe it is impossible to repudiate.*

*3. The names of those taking part in setting up this* internal journal *are Georges Ambrosino, Georges Bataille, Jacques Chavy, René Chenon, Henri Dubief, Pierre Dugan, Henri Dussat, Imre Kelemen and Pierre Klossowski.*

*4. On the occasion of starting this work we look back on the significant dates in the formation of the moral community that exists between us.*

*5. On 15 April 1935, when no formal group yet existed, a meeting took place whose purpose is expressed as follows in the text of the invitation signed by Georges Bataille, Jean Dautry and Pierre Kaan:*

> WHAT IS TO BE DONE?
> IN THE FACE OF FASCISM
> GIVEN THE INADEQUACY OF COMMUNISM

> We propose to meet in order to consider the problems
> encountered by those who are currently
> radically opposed to Fascist aggression,
> unreservedly hostile to bourgeois domination,
> but can no longer trust in Communism.

*6. In July 1935, Roger Caillois and Georges Bataille together planned the founding of an association of revolutionary intellectuals. It was at that moment that those who would go on to found Acéphale renounced the apolitical character of their intentions and conceded that an attempt at action could have meaning.*

*At this meeting, on the occasion of a lecture by Georges Bataille, the Nietzschean theme of the death of God was introduced for the first time, in so far as it dominates our shared mythical existence and thus our actual existence today.*

*7. In October 1935, after Caillois and Bataille split, and having come to an agreement with the Surrealist group, the planned association was formed and published its first manifesto, entitled* Contre-Attaque. *The texts for this manifesto were approved by its first signatories on 17 October 1935. Contre-Attaque promoted the slogan "Death to Slaves!" and undertook to use the weapons created by Fascism for purposes opposed to nationalism.*

*8. On 21 January 1936, a prospectus presenting the* Cahiers de Contre-Attaque *was published; this leaflet announced the forthcoming issue of a* Cahier *devoted to Nietzsche with the following text:*

> It appears that the only people who are allowed to invoke Nietzsche are those who subject him to despicable betrayals. It seems that one of the most revolutionary human voices has spoken in vain.
>
> Must this violent anti-Christian, this scorner of the idiocies of patriotism, remain — for having made *all* demands and *all* acts of pride his own — for ever the victim of Philistines and fools who follow the herd, the victim of universal banality?
>
> We do not believe in the Philistines' future. The proud, all-shattering voice of Nietzsche remains for us the herald of the coming moral Revolution, the voice of he who was in touch with the Earth... The world that will be born tomorrow will be the world heralded by Nietzsche, the world that will call time on *all* moral servitude.

*A single* Cahier, *entitled* The Popular Front in the Streets, *written by Georges Bataille, appeared in May 1936 after Contre-Attaque was brought to a close.*

*9. Encountering only incomprehension outside the group, Contre-Attaque was disbanded in April 1936, following internal disagreements that appeared to be no more than superficial.*

*10. Towards the end of Contre-Attaque's existence, a certain inclination became apparent for the formation, not of a political party or a paramilitary organisation, but of an 'order', analogous to certain secret societies. This tendency reprised aspirations that had been more or less defined earlier by different sections and which were probably a response to the fact that most of the participants in Contre-Attaque were driven by a spirit that was rather more religious than political.*

*Since 1925 (or 1926) Georges Bataille had been planning, along with Michel Leiris, André Masson and a Russian émigré called Bakhtin,*[2] *the founding of an Orphic and Nietzschean secret society — to describe such a vague project in a few brief words. Michel Leiris suggested this society be named "Judas".*

*11. In April 1936, whilst staying with André Masson at his house in Tossa, Georges Bataille wrote two texts which later appeared in the first issue of* Acéphale. *He suggested to Masson that he draw a picture of a man without a head to appear on the cover of the journal, and this headless man then took on in Masson's mind the disoriented and living aspect of a myth; the resonances and almost limitless potential repercussions that are associated with myths were thus assigned to him without anyone having had that specific intention.*

*Masson's reactions at the time were born of a desire not to leave Nietzsche's life without any response. Issue 1 of* Acéphale *was therefore conceived by Masson and Bataille as a straightforward introduction to the planned issue on Nietzsche. Originally the image of the Acéphale simply corresponded in Bataille's mind to a still ill-defined preoccupation with the 'leaderless crowd', and with an existence modelled on a universe that was obviously acephalic, the Universe where God is dead.*

*12. On 4 June 1936, the resolution to found a moral community had its first result, but, deriving from the way political groups tend to be organised, it appeared to be impossible to go beyond the format of a 'study group', and so was given the name — which was never, in fact, actually used — of the 'Sociological Group'.*

*13. The first issue of* Acéphale *appeared on 24 June 1936, in clear contradiction with a form of existence such as a 'study group', but at the same time it was true that no actual internal activities had yet responded to the aims expressed in the texts published in this issue.*

*14. The group met several times without anything of note transpiring during these meetings, with the sole exception of one in which a deep solidarity was expressed with the Spanish Revolution, without this seeming to contradict the group's apolitical spirit. A deep-rooted susceptibility when faced with these currents of political attraction was manifested again by just such an attitude when notions of vital sympathy and the need for limited aggression took on ideological forms.*

*15. In November, the first of the regular meetings was held; for the first time also, during Bataille's lecture, an attitude of violent hostility was expressed unreservedly with regard to deteriorating political concerns.*

*16. In December, the reconciliation between Bataille and Caillois concluded with a meeting at which Monnerot was present, Caillois being absent. A feeling of acute unease ensued, because nothing was clearer than the fact that opportunistic considerations were becoming confused with fundamental concerns.*

*17. These misgivings led to Ambrosino and Dubief writing texts concerning exactly this danger of opportunism and the likelihoods for confusion. An internal meeting was held on 6 February during which the founding of the* journal *was decided upon, because it was becoming clear that given the profile we had assumed we should be taking care to determine all its features. In fact this* journal *marked a retreat towards an internal life that was hostile to all forms of opportunism.*

*18. The following day a meeting was held that had been planned for some two months and in which Caillois took part, [in the course of which he declared] what he considered to be the guiding principles for the establishment of a group. After Caillois's presentation, Bataille sought to show how man caught in the grip of aggression should live in the wake of attempts by Christianity and Socialism to diminish it.*

*20. [*sic*] Just as it is advisable to note in the* journal *each of the elements that brought us together, it is also necessary to take into consideration what has been written in particular in two of Georges Bataille's texts, the contents of which express a state of mind in which we all concur. The first, the "Notion of Expenditure", appeared in 1933 in* La Critique sociale, *and the second, "Sacrifices", was written in the summer of 1933 and published in December 1936, accompanied by André Masson's mythological engravings.*

9 February 1937

*I am not unaware of the fact that the principal effect of sincerity is to supply others with a powerful weapon they can use against us; that is why, incidentally, I was so taken by the idea of more or less public confessions put forward by Ambrosino and Bataille. This is because I like to take a certain amount of risk and think that only these uncensored admissions, which would not exclude the more damaging details, will allow me to determine the extent of my attachment to Acéphale, by giving an account of my past reticence and, in theory, my potential future opposition.*

*I think that first of all I should specify the exact conditions of my participation, and wish to state right away that the experiment I personally am undertaking has nothing at all to do with renouncing the world or life, that it is not a question of destroying and creating, but only of taking part, and simply of putting aside certain utterances in order to make room for others, with the aim of putting pressure on existence according to a coherent and specific approach.*

*By that I mean that I like certain aspects of life, even popular pastimes; for example, I like bridge, I like wine, I like playing rugby and I also like watching it. That is all of no special interest, but other ways in which I participate in existence are at once less personal and less banal and are thereby all the more important to me. My wish is to continue to exist outside your circle in certain respects, and within a community of ideas in other and more important respects.*

*It would, however, be difficult for me to specify what I mean by the sort of community that should be established between us, and so too the tension that would shape it. I am neither a thinker nor a seer, and if, as far as my strengths permit, I wish to contribute to the success of our undertaking, I expect the most important work will be done by others. I have much enthusiasm, but as for what our activity might have in store for us, and concerning which I have such high hopes, it is impossible for me to have any very clear vision.*

*Nevertheless, and to get to the heart of the matter, I believe that I am proceeding in the best way by demonstrating how three of the various forms of existence which have influenced my own — political action, my personal character and friendship — may or may not be in harmony with my relations with you.*

*Less than ten years ago I was a member of the SFIO, ideologically allied with the Étincelle Socialiste, with Maurinist tendencies.*[3] *Then I became friends with Dautry who helped me escape from that leper colony, and since then I have, by working outside and through his friendship, occasionally taken part in your activities. Without being a member of the Democratic Communist Circle, I was, through Jean Dautry, more or less involved in its existence, and can say that since 1930-31 I have never had the slightest political disagreement with my closest friend. It follows that my apolitical stance is more recent. Indeed I joined Contre-Attaque with the most fixed political motivation, but I should have realised from the beginning that I could not be anything but sickened by such a venture. As far as I am concerned, in fact, all political initiatives can only be something put before us to vomit on. Perhaps there was once a time when this sort of politics felt to me like something other than just a mental game. Yet much as I enjoy the game, I know today that politics is nothing more than the unsavoury raging of police and thieves, and it disgusts me.*

*However, I have to say that if I am fully inclined to be rid of this political burden, that does not make it any the less, as far as I am concerned, and to a certain extent, a vital necessity. Whether in reaction to my background or, on the contrary, in conformity with my education, I was born a socialist for life. I am quite willing to spit and vomit, and worse, upon socialism, in your company, you men who are from the same background as me. But in the presence of Fascists, a thousand apologies! I have a reflex instinct to smack them in the mouth. In short, I have a reaction that is both in sympathy and opposed to Puyo's reaction, which was behind his decision to leave us. And I believe that you share my point of view, which is why we judged his so harshly. This is also why we must declare ourselves to be intellectually apolitical, whilst remaining fundamentally political at heart.*

*In practice, I affirm that with my absolute attachment to Acéphale I repudiate all political action that is essential and vital, whilst maintaining deep within me a vital and essential anti-Fascist political purpose which I have no intention of relinquishing under any circumstances.*

*Nor will I renounce my own nature. However, following the breakdown of Contre-Attaque amidst a certain amount of ridicule, I have brought along with me certain mental reservations to my association with this new group. For a long time my nonchalance and a particular sort of critical spirit allowed me to rebel on certain occasions when faced with difficulties associated with the task in hand and the delays involved in carrying them out. But above all, since that evening at the Brasserie Lumina, when Ambrosino made fairly specific suggestions to me, and to a number of others, regarding the collective surrender of body and soul to his influence, suggestions rejected by all of us out of a lack of courage, I have been assailed by doubts. And very recently, in early January 1937, I expressed these doubts in an ironic text that comes very close to being a manifesto for breaking up the group.*

*Note on the materialisation of myths*

*The following story is told.[4] Once upon a time, in the New York Zoological Gardens, a snake was born with two heads, each having a neck about six centimetres long, and thus a certain degree of individuality. There were frequent fights between these two heads, and at mealtimes they had to be kept apart with a piece of cardboard. One day, one of the heads struck the other such a vicious blow that the creature died of septicaemia.*

*There is quite often a desire to break the mirror, or to spit into the pool of water that reflects the pallid and ludicrous image of a face that challenges us regarding our true nature. But the idea that this image might one day come to life, with its own character, and contest our actions in the world, and our life, cannot be tolerated. The enemy head of man, the enemy head of the flesh rising up at its expense, thus becomes the enemy head of the head. And so nature, in this particular case, merely resolves the dilemma by absurdity: either inflict a mortal wound to the head or rip off its genitalia.*

*My taste for self-ridicule, and, make no mistake, for self-ridicule in public, as expressed above, derives from the discouragement I feel at your dilatoriness, your impotence, and at my own. As for my disgust, I don't think that Dugan [Andler] hasn't already noticed this, certainly I think I have been aware of his; I don't think I am the only one to feel like this, and think many of us will admit to having felt the same*

*I only came to an understanding of what it is that unites us during the interview with Caillois — a kind of spinelessness, or to be more accurate, a kind of indifference. That was when I saw various potential realities for Acéphale that I wanted to articulate. When Ambrosino told me of your decisions of Saturday 30 January, I was completely won over.*

*There is no ulterior motive when I reveal with such absolute openness my past attitudes, proving as they do that my enthusiasm, while it was immediate, was also not without a certain holding back; and the degree of hostility I managed to show at the time may be of some interest today; so what I mean to say, exactly and as a result of this, is that I abandoned my doubts without hope of returning to them, even if that was not impossible.*

*If not impossible, I say, because it is no longer a question of disowning a personal objection. I collected and nurtured my doubts but feel no disgust when I reject them today, quite the opposite. I want to abandon myself to an overwhelming enthusiasm, oh yes! But if doubt is no longer appropriate, I know myself well enough to understand that in the case of failure, or deferred success, I am inclined to start criticising again and to bring my bitterness to bear upon those whom, rightly or wrongly, I shall hold responsible for our defeat. My enthusiasm is determined by the future, it depends upon success.*

*I think that in the preceding text I have answered all your questions; I do not believe that the claims I stand by are the kind to divide us. I refuse to renounce what is a great part of the value of my life, but by my mellowing I am fully showing how I intend to be conciliatory, and even wish to make that the reason for my agreement.*

*There is another point upon which I hope to put you at ease regarding my intransigence. I cannot say how much importance you will attach to what follows. Bringing my friendship with Jean Dautry into question might appear unjustified, and in fact it has no relevance today. However, in all honesty and sincerity, I must alert you to an unlikely but not impossible confession. I am extremely fond of Dautry, indeed I have a blind faith in him; I have no need to justify either of these feelings, but both oblige me to declare that if he were one day to confess to an act of hostility towards Acéphale or any of its members, I would not be involved in sorting out any wrongdoings; and the nature of my friendship with him would exclude any assumption of a disavowal on my part and, even more so, of a break with him. You may think that I am pledging a great deal to Dautry and rather little to you. That follows from the deliberately and intentionally blind character of our friendship. We do not envisage that one or other of us could commit an act that would contradict the other's reasons for living, which is what makes it possible for me to make such a commitment.*

*Insurance policies provide for plenty of unlikely outcomes, but I doubt that one day I will have to invoke this clause, though I am none the less anxious to preserve it as the essential point to which I referred at the beginning of this text: those aspects of life and the world of which we are a part and which there is no question of renouncing.*

*In all other respects, nothing will stop me from participating in your activities, but I will do so without altruism and with the most committed egotism. I am fond of children and their games, and also enjoy taking part in them. And I mean games in the broadest sense and not in the petty sense of political manœuvring. By that I mean that I am eager to side with the future, even if for me that means death, which I hardly fear at all. Acéphale in this sense is only a still vague means for ensuring that the present influences the future and is incarnated in it. But let me be clear, I mean the most immediate future, the one which is already almost the present. I am fond of children, but I have no interest in their future children, I am not concerned with posterity.* 1 March 1937

GEORGES BATAILLE Memento[5] 16

*FROM NOW ON, YOUR JOY WILL DEBASE AND TRAMPLE UNDERFOOT YOUR REPOSE, YOUR SLEEP AND EVEN YOUR SUFFERING.*
*REMEMBER THAT TRUTH IS NOT STABLE GROUND BUT THE CEASELESS MOVEMENT THAT DESTROYS ALL THAT YOU ARE AND ALL THAT YOU SEE.*

*REMEMBER THAT IN WAR IS TRUTH*

*YOU WILL NOT CEASE BEFORE YOU RECOGNISE YOURSELF AS A MAN WHO CARRIES WITHIN HIM A HOPE GREAT ENOUGH TO DEMAND ALL SACRIFICES.*
*THIS* MEMENTO *WILL REMIND YOU THAT FROM THIS MOMENT YOU CAN NO LONGER EXPECT ANY PEACE FROM YOURSELF.*

[March 1937]

GEORGES BATAILLE *Prohibitions Regarding the Forest of Acéphale* 18

*1. Do not enter that part of the forest of Yveline, which in ancient times was called the forest of Cruye, other than in such a way as to exclude any possible discord with the spirit of sanctuary we identify in this forest.*

*2. Do not enter one specific area of the forest — whose boundaries will be communicated at a later date — other than for Acéphale's encounters.*

*3. Never utter a single word — not even the slightest allusion — regarding these encounters, not for any reason nor in the presence of anyone whatsoever, unless under exceptional circumstances which will be communicated at a later date.*

*4. If there is sufficient cause, the option exists to put this subject directly into words in a written text for the* internal journal *of Acéphale which may then be handed to one of us.*

*5. Obey all the negative instructions specific to each encounter (including not speaking, not straying from the path, not leaving a place during a given period, not opening the envelope until the time stated).*

[March 1937]

A PARTIR DE MAINTENANT TA JOIE FOULERA AUX PIEDS ET AVILIRA TON REPOS, TON SOMMEIL ET MEME TES SOUFFRANCES.

SOUVIENS-TOI QUE LA VERITE N'EST PAS LE SOL STABLE MAIS LE MOUVEMENT SANS TREVE QUI DETRUIT TOUT CE QUE TU ES ET TOUT CE QUE TU VOIS.

**SOUVIENS-TOI QUE LA VERITE EST DANS LA GUERRE**

TU N'AURAS PLUS DE CESSE AVANT DE T'ETRE FAIT RECONNAITRE COMME UN HOMME PORTANT EN LUI UN ESPOIR ASSEZ GRAND POUR EXIGER TOUS LES SACRIFICES.

CE MEMENTO TE REPRESENTERA MAINTENANT QUE TU N'AS PLUS DE PAIX A ATTENDRE DE TOI-MEME.

16. Georges Bataille, Memento, *and opposite*, 17. *Map of the Forest.*

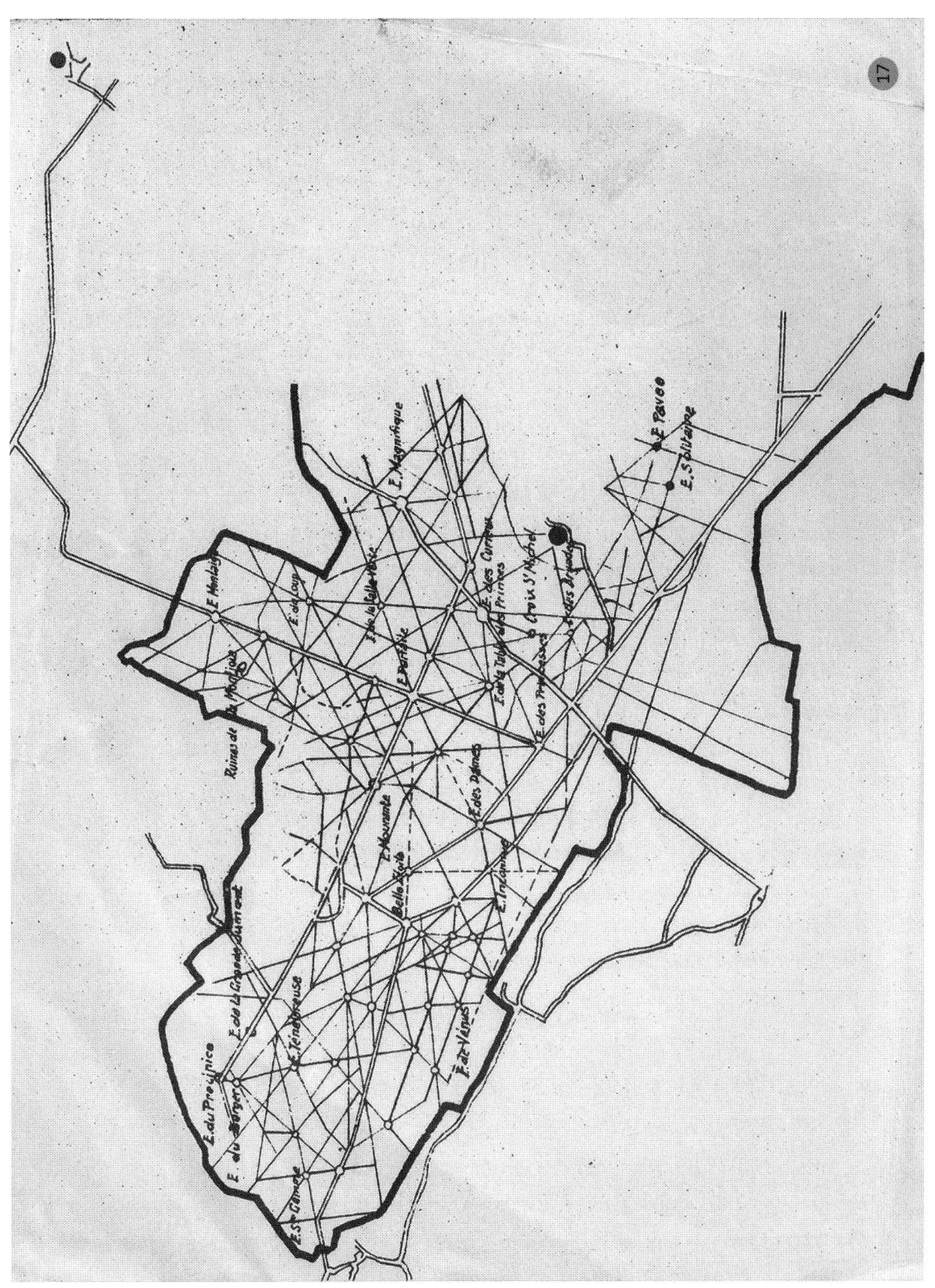
17
E. Magnifique
E. Pavée
E. Solitaire
E. des Curieux
Croix S^t Michel
E. Parfaite
E. de Loup
E. des Dames
E. Mourante
Belle Etoile
E. Ténébreuse
E. de Vénus
E. du Précipice
E. du Berger
Ruines de la Montjoie

19 GEORGES BATAILLE *Instructions for the 'Encounter' in the Forest*

*To be read several times, most carefully, and committed to memory:*

*Purchase a return ticket from a suburban ticket office for Saint-Nom-la-Bretèche. The train leaves at 8 pm.*

*Do not acknowledge anyone, do not speak to anybody, and find a seat away from the others.*

*At Saint-Nom, leave the station, taking the left-hand exit when facing in the direction the train is going.*

*Without asking any questions, follow our colleague who will be waiting by the road, and walk in a group of two or three at most, still without speaking, until you reach the path, from which point you will walk in single file, each person keeping a few metres between himself and the person in front.*

*Back on the road again, walk as before in small groups so as to attract as little attention as possible should there be anyone else around.*

*Once you have arrived at the place of the encounter, stop and wait to be led individually to the spot where you must stand motionless and remain silent until the end.*

*When the encounter is over, follow the others who will leave keeping to the same conditions as when they arrived.*

*Once back on the train, find a seat away from the others and, when you arrive in Paris, go your separate ways.*

*There is no need to adopt a dour or gloomy expression, but it is out of the question to speak at any point, and that should come naturally to us.*

*Afterwards, all conversation on the subject of the 'encounter' is forbidden, under any circumstances whatsoever. If there is something any of us wishes to express it may only take the form of a written text for the* internal journal.

*1. Regarding the appointed area in the forest, each of us must become acquainted with where its boundaries lie. Ambrosino will go first, together with one or two of the rest of us at most. They will be followed by one, then another, and so on, until its extent becomes apparent to everyone.*

*2. Sulphur is a substance produced in the bowels of the earth and only escapes through the mouths of volcanoes. That clearly has a certain meaning in terms of the chthonic character of the mythical reality we are seeking. It also has meaning in relation to the roots of a tree that push deep down into the earth.*

*On an area of marshy ground, in the middle of a forest, where it appears that disturbances have occurred in the familiar order of things, there stands a tree that has been struck by lightning.*

*It is possible to recognise in this tree the silent presence of that which has taken the name of Acéphale, and which is expressed by these arms without a head. The desire to seek out and encounter a presence that infuses our lives with purpose is what gives our proceedings a meaning that sets them apart from those undertaken by others. This* ENCOUNTER *which is* attempted *in the forest will take place in reality only when death manifests itself there. To anticipate that presence is to seek to cast off the vestments that veil our own death.* [25 March 1937]

GEORGES BATAILLE *On an area of marshy ground…* 20

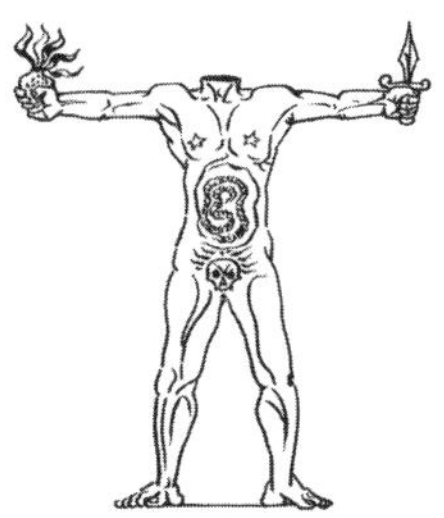

*On an area of marshy ground, in the middle of a forest where the reign of abandon and ruin is slowly being revealed, there stands a tree that has been struck by lightning.*

*It is possible to recognise in this tree the silent presence of that which is expressed to us by the arms without a head of the Acéphale. We have the desire to seek out and encounter what men have always had the possibility of discovering, the vague presence that becomes the recognisable sign of the destiny of each of them. But this first* attempted *encounter on this night in the forest will only take place when death manifests itself there: to go in search of that presence is, as far as we are concerned, to seek to cast off the vestments that veil our own death.*

*Only night and silence were capable of giving a sacred character to the bond that unites us. As for the sulphur produced in the depths of the earth in which the roots of trees push downwards: volcanoes alone produce it, expressing for us the volcanic reality of the earth.* [March 1937]

## 21 GEORGES BATAILLE *For the second time today…*

*For the second time today, we come here together at the foot of this great oak tree that has been struck by lightning.*

*Oaks and thunder were once closely linked in the minds of the earliest inhabitants of Europe. They were the expression of the all-powerful. An oak that has been struck by lightning is like a powerful god that has been torn apart by his own anger.*

*We too can become kings and lacerated oaks within the monastery that has no walls or occupants and where our procession will continue through the night.*

*We have chosen this holy Friday night deliberately in order that we may be brought to that encounter with the great decapitated existence of an oak tree. But there is no lamentation on our part.*

*We want the image of our destiny to rise up before us from the shadows; we want sulphur's fumes to make us breathe in the near or distant faltering of death as it makes its way towards us.*

*But it is the dark hope of the crime, not remorse, which fills us with anguish.*

*What our hope is searching for in this execution is the festival that heralds the coming of EMPIRE.* [Friday 26 March 1937]

## 22 GEORGES BATAILLE *If we are truly united…*

*"If we are truly united, if we are a real community," Caillois assured us, "nothing will be able to resist us." Caillois does not know that we are already a real community but, speaking on the spur of the moment, he expressed a belief which experience shows us is unfounded.*

*Since the community already exists for us, we can see the different sorts of resistance it will have to deal with.*

*In the first instance, there is no doubt that every action we have accomplished, in the sense that each one has connected us, at the same time separates us from other people, and it is inconceivable that it could be any other way. It is even possible to say that Caillois in particular is drifting away from us to the same degree that we are coming together. In this way he is led to think that we are moving away from our goal by isolating ourselves, whereas in fact our opportunity to exist is asserting itself.*

*It would be pointless to associate any sense of unease with this consideration of the* *fatal isolation into which we have entered, or the dividing wall that now surrounds us. However, nothing could better represent our 'duty to be' than this wall. Thus constrained, we are forced to overcome the internal challenges we encounter. It is necessary to isolate oneself in order '*TO BE*'.*

*What meaning might the words* TO BE *now take on for* US*? With what Minotaur shall we be living now, having got so far inside the labyrinth? What bull must we kill now that we have put on again the matador's 'suit of lights'? Doubtless it is out there, and will appear only slowly, in the course of time, shrouded in the inevitable darkness. But the patience required to counter avidity may in no way imply that we are postponing our actions, and the movement towards what is possible today is as strong as it has to be.*

*The first obvious fact that becomes apparent within the labyrinth in which we find ourselves is that everything occurs here in the most contrary fashion. For example, the contemplation of death leads to violent joy. However, I would especially like to talk about* personal depression *because I do not feel it can still be viewed in the way it is outside, where destiny is an individual experience. Personal depression unquestionably admits the meaninglessness of everything that impinges on an individual's existence, and consequently admits the meaninglessness of everything we might attempt as a group. But, at the same time, what we are trying to do would have no meaning if depression did not exist. Even if I had a fairly clear understanding of what might result from such a situation, I would still wait before talking about it because I do not believe there is any other problem quite as laden with anguish as this one. Today I merely want to make a connection between this extreme anguish and the greatest possible irony. Not that I think that irony is the antidote to anguish and must be its cure; indeed, can anguish not persist and even suffocate all existence within the limits of a very cruel irony? And why should everything necessarily be liberated? But when we connect an extreme joy to the terrible contemplation of death, when we connect irony to anguish, we accomplish a liberation that is greater than any other. We deliver religious existence to the naïve and outlandish violence of action. We shatter the gangue of Christian piety.* Rome, 17 July 1937

## PIERRE KLOSSOWSKI *Fragment on Nietzsche* 23

*Nietzsche's reputation rests specifically on the sacrifice of the self that is the murder of God. I mean to say that this murder already implies its own atonement, in the sense that the murderer must put himself in God's place, and no one could doubt that this would be fundamentally dreadful. Bataille said on this subject that Nietzsche was like a man who, having resolved to experience a vice right through to its most extreme consequences, would succeed. Yet I contend that for Nietzsche there was success in atonement: he achieved his madness, the prerequisite for his identification with Dionysus.* [July 1937]

## 24 PIERRE KLOSSOWSKI *On Nietzsche and the Moment*

*While it is true that time cannot be experienced except through its antithesis, the eternal, the desire to effect a leap in time or to fall into it presupposes that we are situated in the eternal. I contend that this leap is impossible since it is obvious that we exist in time and that the fall has happened ever since we have been in this world. The fall is the original condition of man, he is fallen by definition. However, a leap in time can only be made by someone who, standing in the eternal, would have had a negative experience of it; but someone who existed in the eternal must be in possession of the whole, so how could he imagine leaping into the void? To establish an imperative here, the fall we must all inevitably experience is the enactment of a dialectic of time in reverse, with time as the final limit, which amounts purely and simply to eliminating the dialectic of time in order to be able to abolish its antithesis: the eternal. Consequently the Death of God, for Bataille, would result in a condition of immanence which would cease to be an immanence because no transcendent current would be able to raise it any further outside itself. This would be a life in the present pure and simple, which in my view would take on the character of nihilism from the moment it ceased to be denied by dissatisfaction and spiritual anguish. For Nietzsche, the Death of God was quite the opposite, and signified for him that God had lost all transcendental virtue, since God had fallen to the level of the present pure and simple; hence the birth of Dionysus, hence the deepening of the moment and freedom from immediate necessity through the eternal return of the moment. The moment experienced at the Death of God as a fall into the abyss is felt as an elevation, as the possession of the whole in the anticipation of his eternal return.*

*If everything is only appearance, and if time is the sole reality, the idea of the eternal return is an expression of the desire to go beyond appearance: things then acquire an intense degree of reality in their eternal return, in the desire for their eternal return. And also, would the importance of the moment not be the same with or without the eternal return; with the new weight of the moment dissolving firstly into the nothingness opened up by the Death of God, this new weight of the moment is assured either because that is where the eternal return is perceived, or because that is where the eternal is revealed.*

*Otherwise, the moment would become mixed up with what follows etc. Henceforth, when I say: this moment is unique, it will never return — I will already have noted that it contains the eternal; it will not return for me, I who am in time, even though the moment was a vision of the eternal or of the eternal cycle of time. It is rather I who would be transported in the moment, and for that to happen I would have to step out of time, or else the eternal return would bring me back to that moment.* [July 1937]

## PIERRE KLOSSOWSKI *On the Master and the Slave* 25

*The relationship between man and God corresponds in social terms to the relationship between Lord and Servant. The Lord's revolt against God re-establishes the ancient relationship between Master and Slave and leads to the Slave's revolt against his Master. The death of God desired by the Master supplies the template for the Master being put to death by the Slave. However, the Master can only kill God in his dreams: dreams that God himself has sent him; he can only provoke God into single combat by provoking his Slave against himself; and the Slave, thus provoked, in putting his Master to death rejoices for a moment, drunk on freedom, transformed into a god himself, and powerless to suspect that he was merely the blind instrument of divine will.*

*God bestows both eternal life and death. And in the presence of God, the Lord decides upon the life and death of his Servant. The moment he aspires to usurp the functions of Providence, and hopes and convinces himself that God does not or no longer exists, he assumes responsibility for the crime before God. He thus re-establishes the ancient situation of Master and Slave, but re-establishes it beneath the gaze of God, hoping that this gaze has been extinguished. The Servant, now once again the Slave, believes he understands that the Master's prerogatives allowed him to carry out the crime with impunity. But when the rebellious Slave sets about taking his Master to trial, he immediately becomes an accessory in the Master's revolt against God, and because of this he in turn arrogates to himself the committing of the crime — for he thus makes a claim to extend his own prerogatives by what he considered to be his Lord's. The proceedings he brings against his Master have no other objective than to put these prerogatives into practice for his own benefit, by killing his Master.* The justice of Slaves can only be the shared practice of individual iniquity. *In rebelling against iniquity the rebellious slave can only answer back with iniquity, and whilst he assumes all manifest guilt in the dream of the Death of God, the Master in his humiliation and his torment atones for the dream the slave wants to make real, and atones for his crimes committed before God against the person of his slave. After having overthrown his Master, the slave appeals in vain, if not to God then at least to an identical order of being, that he might be allowed to enjoy the benefits of his rebellion in peace. Henceforth, everything he does bears the stamp of murder. He never obtains redemption, or pardon; he simply gets moments of respite, granted with bad grace by the Destiny that is impatient to destroy both him and his work; soon he is reduced to re-establishing through his own efforts the different forms of his Master's life: the Slave recreates slavery, but where the Lord could feel no hatred for his Servant, the Slave who has re-established slavery in order to maintain his position as usurper does not feel that he has enough strength to overpower those who, at every moment, remind him of his own origins and the fragility of his position.* [July 1937]

## 26 JACQUES CHAVY *On Authority*

PRELIMINARY REMARKS: *I am sorry I haven't organised and worked up these notes, in a word, to have explained any better what I mean. I don't have the technical vocabulary and my clumsy style of writing will draw attention even more to the sketchy nature of what follows. I have considered the issue of authority only within a framework that one might term political, within a moral framework it would probably not develop very differently.*

A QUESTION THAT DOES NOT REQUIRE AN ANSWER

*If in what concerns their individual lives men have the impression that they decide their actions, for everything related to living in groups, to living in society or between one society and another, they either rely on the government or at any rate put up with it. It is government that makes the laws that regulate relationships between individuals and which makes decisions in relations between different societies (nations).*

*Without listing all the types of government that exist or have existed, it must be acknowledged that governments have no power, whatever form they exist in, unless they possess authority.*

*Authority is a principle that takes hold of any man regardless who he is from the moment he becomes active in government and which he possesses only for acts relating to government; the fact must be admitted that some individuals without even a scrap of power can still have influence over their fellow men, for they have a natural authority, they possess Mana,*[6] *they possess authority even without holding any power, just as men in power may be devoid of any authority, or any influence (the difference between having authority and being dressed in authority in order to exercise power).*

*But where does authority come from? I believe that in the societies that have existed up until now authority is not the imperious desire of a man to govern and to lead other men because he has a taste for exercising power, because that is what he enjoys. A man cannot put on authority like he can his clothes — authority is granted to the king or the leader by God (without going into all the details concerning the religions in different societies) or by whoever has replaced God in democratic countries: the sovereign people (in this case the authority comes from an impersonal being — a man like Hitler wields absolute power, but also power from the German people, from his race, his blood, a more religious form of the sovereign people).*

*There is not a man in existence who is the source of his own authority, who governs for himself; a leader is a person interposed between God and men, a mediator. God has given him authority, and in exchange he must maintain, conserve and, as far as he can, increase the power of the group that God has entrusted him with leading. This leader does not govern by himself, but because God has bestowed upon him a scrap of his omnipotence. But if, in a society with a single leader, authority has a divine origin, where would authority come from in a society based on initiation, which is the basis of its hierarchy, and which chooses not to have a head? To put it another way, if there are mysteries, they have to have been revealed. The death of God has been revealed. Does God only exist in that moment when he dies?*

NOTE 1. *One might think that men with influence are natural leaders, that authority is a personal quality. But how do we explain that leaders have always justified their use of power by invoking the divine will that put them in the position they occupy not for their pleasure but for the glory of their God, and therefore, of their people?*

*This constant justification throughout history leads us to think that what man fears most is to command, and that his need for submission and obedience is such that even someone who takes on the greatest responsibilities is afraid of being held responsible for his authority (in other words, its source, its origin) and so he justifies his actions, and excuses them as being the will of God.*

NOTE 2. *Just as men bow down to their leader, the leader bows down to God. But is God also afraid of his omnipotence? What is God's justification?* 16 August 1937

DIONYSOS

# DIONYSUS 27

(Extracts from *Dionysus* by Walter Otto, apart from the final citation.)

**All of Antiquity viewed Dionysus as the provider of wine. However, he was also known as the Frenzied One who makes men possessed, who incites them to savagery and even bloodshed. Dionysus was the guardian and companion of the spirits of the dead, and his was the most important name in the dedications made in the sacred mysteries. Dramatic performance was associated in particular with his worship and cult practice [...] It was he who made the flowers come out in the springtime; ivy, pine and fig were all associated with him; yet far higher than all these examples of the bounty of nature must be placed the thousandfold-blessed gift of the vine. Dionysus was the god of joyful drunkenness and ecstatic love. But he was also the Persecuted, the Suffering and the Dying, and all those he loved and who attended him shared as a result in his tragic fate.**

**Who was Dionysus?**

**The god of ecstasy and terror, of savagery and joyful deliverance, the mad god, whose appearance sent men into a state of delirium, already manifested the mysterious and paradoxical nature of his being in the circumstances of his conception and birth.**

**He was the son of Zeus and a mortal woman, who even before she gave birth was consumed by the lightning-fire of her celestial bridegroom.**

André Masson, *Greek Tragedy*.

Like the myths connected with his birth, the myths relating to the appearance of Dionysus also reveal much about his nature.

At the point when he was conceived the element of earth was touched by a blast from the divine sky. But from this union of the celestial and the earthly, which was expressed in the myth of the god's double birth, the arduous and tearful aspect of human life was not lifted, but kept in stark contrast with such superhuman splendour. The one who was born in this way was not only the one who cried for joy, and the bringer of joy, but the tormented and dying god, the god of tragic contradiction. The inner conflict of this dual nature was so great that like a violent storm he appeared amongst men right in their midst and terrified them, beating down all resistance with the scourge of madness. Everything that was usual and ordered must be shattered into myriad fragments. Existence suddenly became an intoxication, an intoxication of dazzling happiness, but one that was also marked by fear.

When Dionysus arrived at the city of Argos, because the people there did not wish to celebrate his cult, he drove the women mad to such extent that they took themselves off to the mountains and there tore the flesh from the bodies of their newborn children [...] Aura, the beloved of Dionysus, killed one of her young children and devoured it...

A god of frenzy! A god, whose nature it is to be mad! What did they experience or see, those men who were exposed to the impossible nature of this image?

The face of this true god is the face of a whole world. There can only be a god who is mad if there is a

André Masson, *The Dionysian Universe*.

world that is mad which reveals itself through him. Where is this world? Can it still be found and recognised by us? Only the god himself can help us find the way...

Whoever wishes to beget something which is alive must descend into the primordial depths wherein the very forces of life reside. And when he returns to the surface, there is a gleam of madness in his eyes because there, down below, life and death live together as one. The original mystery is itself mad — the bosom of laceration and of unity torn asunder. On this matter we have no need to consult the philosophers [...] The experience of life and the rites of all peoples and of all times are proof enough.

The experience of these peoples declares that wherever there are signs of life, death lies close by. And the more alive this life becomes, the more death draws near, until the supreme moment, the moment of magic when something new is created — when life and death collide in joyful madness. The thrill and the whirl of life is so profound because it is dead drunk. Each time life renews itself, the wall which separates it from death is breached for a moment.

Taurus was one of the forms of Dionysus not only because of its fertility and abundance of life, but also because of its raging madness, its dangerous nature...

Its oft-mentioned lasciviousness must have been what made the goat one of the Dionysian animals...

*Nietzsche Dionysus*

An intoxicated god, a demented god [...] The hastily assembled hypotheses which reduce all significant meaning to the level of the commonplace have only served to keep us from seeing this representation. History, however, bears witness to its strength and truth. To the Greeks it provided a feeling of intoxication that was so powerful and so all-embracing that, thousands of years after their civilisation had fallen into ruin, a Hölderlin or a Nietzsche could still express their ultimate and most profound thought in the name of Dionysus. So too Hegel, who represented the knowledge of truth by means of a Dionysian image, declaring that it was "the bacchanalian revel, in which there is not one person who is not intoxicated."

Here is my Dionysian universe that creates and destroys itself eternally, this mysterious world of double pleasures, this, my "beyond good and evil", without purpose, unless the contentment at having accomplished the cycle is itself a purpose, without wishing it so, unless a ring has the good will to turn eternally on itself, and on nothing but itself, in its own orbit. This universe that is *mine*, which is therefore lucid enough for me to be able to see it without straining and risk losing my sight? Strong enough to reveal its soul to this mirror? To place its own mirror opposite the mirror of Dionysus? To propose its own solution to the enigma of Dionysus? And being able to do so would it not have to do it all over again? Becoming wedded to the "cycle of cycles"? Yet vowing its own return? Accepting the cycle in which ever and eternally it will glorify itself, and assert itself? With the will to want all things again? To see all the things that have been return again? To want to go to everything there must ever be? Do you know now what the world is for me? And what I want when I want this world?

(Nietzsche, *The Will to Power*)

ROGER CAILLOIS

# DIONYSIAN VIRTUES 

It seems that to the exact extent that the mind is set upon a rather narrow form of discipline and rules that are *at least very severe*, it must take an equivalent approach to the various forms of intoxication and be disturbed by their very existence, because it can never be sure that it will not experience temptation or remorse. In private, it can keep a tight rein on itself at all times and always maintain the most exact control over its instinctual inclinations; and in public, restrict the exercise of its faculties to stating the obvious, promulgating only the minimum of what can be expressed and defined, advancing only on to ground already fully conquered and assimilated, and putting forward nothing that cannot be proven and which is not a fixed part of a system. The power granted by this austerity for the mind that adopts it is strictly speaking almost boundless. In fact, through this power the mind acquires such a cohesiveness that it becomes unshakable, rather like an army in which each tactical element at any particular point benefits from the collective strength of its massed forces. Even so, it does not feel any the less the ever-present attraction of intoxications. More to the point, a mind connected in this way must without doubt be an easier target for intoxications, and be carried off by them completely. It is too unified to become divided or *to make concessions* at the point when vertigo takes hold: it is inconceivable that such a mind would not remain just as whole when afflicted by mental convulsions as when occupied with arithmetic. Being inclined to one of these in equal measure as it is disrupted by the other, it would appear that the release was only so explosive because it followed an excessive state of tension.

Intoxication, moreover, manifests itself as *a total state*, capable, at least potentially, of overwhelming the whole range of functions of an individual, since all of them give way and become still during the time when intoxication is providing stimulation to one of the others. If we add the *semi-intoxication of extra lucidity* spoken of by Baudelaire to the other forms identified by Nietzsche, i.e. the three intoxications of strong alcohol, love and cruelty, it is easy to see that there is no point from which ecstasy is unable to obtain its bearings, and that the extreme sensation of power which characterises it will continue to be identical with it. Whatever its personal effects, and whatever worth they are granted, it is certain that individuals find themselves transported and — except in the case of a few paralysing toxins which nevertheless also produce feelings of intense yet calm superiority, albeit of a contemplative nature — that an impression has been imparted to them of the fullest sense of being, causing them to prefer in comparison with the rest of their lives these rare moments they long for and yearn to experience anew.

Thus, while affecting the individual in the part that is least likely to be surrendered, the various intoxications naturally seem to represent a *violent* state when compared with society, and perhaps indicate certain difficulties the individual may have in adapting to living as part of a group. Here again then, and perhaps not the least of such cases, there is a conflict between the forms of intoxication and the intellect: the imperialistic destiny of the latter and the disdainful resignation of the former which seek to indulge their enthusiasm to the exclusion of all else.

History, however, suggests that there is no absolute character to this conflict. As much as society does not know how to incorporate Dionysian forces, distrusting and persecuting them instead of integrating them, the individual is reduced to finding his gratifications in spite of society, when it is society alone that should be providing them. The essential value of Dionysism is in fact based on precisely this point, that it united people by socialising the thing which, more than anything else, causes separation when its pleasures are enjoyed individually. More specifically, it made participation in ecstatic rites and the communal understanding of the sacred into the *unique* cement of the collectivity it established, for, in contrast to the closed local cults of the cities, the mysteries of Dionysus were universal and open to everyone. In this way the mysteries placed at the centre of the social organism those sovereign forms of unrest which, once they had dispersed, would in due course be hunted down by society in the no man's land on its margins where any threats to social harmony were cast out.*
This approach represented nothing less than the most radical of revolutions, and

that Dionysism coincided with the revolt of rural elements against the urban nobility, and that the spread of cults associated with the underworld, at the expense of the Uranian[1] religion, had been brought about by the victory of the populace over the traditional aristocracies. At the same time, certain values were inverted: the poles of the sacred, the base and the holy, switched over. What was once marginal, with all the appealing discredit associated with that expression, became a part of the new order and, in some way, the point on which it turned: the asocial (or what had seemed to be so) focused collective energies, crystallising and setting them in motion, and became a force of *super-socialisation*.

It follows from this general discussion that we may now employ the term *Dionysian virtues*, with virtue to be understood as something *that connects*, and vice as something *that brings about separation*. These virtues were sufficient in themselves to enable a collectivity to create its emotional foundation and to establish the solidarity of its members on these virtues alone while excluding any prior affiliations based on locality, history, race or language;† this would affirm, for those drawn to them, the conviction that these virtues were unfairly mistreated in a society that chose not to recognise them and which did not know how to suppress them; so too to give them a taste and show how they might group themselves together in an organic formation that was irreducible and resistant to assimilation; and finally, to strengthen their resolve to adopt this strategy which is always available.

* In fact, in Rome, the Bacchanalia were prohibited for being both immoral and a threat to the *security of the state*. In Greece, Euripides' *Bacchae*, a document which should indeed only be used as evidence with great caution, shows to some extent that the spread of the Dionysian cult did not take place without resistance from the established powers.

† On this aspect we should be able to refer to a whole body of work on the sociology of *brotherhoods*, but unfortunately this is still only in its early stages. Two features ought to be noted, however: brotherhoods exist as a solid structure within a weak social environment. They are formed by substituting in place of the factual qualifications (birth etc.) on which the cohesion of the social environment depends, a free choice consecrated by some sort of initiation and formal admission to the group, and so tend to consider this acquired kinship as equivalent to kinship by blood (hence the continuing use of the term *brother* among adepts), which makes the bond thus created stronger than any other and assures that it is the one to be favoured in the event of conflict.

GEORGES BATAILLE

# 29 *What we undertook a few months ago…*

What we undertook a few months ago, we undertook at least in agreement that it was impossible for us to go into any great detail. We were well aware of our starting point and also knew that we had to turn our backs on what was already only the past. But we did not know, and could not know, where we were heading. The only publication[1] which up until now has served as an indicator of our activity has also by its nature responded to these conditions: its merit was that it indicated — even if in a seemingly absurd and brief manner — that we were taking our leave from what we had apparently been engaged upon until that point. Yet there was nothing in its pages that might satisfy, however feebly, those who insist that action should have a precise goal. The only valid response we could offer to such irony — all the more valid because we kept it to ourselves — is that action, as we understand it, cannot be limited to predefined goals.

I am not seeking a more encouraging path today any more than I was a few months ago. On the contrary, I am possessed by the idea that the path we are following ought to be more disheartening, that the advances we have made run counter to our rigorous demands. When I consider the sometimes dreadful, often harrowing demands that men everywhere have managed to respond to with a sort of outburst of joy, it saddens me to acknowledge how little it is possible to get from us. If we are bound only to bear witness to the debility of today's existence, it would be better if people like us had never lived… I hope that one day we might live with such explosive strength of will that the life of a Trappist monk would make us laugh. Trappists certainly "exist", Tibetan hermits "exist"…

But what matters now is not any desire to make things easy, nor admit to any limit, so much as attempting to specify the directions in which we now find ourselves engaged.

Furthermore, it is less a matter of fixing a set of principles than of defining a state of affairs. In the midst of the current breakdown there cannot in fact be any question of rediscovering the conditions of a collective emotional life while moving forward according to arbitrary decisions or simple guesswork. We know of no authority that can give any weight to such decisions. We cannot under any circumstances allow ourselves to remain attached to a past of any kind. Nothing can gainsay the fact that not one of us, in isolation, has ever known any guide outside himself other than science. Science is the sole authority we rely on. This means, among other things, that we acknowledge no higher authority capable of preventing us from blaspheming or laughing at it.

The objectivity of science does not stop existing within us whenever we make a stand against ordinary rationalism. And at times when our position is irrational, when it results directly from spontaneous instincts, we can relate this position and these instincts to a set of facts whose consequences and precursors are already known. The consciousness that results from an extensive knowledge of the different possible forms of emotional life is one element of an absolute originality within an elaboration of the collective and passionate forms of this life, a paradoxical element that specifically gives a precise character, and a particular direction for all our potential activity.

This is how mythology became part of our way of thinking from the beginning, as the cornerstone of a science of society perhaps even before it became the bewitching play of images that fed into our feelings of disquiet. There is in myth a quality that must seem irreconcilable with a religious conviction that can only proceed from unconsciousness and naïveté. Yet it is quite enough to counter this pessimistic way of thinking with an overview of all the things that are different in today's existence compared with during the earlier Buddhist or Christian eras. Buddhism and Christianity were products of their times, and naturally drew inspiration from the history of ideas that were then current. "The Gospel according to St. John is an understandable testimony."[2] It would be foolish to imagine today, on the grounds that collective exaltation needs to be rediscovered, at a time when the secret of it has been lost and seems to belong to the past, that only regressive forms are possible. The requirements of religion, however sour they may one day or another reveal themselves to be, do not demand of anyone that they play at being inspired or being a prophet. There can be no disputing the fact that Nietzsche, paralysed by the impoverished forms of existence in his day, was obliged to resort to the fiction of Zarathustra in order to be able to express himself fully. But Nietzsche did not express himself only through the voice of Zarathustra — even if the burning passion of Zarathustra is essential to his teachings — and since then, everything in this world has been so thoroughly shaken up that it has become possible to bite using his teeth, to make a fire out of his bones; taking off all one's clothes in order to be able to exist fully is a necessity born out of a state of affairs even more debased than our own, and a state of affairs that has disappeared.

All the various aspects of modern activity stretch out in front of us and there is nothing amongst it that creates any sense of unease; the traditional forms of poetry and mythology are dead. As much as that might depend on human will, this world has become like the suburb of a large city — at the very least, these large city suburbs with their factories and nondescript residential buildings represent the only human material that can be reproduced indefinitely. Setting aside the disgust we feel for theatricality, we know that a world as empty as this should not be entered with the lofty contempt of a magus but that of a surgeon, which is to say, with a more active, indeed a more cutting style of scornful sympathy. The disintegrated human material we are focusing on here, with the view of subordinating it to these elusive values, can only be reduced by clear-headed men.

I cannot even begin to imagine that any such hope could be conceived if we ourselves were not precisely in a position to take this clear-headedness to its ultimate limits. With respect to the one who grasps in an instant what he sees before him, in his eyes there can be nothing to hope for. He who aimlessly observes the human beings around him, who in his anguish and in spite of himself eavesdrops on their strange conversation, if, as is natural, he is feverish for something else, then all that is left to him is to give in to nervous breakdown. But if there is something in him analogous to the aloof and aggressive coldness of science, then all these vague movements of bones and lips will be no more than a mask to tear off, a mask that conceals nothing but an inner conflagration. Beneath the ashes and the burnt remains he discerns a movement which is difficult to detect, yet all the more likely to make him catch his breath — all of life in slow formation, little by little revealing to his eye its incandescent traces and endlessly fractured structure, seeming more like a mortal wound or a cry of hunger than all that the strange heart-rendings of poetic inspiration had allowed us to believe existed in the night.

Of course, I am speaking of a vision it is not yet possible to attain. But I mention it precisely because I am aware that this unattainable aspect of why men exist — which cannot be described any more exactly — is the very obstacle we must overcome, it is the fog which must be dissipated so that this ungodly promised land may be revealed, bathed in sunlight, to the most feverish.

But this obstacle is not one that can be reached and overcome only after long and patient waiting; this promised land is not yet attainable, but, in order for it to become so — and this must be stated categorically — little more is needed at this moment. The responsibility that falls to us in particular is limited, although these limits are not of our own choosing, but result from the current state of knowledge. There are now methods of investigation which have led to a precise understanding of the emotional structure of primitive societies. These societies appear to be constructed, in so far as man does not exist within them as a single brick in isolation, according to myth and ritual. The images and rites, heavily charged with the emotional content of primitive or uncivilised communities, represent to us the fabric of these communities. And, as we pass to a philosophical interpretation of these facts, we realise that the myths and rituals constitute the very soul of these communities. However, the methods which have led to these key representations have not yet found their exact point of application for our purposes because they have only ever had as their object certain forms of human existence that are unfamiliar to us; with rare exceptions, no one has dared to make today's society, the society in which we "exist", the object of a structural analysis.

It is possible that a sort of unspoken taboo might be blocking any such attempt. However, until recently, the difficulties being faced had nothing to do with religion. The social community's existence was profoundly fragmented, and everything that could be called structural fabric seemed to be only a relic from the past — not a truly living fabric, and still less a fabric that was in the process of being created. But the shared existence of which we are also a part has, for some twenty years now, undergone certain transformations that are some of the most rapid, according to our information, seen in the whole course of history. The facts we are able to analyse first-hand because of their topicality indicate a surprising wealth of such material for further analysis, a wealth which, moreover, contrasts with the exceptional dearth of material from the earliest years of the twentieth century. The fabric that makes up the social structure has proliferated before our eyes with an extraordinary energy, and principles that had been established in crumbling societies have found themselves treated as roughly, in certain cases, as if they were lifeless waste. However, this new fabric has precisely the same nature as that found in primitive societies; it is mythical and ritual, and forms with vigour around images charged with the most powerful emotional values; it forms in the great movements of the crowd that are regulated by the ceremonial which introduces the symbols of its subjugation.

Fortunately for our purposes, however, a method has already been introduced by Freud for the specific interpretation of these facts. The analysis of the emotional structure of the army and the Church, set out by Freud in his *Group Psychology and the Analysis of the Ego*, is perhaps one of the most surprising and most important revelations in the science of the nature of life. This is because it is not only an introduction to the understanding of the great unitarist structures — once the requisite understanding of primitive facts have been established, the data from Freud's analysis can open the way to a general understanding of social structures of all kinds, whether Church or religious order, army or militia, secret society or political party. And if Freud himself did not go so far as to undertake a general analysis of living forms, he did, as it were, leave the possibility of making that leap to those who have followed him. Thus, not only has the analysis of what is been opened up in several respects, but it has now become possible to examine experience itself, by which I mean the attempt to pass from knowledge to action; and oppose the great unitary formations which in other countries have brutally closed off and fixed existence, and attempt to form a religious movement, or perhaps more exactly a 'Church', which would unite existence not only in order to respond to the immediate need for an arrangement of forces, but also to *liberate* it.

It is essential at this point to set down quite clearly, even brutally, how the various possibilities present themselves. I began by talking about science. Now I want to talk about experience. But it is obvious that the vocabulary might introduce a misunderstanding here, if something were to be retained of that subordination of experience to science, which is self-evident when it is not concerned with human life. Experience, in the way we envisage it, takes precedence in such an imperious manner that it would be laughable to compare such a situation to that of medicine.

Medicine is in fact concerned only with the medium term, with organs and bodily functions, which may be indispensable to life but which do not in themselves signify the end of that life. Sociology — more precisely mythological sociology — is on the contrary only concerned with this *end* of man, which can only be discovered beyond him. Myths are more than the focus of social cohesion for individual beings: they are the reason why a man is able to give what is most precious to him, his blood. Existence gains access here, and only here, to the *totality of being*, and in that moment of vertigo and gravity everything that remains only function — science itself — enters a region of silence. For even if it is the only means we can resort to in order to discern in the half-light precisely *what matters to us*, this means of discerning must not be confused with what is being discerned. All that we should assert at the outset is: (1) that in the situation we find ourselves in, science cannot prevent us from discovering within its purpose those values it is reduced to recording without being able to establish them rationally; (2) that, reciprocally, there exists no prior emotional determination within us which by its nature might lessen for us the cold objectivity of science.

And without doubt this last point is essential at precisely the moment when I must insist on the necessity of making a choice. Two radically opposed methods would appear *a priori* to be possible. If we employed one of these methods, we would proceed with a somewhat random potential experiment, in other words we would have no other goal except to create a common existence, a 'Church', which might in the end be no more than a political party; if we were to employ the other one, we would be starting from certain principles that have been authoritatively demonstrated. However, there is a way of avoiding both these approaches. There is one objective that may be determined in advance without the intervention of any revelation: this objective is the discovery or the rediscovery of the *totality of being*. I do not believe it is necessary or even useful to bring any other limitation to bear, but in and of itself such an ambition would exclude a large number of other potential experiments. Doubtless something still remains of the enormous liberty that continues to preside over the development of human cohesion — for individual beings are always open to being combined into more than one grouping. But in any given circumstances, the search for this totality depends on the whole set of modifications to which the lives of men are subject — precisely at that moment.

What is more, totality always demands from men what they reject under the dominion of what is called "common sense", which is no more than a sort of senility. Totality demands that life comes together and, so to speak, loses itself in the orgy with death. The purpose of the experiment should thus be to pass from a certain fragmented and empty state, from a life freed from the fear of death, to this sort of brutal and suffocating refusal of everything that is, everything that very likely occurs in many death throes.

Beyond these and other similar considerations, make space for liberty! Myths — or to speak more precisely — the mythical images we have at our disposal, are not disqualified from the debate. Earlier I spoke of Trappist monks. Of course, we are not going to become Trappists; we want nothing to do with Christian avarice. We are free spirits, having a boundless generosity combined with a Greek naïveté, in other words happy, and with occasional impulses of outlandish humour… that sort of childish greed we feel when approaching the tragic site wherein our existence surrenders, frolics, and would, without generosity, be merely a new form of Christian avarice. Let myths destroy themselves, fester away and show their hatred for one another! And if they can, before a universe emptied of its servile function, emptied of God, let them make human life into a festival and a game that is every bit as free!

I know that once again I have only said part of what is necessary; I think that if I could communicate, really communicate what I see, and at the same time the rapture that I feel in the presence of what I see, for my listeners it would be bound to result in an unburdening, a liberation, a need to act and to stir up others, a long-suffering yet dreadfully happy need. But what is clear to me, whatever I do, I can only make a little less obscure to others. I would just like to add what I feel so deeply: that in all that I experience in this way, I disappear, like the tiniest little cry. [Spring 1937]

ROGER CAILLOIS

# *The Winter Wind* 30

*Extra ecclesiam nulla salus*[1]

Up against a world that gives them little satisfaction, the various different dissenters share in feeling the same need for action but the same inability to act. They realise that they must unite in order to be strong, but, fearing that this will prove more burdensome than the weakness which already weighs upon their shoulders, they dread the prospect that unity will make them concede to more sacrifices than their powerlessness had imposed by what it made them give up. Following in the footsteps of the great individualists of the last century, they forecast only ill from following a path on which the demands of solidarity would soon set limits on their independence. In short, they fear that in gaining strength they will lose their reason for being, and at this juncture they are seized by a sudden foreboding. The stakes are indeed high.

## I. THE FATE OF INDIVIDUALISM

> The disintegration of a society's morals is a situation in which the new ovule appears, or new ovules — ovules (individuals) containing the germ of new societies and unities. The appearance of individuals is the sign that society has become fit to reproduce.
>
> Nietzsche, *The Will to Power*

If we examine the evolution of ideas not only in France but throughout the whole of Europe, from the beginnings of Romanticism onwards, it is impossible not to be struck by the increasing and increasingly significant influence, quite out of proportion with any other phenomena of a similar order, of the great individualists whose supreme representative was Stirner but in Nietzsche found its richest expression. It is noticeable that written works in this vein seem to situate themselves outside of any aesthetic considerations on purpose, while gladly presenting themselves as good examples and placing a certain value on the use of slogans. While the ultimate consequences of this way of thinking have not been generally accepted, people have been less and less able to tolerate the fact that its principles were discredited at the start; the autonomy of the moral individual has become the very foundation of society. However, little by little, a crisis of individualism has begun to emerge, to which a number of substantial external and immediately obvious causes have contributed. The development of sociological research has undermined the fundamental assumptions on which individualism is built and, more urgently, political and social developments themselves — which allow scarcely any possibility of living apart from society, but all the more of dying that way — have in their combined effects gradually made a sheltered existence in ivory towers seem only dull and dusty. These factors are sufficient to induce the faithful followers of the great individualists to reconsider their approach and to inspire them to take part in an activity of a distinctly collective nature, but not, however, to abandon all their scruples, nor prevent them from questioning whether this temptation will lead to a consolidation of their position, or to making concessions to the tribal group, or quite simply to their surrender.

There can be no hope of solving this problem without first examining the reasons which have led intellectuals to withdraw from their social group, falling back to the Aventine Hill[2] and at once adopting a position that is directly hostile to any constituted society. The act of resigning in this way coincides historically with an ideology that strangely denies the instinctive phenomena of attraction and cohesion in which later on will be sought the vital force of social groups. The only salient features associated with these social groups have been their enlightened self-interest together with their preoccupations for distributive justice, neither of which find any common ground with man's deep sense of being and which tend just as much to deter him from the idea of social existence, especially when such determining factors are evidently missing from a society that is founded only on injustice and the sort of privileges which immediately make it seem scandalous and detestable. Thus conscious individuals of a contemplative nature have cultivated only indifference to it, while those of a cantankerous disposition have shown open and ill-tempered hostility towards the restrictions imposed on them by the group, which they find unbearable because they see them simply as persecution and bullying. Feeling nothing towards society other than defensive reactions, such individuals naturally reserve their sympathy for all those society keeps on the margins, the vagabonds, streetwalkers and outcasts, and gradually makes a hero of *the hardened criminal on whom the prison gates will always close.*[3] It would be a mistake to see those themes of romantic literature, the prostitute with a heart of gold or the noble thief, as signs of crude sentimentality, when there are few better indicators of the essential novelty of the times in which we live, i.e. the consummation of the divorce, in terms of values and before long morals too, between the writer and the close-knit, stable part of the social body.

The individualist, however, quickly taking his point of view to its furthest limits, starts proclaiming as fallacious and tyrannical everything he sees as the constituent parts of society: family, state, nation, morality, religion, sometimes even adding reason, truth and science, either because the connections they create seem to be just as much of a constraint, or because they are to some extent garbed with the sacred in the manner of the preceding categories. Thus was born a type of methodical iconoclast, the hopeless character seeking the profane as described by Stirner: "Tortured by a gnawing hunger, crying out in distress, you wander right round the walls that enclose you in search of the profane. But in vain. Soon the Church will cover the whole Earth and the *world of the sacred* will be victorious."[4] In these conditions, there is only one possible moral reaction: profanation, the full-blooded destruction of the sacred, is the only course of action that can give the anarchist the sense of effective freedom.

In actual fact, this is only illusion: the sacrilege never goes beyond sarcasm or blasphemy, and their actions fall so far short of fulfilling the promise of their words that sometimes the sheer quantity and self-importance of what is said seems designed only to paper over the absence of any actions. The greatest of the individualists were also feeble, insignificant or maladjusted, deprived of the only things that would have given them real pleasure, yet being obsessed by them to the point of feverish excitement: Sade, conjuring up his debaucheries within the walls of his dungeon; Nietzsche, at Sils Maria, the solitary and sickly theorist of violence; Stirner, the state employee living his well-ordered life while constructing his justifications for crime.

At the same time, poetry too was exalting all forms of liberation, but this was, more than anything else, a poetry of *refuge*, which lulled and consoled, brought oblivion and painted a harsh world with the soothing colours of dreams. This blind alley could not offer satisfaction for ever. More than simple *avoidance*, it must be conquest that captivates us. Today, the problem appears even more urgent, yet it has become clear that society, through its cohesiveness, wields a strength that breaks all individual efforts as easily as glass; the time has also come to communicate to those who are not resistant to the idea, whether out of fear or self-interest, that the individuals who are truly determined to undertake this struggle — on an infinitesimal scale if need be, but in an effective way when their attempt looked as if it might spread like an epidemic — must stand up to society on its own ground and attack it with its own weapons, that is to say by forming themselves into a community, and still more, by ceasing to allow the values they defend to become the prerogatives of rebels and insurgents, but on the contrary regarding them as the chief values of the society they wish to see established and as the most social values of all, even if they are just a little implacable.

Such a plan assumes a certain amount of education in the understanding of revolt on the part of this individual, which would enable him to proceed from the simple instinct for rioting to a more broadly imperialist position and show that he should suppress his unruly and impulsive reactions in the interests of discipline, forward thinking and patience. In a word, rather than *Satanic* he must become *Luciferian*.

In a similar manner, the committed individualist should completely change his way of thinking with regard to power and the sacred in general. In this respect it is almost necessary to adopt the opposite course to what Stirner enjoins and direct all efforts not at profanation, but at making sacred. It is, moreover, this impulse that will enable him to establish his most deeply rooted opposition to a society which has been profaned to an extreme degree by its own actions, in such a way that nothing could be more antagonistic to it than the intervention of these values, and there is nothing against which it would be less capable of defending itself. Still more than this: what directs any group thus formed is the desire to fight society as a society, while the plan to attack it as a surer and more compact body aims for it to become established like a cancer within the more unstable and less close-knit organism, albeit one that is incomparably larger. This is a process of *super-socialisation*, and as such the community envisaged is already naturally set on the path of making sacred as much as it can, in order to increase to the greatest conceivable extent the singularity of its being, and the impact of its actions.

Individualists are now in a position to ease their scruples. Undertaking collective action would not mean renouncing their faith, but rather committing themselves to the only way available, and from the moment they made the decision to move on from theoretical recriminations to effective struggle they would be doing no more than progressing from skirmishes to pitched battle. They would be fomenting their holy war. And war, as Clausewitz said, is the continuation of politics by other means.

## II. THE FOUNDATION OF COLLECTIVE EFFORT

> I do not know whether I have already said it in this work but what has distinguished men the most is that those who have performed great deeds have simply seen what could be done before others did. *Memoirs* of Cardinal de Retz

Just as there is an irreducible primitive experience of the *self*, which is the fundamental basis of anarchist individualism, so too the inalienable and existential foundation of collective effort must also be brought forth. It cannot, under any circumstances, establish its emotional basis upon something as entirely backward-looking as factual categories — race or language, historical homeland or tradition — which shape the existence of nations and fuel their patriotism. To do so would be to sanction precisely what we are plotting together to change, and to reinforce what we wish to see weakened. It is readily understood that a movement originating *within* a society and which is directed against it cannot be founded on what defines and holds that society together by setting it against its rivals.

A social nucleus of the type I am proposing here must be built from elements of a totally different nature: a common will to carry out an identical task already entails elective affinities that are capable in themselves of directing the formation of a community and making that their necessary and sufficient reason by supplying each member, as distinct from his fellows, with a twin series of complementary experiences of attractions and repulsions.[5] This implies a fact of everyday life beyond any argument, which had already become apparent even to the originators of individualism: the essential ethical opposition between at least two classes of people, with such contrasting reactions it is as if they belonged to different species, and which result in both conflicting conceptions of the world and irreconcilable sets of values.

Indeed each of us, in our relations with our fellow men, encounters others who seem to belong to another moral species, almost another race. There is no avoiding the feeling that we recoil from such people as though from some harmful foreign body. Their behaviour is always what we fear it might be, never what we hope for, and their vulgarity surpasses expectations. In contrast to these there are others who, when they are put to the test, act exactly as expected, as indeed we would behave too when at our best and precisely as we would wish they should behave. So it is that, confirmed by the behaviour of these individuals, in other words in a world without any deception as to what actions have been carried out and with the pressure of realities it would be rash to avoid and which in fact constantly bring us back to order, there is an ideal demarcation according to which each one of us allocates a position to our fellows and to all the rest. On this side of the line, a community of closely connected people is established by the very fact of the line's existence, people who have spontaneously recognised each other as allies and who are willing to provide unconditional mutual assistance. Meanwhile on the other side, living according to their own laws is a crowd of unfortunates with whom we have nothing in common, for whom there are justifiable grounds for treating them with contempt and from whom we instinctively distance ourselves as if they were something impure, radiating like a sort of dangerous contagion their particular appeal, this latent temptation which the lowest levels always exert on the most elevated and which alone would justify for those at the top their pride in such a position and their will to stay there.

These are distinctions not of degree, but of nature. No one is responsible for the place he occupies in this hierarchy of qualities of the soul: the defaulter is not condemned by trial, but kept apart as a sanitary measure, to protect the integrity of the whole. For the same reason that at harvest-time the unblemished fruits must be separated from the diseased ones, an armed yet distant neutrality is no more than the basic practice of legitimate defence with regard to untrustworthy individuals, something that is absolutely essential to avoid contamination. A society, like an organism, must know how to eliminate its waste.

Sympathies and antipathies, which, as we know, are *beyond our control*, may pass for the individual and ephemeral rudiments, weak in the extreme on account of their subjective and fragmentary nature, of a living system of this kind. Moreover, it is by no means accidental that the collective opinion chooses to represent them as misleading, advises that we disregard them and stipulates that we pay them no heed, all on the pretext of impartiality, when it comes to decisions of even the mildest interest concerning society itself, and more specifically its public services. Society, it seems, thus feels the necessity to obstruct the formation of any *endogenous* aggregation based on reflexes of discrimination, with the idea being that this is the source of both a ferment capable of breaking down its structure and a beginning for the recomposition of its living forces, which is liable to improve its situation by degrees, and all the more as intended, by subverting the social equilibrium to its own advantage, which it would then distribute within its own framework. This is why the *socialisation* of direct individual reactions[6] appears, on the contrary, to constitute the first phase of development of one social existence within another. Duly elaborated and systematised, and treated as the expression of a fundamental reality, it is a sure outcome that they will succeed in giving even the most fiercely independent individual an extremely powerful sense of group consciousness, including, if needs be, total alienation from himself.

Indeed, when the individualists of the last century imagined (they never made even the slightest initial attempts at putting anything into practice) some sort of conquest of society, their hopes were always invested in formations of just this type. It cannot be over-emphasised how important it is that Balzac and Baudelaire not only regarded with sympathy but also put forward as models Loyola and the *perinde ac cadaver*[7] of the Society of Jesus, and the Old Man of the Mountain and his Hashisheen, and how significant it is that one of them was content to describe the dealings of a mysterious association within the society of his day, and the other to foretell the constitution of a new aristocracy based on a mysterious grace that would entail neither work nor money.[8]

Taken to their limits, these ideas allow us to determine what in particular is required for the struggle by a closed and militant association that models its way of thinking on an active monastic order, its discipline on a paramilitary group and its modes of existence and action, if needs be, on a secret society.

These three types of community can immediately be seen to resemble one another by the strict separation which divides their members from the rest of society. Further analysis would show that the differences between them are not so much defined by their respective aims as by the external conditions which affect their development — thus whether they enjoy the support of the authorities, are tolerated reluctantly or are reduced to the status of criminals. Each gains affiliate members by volunteering or by novitiate. Members are distinguished from outsiders and connected to each other by a complete uniform or some imperceptible sign. Their whole ethic depends on this arrangement, setting up strict obligations for members and compelling them to regard all other people not so much as their equals in rights, but rather as raw material for the work they undertake.

Thus, within the social structure it is not only individual attractions and repulsions that tend to be approved, but before very long too a distinction of the kind laid down by Nietzsche as regards Masters and Slaves. We should perhaps update our vocabulary at this point, so that the terms we use are no longer borrowed from a situation that is past and which therefore distance our thoughts from the present situation, and also so as to stop these terms from seeming paradoxical when the consequences of this doctrine show that the slaves have become the oppressors, and the masters poor unfortunates who are powerless to protect themselves against their assaults.

There is therefore something to be gained by updating this opposition with terms which are more closely related to present-day reality, such as "producers" and "consumers", for example. These not only call to mind the economic substratum but also express a vital position which, while being not entirely determined by it, is often, in the simplest cases, no more than its direct outcome.[9] By consumers, we mean, broadly speaking, those who are oriented towards their own enjoyment, being themselves unproductive and merely using things up, parasites of others, who judge everything only according to whether it will bring them pleasure; they are incapable of generosity, all the more so when it comes to the gift the producer is obliged to make according to his very nature out of what he manufactures and which is not for his own use, for his penchant to produce grips him so strongly that he scorns all leisure and any payment.

A creator by fate, it is he who sets the standards to which others conform. He initiates the practices that others adopt, in such a way that even when he is stifled and forced into the servitude of the mass of his enemies he still retains the full range of his bold instincts and initiatives, while by exercising his marvellous abilities for influencing people he retains the certainty of his imprescriptible superiority, which consumers themselves, in their triumphant satiation, cannot block from their own *conscience*, well aware as they are that they lack any such active, effective and creative drive. Being thus identified only with their own *self*, whilst the producers fulfil their creative needs, they are bereft of that sense of *sovereign irony when a person is able to see themselves alive in the very moment of tragedy*, along with that supreme detachment that is the mark of the strong, as pointed out by Stirner, which shows what they are made of and assures them how worthless all those others are who are incapable of such elegance.

## III. MORALITY OF THE CLOSED COMMUNITY

> I had always thought that something could be built upon contempt; now I know what: morality.
>
> Henry de Montherlant, *Service inutile*

The nature of the Masters, which scarcely allows them to have any dealings with others, by the same token forces them into a vivid sense of the alliance that exists among their number, which soon enough they come to feel as a sort of complicity, since even their slightest reflexes may be deemed a criminal act. From the outset, this situation leads to an awareness of a specific code of ethics which can only emerge fully in the course of the structural development of the aristocracy, although its earliest forms may be discerned from the moment it first came into being.

A brief description of this situation must be given at this point. It is not enough to see honesty as the unconditional basis of all morality. There can be no doubt that honesty is an instinct which expresses the imperative of an individual's unity and totality, the convergence of all his various postulations towards a single principle, a single integrity. It is the active proof that an individual wishes to be at peace, that he tolerates internal discord as unwillingly as an organism does infectious attacks, that he represses the gnawing disturbances within him and knows how to defend himself from the times when he is tempted to give up, or when this would degrade or weaken him. Honesty is that quality which grants a man only one face and silences the *raging dogs that tremble in these kings*.[10] But may I remind you that a hero is great only after he has fought monsters, and before he has been defeated by them. There is nothing to hope for from those who have nothing to oppress within themselves.

Next come contempt, love of power, and courtesy, virtues which, while not necessarily being cardinal, stem directly from the position described and eminently characterise its originality.

Starting from the experience that individuals are not equal, the virtue of contempt safeguards, gives expression to and sanctions that inequality. In presenting a real situation it does not do so with any degree of pride, but even if it did, that should not be any cause for alarm. The fact that an individual is not contemptible through any fault of his own does not mean he should be regarded with any less contempt, since it follows that he should be treated as his nature demands. In essence, contempt is directed at those who engage in or agree with actions we would utterly detest to carry out or endorse. There would be no point in trying to conceal the fact that such a feeling also has an unreliable, or at the very least ungovernable side, since no one would be able to declare that, if they were placed in the same conditions and forced to act, their behaviour would not be exactly the same as what they had originally held in contempt. Furthermore, contempt is only productive when it is demanding. It is nothing if it does not directly impose a certain harshness on itself. Once experienced, it must be considered in line with the obligation it imposes, that it should never be called for again in similar circumstances, so that each act of contempt becomes a pledge of honour and a down-payment on future conduct. But it must also be seen in terms of the right it offers that those who are duly cut off from us should not be treated as equals, nor as enemies with whom we must respect the rules of war or observe the courtesies appropriate between peers.

As for power, it is important to treat it as a force of nature against which all sense of reproach has been removed, but which we are still free to fight against and perhaps bring within our control.

There is nothing more futile or pitiful than the hatred of the principle of power, which saps the strength of the bravest spirits in vain and unequal struggles, confirming them in their hatred and behaviour and ultimately turning their capricious attitude and obstinacy into objects of worship. It is healthy to desire power, whether over souls or bodies, for prestige or tyranny. Every one of us, moreover, uses power within a limited sphere which it may unexpectedly become possible to extend considerably, for human relations are such that we may often acquire the ability when all we desired was freedom, so much so that the strong seem destined for domination, and that, even when they are bound in irons, they instinctively regard it with respect and treat it seriously, thereby demonstrating that it is the love of power that distinguishes conquerors from slaves.

As precise and punctilious as court etiquette, the courtesy which ritualises the secondary aspects of the mutual relations between people lightens the mind in the process and so puts people more at ease. Furthermore, it helps maintain a certain internal tension which would be difficult to keep up if basic manners were neglected. In an association of the closed variety, which is intended to increase separation, courtesy is part of its ethical code and becomes almost an institution. By codifying the relations of initiates, its esoteric yet conventional nature is reinforced by the fact that it has to work to differentiate these relations even more from relations that are profane. The discourteous person, in fact, is not so much the one who neglects certain usages as the one who is unaware of them, or who practises those of another group. And so courtesy, a way of being recognised amongst ourselves and of recognising outsiders, becomes a practical means of maintaining our distance. In fact, at times when it becomes necessary to express hostility or contempt towards someone, it is sufficient, as we all know, to assume an air of excessive courtesy which will prove as hurtful as any reprimand and immediately rules out all familiarity. On this subject we should not forget that absolutely characteristic way in which certain notable individualists, such as Baudelaire, as they guessed which implacable weapon yet concealed a perfect propriety, made dandyism into the preferred mode of modern heroism.

These are the initial virtues that must be developed right from the start by a community which finds its purpose from within. There is nothing in them the individual could not take on that would cause him to have reservations later. On the contrary, he will recognise in them the development of certain of his inclinations, things that were felt but without him being able to define them, before they had found the fuller scope that would allow them to become explicit. Their transposition to the social scale, far from blunting their effect, has imparted to them, by the fact of their being revealed to themselves, the increase of decision and force which sets out the superiority of a clear conscience over a vague, confused and groping presentiment. In conjunction with this, within the group these virtues tend to sharpen its outlines and deepen the rift that isolates it from the society within which it originated; those who practise these virtues with this in mind will soon, in turn, find that they have formed a veritable *milieu*, in the organic sense of the word, a small island of solid density, which as a result is able to draw towards it the floating bodies set adrift in an extended society, and thus to provide its active cells with a genuinely positive role instead of the sterile and unbalanced agitation in which they had previously indulged.

★

The weather is no longer quite so mild. There is now a great wind of insurrection in the world, a cold, harsh, arctic wind, one of those murderous but thoroughly bracing winds which kill off the frail, the sick and small birds, not letting them make it through the winter. So it is that in nature there is a slow, silent and inescapable cleansing, like the imperceptible approach of a tide of death. The sedentary population, in the shelter of their overheated homes, are too exhausted to revive their limbs where the blood has clotted in their veins and stopped circulating. They nurse their chapped skin and chilblains — and shiver. They dare not venture outside where the sturdy, bare-headed nomad, exulting all over, has come to laugh at the wind, intoxicated by this icy and refreshing violence which slaps his stiffened hair against his face.

The winter months, perhaps a quaternary period — when the glaciers advance — is beginning for this broken-down, senile, half-crumbling society. It is a spirit of enquiry, a ruthless and disrespectful incredulity, which is attracted by force and passes judgement on our capacity for resistance; it is also cunning enough that it can expose our own cunning tricks in a trice. This climate will be very hard, the cull highly selective. Everyone will have to prove their worth to ears that are deaf to song, although still vigilant and attuned, to eyes that are blind to ornament, yet still are piercing; they will have to pass from one pair of nimble, clutching hands to another, by exercising an extraordinarily well-trained tact, a sense that is more material, more realistic than the others, which is not misled by appearance and which separates with such accomplishment the empty from the full.

Those with good circulation will be easily recognised, in these very low temperatures, by their rosy complexion, the bloom on their skin, the way they are at ease, their cheerfulness in at last enjoying their living conditions and by the great inhalations of oxygen their lungs require. The others, duly given over to their weakness and driven from the stage, wither, shrivel up and cower in their holes; the restless become motionless, fine speakers fall silent, actors become invisible. The field is wide open for the fittest: no obstacles on the path will trouble their progress, no tuneful chirping from countless throats will smother their voices. Let them be counted and let them recognise one another in this rarefied air, so that winter leaves them united and close, elbow to elbow, in the full awareness of their strength, and when spring arrives it will consecrate their destiny.

ROGER CAILLOIS

# 31 *Note on the Foundation of a College of Sociology*

1. As soon as the study of social structures is credited with having any special importance it can be seen that the few results obtained by science in this field are not only generally unknown, but also directly contradict current ways of thinking on this subject. These results, such as they are presented, appear to be extremely promising and open up unforeseen perspectives for the study of human behaviour. However, they are still tentative and incomplete, on the one hand because science has limited itself too much to analysing the structures of so-called primitive societies, while ignoring modern societies, and on the other hand because the discoveries that have been made have not yet affected the assumptions and spirit of this research as deeply as might have been expected. It even appears that there are obstacles of a specific nature that stand in the way of the development of our knowledge of the vital elements of society; this would seem to be down to the necessarily infectious and *activist* character of the representations brought to light by this work.

2. It follows that there is cause to develop, amongst those who intend to pursue investigations in this direction as far as proves possible, a moral community, somewhat different from the one that typically unites researchers and which is bound very precisely to the infectious nature of the field to be studied and the individual facts as they are gradually revealed.

Even so, this community will have the same free access as that of any other established scientific body, and anyone may contribute their personal point of view regardless of the particular concerns that have led them to become more specifically aware of various essential aspects of social existence. Whatever motives or aims are involved, such an interest will be considered sufficient on its own to establish the necessary connections for joint action.

3. The specific object of the activity being contemplated may be called *sacred sociology*, in so far as that implies the study of social existence in all its manifestations in which the active presence of the sacred is clearly to be found. It thus intends to establish points of coincidence between the fundamental obsessive tendencies of individual psychology and the guiding structures which govern social organisation and drive its revolutions.

GEORGES AMBROSINO, GEORGES BATAILLE, ROGER CAILLOIS,
PIERRE KLOSSOWSKI, PIERRE LIBRA, JULES MONNEROT

This declaration was drawn up during the month of March 1937. The activities of the College will begin in October, comprising first of all a course of theoretical instruction in the form of weekly lectures. All correspondence should be addressed for the time being to Georges Bataille, 76 *bis* rue de Rennes (6$^{e.}$).

# THE SACRED CONSPIRACY

# IV

September 1937 – December 1937

*Chronology*
*Commentaries*

## THE SECRET SOCIETY OF ACÉPHALE

- 32. Georges Ambrosino and Georges Bataille *To Pierre Andler, Interview*
- 33. Georges Bataille *The Crucified Christ*
- 34. Pierre Andler *The Useless Death of the Crucified Christ*
- 35. Georges Bataille *Meditation*
- 36. Pierre Andler *The Way of Necessary Harshness*
- 37. Henri Dussat *An Order*
- 38. Georges Bataille *Rules as of 24 September 1937*
- 39. Georges Bataille *Annual Summation, 24 September 1937*
- 40. Georges Bataille *Concerning the first encounter we attempted...*
- 41. The Members of Acéphale *Statement of Commitment of 1 October 1937*
- 42. Georges Bataille *The Ruins of Montjoie*
- 43. Henri Dussat *Meditation before the Cross*
- 44. Georges Ambrosino and Georges Bataille *To Pierre Andler, Interview*
- 45. Georges Bataille *Rules as of 28 December 1937*
- 46. Imre Kelemen *Statement to the Sessional Meeting of December 1937*

# CHRONOLOGY

## 1937

**5 September.** Bataille and Ambrosino send Andler a summons for a first interview at the Café Mal-Assis.

**11 September.** A meeting of Acéphale is held at rue Séguier, to discuss a proposed issue of *Acéphale* on "The Crucified Christ".

**17 September.** Date of an unpublished text by Andler, "The Way of Necessary Harshness", ●36, written in anticipation of a meeting with Ambrosino and Bataille (probably the one set for "Friday evening at 9.30 in the Café Le Chat Botté, on the corner of rue Étienne Marcel and rue Saint-Denis") and which responds to Bataille's "Meditation", ●35, on the exercises of Loyola. Written the same month, Bataille's text was a prelude to the technical approach to ecstasy he would follow from May 1938.

**19 September.** Date of Dussat's "An Order", ●37.

**22 September.** A coup is attempted by La Cagoule, the military wing of Action Française, the far-right political movement. Hundreds of the group's members are arrested the following month when a second, more serious plot is uncovered.

**24 September.** A meeting of Acéphale is held at which the Rules of the Society are given out, ●38. The "Annual Summation", ●39, stresses the importance of the collection of texts they have put together on the theme of the Crucified Christ. This probably includes Andler's unpublished "The Useless Death of the Crucified Christ", ●34, of 2 September, and Dussat's "Meditation before the Cross", ●43, of 3 October. Various publishing projects are discussed in the context of two future issues of *Acéphale* which, in the event, do not appear.

**End of September / beginning of October.** Caillois sends Paulhan the definitive version of "The Winter Wind", ○30,[1] which appears in the *NRF* on 1 July 1938, with a text each by Bataille and Leiris, in a special section of the journal on the College of Sociology.

**October.** Leiris attends bullfights in Nîmes and Marseille, having been an aficionado since the mid-Twenties, and begins writing *Mirror of Tauromachy*.[2]

**1 October.** The second encounter in the forest takes place, described in the texts "Concerning the first encounter we attempted...", ●40, and the "Statement of Commitment of 1 October 1937", ●41. This last, signed by Ambrosino, Andler, Bataille, Chavy, Chenon, Dussat and Kelemen, constitutes the second vow of engagement of these members of Acéphale, sworn at the ruins of Montjoie, the place where adepts were inducted into the Society by the pact of blood. There are various accounts of this ritual, from Patrick Waldberg, ●68, Okamoto and Rollin (who was inducted in the forest during one of his visits to Paris). The most detailed account, however, is from "X", an adept who agreed to be interviewed by Claudine Frank so long as he remained anonymous. He revealed that his initiation concluded with "a small cut to the left arm" and a "compact" whereby one agreed "to be the *possible* victim or the *possible* murderer, but without any other details being specified [...]; indeed, everybody who participated in Acéphale *could* be the possible victim". It was signed in blood.[3]

**2 October.** Bataille writes "The Ruins of Montjoie", ●42.

**16 October.** Bataille reconnects with Rollin; a phrase in his letter suggests that Bataille is presuming Caillois will not join Acéphale.

**Early November.** The College issues its first programme. Almost from the beginning of its activities, repeated ill-health often prevents Caillois from giving his scheduled lectures.

**10 November.** Bataille sends Andler four statements, which represent the first draft of *The Seven Aggressions*, and writes to invite Caillois to his apartment the next day at 5.30 in the afternoon to discuss the College with Rougemont and Chevalley, and the possibility of producing abstracts of lectures. Bataille also asks Caillois to clarify the subject of his address to be given at the opening session of the College.

**11 November.** Probable date of an internal meeting that was to have been chaired by Ambrosino, who in the event cannot attend, so that a further meeting is called for the 13th.

Dussat writes to Chavy to tell him that on Sunday 28th he will go with him to the forest so that Chavy, "guided by Bataille", can henceforth "recognise the boundaries of the forbidden".[4]

**13 November.** An internal meeting of Acéphale is held at the Brasserie Lumina at 7 in the evening; Bataille, Andler and Kelemen discuss the four statements sent to Andler on the 10th.

**20 November.** The inaugural session of the College of Sociology takes place in the back room of the bookshop in the rue Gay-Lussac: Bataille and Caillois lecture on "Sacred Sociology and the Relationships between 'Society', 'Organism' and 'Being'".

**21 November.** Bataille writes to Caillois with certain reservations about the previous evening.

**4 December.** Kojève lectures to the College on "Hegelian Concepts".

**5 December.** Bataille, Laure and Heine make a trip to Malmaison, near Épernon, 40 kilometres outside Paris, where Sade had stipulated in his will that he should be buried in a ditch, as per the instructions quoted in the epigraph to ●2. On their return, having bid farewell to Heine, Bataille and Laure have arranged a supper and orgy with two guests who are as yet unidentified: "Ivanov et Odoïevtsova".[5]

**6 December.** Bataille responds to Kojève's lecture with his "Letter to X".

**8 December.** Bataille breaks with Monnerot. From Bataille's letter to Caillois the same evening, the problem seems to be in part the result of a personal antipathy between the two, with Bataille unconvinced by Monnerot's commitment. He also refers to "the unacceptable way he conducted the meeting on Nietzsche in March".[6]

**19 December.** Caillois lectures to the College on "Animal Societies", which is followed by comments by Bataille. Caillois's lecture has survived only as rough notes.

**27 December.** Bataille and Ambrosino summon Andler for an interview at the Chat Botté, at 9.30 pm.

**28 December.** Sessional meeting of Acéphale. Texts are read by Kelemen, "Statement...", ●46, and Bataille, "Rules as of 28 December 1937", ●45, which defines the status of participants and the rules for their taking part in encounters in the forest. According to ●48, new members are proposed to the Society.

# COMMENTARIES

## ACÉPHALE [MG]

The texts in this section document the resumption of the Society's activities after the summer break, marked both by the implementation of a new practice and a meeting for *Acéphale*. The new practice, which involved the adepts as individuals, was the ritual of interviews which, like the meditations before the acephalous tree, required not only obedience to rules previously agreed upon, but also observance of "all the negative instructions specific to each encounter", ●18 §5. Prior to an encounter in the forest, each adept would now receive an envelope containing instructions giving the day and time of departure from the Gare Saint-Lazare, and how to reach their destination in the forest. When it came to interviews, the required formalities were fixed in the "Rules as of 24 September 1937", ●38, which had been passed during the meeting held the same day, while the negative observances were generally laid out in the letter of summons, and involved the adept abandoning habits "such as saying hello, smoking or making small talk...", as we read in the summons to Andler of 5 September, ●32.

The meeting for *Acéphale* took place on Saturday 11 September at rue Séguier and concerned an issue of the journal about the Crucified Christ, which was intended for adepts only, as described in ●33. It was a question, wrote Bataille, of refusing to endorse the perversion of death promulgated by Christianity, and "of concluding the atheist's meditation before the cross", in other words to make torture into a way of accessing a new form of laughter and even "the violent pain of erotic satisfaction". This issue was probably intended to contain "the various texts on the *Crucified Christ*" referred to in the "Annual Summation" of 24 September 1937, ●39, which must have the "value of a formal covenant" for members, being capable of transforming, according to Bataille, "our vast and aged weakness into the will to power". Although no trace of this issue has survived, two texts related to the project are published here. "The Useless Death of the Crucified Christ", ●34, by Andler, dates from 11 September 1937 and introduced a stance "beyond all hope", that was as distant from the attitudes of believers, for whom "the crucifix is hope", as it was from those of atheists. At the conclusion of Dussat's "Meditation before the Cross", ●43, dated 3 October 1937, the "gloating joy" of the murderers of God is associated with their contempt for the piety of their own fathers. It was probably ideas such as this within Acéphale that induced Klossowski, in 1985, to refer to Bataille as "an atheist mystic" and to link his "heterodoxy with regard to faith" — which he himself shared, while "never being anything but a Catholic"— to "the same certainty outlined by Kierkegaard in *Either/Or*: that Christianity, through the Incarnation and the Resurrection, preaches the *assumption of sensuality*, and the kingdom of the flesh".[1] In "Le Corps du néant", Klossowski described Acéphale, the "Church of the Death of God", as one of "those anti-churches [...] that across from Golgotha raise up an anti-Golgotha, at the foot of which they celebrate an eternal Good Friday",[2] and later affirmed that: "Acéphale's whole a-theology is based on the idea that the death of God does not result in a form of atheism; this is the legacy of Golgotha, death is not final, it is a continuing process [...] any belief that we might somehow be able to dispense with killing the Man-God would only have meant a return to the charnel-house."[3]

The Society's will to power was the main thread connecting three other texts that date from September. Bataille's "Meditation", ●35, raised the question of the need to link the "risible lack of conscience of the universe" to a "rigour equivalent to that in the *Exercises*" of St. Ignatius of Loyola, which Bataille had practised in 1918 during a retreat with the Jesuits of La Barde in the Dordogne[4] (as recalled by him in his "Nietzschean Chronicle" in *Acéphale* 3/4). Andler's meditation of 17 September, ●36, written while waiting for another interview (a third, the content of which is unknown, took place on 27 December), offset the rigour preached by Loyola with an even greater "harshness". This, he asserted, provided the only possibility of replacing the "absurdity of a world willed and created by God" with the revelation of "absurdity itself", only to be made known to those with sufficient strength, and "not just to all those who might be qualified to understand it". Dussat's "An Order", ●37, developed the idea of the possibility of an organisation opposed to "bonds of birth and blood" that would exercise "its natural inclinations to power" according to the nature of the social and political structure within which it was situated. *Acéphale* 3/4 had already considered this problem in "Dionysian Virtues", ●28, where Caillois had drawn attention to the need for a sociology of brotherhoods, which "exist as a solid structure within a weak social environment" and found their cohesion by, as noted earlier, "excluding any prior affiliations based on locality, history, race or language". This topic was also addressed in a general way in the Society's "Annual Summation" of 24 September, ●39, by the attempt to define the "conditions necessary for an *order* to revitalise the structure of a decomposed society", and more specifically, within the context of the politics of the time, by the College. Two of its lectures from 1939 were particularly relevant in this respect: Bataille's on "Hitler and the Teutonic Order" and Hans Mayer's on

"Rites of Political Associations in Germany during the Romantic Period", which demonstrated how such rites had contributed to the rise of Nazism.

The Society's records show that after the meeting of 11 September two further meetings were held, one on 24 September and another on 13 November. The "Annual Summation" of 24 September is informative in this regard, since it provides an overview of the various stages of the Society's development: from the publication of the two double issues of *Acéphale* in 1937, subsidised by Andler, Dussat and Laure,[5] to the compilation of the texts on the Crucified Christ and the drafting of the next two issues.[6] This was all done — and here Bataille noted the difficulties encountered by the adepts after Rollin's departure for Spain and the resignations of Dautry, Dubief,[7] Klossowski[8] and Puyo,[9] which reduced the number of members from twelve to seven — in conjunction with the creation of the College, which was intended to bolster the Society's influence and to act as a "recruiting ground for new affiliates".[10]

The need for Acéphale to assert its authority is reflected in the second formal act connected to its founding, the commitment "to uphold the first bond of our community: the prohibitions regarding the forest". This document, ●41, was signed by the seven adepts on 1 October at Montjoie, the site whose history connected it with the celebration of regicide (see pp.20 and 55).

At the internal meeting on 13 November, discussions centred upon the first draft of the "Eleven Aggressions" of the *Anti-Christian's Manual* (these discussions continued in meetings the following year, on 25 July and 29 September), while the scheduling of the first lectures at the College and its initial programme (p.225) were also considered.

The final meeting of 1937 took place on 28 December (see ●45). According to the "Rules as of 24 September 1937", ●38, this, unlike the principal meetings fixed for Easter and in September, was a "secondary" meeting with the same status as the one held in July. Taking place a month after the inauguration of the sessions of the College of Sociology, it dealt with the rules governing a "participant", which from now on would be a first initiatory stage prior to becoming an adept (see p.44). One of the adepts, Kelemen, read a statement, ●46, in which he contrasted the image of Acéphale as a representation of "the leaderless crowd", as introduced in ●14 and referred to in the 21st of the "Propositions on the Death of God", ●65, with the empty lure "of an idyllic society" put forward by Marxism and Socialism. Because of Kelemen's rejection of his past Socialist militancy in Hungary, his echoing of Bataille's criticism, in *La Critique sociale*,[11] of the optimistic messianism of Marx and Socialism leads to the poignant image of Acéphale as "the sole object of the consuming love felt by those who desire existence in its entirety" and of chance seized upon when "emerging from my depression".

## THE COLLEGE OF SOCIOLOGY [AB]

The College of Sociology "opened its doors" on 20 November 1937. Its original ambition to hold weekly lectures was reduced to holding them once a fortnight, on Saturday evenings, and its beginnings also appear somewhat tentative in other respects. From what we know of them, the first three lectures approach the project rather warily, or in Kojève's case, with some hostility. Only Bataille's text has survived though, and that only in part.

These lectures were intended in the main as an introduction to sociology, and then specifically to sacred sociology. Caillois spoke first on 20 November, and presented what was, apparently, a fairly conventional history of the science of sociology. Bataille followed this by outlining its relations as indicated in the title to his lecture, "Sacred Sociology and the Relationships between 'Society', 'Organism' and 'Being'". Sacred sociology was uncontroversially defined as the study of everything that created unity within society, and Bataille asserted that the College, like Durkheim, did not accept a strictly utilitarian interpretation of society as a system of contracts between individuals.

He then presented an overall view of social organisation as a series of structures of ever increasing complexity, from atom and molecule to cell, then organism (the individual), and finally to communities and society. Bataille asked, where on this scale does *conscience* begin and end? For example, does a social community possess *conscience*? He discussed various types of community — church, army, country — and distinguished between those that are "traditional" (whose membership is involuntary, but from which the individual may disassociate) and those to which the individual chooses to belong, those that are "elective" (which included both the College and Acéphale). Elsewhere, in his and Caillois's writings, this is what distinguishes "primary" from "secondary" communities.

Bataille also situated the work of the College in a political context, and argued that it must give an adequately vivid account of society, since society is not a place of barren intellectual debate but "precisely the theatre in which political tragedy is played out".[12] Moreover, society is composed of communities, traditional and elective, whose members either feel that the associations to which they belong have rights over them, or that they do not, and accordingly will "take up arms and ally themselves with one faction or the other, and then the game of death begins between them".[13]

The day after this lecture, Bataille wrote to Caillois with a critique of the evening, noting that their lectures suffered from having been too improvised and not well enough thought through. He blames himself for this, but does take Caillois to task for his

# COLLÈGE DE SOCIOLOGIE

## ANNÉE 1937-1938 .. LISTE DES EXPOSÉS

Samedi 20 novembre 1937
**LA SOCIOLOGIE SACRÉE** et les rapports entre "société", "organisme", "être", par Georges Bataille et Roger Caillois.

Samedi 4 décembre 1937
**LES CONCEPTIONS HÉGÉLIENNES**, par Alexandre Kojève.

Samedi 19 décembre 1937
**LES SOCIÉTÉS ANIMALES**, par Roger Caillois.

Samedi 8 janvier 1938
**LE SACRÉ**, dans la vie quotidienne, par Michel Leiris.

Samedi 22 janvier 1938
**ATTRACTION ET RÉPULSION.**
I. Tropismes, sexualité, rire et larmes, par Georges Bataille.

Samedi 5 février 1938
**ATTRACTION ET RÉPULSION.**
II. La structure sociale, par Georges Bataille.

Samedi 19 février 1938
**LE POUVOIR**, par Roger Caillois.

Samedi 5 mars 1938
**STRUCTURE ET FONCTION DE L'ARMÉE**, par Georges Bataille.

Samedi 19 mars 1938
**CONFRÉRIES, ORDRES, SOCIÉTÉS SECRÈTES, ÉGLISES,** par Roger Caillois.

Samedi 2 avril 1938
**LA SOCIOLOGIE SACRÉE** du monde contemporain, par Georges Bataille et Roger Caillois.

■ Les exposés des mois de mai et juin 1938 seront entièrement consacrés à la MYTHOLOGIE.

■ Le COLLÈGE DE SOCIOLOGIE se réunira dans la Salle des Galeries du Livre, 15, rue Gay-Lussac (5e). Les exposés commenceront à 21 h. 30 précises ; ils seront suivis d'une discussion. L'entrée de la salle sera réservée aux membres du Collège, aux porteurs d'une invitation nominale et (une seule fois) aux personnes présentées par un membre inscrit. L'inscription est de 5 fr. par mois (8 mois par an) ou de 30 fr. par an (payables en novembre). La correspondance doit être adressée à G. Bataille, 76 bis, rue de Rennes (6e).

**INVITATION NOMINALE** valable le ______________ ■______________________

College of Sociology, programme for the year 1937-1938.

"biologism", a criticism similar to Adorno's objection to "The Praying Mantis" (see p.77). He also mentions the proposed "Bibliographical Summary" of the College's activities, which was intended to appear periodically, but this, like the College journal, did not happen.[14]

Although Kojève's lecture is rumoured to have been recently rediscovered, little is yet known of it. The lecture itself was not well received by Bataille who later referred to the negative intentions behind its critique of the foundations of a science of sociology.[15] On this point he was supported by Benjamin, whose report on it to Horkheimer noted that "much of its purpose was to annoy the organisers of his presentation."[16] This appears to have been accomplished by Kojève's support for Stalin, whom he now revealed to be the man who signalled the end of history (rather than Napoleon, as asserted by Hegel).[17] According to Bataille's letter to Caillois on this matter, a part of Kojève's objection was that the subject matter of sociology remained too much in development to be studied scientifically, but as was pointed out by a member of the audience, all scientific theories apart from those of mathematics are similarly only provisionally correct, that being the basis of the scientific method.[18] However, Bataille was not content with his answer to Kojève after the lecture and wrote him a long letter, the "Letter to X", which was published in *Guilty*, his diary. Too complex to summarise here, it is nevertheless worth noting that in part it was an attempt to find a loophole in Hegel's eschatology, which foresaw three possible roles for human beings at the end of history: happy automatons, mad people and philosophers. These were all roles that held little appeal for Bataille.

Caillois's lecture on "Animal Societies" was presumably intended to delineate further the boundaries of which societies might be relevant for study in terms of sacred sociology by considering certain extra-human social structures. Not even his notes survive, so Hollier in this part of his book on the College made use of Bataille's notes on the same subject. Bataille seems to have confirmed Caillois's negative conclusion since: "It seems that on the surface of this planet, existence gravitates around things that are, so to speak, charged with the dread they provoke, a dread that is indistinguishable from the dread of death."[19]

# TEXTS

September 1937 — December 1937

Nous te demandons de te rendre le dimanche 5 septembre à 21h 1/2 au Café Mal-Assis, à l'angle de la Rue St. Denis et de la Rue des Cygnes afin d'avoir avec toi un premier <u>entretien</u>.

Nous te demandons d'abandonner dimanche les habitudes telles que dire bonjour, fumer, parler de choses et d'autres ....

Georges Bataille G. Ambrosino

Prière de prévenir Bataille en cas d'impossibilité absolue et d'indiquer trois jours libres.

32. Georges Ambrosino and Georges Bataille, *To Pierre Andler, Interview.*

GEORGES AMBROSINO AND GEORGES BATAILLE *To Pierre Andler, Interview* 32

*Please come on Sunday 5 September at 9.30 pm to the Café Mal-Assis, on the corner of rue Saint-Denis and rue des Cygnes, for a first interview.*

*We request that on Sunday you disregard your normal habits such as saying hello, smoking or making small talk…*

*Georges Bataille*
*G. Ambrosino*

*Please inform Bataille if you absolutely cannot be present, and let him know which days you can be available.*

GEORGES BATAILLE *The Crucified Christ* 

*The next meeting of ACÉPHALE will be held on Saturday 11th, at 17 rue Séguier.*

*The purpose of the meeting will be to put together an issue of* Acéphale *on the CRUCIFIED CHRIST, an issue intended for internal circulation only; any proposals must be brought up on the day.*

*We cannot contemplate the Crucified Christ with the cold or kindly irony of men of reason: we cannot remain so indifferent to such agonies, still less endure such fear. We cannot rejoice in torture: it may become an object of laughter for us. It might even be used by us to taint the innocent nature of laughter; through it we might try to find the laughter of a happier man than the one who stupidly accepts the irrelevance of his greatest joys. And why too might it not also yield access to the violent pain of erotic satisfaction?*

*It does not seem likely that we will go beyond our disgust. Nietzsche managed to step aside from so much sick flesh with feelings of the greatest repulsion. But we cannot allow this flesh to remain at that summit we perceive as being behind us. Why would we try to eradicate an obsession that is so deeply marked with blood? We must make use of it.*

*This is the reason why we should make more of an effort to favour Chenon's proposal than any of the others, since it rouses each of us to the point where deep shocks have opened up the first cracks.*

*This is not a matter of starting all over again to criticise Christianity, but of concluding the atheist's meditation before the cross. Christianity has perverted the best of man's possessions: it has perverted death, but without entering into any difficult arguments it is time to snatch back its final treasures by violent means.*

[11 September 1937]

34 PIERRE ANDLER *The Useless Death of the Crucified Christ*

*The whole attraction exerted for centuries by Christ's religion is born out of the horror and absolute improbability of his death throes. We do not necessarily turn away in disgust from men's devotion to such an improbability, to such folly — which after all recalls other follies to which we adhere. But the blood of Christ is both sin and redemption. The crucifix is hope.*

*We who do not wish to cleanse ourselves of all filth and who are beyond all hope may reflect, with neither pity nor hatred, on the useless death of the Crucified Christ. Faced with this blood and this body in death, men today have no further need to deny their miraculous qualities in order to be able to free themselves from their grip, smiling as they do so. Our smile before the cross has nothing of the secular sneer about it: our smile is the mocking, almost imperceptible smile of men who have glimpsed utterly different chasms from that of sin, and who are not even trying any more not to fall in. But in this smile there can be nothing irreverent. In terms of who we are today, irreverence is as incompatible with our profound existence as it is with the existence of the gods.*

II.IX.37

35 GEORGES BATAILLE *Meditation*

*How can meditation, as applied to finding strength for the path ahead, find a rigour equivalent to that in the* Exercises*?*

*Science tells us that the sun, stars and atoms are as easy to understand as a table and the plates upon it. But science was then led to add: the table and its plates are as easy to understand as the sun and the stars. It was just a question of which moments of under-*

*standing were brought into focus during the course of a long process. It is less arbitrary to take heed only of moments of total incomprehension. Hence it appears that to explain something means to reduce it to a particular sort of unintelligibility, to be precise, to a sequence of facts, such that there is nothing about them that seems — at least at first glance — to be hidden. In this way it will be seen that we have simply brought out 'into the open' all that was possible to bring out 'into the open'. And at the same time, we will believe that we are wonderfully brave and wonderfully motivated, when we cry out: I see! And this cry will be one of final despair and hilarity that cannot yield to anything. What is called happiness is wretched beside such an absence of hope.*

*There are no representations of the world, showing its origin or how it came into being, that have even a hint of seriousness about them. Where does this idea come from that jocularity might be more suited to the world than seriousness? Although in fact, any joke at all has one virtue that is lacking in the usual kinds of representation: it breaks the circle of conscientious ideas. There is a need for at least one man 'without* conscience*' to respond to the eternal silence of space… because while eternal silence is everything one may imagine to be strange, there is no doubt whatsoever that it has no conscience. Turning to human power, we must consider that man a Judas who is not committed to bearing witness to the happy, indeed risible lack of conscience of the universe, to bear witness if need be under torture. As long as a man has not* laughed *even once, whatever torture he has been subjected to, about the wrongness of everything, existence will have some weight to it.*

*There is no place for mockery in any discussion about laughter. What matters is still having the strength to look upon what laughter reveals. The reality revealed by laughter is generally thought to be random and lacking in meaning. It can only have meaning if a man holds it in sufficient esteem to affirm it, despite all opposition — even as others have died in order to affirm through their virility whatever principles were at stake.*

[September 1937]

## PIERRE ANDLER *The Way of Necessary Harshness* 36

*It is quite pointless, especially amongst ourselves, to claim to be something one is not, or has not yet become. The personal inadequacy that exists within each of us is in no danger of being lost from sight any moment soon, and it is not perhaps a useless exercise to recognise that, duly isolated, there probably wouldn't be any such inadequacy. I say this without bitterness or any feeling of weakness. I cannot say that I like either my inadequacy or my cowardice, they do not overwhelm me but nor do I wallow in them. The solution is to be found in an even greater difficulty, and one that should probably be sought more in temptation than in its absence. Despite the little I have read of them, the exercises of Loyola come across to me more than anything else as a way of chasing off temptation. I do not think that once I have studied them more closely I will find in them anything other than a marvellously specialised tool for combating man's weakness. Up until this point I feel that I have disclosed something of the rigour involved, but not the rigour itself.*

*What we want, above all else, is rigour, what I earlier referred to as difficulty. To men like me, destined by their character, work or individual intelligence to be asked to do things or diverted from their own activity more than other men are, the conditions in which the exercises are supposed to have come together seem idyllic. For us, who live in the secular world, other conditions are required and these still remain to be created.*

*Up until now we have been tempted to think that exaltation, whether or not it is continuous, would be enough for us to achieve the necessary rigour. I have reflected upon my death and on the lacerations love has caused me, in order to understand my destiny as something that is worthwhile and, all things considered, unique.*

*I no longer think the path to the required difficulty should be sought in the "irregularity of meanings" that results from personal meditations. For men who face such demands, it takes more than the rigour of the exercises (which after all is only rigour), more than the absence of temptation for the smoothness of a retreat to succeed in the same way as a strict initiation. So that one day we will no longer ask what the world has in store for us, in order that we can say what we have in store for the world, we must destroy the fear of personal inadequacy within us — which does not stop us from destroying the inadequacy itself — by seeking the power of 'us', of our community. Everything must be subordinated to this, and no tyranny could be more terrible than the tyranny we inflict on ourselves.*

*I write this almost without any emotion, as I wait for it to be time for our meeting. And I write without particularly weighing my words, feeling all too aware, on the contrary, of the megalomania that is always possible, and the obvious inadequacy of what I have to say. I know that the world is ridiculous and oblivious, I know that I have always known it, and I also know that I would never have dared to think it if I had not been set on this path. Laughter for me has always been the challenge and the irony, the desire to hurl myself into time, a death that is projected, and happy. I have laughed in despicable ways as well, but I have never confused that with proper laughter. However, it has never seemed to me that a person had to know how to die in order to assert how ridiculous the world is. Now that I know it, I have come to ask myself why I thought even up until a fortnight ago that someone might die in this way.*

*The absurdity of a world willed and created by God collapses in the face of absurdity itself. I believe that this revelation can be compared to all the rest that have already swept men off to other things. But I do not think I am saying something unimportant when I add that this revelation only deserves to be made known to the strongest and most powerful.* I cannot imagine myself as being in any way superior.*

**And not just to all those who might be qualified to understand it.*

Written while waiting for a meeting, 17 September 1937.

HENRI DUSSAT *An Order* 37

*(A problem of political theory)*

*A society in which authority is at its most imperious, at those times when its bedrock is absolutely secure, seems more likely than any other to be able to tolerate the worthlessness of people; to the same extent, the requirements of its structure would not permit it to grant an* ORDER *(roughly, a* constituted *caste that ignores the bonds of birth and blood) the right to practise what the latter is inexorably drawn to see as its function, which is to say its natural inclinations to power.*

*Can we infer from this statement that, in so far as external conditions come into play, the greatest opportunities for an order to be born and to develop are to be found amongst societies that have a democratic structure, or during times of revolution or periods of serious disturbance, when dictatorial power is falling apart? It would probably be rash to make such a claim.*

*This presents the problem in all its complexity, and suggests examples of various responses, even if they would not be satisfactory in legal terms.*

*Any consideration of such conflicts must, however, for us be at the root of a wealth of* deep perspectives *to which we cannot neglect to lay claim.*

19 September 1937

38 GEORGES BATAILLE *Rules as of 24 September 1937*

*1. Meetings will be limited in principle to two principal sessional meetings at Easter and in September and two secondary sessional meetings at Christmas and at the beginning of July.*

*2. The sessional meeting at Easter will incorporate an external meeting and the sessional meeting of September will include an "annual summation".*

*3. At each sessional meeting, each of us will be expected to provide an account of the various conversations he has had with strangers about our ideas.*

*4. A meeting can always be called if two of us judge it necessary, but they will have to specify the reason and the agenda. Summons to meetings can only be sent out after Ambrosino or Bataille have been notified and have been able to give their consent.*

*5. Outside of meetings, informal* appointments *may be arranged anywhere, and require only one of us to set them up.*

*6. An interview can always be requested by two of us with one of the others.*

*7. Any of us who is in a state of severe depression will always be able to obtain an interview with two others.*

*8. After each sessional meeting, from a starting date that has been fixed on each occasion, for two weeks we vow not to meet, whether just two of us or more, other than for the most important of reasons.*

*Rules as of 24 September 1937*

*1. It is understood that any references to* encounters *must be limited, outside meetings, and between us, to all but the most unavoidable.*

*2. In meetings they can only be on the agenda for serious or exceptional reasons.*

*3. During* interviews *each of us may speak freely.*

*4. Amongst strangers, the greatest caution is required when making any references to them.*

*Closing Text of the Meeting of 24 September*

*Now that we have talked through everything that our discussion could foresee, henceforth our encounters will take place only in silence. If all that we have said up until now has any meaning, it goes without saying that we have now only to enter into the silence of death. What words do not allow us to meet in its nakedness is now the thing towards which our steps are leading us.*

### GEORGES BATAILLE *Annual Summation, 24 September 1937* 39

*It is more than a year ago since we first met, and now, at the end of September 1937, a month that will perhaps be seen to have had decisive significance for us, this gives us the sense of looking backwards, which at the same time makes it possible to look ahead.*

*There is no need to dwell on what we have achieved externally, with the publication of our journal and the results that have already transpired from that. Nor is there any need to dwell on the ambiguous nature of these results, or on the still vague level of interest aroused by what we have written and published. All that is worth repeating in this respect — since we must learn to draw lessons from experience — is that shared wisdom does not appear to be any more reliable in this case than in plenty of others; this is the reason why, at least for the people we are trying to affect directly, what we published on Dionysus, which seemed more hermetic, has often seemed more intelligible than what we published at the start on Fascism and Nietzsche.*

*We would like to emphasise the fact that we have produced these few publications in the most unfavourable material circumstances — in other words with such completely uncertain resources that only true* faith *has made possible an undertaking that did not appear to be viable. We have not resorted to anything as contemptible and underhand as doing anything about this; no literary vanity has played a part for us, and any outside financial support we have benefited from has been tiny — there are only seven of us, let that be the measure of the* faith *that drives us on.*

*Nevertheless, that doesn't mean we can treat this* faith *as being sufficient in itself, or that we may regard it as a point of pride, however justified. We must also recognise our weakness and it goes without saying that the few difficulties we have overcome are as nothing compared to what lies ahead.*

*The most pressing difficulties we will run into are perhaps the most subtle and imperceptible. They also relate to our understanding of what brings us together. We know that we are nothing without the* presence *of that which brings us together and which is necessarily external to each of us. This is what gives the word* encounter, *saved for referring to that essential aspect of our activities, its most charged meaning. Each time we get together and this* presence *is not perceptible to every one of us — even if only weakly — it would be better that we had not met at all. And so, by establishing the slow change that has been able to come about in this respect we can establish the distance we have travelled in the more than a year since we have been meeting.*

*When we first started meeting there were twelve of us: today we are only seven. It is true that one of us, Rollin, is not here because of physical distance,*[1] *but such is not the case for the other absentees, even if another one of us is now living some way from Paris.*[2] *We have split with Puyo. Dautry very quickly ceased to feel he was in agreement with us and we can have no specific reactions to his recent vague attempts at reconciliation. Dubief seemed to have disappeared for a while and, although he has recently shown interest in reaffirming the lasting value of the bonds that tie him to our community, he has postponed any actual renewal of his participation. Klossowski has gone so far as to interpose God between himself and us. If this summary represented an actual loss of strength in accordance with the way it sounds, we would be horrified. Instead we propose, in the most paradoxical fashion possible, and* without further explanation, *to find in the consideration of these facts and at the same time in consideration of our presence here, which is so vigorous of spirit, the very proof of our reality. For whoever can hear it, there is in this situation a place for laughter — happy laughter, it goes without saying.*

*There is no doubt that we have the strength to withdraw into ourselves. We are weak too, that is clear, but we have discovered the secret of looking upon the rest of the world with simple calmness. This secret is certainly linked to the presence that we have* encountered. *The extent to which this* presence *is there is what makes us real: we have managed to lose almost half our number in thus becoming real.*

*We can therefore attribute the greatest importance and significance to everything that happens between us, in isolation from the rest of the world. The* encounters *that we have had or that we will have may be more important for us than any external reality. The same applies to all that we can do to give these* encounters *meaning within ourselves, in other words the permanent formal covenant between each of us that we mean to enforce from now on in the most aggressive manner.*

*Henceforth, in fact, this covenant will be enforced in such a way that none of us will be able to escape it, and, as each of us is already aware, this applies both for individuals and the group. Naturally, we are only planning, at this meeting, a* general *covenant and will put it into practice later on — while* generally *seeking to habituate ourselves to the obsession with torture — as if the representation of genuinely appalling tortures were for us the portal by which we might enter into the world that will be ours. It goes without saying that what we undertook with the various texts on the* Crucified Christ, *which will in principle have meaning only for us, must equally have value as a covenant — we stress this with the utmost emphasis — because existence, a particular existence unknown to others, must now develop within us the wealth of its forms, in the same way as in a hothouse. We will then have the strength to transform into joy within us the torture that exists in the world — the* Crucified Christ *into happy laughter — and our vast and aged weakness into the will to power.*

*Once this has been recognised and put forward as an essential principle, we must guard against any tendency that might develop from it, or act against us and lead us little by little into the void. If it is true that we find our strength by turning in on ourselves, such a withdrawal may in no sense imply that we are blinding ourselves to the rest of the world: a strong internal existence remains an existence only to the extent that it grows and radiates outwards — in other words to the extent that it is outwardly aggressive. That is why we cannot be indifferent to the radiance spreading out from us; we must also commit the greatest part of our strength to this radiance — if only in the profound awareness each of us may gain from what causes the tension that holds him in solidarity with this expenditure.*

*Thus we are led to attach great importance to the fact that in the next two publications we are planning and which will appear, the first in November and the second early next year, we will have the opportunity to state there the principles of our shared existence. In the text to be entitled "Nietzschean Politics" we shall contrast the Nietzschean concept of struggle with the corresponding Marxist concept; we shall declare that our struggle must be brought against the masses upon whom we feel obliged to impose chance; and we shall define the conditions necessary for an* order *to revitalise the structure of a decomposed society. In the issue devoted to eroticism, we shall show what the nature of the erotic object reveals about nature itself; at the same time we shall establish what binds man today to such a revelation, to the point that he must now understand that he must either renounce being or else impose himself on the masses who are at present still unaware of it.*

*However, we shall not be satisfied with merely defining what we have undertaken; we intend to give this undertaking a theoretical basis that is underpinned by a perfectly mastered understanding; this is what we shall undertake in the context of the College of Sociology, which will represent the other element of the framework within which may be found the least unfavourable* milieu *we can meet with.*

*Within such a* milieu *it will be easiest for us to pick out those likely to help us identify what we are faced with in the depressions and extreme tensions in the world around us — in this* milieu, *but also, of course, in all places where we might come across fellow travellers; and, clearly, not one of us may consider himself exempt; each of us must be borne, however aggressively, towards the encounter with one who resembles him.*

## 40 GEORGES BATAILLE *Concerning the first encounter we attempted…*

*Concerning the first* ENCOUNTER *we attempted in the forest we said that it would take place only when death manifested itself there. Today, however, we can say that it did indeed take place.*

*This evening we are going to* recognise *what we have already* encountered. *And yet we do not want to advance any further into this world where we have discovered a presence.*

*That there was a birth, with all the shattering weakness the word implies but at the same time a hope of strength, and that there was a birth in our own life as well, is what we experienced before this presence, and tonight, in the darkness, we are searching again for that birth and our birth,* in the same way *as the first time it was revealed.*

*"On an area of marshy ground, in the middle of a forest, where it appears that disturbances have occurred in the familiar order of things, there stands a tree that has been struck by lightning.*

*"It is possible to recognise in this tree the silent presence of that which has taken the name of* ACÉPHALE *and which is expressed by these arms without a head. The desire to seek out and encounter a presence that infuses our lives with purpose is what gives our proceedings a meaning that sets them apart from those undertaken by others.*

*"This* ENCOUNTER *which is* attempted *in the forest will take place only when death manifests itself there. To anticipate that presence is to seek to cast off the vestments that veil our own death."* [1 October 1937]

## 41 THE MEMBERS OF ACÉPHALE *Statement of Commitment of 1 October 1937*

*We enter here into the* EMPIRE *to which our breath, our actions and even our most secret absurdity belongs — the* EMPIRE *where death is present in a spectral guise, where everything is finally surrendered to the tragedy of time and its endless flight.*

*We pledge to offer our existence to that of this* EMPIRE *— in such a way that it makes life into a power and an eruption.*

*Today we solemnly pledge, for the second time, to uphold the first bond of our community: the prohibitions regarding the forest in which we founded it.*

*Ruins of Montjoie, 1 October 1937*

*Henri Dussat, Georges Bataille, Jacques Chavy, Georges Ambrosino, René Chenon, Imre Kelemen, Pierre Andler.*

## GEORGES BATAILLE *The Ruins of Montjoie* 42

*Owing to the fact that we let ourselves get caught out by the lack of any form of light, we got lost yesterday on several occasions and the encounter we attempted could take place only in part; for the same reason we also forfeited the virtue of silence. We cannot complain that we got lost: we will learn as a result that nothing can be found in the domain we were moving through other than by wandering, but we will also learn slowly to take* possession *of this domain along with all its radiating paths. Each of us will have to return to the forest in the course of the next few weeks in order to find what we did not encounter yesterday, but we shall not return there together, and, this time, there will again be a deathly silence.*

*The abandoned ruins where we met are what remains of the tower of Montjoie, the name of which comes from the original war cry of the people who gave birth to most of us here. "Montjoie" is thus one of the names that expressed the strength and the presence of what was the heart and soul of a kingdom, and yet it remains a forgotten treasure, lost to this kingdom. It seems that for a long time a curse has afflicted this tower, and being abandoned it was used for certain necromantic practices directed against the royal person himself. We met amongst these ruins, today so abjectly abandoned, solely in order to seize [them] in the name of the hostile* EMPIRE, *whose authority can only be based on abduction and crime — since it is the* EMPIRE *of the murderers of God.*

[2 October 1937]

## HENRI DUSSAT *Meditation before the Cross* 43

*Meditation before the Cross rightly leads to thoughts, for those who do not turn away from them, on the problem of the death of God.*

*The image of the Crucified Christ is in turn associated with this theme as an approximate value that has a quality of revelation so intense that we might indeed attempt to understand this idea of the death of God in an entirely different way from that which dresses the joint of the cross with its victim.*

*1. The self-consuming torture on Calvary is put forward as a representation of the death of a part of the divine person — a death offered to men for their atonement, a death preached by the victim himself, which is to say as well a death that is desired, and premeditated by man's nature, as a consequence of his sin, which is his innate quality.*

*But it is important not only to attribute to the Crucified Christ the role of supreme outlet for authority. He is the liberated projection — and must therefore be happy — of sin revealed unto himself, consumed by a new thirst. This victim of torture, slumping under the golds of his halo, in the unreality of a night that weighs down on him without respite yet is heavy with promises of an unknown sweetness, offers himself up, in his still twitching perfection, like the brightly lit path along which rushes the sinner's heart, eager for its own interests. It is only through the Passion, whereby he seeks to take all horror upon himself alone, that the ends offered to this heart arrive at a state of beatitude, but even so, in the moment of this death agony the relationship between sinner and God becomes confused with the one that is presented in the death on the cross, seen as an assumed existence, as a victim for all eternity.*

*2. Bodies have been eviscerated and blood has flowed. Empty space is created around the act, the better to express the horror of it; only the heart of the sinner is present and looking on.*

*In the suspended silence of creation the lamentation is murmured in vain but echoes delightfully, through all the tears, in the sinner's heart. Another pledge is made to him, and the bonds of complicity unite as one in the dying Lord.*

*Thus a pact is forged; what happens here is fulfilled according to its own law, and from the* conscience *of its empire there may burst forth a joy without equal: in the solitude of the Crucified Christ the solitude of the sinner's heart is shattered.*

*First of all comes the projection of sin — in terms of the sinner's heart picturing its own subject to be what could be referred to as the category of* amor fati[3] *and in this transference the crucifixion is a happy event, carried out in a direction that corresponds to human nature; at the same time the sinner withdraws from the scene of the tragedy, knowing full well that it is his own tragedy playing out there, whose purpose is to deliver him to a state of happiness marked by infinite troubles (which may be the pretext for the severest repentance). So the sinner's heart appears to have given way to itself in the deepest part of its disgrace, but even so it knows nothing of what is meant by fidelity in the world which has just come into being — fidelity without any loss, without the slightest hope of remission, the fidelity of the subject to its object, and of the object to its subject. This brief isolation, this moment of delight which is quickly stifled, almost takes place moreover as if it had done so unbeknownst to the sinner, but in reality nothing deceives him, he knows its slightest deviations, its slightest roughness and its slightest hollows, its slightest disguise, and if he could submit to what he knows is not a false illusion, but to what it might have been, it is because he has already measured the depth of fidelity which is not misled by anything and which reserves for whoever seeks it out the one who is revealed as custodian of his reality and his salvation. At last there is connection, joining, reuniting, the bewildered embrace between the sinner and the Man-God who doubted, between the anguish of the sinner who is suddenly cast far beyond his limits towards his objective, and the cross on which the tortured figure dies; and at that moment the sinner's heart, lying broken at the feet of the corpse, having tasted for one brief moment, with a feeling of complicity, the infinite joy of no longer being alone, is confronted with the stark and unbearable image of its death.*

*3. The blood was shed for a long time; the body of the Lord slumped, exhausted and no longer resisting, hanging heavily from the joint formed where the wood met the wound of his nailed hands.*

*The blood had been offered up to the gaze of the executioners for a long time, along with the insides of his tormented flesh; the body of the Lord had been violated again and again. His groans had made the people laugh and his words of mercy brought sarcastic remarks from the rabble and the soldiers. His offer of infinite love had been cast back at him and the burden of all this scorn was centred on the head of the Son of Man as he endured tortures that put everything in danger.*

*The image of death — of his own death — which seized hold of the sinner's heart was such that it demanded that the whole of his life leading up to it should be damned; in the same way, the whole of his life, set before the boundless threat manifested by an ending glimpsed in a revelation that was equally terrible, damns death.*

*The beneficent attire which clothes the promise of passage and trespass into a world proclaimed as one of bliss and eternal tranquillity is not itself endowed with the quality of being able to lift this curse.*

*The wretched wounds, the vanquished blood and the quivering flesh are all attributes of the ghastly image of destiny inflicted on being. Yet the sinner's heart continues on its endless journey from bottomless despair to the hope that is enjoined while awaiting death's hideous arrival; above and beyond all its lacerations suffered hitherto it is thus lacerated without release and without ever being able to resolve itself. In this way it appeases the deep-seated imperatives of its essence and existence.*

*The identification of the Crucified Christ with the vision of the death of God could be discarded before being taken up again during the description of the image of his torture; the persons of the Father and the Son may be represented as if they were unable to become reunited; the All-Powerful may appear as if unchanged with regard to his integrity by the fulfilment of the Passion. And from this we are authorised to see in the spirit of the Passion a distant challenge to the courage of those men who will be viewed as the murderers of God and who will appear as such.*

*We who can stand in our own presence and in the presence of being in all its totality without flinching, and we others without sin, have plenty of time to attribute the Christian effigy with the value of this or that representation; for example, the value associated with the swift but inevitably cruel pursuit of erotic desires.*

*We cannot but be led to feel a sense of gloating joy at the wretched spectacle of sin — a wretchedness from which myth cannot manage to extricate itself. Despite this, we shall not forget that our contempt is directed every bit as much towards those who profess to scorn God only because they are weak or mean-spirited, as it is directed towards those who worship this same God, and whose religion is that of our fathers; in this respect, in particular, we may feel shame for our fathers, a valid, but not unhappy shame; we entertain a vigilant hatred for whatever stops at the threshold of a past in the presence of responsibilities at which we laugh and turn away.* 3 October 1937

## 44 GEORGES AMBROSINO AND GEORGES BATAILLE *To Pierre Andler, Interview*

*Please come on Monday 27 December at 9.30 pm to the Café Le Chat Botté (on the corner of rue Étienne Marcel and rue Saint-Denis) for an interview with us.*

*G. Ambrosino*

*Georges Bataille*

*If you cannot be present, telephone Bataille at the Bibliothèque Nationale Ric. 00-06 between 1.30 and 2.* [27 December 1937]

## 45 GEORGES BATAILLE *Rules as of 28 December 1937*

*1. A new participant in Acéphale may only attend internal meetings after he has signed the first commitment (the clause concerning the second one does not apply) and been once to the forest.*

*2. The names of those who are likely to participate must be given in advance, either during a sessional meeting or in a letter sent to each of the adepts. If there is no objection at the meeting or if no objection is received in the week following the letter being sent out, Ambrosino and Bataille, acting jointly, shall take it upon themselves to lead the new participant into the forest. They must then bring this encounter to the attention of each of the adepts, either verbally or in a letter simply containing the name of the new participant preceded by the sign of the labyrinth.*[4]

*3. Participation assumes, first of all, a personal rigour sufficient for the secret to be kept; and second of all, an interest in, and a profound sympathy for what Acéphale means. It does not necessarily assume a formal attachment to our precise proposals nor any resolution to devote one's strength to a defined task, all of which are things that are required only of adepts.*

*4. A participant may only be received among the adepts — that is to say will only be permitted to sign the second commitment — a minimum of three months after the first encounter at which he was present.*

*5. Encounters may take place during sessional meetings or outside them; the whole corps of adepts may be present; or only some may be present, but sulphurous fire may only feature if at least two adepts or participants, including either Ambrosino or Bataille, are present. An encounter may also be conducted with only one adept or participant — proceeding at night to the specified location in the forest.*

*6. When no general or partial encounter has been organised during a sessional meeting, each of the* adepts *will perform an encounter on his own without sulphurous fire and within the two weeks that follow. They will therefore need to be acquainted with the forest paths.*

## IMRE KELEMEN *Statement to the Sessional Meeting of December 1937* 46

*The image of the Acéphale was created to represent the leaderless crowd. But since it was created it has also come to represent the will to be, the unnamed effort and also the cost of this effort for the men who are bound together by this will and by this effort, and by the secret.*

*Revolutionary doctrines which originally sprang from anguish and internal lacerations set before this anguish and laceration the lure, quite empty of meaning, of an idyllic society. These doctrines can never bring about a society whose representation corresponds exactly to the blind, vain flight of the mass in the face of tragedy. This tragedy is such that the flight from it or any representation of an idyllic state are both a part of it, like unimportant backdrops.*

*An image representing a headless man, an image of reality, of life and the Universe, a reality that is unbearable to contemplate and closed to intellectual speculation, but the sole object of the consuming love felt by those who desire existence in its entirety — Acéphale* is *the tragedy itself.*

*To aspire to existence in its entirety is to carry tragedy within oneself. Acéphale was not born to replace, in the confused and feeble minds of the mass, the impoverished mirage of a paradise, earthly or otherwise. Acéphale cannot replace anything whatsoever, and especially not something that does not exist, for Acéphale does exist.*

*The private depression that lies in wait for me, in the world of useful labour in which I live, humiliates me. It corresponds to my desire for failure, and is a manifestation of it. I am alone, humiliated and sometimes weak, wasteful and indecisive, on the brink of this abyss where escaping or falling in amount to the same thing. I was alone in my failure: now I want my existence.*

*What I want is not situated in any future. The muddled elements of it are within me; everything is within me. At the edge of the abyss, torn between the temptation of falling and escaping, braced and tense and emerging from my depression, I seize the chance, MY CHANCE, having abandoned all that was of value to me — both the precious and the contemptible — from my past life.*

# THE SACRED CONSPIRACY

# V

January 1938 – August 1938

# CHRONOLOGY

## 1938

The activities of the secret society and the College reach their peak during this year.

**8 January.** Leiris lectures to the College on "The Sacred in Everyday Life", ○60. Laure attends this lecture and over the course of the summer writes notes on her own idea of the sacred, which Bataille and Leiris describe as distinct from "the notions derived by social scientists from their studies of societies less developed than ours", because it "testifies to lived experience".[1]

**13 January.** Dussat's "Meditation in the Forest", ●47.

**17 or 18 January.** Bataille speaks at the inaugural session of the Society of Group Psychology, whose theme this year is to be "Attitudes to Death".

**22 January.** Bataille lectures to the College on "Attraction and Repulsion I. Tropisms, Sexuality, Laughter and Tears".

An entry in Leiris's *Journal* records long conversations with Laure, that presumably took place over several weeks.

**28 January.** A meeting of the members of Acéphale is held at the Brasserie Lumina at 9.30 pm.

**5 February.** Bataille lectures to the College on "Attraction and Repulsion II. Social Structure".

**19 February.** Bataille speaks again at the College on behalf of Caillois, who is ill. The topic is "Power".

**2 March.** Caillois sends Bataille his notes for the lecture on "Brotherhoods, Orders, Secret Societies and Churches" to be given on the 19th. He also tells him that he is to edit a series of books for Gallimard on the theme of "Tyrants and Tyrannies. Studies on Extreme Forms of Power".

**3 March.** Bataille proposes to Caillois a book to be called *Tragic Destiny. Essays on the Sacred Sociology of Fascist Europe*, to be based around two articles from *La Critique sociale*, presumably "The Problem of the State" and "The Psychological Structure of Fascism", prefaced by a long introduction on the "development of Fascism, its significance and consequences".[2] He also suggests they put together a special issue of *Acéphale* on the topic of secret societies for the following month, a project that does not come to fruition, and writes that he is working on "The Sorcerer's Apprentice", ○61, for the *NRF* and hopes to finish it the following week.[3]

**5 March.** Bataille lectures to the College on "The Structure and Function of the Army". The text is lost.

**8 March.** A document listing the initials of those involved is distributed within the secret society, and includes those of Leiris, Masson and Colette Peignot, ●48.

**Early March.** In the second week of March Bataille writes his text for the *NRF*: "The Failure of the Popular Front". Published posthumously,

Michel Leiris and Laure, undated.

this was a response to Paulhan's open letter, dated 9 March, "What Constitutes a Perfect Failure?", an analysis of the catastrophic political and economic situation not only in France, but also in Spain, Germany and Austria.

**12 March.** German troops cross the Austrian border and annex the country the day after.

**13 March.** Blum is elected prime minister of a leftist coalition government for a second time.

**14 March.** Bataille and Laure again visit the site where Sade had wished to be buried outside Paris, on this occasion with Leiris and Zette, whom Laure hoped to inveigle into an orgy over supper at their home.[4] Soon after they get back there, Laure's tuberculosis enters its decisive phase: "She walked through the day as if death was not eating away at her and in bright sunlight we came to the edge of the small lake Sade had chosen. The Germans had just entered Vienna and the atmosphere was charged with the smell of war [...] Soon after we returned Laure felt the first attack of the illness that would kill her. She had a high fever and took to her bed without realising she would never leave it."[5]

**19 March.** Caillois is still unwell, so at the College Bataille reads his intended response to Caillois's notes on "Brotherhoods...", and then reads the notes of Caillois's lecture themselves.

**25 March.** Dussat, in Toulon, writes "Moving within Ethics" for Acéphale (not included here).

**28 March.** Caillois publishes *Man and Myth*, a series of studies intended to be a methodical investigation of the nature and function of myth, where the demands of the individual psyche and social pressures collide.

Leiris and Denise Schaeffner lecture to the Society of Group Psychology on "The Funeral Rites and Successional Costumes of the Dogon".

**29 March.** Laure enters hospital with a collapsed lung. Around this time she writes: "My illness is so deeply connected to my life that it cannot be separated from everything I have lived".[6]

**March.** In *Sur*, the most important literary journal in South America, Leiris publishes "La Cabeza de Holofernes", a Spanish translation of part of the fifth chapter of *Manhood*.

**2 April.** Bataille and Caillois, now recovered, lecture jointly to the College on "Sacred Sociology of the Contemporary World".

**3 April.** Leiris has second thoughts about "The Sacred in Everyday Life", and in a letter to Paulhan suggests it should be "thrown in the wastepaper bin"[7] (see also p.261).

**4 April.** Dussat, in Menton, writes "The Labyrinth" for Acéphale, ●49.

**10 April.** Fall of the Socialist government under Blum after less than a month (during which time they supplied armaments to the Spanish Republic). Daladier forms another left coalition.

**15 April.** Publication in *Mesures* of Bataille's article "The Obelisk", in which the monument that marks the place of execution of Louis XVI is seen as an architectural expression of the radiation of power, and together with the sacred sites in the forest is interpreted as one of the places that most resounds with the "mystery of the death of God".

**14 May.** Letter from Paulhan to Caillois: he has at last received Bataille's "The Sorcerer's Apprentice" but it is too long and too late for the proposed publication date of June.[8]

**17 May.** Bataille writes to Caillois inviting him to a meeting at his apartment concerning the College on 25 May at 9 pm. He has also invited Klossowski, Kojève, Leiris and Jean Wahl (the philosopher and contributor to *Acéphale*), along with Benjamin and Moré. There is some doubt about the viability of the College's activities. The programme for 1937-8 states that the May and June lectures would be on mythology,[9] but these lectures do not happen and only Klossowski's lecture takes place until a new programme can be decided upon, beginning in November. Bataille also writes about the practicalities of the *NRF* publication on the College and hopes Caillois can retrieve his manuscript for "The Sorcerer's Apprentice", ○61, when he sees

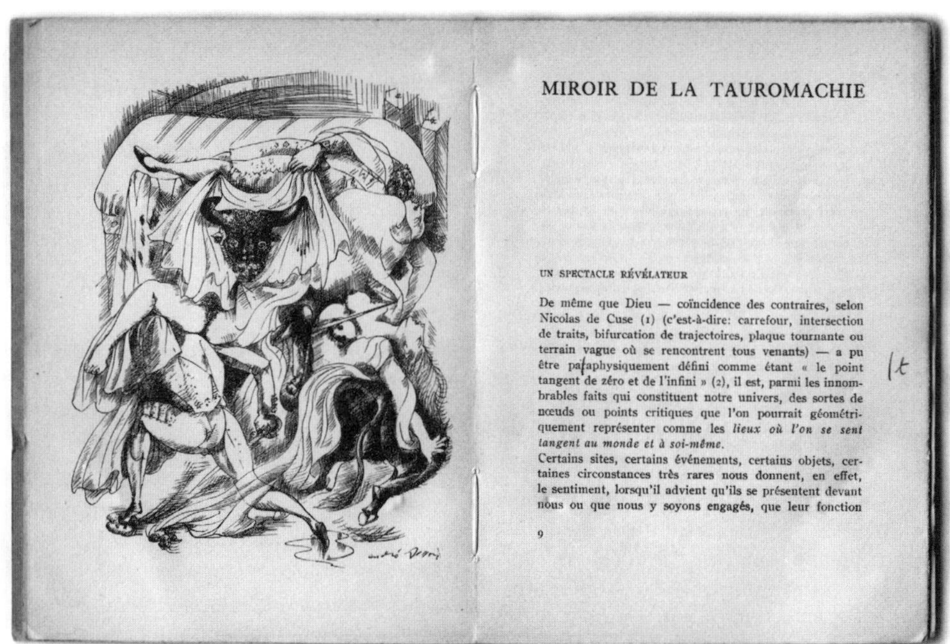

MIROIR DE LA TAUROMACHIE

UN SPECTACLE RÉVÉLATEUR

De même que Dieu — coïncidence des contraires, selon Nicolas de Cuse (1) (c'est-à-dire: carrefour, intersection de traits, bifurcation de trajectoires, plaque tournante ou terrain vague où se rencontrent tous venants) — a pu être paraphysiquement défini comme étant « le point tangent de zéro et de l'infini » (2), il est, parmi les innombrables faits qui constituent notre univers, des sortes de nœuds ou points critiques que l'on pourrait géométriquement représenter comme les *lieux où l'on se sent tangent au monde et à soi-même.*
Certains sites, certains événements, certains objets, certaines circonstances très rares nous donnent, en effet, le sentiment, lorsqu'il advient qu'ils se présentent devant nous ou que nous y soyons engagés, que leur fonction

9

Paulhan as he wishes to make further changes to it.[10]

**19 May.** Klossowski lectures to the College on "Tragedy".

**May to November.** In the Spanish pavilion at the Paris International Exhibition, Picasso's *Guernica* is exhibited for the first time. Leiris writes: "On a black and white canvas that depicts ancient tragedy [...] Picasso also writes our letter of doom: all that we love is about to be lost."[11]

**Late Spring.** Leiris submits his thesis to the École Pratique des Hautes Études on *The Secret Language of the Dogon of Sangha*.

**27 June.** Opening of the new Musée de l'Homme, a modern ethnographic museum based on the previously chaotic collections of the Trocadéro; this is an act of defiance in the face of Nazi racial theories. Its director, Georges Henri Rivière, is an old contributor to *Documents* and Leiris later worked here for many years.

**July.** Publication by GLM of Leiris's *Mirror of Tauromachy* with illustrations by Masson, the only book to appear in the Collection Acéphale (*above*). For the translation published by Atlas Press, see p.479.

**1 July.** At Paulhan's suggestion, the College of Sociology publishes in the *NRF* a brief selection of texts "intended to define their aims"[12] under the collective title of "Towards a College of Sociology": "The Sorcerer's Apprentice" by Bataille, ○61, "The Sacred in Everyday Life" by Leiris, ○60, and "The Winter Wind" by Caillois, ○30, preceded by Caillois's "Introduction", ○59.

**15 July.** Laure, after a stay in the sanatorium at Avon and two months in a Paris clinic on rue Boileau, moves in with Bataille into the house "surrounded by large trees" that he has rented

Fourqueux, with the forest of Marly in the distance.
Laure is buried in the graveyard of the church.

in Saint-Germain-en-Laye, at 59 *bis* rue de Mareil, which she called, "with bitterness, the nunnery" owing to Bataille's ascetic tastes in decoration. It has views overlooking the ancient priory and the roofs of the town towards the village of Fourqueux in the valley below, and beyond that, the forest of Marly.[13]

**25 July.** Sessional meeting of Acéphale at which various projects are discussed, including the creation of a publishing arm to be called the Society of the Friends of Acéphale, and the publication of a selection of texts from Nietzsche (later published in 1945 under the title of *Memorandum*). These projects are described in the advance letter and agenda of ●52, Bataille's "Statement", ●51, and "Decisions", ●53. New names are added to the list of those who had been proposed for membership in March, ●48, including the Swiss sculptor Isabelle Farner who, according to Koch, was the only woman to take part in what he referred to as the "Männerbund" (male society) of Acéphale, even though women were not specifically excluded. The text by Andler, "It was about resisting boredom...", ●50, was probably written for this meeting.

**Summer 1938.** This is the approximate date of a text by Bataille recommending to Acéphale a passage from Nietzsche's *Will to Power* because of its ability to "shake us to the core", ●54.

**August.** Discussions take place between members of Acéphale on the procedure to be followed for the final admission of Patrick Waldberg, which is scheduled, according to a letter from Dussat to Chavy, for "mid-September, shortly before the end of the autumn session."[14]

Bataille begins writing "The Sacred", which appears in the *Cahiers d'art* in 1939, and was intended for a book on the same theme that

The house in Saint-Germain-en-Laye.

had been conceived "as a series of explanations of his novel of 1928, *The Story of the Eye*",[15] to be published "perhaps under the name of Lord Auch, with notes on the sacred by Laure". Dussat writes "The Acéphale", ●55, on the 8th, and Waldberg "The Image of Death", ●58, on the 30th, both texts being for the Society.

**16 August.** Ambrosino and Bataille summon Andler to another interview at 17 rue Séguier, at 5 pm. The subject under discussion is a questionnaire about religious experience, ●57.

**End of August.** From Bataille's diary: "Since coming back from Sade's 'tomb', Laure has only been out once, towards the end of August. I took her by car from the house in Saint-Germain into the forest. She got out only once, in front of the stricken tree. On our way there we crossed the plain of Montaigu where she was intoxicated by the beauty of the hills and fields. But just as we entered the forest, on the left she saw two dead *crows* hanging from a branch in a coppice. *I wanted it to accompany me every-where / and always to go before me / like the herald for his knight...*"[16] Soon afterwards, according to Bataille, the "vague resemblance" of Laure's face to the face of his father became more pronounced. Later recalling her sudden feelings of hatred for him, Bataille wrote in *Guilty*: "I fled from my father (twenty-five years ago, I abandoned him to his fate during the German invasion [...] he was blind and paralysed and in his suffering he cried almost continuously); I fled from Laure (I fled her morally, overcome with terror [...])".

# COMMENTARIES

## ACÉPHALE [MG]

Having established its structure in 1937, Acéphale initiated a new phase in its activities in the year that followed, intended to facilitate the adepts' journey towards what Andler called the need for "being and thus becoming whole" in his text of 24 July, ●50. The writings from the Society in 1938 bear witness both to this collective journey, and to its expansion through the recruitment of new affiliates, primarily from the College of Sociology.

The first text here, "Meditation in the Forest", ●47, of 13 January, recounts Dussat's trek one night into the forest of Marly and an ecstatic experience at the foot of the acephalous tree, where death appeared to him "in the guise of his own death" and seized him "with a violent strength, like an image as fleeting as one of the piercing shrieks of the wind".

Bataille's "List of Names", ●48, dated 8 March 1938, was found among Andler's papers, and relates to possible "participants" in the Society as already discussed.[1] Here Bataille reconfigures Acéphale into two initiatory degrees: the adepts, whose initials correspond to the seven members who signed the second commitment at Montjoie, ●41; and the neophytes, those "almost uninitiated",[2] whose initials are divided into three lists. The first, numbered 2, lists actual participants, naming only Patrick Waldberg; the next lists participants proposed at the meeting of 28 December 1937 (the date in the document is erroneous). Among them is Michel Leiris, who had just given his first lecture at the College and who, according to Andler and Chavy, was close to the group, although he always denied he was ever a member. André Masson too appears, whose involvement with the Society included illustrating two volumes for the "Collection Acéphale". The other initials are those of Jean Rollin, Saint-Paul (i.e. Robert Folio), H.W. (unidentified), Colette Peignot and Esther Tabacman, the wife of Ambrosino, who remained outside the Society. List 4 contains the initials of participants to be proposed by Bataille at the next meeting: the poet and painter Jean Atlan, who did not join Acéphale; the Japanese painter and sculptor Taro Okamoto, a student of Mauss and Kojève; and the initials C.B., which according to Camille Morando are probably those of Camille Bryen, then close to Atlan, Okamoto and Waldberg.[3]

Dussat's "The Labyrinth", ●49, dated 4 April, is a variation on the theme of the structure of social existence explored by Bataille in his text of the same name.[4] Bataille had inverted the ancient version of the myth which represented the birth of mankind as issuing from the murder of "this hybrid being, at once man and bull, that is the Minotaur".[5] The labyrinth according to Bataille, however, has no exit, and delivers man to the Minotaur to be torn apart so as to open him up to "monstrous repressed metamorphoses"[6] at the risk of his very life. As the symbol of the Acéphale both on the cover of the journal and on the notification of the adepts' initiation (see p.321), the labyrinth in Dussat's text takes the form of a snake that devours itself, which is the "goal and destiny of he that seeks", according to Jaspers in *Acéphale*.[7] Furthermore, like the arena of the matador-adept, the labyrinth updates the link obliterated by Christianity between the horror of death and "extreme joy", according to the image previously proposed by Bataille to the Society in ●22 and which he continued to develop in his early lectures to the College at the beginning of 1938, on "Attraction and Repulsion" and in his response to Caillois's lecture on "Animal Societies". Here Bataille introduced the idea of a social nucleus of the left sacred, where "existence revolves around things that are charged with the dread they provoke, a dread indistinguishable from that of death". The laughter "mediated" by this nucleus of the sacred became for him "the form of interaction that is specific to the human."[8]

Andler's "It was about resisting boredom...", ●50, dated 24 July, was an appeal to the adepts to become "truly imperious". The same concern informs the "Statement" made by Bataille before the sessional meeting of 25 July, ●51, while the other two documents associated with this meeting are the agenda, ●52, which is preceded by a letter that establishes the new rules for meetings, and "Decisions", ●53. According to Andler, the letter revealed the central role assumed by Ambrosino in the community, alongside Bataille, although Koch, in one of our conversations, recalled that "he lacked the communicative pathos of Bataille". The meeting's agenda testifies to the Society's intention to increase both its internal and outwardly directed activities. Internally, the drafting of common letters to Chenon, Rollin, Dubief and Klossowski questions the genuine commitment of absent members, and from now on if they cannot attend a main sessional meeting they must send a letter of solidarity. Looking outwards, there are additions to the list of possible participants, including Alain Girard who, according to Koch, did not join the Society, and two who did: Isabelle Farner and Koch himself. In connection with this, Dautry is to be readmitted, and Atlan expelled, ●53. Also on the agenda are two projects which were central to the sessional meeting of 29 September (●69): the founding of a teaching programme and of a Society of the Friends of Acéphale.

The new strategy of Acéphale, neither literary nor political, was mostly to direct itself outwards, and was to be achieved in part through two publications. *The Seven*

*Aggressions* was intended to be the first of a series of occasional pamphlets that would be collected together to make an *Acéphale Yearbook*. The augmented version, that appeared in the agenda of the meeting of 29 September, later became one of the manuscript fragments of Bataille's *Anti-Christian's Manual*[9] which also included a "Plan" that described the work as an "introduction to a doctrine" founded upon "human prodigality". The summary of chapter IV, "Aggressiveness", reads: "The new aggressions. In addition to the struggles we see at present and which are drowning amongst an ever increasing meaninglessness, new aggressions are necessary, and a new struggle must be undertaken". The "Plan", however, makes no mention of the statutes of the Society of the Friends of Acéphale, which according to the agenda were to be a part of the *Manual*.

The second planned publication was to be a *Memorandum* of Nietzsche, a selection of texts that was eventually published in April 1945 by Gallimard, with the sub-title "Maxims and texts collected and presented by Georges Bataille". Divided into four sections, the second, called "Morality (The Death of God and the value of the perishable moment)", contains the aphoristic paragraph "The types of my disciples" from *The Will to Power* which was offered in the summer of 1938 to the adepts, as responding to their aggressiveness, ●54. Bataille used the same text in the first part of his *On Nietzsche*, written between February and August 1944, and also published by Gallimard in 1945.[10]

The letter sent by the adepts to Rollin, ●56, also concerns these two aspects of Acéphale's activity. The "importance of demonstrating a moral bond" is joined to the possibility of some sort of agreement with Rollin's "anarchist friends", in particular Miguel González Inestal, of the National Confederation of Labour (CNT). In 1937 this group had affiliated to the Iberian Anarchist Federation (FAI), an underground revolutionary organisation which was then one of the most important military forces opposing Franco in the Spanish Civil War. According to Koch, who knew Inestal through Rollin, Inestal had expressed interest in Acéphale, and had "written a text responding to those by the group", which Rollin translated but then lost. Also missing is the "letter to the anarchists" mentioned by Bataille in two letters to Rollin,[11] which was intended to appear in an appendix to the *Anti-Christian's Manual*, suggesting that Bataille still had a copy of it.[12]

The remaining texts in this section are by Dussat, Ambrosino and Bataille, and Waldberg. Dussat's "The Acéphale", ●55, of 8 August, is another meditation before the tree, in which again he encounters his own death, in a sort of overcoming of individual consciousness in the experiencing of the *"it is"*. Ambrosino and Bataille's "Questions", ●57, for Andler relate to his summons to a new interview on 16 August, and ask him to reflect upon a number of themes bearing on the search for inner fulfilment: religious experience, anguish, power and ascesis. Ambrosino and Bataille also asked the same questions of another adept, Chavy (p.309, *9 September*). In the final text, dated 30

August, "The Image of Death", ●58, appears as something "terrible and magnificent" at the most intense moment of sexual passion, and from the standpoint of "Masters" claims its intimate connection with laughter.

## THE COLLEGE OF SOCIOLOGY [AB]

The lectures given in the course of 1938 rapidly became more original, and the end of the first academic year was marked with the College's only joint publication: "Towards a College of Sociology" (see p.250, *1 July*), a separate section within the July issue of the *NRF*, with texts by Bataille, Caillois and Leiris.

The first lecture this year, Leiris's "The Sacred in Everyday Life", had a very different tone from those given previously by Bataille and Caillois. It avoids generalities until near the end and is firmly situated in Leiris's personal experience, something which would have made it unacceptable in Durkheimian terms. Bataille later described it as demonstrating how "in some societies, those having the advanced civilisation in which we live, the sacred seems, at least initially, to be in the process of disappearing."[13] Direct and vivid, this text does not require much comment here, except to say that it would later be seen as the first sketch of what would become a major part of Leiris's future autobiographical works, *Manhood* and the multi-volume *Rules of the Game*.

With the two lectures on "Attraction and Repulsion", Bataille resumed the work of explaining the foundational ideas of sacred, as opposed to profane sociology. These lectures are considered together here because they share the same theme, and because only in the second does it become clear that Bataille is erecting his ideas of human urges and interaction upon the theory of social structures outlined in his first lecture, on 20 November. He imposes on these structures a morphology based upon the primitive biological cell, and it has to be admitted that this works better as a metaphor than as a scientific proposition.

Bataille begins with a reiteration of his summation of "Animal Societies": "Everything leads us to believe that in earlier times human beings were brought together by disgust and mutual terror, by an insurmountable horror focused exactly on what originally was the central attraction of their union."[14] Societies have at their core a conglomeration of social facts, consisting of the left sacred, that forms a central "nucleus", a "terrifying" concentration of taboos, objects, beliefs, practices and constraints that mediates all interaction in the outer ring of profane everyday life. The relationship between the two domains is reciprocal, however. Society banishes what it finds repulsive to the nucleus — which Bataille associates with repression in the psychoanalytic meaning of the word, with guilt and therefore crime — but it is the practices and power of the nucleus that binds society together. At its centre are rituals of elevation and of putting to death associated with sacrifice, which are conducted in the "violent silence" that accompanies the meeting of sacred and profane. The purpose of these rituals is to transform what we find repulsive into the attractive, from impure to pure, a process that preserves the sacred character these objects have acquired by their banishment. According to Bataille this situation exists, albeit in an "obviously degenerate"[15] form, even in a small French village. The church at its centre has a repulsive force that keeps "the noise of life at a distance", and a force of attraction when its central rite is enacted: a sacrifice symbolically represented by the transformation of bread and wine into flesh and blood. Here the repulsive putrefying corpses of saints are turned into objects of attraction and veneration — bleached bones — while the divine person of Christ himself is represented as issuing from "a tortured body, that has been beaten and abused".[16]

Repulsion at the core of society was originally focused upon bodily expenditure, and thus around a fear of expenditure in general, and the object that embodies the greatest repulsion and the greatest possible expenditure is death. Even so, what repels also attracts, and here Bataille instances collective laughter at representations of death or erotic images that resemble "wounds open to life",[17] since it is in sexuality and laughter that this attraction is most apparent, with laughter being the specifically human form of social interaction. He supposes that the balance of repulsion and attraction within the nucleus is simultaneously a balance of prohibition and licence, but licence can only be accessed by the periodic breaking of prohibitive taboos and it is this that allows the expenditure "essential for maintaining the integrity of the social whole".[18] Yet this expenditure, which is again a transformation of impure repression into pure exuberance, must in turn reinstate the prohibition that forbade it, and even deny the crime that freed it, so as to forestall a possible expenditure to the point of total loss. And so: "All of our existence, which is to say all of our expenditure, is thereby produced in a swirling tumult in which death is joined with the most explosive tension of life."[19] It is worth noting, however, that nowhere does Bataille cite attraction and repulsion as a means of dividing people into categories of admired and repellent as Caillois proposed in "The Winter Wind", ○30.

On 19 February Caillois was supposed to give a lecture on "Power", and as we will see in his "Introduction", ○59, this subject was considered one of the three central topics for investigation by the College, and once again returns to theses originally developed at the time of Contre-Attaque. Illness prevented Caillois from giving his lecture based on these notes, but Bataille had prepared a response to them and it is this that survives and which he read, although in his preamble to it he stated that he had subsequently incorporated what he could from Caillois. The lecture attempted to identify movements of power between the secular and sacred realms and, one suspects, to account for the emergence of a distinctive cult of total negativity: Hitler and Nazism.

The exercising of power is a social fact *par excellence*, since an individual cannot have power over himself alone, and in this lecture Bataille returned to the themes of expenditure and sacrifice, in particular the ultimate expenditure, death, as applied to its ultimate victim, the king. The notion of power combines the religious and the political, both mythically and literally in Bataille's schema. By its nature, it partakes of the tragedy of existence in an especially poignant form, because the possessor of power has but one fate, to lose it, a sacrificial expenditure Bataille associates with the "*me* that dies" in his text "Sacrifices". Frazer had thus selected the perfect exemplar: the priest-king who gains power by a criminal act and who will lose it by being murdered in his turn. This putting to death of the king is the fundamental sacred rite and the source of all tragedy and religious power, since (again following Frazer) the king "represents a dynamic concentration of all the impulses that socially animate individuals. [...] The power to realise the common desire is transferred to the king, who becomes solely responsible for it. It is precisely the king who guarantees the order of things, and who must be incriminated if this order is disrupted."[20] Bataille analyses the phenomenon chronologically and his description of the central event of Christianity demonstrates very clearly his idea of the transformation of left, impure sacred into right, pure sacred, and also relates directly to various documents of Acéphale from recent months, including ●33, 34 and 43.[21]

According to Bataille, we can date the birth of power in the modern sense of the term to the triumph of Christianity within the Roman Empire, an "institutional union of sacred force and military strength".[22] As it becomes increasingly hierarchical, the Church gradually corrupts the sacred by denying its central crime and diverting expenditure towards both its own conservation and the conservation of its power. Bolstered by this formidable coalition, as exemplified in the alliance between the fortress of Montjoie and the abbey of Joyenval, the killing of the king would become the central myth of European civilisation, and remain undiminished until recent times when it was inverted by Fascism. This inversion is seen in the symbols of both Christianity and Fascism: the cross, on which the *king* was tortured to death, and the fasces, bound about the lictor's axe used to behead *subjects* who had disobeyed the institution's laws. This dichotomy matches the original representations of killing the king, in which Christianity identified itself with the victim, but tragedy with the killers. It is tragedy that must be embraced, in opposition to the servility imposed by both Christianity and Fascism, and no remorse should be felt for the crime, ●22. In the political realm, the central foundational myth of the French Revolution, the guillotining of Louis XVI, embodied all the profane and sacred meanings of the killing of the king, which is why Bataille envisaged an annual rite to celebrate it.

In modern times, however, such representations have been bypassed. Temporal power finds itself unsupported by the sacred it has degraded, and the dominant classes, nostalgic "for that power which allowed them to arrange the order of things to their own advantage",[23] must resort to less authentic forms, to military force and to representations such as patriotism and the fatherland. Bataille concludes by announcing that the following two lectures will cover "present-day forms" that oppose all movement (the army) and, on the other hand, certain "secondary dynamic forms that [have] the possibility of reactivating the social tragedy", i.e. elective brotherhoods, a category we may take to include both Acéphale and the College.

Bataille's lecture on "The Structure and Function of the Army" is lost, but he summarised its content at the start of the next lecture, on 19 March:

> I would like to emphasise at this point the opposition I have tried to set up between the religious world, a world of tragedy and *internal* conflict, and the military world, which is so radically hostile to the spirit of tragedy and constantly directing aggressiveness outside — *exteriorising* conflict. In the last session I discussed the revolutionary upheavals that have racked Europe for several centuries as a development of religious agitation, that is to say, of tragic agitation. I showed that this development was based upon the capacity of the tragic world for a destruction that spared nothing, and I argued that this world had worked endlessly towards its own annihilation, and that before our very eyes this annihilation leads only to the death of the revolutionary spirit itself, which can no longer exist in man without him becoming the scene of heart-breaking contradiction. But above all I insisted that revolutionary struggles, by annihilating a religious world that had become empty and then annihilating themselves, have left the field free to the military world: in other words it is possible to say that the chief effect of the great revolutions of Europe has been the development of military nationalism. At this very moment, in the face of our powerless recriminations, the military spirit alone dictates the destiny of the human masses who are in a state of hypnosis; some euphoric, and others dumbfounded.[24]

Caillois's lecture on "Brotherhoods, Orders, Secret Societies and Churches" was evidently significant in the context of Acéphale and the College, but Caillois was still unwell and Bataille again had to step in. Having prefaced this lecture by expanding upon his previous conclusions on the army, he now characterised the man open to inner conflict as the "man of tragedy", and he who externalises it as "the military man". He then added a third category, the "man of comedy", essentially a man of bluster, whether legal, political or literary, who does not necessarily deny these conflicts, but sublimates them, consciously or otherwise. Thus the result of the revolutionary struggles of the past century, directed by these last two representatives of humanity, has been to destroy the religious order, and then the possibility of revolutionary struggle itself, but the resulting military power is fragile, since it suffers from an inbuilt contradiction. The military realm can exist only as an opposition and once victorious it loses its meaning, thereby proving itself unable to resolve the contradictions of life. The question, therefore, is one of establishing a secondary order that will prepare for the time when "the primary organisation of society is no longer able to satisfy all the aspirations that rise up in it".[25]

These contradictions, and aspirations, are associated by Bataille with the man of tragedy, able to "bear within himself the reality of human existence that is profoundly lost within the vastness of the universe".[26] Tragedy and existence are bound together and only a community that acknowledges this can have any value. Suppose, he asks, "there was a contagious religious organisation, new and entirely incongruous within its milieu, and sustained by a spirit incapable of servility, then a man might yet learn — and remember — that there is something else to love apart from this barely veiled image of financial necessity which is the fatherland having taken up arms: something else worth living for, and something else worth dying for! And although it is true that such an organisation can in no way prevent the firestorm into which it seems we have already entered, its presence in the world could be regarded from now on as a pledge for the future victories of MAN over his weaponry!"[27] This organisation was of course Acéphale, but also, to the extent that it was "active", and a community, the College.

The final section asserts that only existential societies, ●14 §1, can maintain themselves in total opposition to the established order, since their refusal of utility is "the sole negation, which does not consist merely of words, of that principle of necessity in the name of which the majority of present-day humanity collaborates to deplete existence."[28] This leads to the first public acknowledgement at the College of the notion of "active" sociology:

> Only the wholeness of *existence*, with all its tumult and its explosive will to be, that even the threat of death cannot impede, can be that thing which, since it is itself impossible to subjugate, must necessarily subjugate all that consents to work for others: ultimately the empire will belong to those whose life is such an outpouring that they love death. I am not unaware of how objectionable all this is. I know that I have gone beyond the limits of sociological study. But I must say in all honesty that these limits seem arbitrary to me. The field of sociology is the domain, in fact the only true domain, of the crucial decisions of life.[29]

On 2 April, Bataille lectured on "Sacred Sociology of the Contemporary World". He began with a summary of the year's activities, although in the event there was still to be at least one further lecture. He then read "the text which first united us", which we presume to be ○29, before reaffirming the College's faith in Durkheim and the profound reality of social phenomena. Next came an overview of the international situation, where, according to Bataille, the current level of agitation was something not seen since the Middle Ages. Certain trends were perceptible within this ferment, with individuals having an apparently increasing autonomy from social movements, but no more than apparent since it was quickly subsumed into the world of work. The second outcome was the founding of three new monarchies "much more than dictatorships, veritable divine powers",[30] namely Nazism, Communism and Fascism. Both of these tendencies combined to elevate work into an aim in itself, something that proved insufficient to sustain social cohesion when labour divorces its workforce from tragedy and real existence. The progressive collapse of these structures could only be (temporarily) halted by "reducing the world of labour to servitude to the military world",[31] which was now the situation for the social structures set up under Fascism or Nazism.

Thus the College reached the end of the lectures listed in its first prospectus, but this had also carried the announcement that the lectures "in May and June 1938 will be devoted solely to MYTHOLOGY". These never took place, however, probably because Bataille and Caillois were unable to keep up with the demands of the College, demands that were exacerbated by the fact that Paulhan had offered to publish their texts in the *NRF*. This precipitated something of a crisis (see p.249, *17 May*). Klossowski in part filled the hiatus with a lecture on "Tragedy", which was a reading of his translation of Kierkegaard's "Ancient Tragedy's Reflection in the Modern" from his *Either/Or*.

Publication in the *NRF* was obviously important for the College, but both Leiris and Caillois proposed publishing texts they had already publicly read, with, it seems, minimal editing. Bataille, on the contrary, laboured for several months over his contribution, missing several deadlines. Having thought it would be finished in the second week of March,[32] he finally delivered it in mid-May, and it stands as a dense and eloquent summation of his ideas from the last few years, and of his experiences in trying to act upon them, within both the Society and the College: "The Sorcerer's Apprentice", ○61.

Caillois contributed "The Winter Wind", ○30, and an "Introduction", ○59, that incorporated his "Note", ○31, of the year before. Leiris offered "The Sacred In Everyday Life", ○60, but he was now engaged in a more conventional career in sociology and ethnology and attempted to pull his contribution and substitute a more orthodox ethnological text, a lecture on the Dogon he had given to the Society of Group Psychology. Paulhan refused his suggestion.

# TEXTS

## January 1938 — August 1938

*Left:* André Masson, *Osiris*, etching from *Sacrifices*, 1936.

8.- III.- 1939.

**LISTE DE NOMS**

1. Adeptes.

G.A.
P.A.
G.B.
J.C.
R.C.
H.D.
I.K.

2. Participants.

P.W.

3. Proposés le 28.-XII.-38.

M.L.
A.M.
J.R.
S.
H.W.

C.P.
E.T.

4. Seront proposés en principe lors de la prochaine session par G.B.

J.A.
C.B.
T.O.

48. Georges Bataille, *List of Names*.

## HENRI DUSSAT *Meditation in the Forest* 47

*I am here.*

*I came here, slowly, as though following a slow, calculated rhythm, built in to the beat of time.*

*I am alone, I am trying to be still more alone.*

*Elsewhere, I know, insects are dancing in the lanterns' halos. Insects twirling around and around, here a glint of gold, sometimes a wing catches fire and burns.*

*I know that this spectacle runs the risk — at certain moments, more or less frequent or more or less fleeting, for many men, and for me too — of resembling the spectacle of life.*

*In the haze of the lantern light, amidst the lost flailing of empty gestures, before the shifting night horizon that was yet brightly lit, like the interior of a bedroom with its door flung wide open, its walls melted into thin air, a room that would be found right in the centre of town, in the flux where hands, smiles and kisses are offered, where nothing has any real impact, I can clearly make out an impression that resembles my own footprint.*

*Such recognition is not experienced on any other level than that of the greatest aptitude; but from now on perhaps it will be possible to trick oneself into using it freely with regard to such forms of being.*

*Nevertheless, nothing has been resolved for me, I believe, and to find myself often face to face with my own image, in the grip of vanity, and the loss that is linked to participation in external life, to encounter myself like that, to stop, to get a grip on myself, to act with myself as far as I am able, well, to me that is the certain proof that this is the way of things, today, that things have not yet come apart with a certain feeling of misfortune.*

*I do not intend to hide, confident of how obviously, as I am writing this, I may be far from that freedom, specifically from that calm and secure freedom that has no need to resort to caution, from freedom unquestionably considered to be a desirable goal, faced with a shimmering jumble of shapes and colours whose sparkling flashes draw the spirited gaze into the lanterns' halo.*

*Today I am far from that, I am here; I am walking in the dark. It is the first time that I have braved the forest alone. First of all the approach, this evening, is more difficult than it has been before; rain is falling, the wind is blowing, the sky is lowering and very dark. I feel, so close to me, the presence of the elements, and it is as though all around me everything is moving. I have the intense feeling, as if held in the grip of something, that I need to let myself be exposed to the idea of danger.*

*I have been here before, I have already walked with other men along these same paths, in the same direction. I am bound to these men by the forest, by the route we followed together — in silence, in the dark — and by the tree. Walking with them before, proceeding, like them, with all my strength, towards the presence, I felt bound to them and knew what it was we were all attempting to bind ourselves to, by taking hold of it. Together we forced ourselves to walk at the same demanding pace; perhaps it was already possible to a certain extent, and to that extent with a certain ease, for us to gain access to a feeling — not pleasant or happy, on the contrary, harsh and brutal, as if we were moving too quickly, and were out of breath — a feeling that, ahead of us, in a way that perhaps hadn't been considered, things were opening up.*

*Now, being here alone, walking alone, the most alone it is possible for me to be, I know that if I feel bound to what I call the presence it will be without anyone else having introduced me to it, or interceding on my behalf, with no question of putting a foot wrong, like someone making their way along a ridge in the high mountains, or running along the edge of a precipice. And, more supremely than it has ever been possible to sense before, I am aroused by the thought that in this way nothing is as close to me as danger.*

*It is impossible for me to think of anything that is genuinely meaningful, that is conquering and rich in bloody virtues; it is impossible for me to think of what we might undertake, of what imperious thing might be born of us, here in the present or in the future, other than by allowing my thoughts to take on a form all of their own as they attempt to grasp what constitutes the essence of actions — and amongst the actions resulting from the form my thoughts take, as they aspire to seize on the essence of the densest ones, those whose completion results in death arriving unexpectedly in the thing at which they were directed. In the same way, the thought we have to hold on to with all our strength, with all our power, in order to implement everything, and to ensure that everything commits us more to our path, this thought, which I sense in all its reality and power, tonight, alone, in the forest, is to me indistinguishable, in its form, from the exhilarating thought of danger.*

*For us there are different kinds of danger whose existence must be revealed to us, elsewhere, by the world of agitated humanity, whether as the result of its hostility or its complacency. But it is clear that what is manifesting itself here, at this hour, is of a quite different nature. In the world our hands are seeking to prise open, the world to which our steps, in their dogged effort, to which all our advances are straining to give us access, this world of shadows amongst which we can nevertheless make out the beating heart of flames, the nature of the danger it has in store for us is such that, even from far away, its presence is revealed to our burning passion, and may be revealed as either dense and heavy with threat, or transparent, and overlaid with veils.*

*In the night of shadows and flames, that which has taken on the form of existence, in a being blessed with life, with human traits that are the same as my own, goes forth and beseeches death to appear to him in the guise of his own death.*

*My own death has not appeared to me, this evening, at the end of a meditation undertaken and undergone with great effort; rather it has seized me, like an image, with a violent strength, like an image as fleeting as one of the piercing shrieks of the wind around me. In a forest such as this one, in this very forest, a man is moving. He has taken off all his clothes, he is completely naked. He leaves the thick shadow of the trees and starts to walk across a broad clearing that is violently lit by an intense light, falling from the sky. He starts to run into this clearing, waving his arms and legs about, jumping and leaping as he runs, laughing and weeping. Suddenly, cleaving asunder the blazing clouds, lightning bursts forth from a sun and strikes him full in the chest, like a dagger, and he falls to the ground. He is dead.* 13 January 1938

## GEORGES BATAILLE *List of Names* 48

*1. Adepts*

*G.A.*
*P.A.*
*G.B.*
*J.C.*
*R.C.*
*H.D.*
*I.K.*

*2. Participants*

*P.W.*

*3. Proposed on 28-XII-38*[1]

*M.L.*
*A.M.*
*J.R.*
*S.*
*H.W.*
*C.P.*
*E.T.*

*4. To be proposed in principle by G.B. at the next session*

*J.A.*
*C.B.*
*T.O.*

8.III.1938

49 HENRI DUSSAT *The Labyrinth*

*In the course of a frantic chase, the life which is, in a human form, me, tries to seize hold of this form, that goes by the name it is called amongst men, tries to seize hold of this reality constituted by the unbelievable fact that this human form animated by life — in other words that which is not total absence, silence or the void — that this human form, my person, is moving, shifting position, walking at this moment, at this time, down this road in a city where life fills a profusion of human forms in the same way so as to attempt to understand that the encounter, the coincidence of existence with this human form that is itself, must signify, just as it does for me, a pledge to an all-consuming anguish.*

*In a flash, the serpent coiled itself up into a tight knot; but its head, right in the centre of the shape it now forms, is simply caught in a new seizure, in which every moment of its existence is called into action and which then annuls each movement it has just completed; it is only through this seizure that it can bite its own tail with its own head, joining itself together — thus presenting the image of the labyrinth.*

Menton, 4-IV-1938

*It was about resisting boredom and escaping the void. But friendship has brought us only impunity.*

*The air that we found unbreathable though is not the air of friendship. So it is not those who kept themselves at a distance who should be throwing stones. Sober resolution has not, as it happens, served them any better. It is, like friendship, just another stage in the fear of remaining inadequate. This fear is the matter in question today.*

*We allowed ourselves to be possessed by the hope that we might become impregnated: but we are the ones who already do the impregnating, during puberty. To be ignorant of this function is another form of fear. It derives from our desire for wealth.*

*Art can take many forms — psychology is undoubtedly an art — but for us it was to do with being and thus becoming whole. We must therefore leave art behind where we left everything else that divides us. Because we have chosen ourselves.*

*This choice could be arbitrary, but it assumes that certain things have been learned, and in particular that it is not always necessary to explain everything. This will undoubtedly need to be demonstrated before anything else.*

*In order to give others — ourselves — the right to be more demanding, we ourselves must also demand more. Today it is a question of educating ourselves, because we have made way for illiterates and pedagogues (each one of us is an illiterate and a pedagogue). We have taken our time, but then this is not something that should be rushed into head first.*

*What we have taken for modesty is only laziness. But let that not be of any further concern, under the pretext of shaking it up with our individual* conscience. *Find in favour of simplicity — but so that it is protected on both sides simplicity must be up to its task, so that individual* conscience *stops speaking out at length. If I am being obscure, it should nevertheless be understood that I have set my sights on writing texts.*

*Ultimately, this text is addressed to everyone. Simplicity should not be confused any more with mental deficiency. It has nothing to do with surrendering, it means becoming truly imperious, no more to leave our aggression without an objective. This should happen without breaking glass. To my mind it is a question only of the forest.*

24.VII.[19]38

## 51 GEORGES BATAILLE *Statement to the Sessional Meeting of 25 July 1938*

*At the start of this meeting I would like to make a preliminary statement. One concern for us has been that there was only a single sessional meeting, a long one, covering the period from July to September. In addition, some things have appeared to be more difficult when looked at more closely. That said, there would be no point going into details about the facts of the matter. As a result, we have abandoned the first project. One principle remains, however, that I do want to insist upon: it is that [ ] a clear and simple necessity, for many reasons, some of which touch me to the innermost core of my being, this revival of our activity at the end of July 1938 must bring to our undertakings not only perseverance, but an awareness that is much more earnest and above all more unpleasant than what these undertakings signify. The means, which have been lacking up until now, by which we could increase our still embryonic cohesion, may be within our reach very soon. I do not believe that the seriousness of purpose we have accepted will be permanently without issue. Sometimes it happens that an initiative has already begun before it abruptly reveals itself to be very much more onerous than was originally supposed — sometimes even almost to the point of ruin. Some people withdraw in confusion. Others carry on. For the latter, it is only then that the serious work begins. Anyone who is still concerned with the kind of trivia that up until now has been remorseless and unavoidable will just seem like an irrelevant gossip, and stupidly muddle-headed, when it is at last a question of the reality of existence, of life and death. Many of our abilities may become completely displaced, or may become the focus of other people's anger, in particular, everything that is related to the self and its stubborn demands, its grating conceits and lethargies. I know perfectly well that this is all rather arcane; besides, we haven't yet arrived at that exact point when we are forced, literally forced, to eliminate wholesale the minor, paralysing abilities. All I am asking is whether we can really envisage everything continuing as it is for any length of time.*

*The tacit excuse behind which each of us has entrenched himself thus far — I exclude no one from this and, of course, I do not exclude myself either — depends on what might result from the simple question: "But what can I do? What could I do?" Such a question would, however, be strange in our case: have we not found the essential point of our disagreement with all politicians in the principle that* existing, being, *is the only thing that counts for us, and that the primordial concern with* taking action, *with* doing, *is to us commensurate with abdication. Yet what have we done up until now, in order* to be, to exist? *The main point — perhaps... but overall, what is the* existence *that has come about in relation to this point? Have we not encountered the essential only to discover that we are incapable of meeting its demands?*

*I am not expressing any impatience here, still less any particular acrimony. The requirement expressed amongst us in the severity of my language calls for* being *to ensue from our unity. Sooner or later it was inevitable that this requirement, which, once we were making some progress, had something unstoppable about it, sooner or later it was inevitable that this requirement would be expressed with some kind of violence. On condition, however, that this violence was accompanied by a strength of mind that would immediately recover all of life's joyful sympathies and all its harsh ironies. It is enough that the mask be removed for a moment. What must come out of all this can be nothing but clarification, an endeavour systematically accomplished by slowly picking up our every bout of tiredness in reaction to the brick walls it has come up against, and by insisting that decisive steps should only be taken with absolute certainty.*

## GEORGES BATAILLE *Sessional Meeting of 25 July 1938* 52

*The time has come for us to consolidate our inclinations to form a quasi-religious order and even a sort of military stability.*

*This is why we propose the immediate adoption of the following rules (which have, it is true, only a preliminary value):*

*I. Each of us shall commit to attending the primary sessional meetings. In the event that this is not possible — because of illness or distance — a letter of solidarity must be sent. If this letter is not sent, a joint letter will be written and sent during the meeting, in which the consequences of failing to attend will be made clear, with all appropriate severity.*

*II. Each meeting will start exactly on time. Each of us commits to arriving exactly on time. Each of us is aware of the fundamental importance of punctuality. Those present must take their seats at the table about two minutes before the meeting begins. From then on they must observe the rule of silence. Leaving afterwards must be done as swiftly as possible. We must avoid as far as we can any routine conversation and, apart from obvious reasons, not leave in groups of more than two.*

*III. It makes no sense for us to meet for debate. Discussions can easily, and therefore should take place outside these meetings. Each proposal may be followed by requests for clarification, objections or responses, all brief, but these may be overruled. Objectors can demand a further face-to-face meeting, but proposals* can *be passed immediately, subject to ongoing objection, in other words clauses may be inserted forthwith, at least where this is necessary or urgent.*

*IV. Ambrosino and Bataille have the right to make preliminary objections at the meeting. This means that no proposal can be presented without the prior agreement of one of them, but each of us then has the right to object. On the other hand, Ambrosino and Bataille must make sure beforehand to address everyone's feelings in their proposals.*

*V. The state of mind that must be seen to prevail in these meetings may only be a religious one. Consequently, what is required of each of us is the profound silencing of his normal interests and the radical abnegation of his individual points of view. Even a revelation as serious as he is capable of presenting to us from the most secret depths of his person: even if the most violent tragedy has taken place just before.*

*Agenda for the sessional meeting of 25 July 1938, to begin at 9 o'clock sharp, to deal with the following proposals:*

I. Internal activities
*Establishment of a teaching programme (gradually assuming a fixed timetable)*
*Formal agreement to rent a workshop*
*Planned writing of common letters to Chenon, Rollin, Atlan, Dubief and Klossowski*
*Adding to the list the names of Isabelle Farner, Girard and Koch*
*Establishment of a* Society of the Friends of Acéphale

II. Publications and definition of Acéphale's position
*Proposed publication of occasional pamphlets of 4, 8 or 12 pages in 16mo format, intended to be bound together as a whole at the end of each year to make an* Acéphale Yearbook.

*Proposed publication in August or September of a first pamphlet, entitled* The Seven Aggressions, *to set forth seven basic principles:*

*1. Chance against the mass*[2]
*2. The truth of human communion against the lies and impostures of the individual*
*3. An elective community against all communities based on blood or land*
*4. The tragic brilliance of existence against servile abdication*
*5. Becoming criminal against becoming a victim*
*6. Joy in the face of death against all forms of immortality*
*7. The empire of tragedy against the omnipotence of God and the Army*

*(Inclusion of the statutes of a* Society of the Friends of Acéphale *at the end of this first pamphlet).*

*Drafting of a* Memorandum *(collection of selected texts) by Nietzsche.*

III. Preliminary verdicts regarding July encounters.

THE MEMBERS OF ACÉPHALE *Decisions* 53

*1. The proposals in the advance letter are adopted. However, items III and IV, although adopted without objection, have been deferred for possible modification at the next meeting.*

*2. It is agreed that another name will be given to what was to have been called the* Society of the Friends of Acéphale.

*3. For the time being, no letters will be sent to Atlan, and he will be struck from the list.*

*4. Dautry will be added to the list.*

*5. "Or other interests" will be added to the third aggression.*

*Furthermore:*

*1. Letters sent out in advance of sessional meetings, which must, according to the rules, include an agenda, should be sent at least four full days before the meeting.*

*2. Letters of solidarity must include a response to the agenda.*

*3. The proposed teaching programme will be open to every individual on the list.*

[25 July 1938]

## 54 GEORGES BATAILLE *The Types of My Disciples*

*In the recent edition of* The Will to Power *there are a large number of passages that are so cruel they could be said to embody for us the aggression in whose grip we inevitably find ourselves, and it would not be a bad thing for each of us to be reminded of them in the hope that this aggression will shake us to the core.*

*To give an example of one reference here:*

"The types of my disciples — *To all those* who are of any concern to me, *I wish suffering, neglect, sickness, ill-treatment and dishonour; I wish that they will be spared neither the profound self-contempt, nor the torture of the self's mistrust; I have no pity for them, for I wish them the only thing that can prove today if a man has* value *or not* — to stand his ground.*"*[3]

[Summer 1938]

## 55 HENRI DUSSAT *The Acéphale*

*I exist in so far as the tree, in front of me, rising up out of the deep earth, rises up out of that which, first of all, I perceive as being as old as time.*

*That which rises up from the most remote human blood takes the form of a fusion between all human lives and deaths, and there is nothing more of agitation or the memory of agitation. There is no head or body that yields to anything.*

*In this moment I plunge into the earth as if diving into the waves, at the same time as the symbol grows bigger, and as my stark-naked and living death stands before me.*

*And when I leave I am not alone: what I have invoked will not abandon me. In my human form that is. This edifice of bones will one day turn to dust, but today, now,* it is.

8-VIII-1938

## 56 THE MEMBERS OF ACÉPHALE *To Jean Rollin*

[August 1938]

*We are forwarding you the advance letter from our last meeting — in accordance with the principle stated in the texts included therein, which emphasises the importance of demonstrating a moral bond.*

*At this meeting all the proposals put forward were adopted without exception.*[4]

*We look forward to your response.*

*However slight the hope we might have of being understood by those outside, we have a genuine interest in the reactions of your anarchist friends. We hope you can come to Paris soon, and, when you do, that you can participate fully in what unites us.*

*Please send your reply to Bataille*

*59* bis *rue de Mareil, Saint-Germain-en-Laye (Seine et Oise)*

## GEORGES AMBROSINO AND GEORGES BATAILLE *To Pierre Andler* 57

*Questions*

*Once more, we are asking you to attend an interview. It will take place on Tuesday 16 August 1938 at 5 pm, at 17 rue Séguier.*

*Allow us to remind you of the rules of our interviews: no greeting, and no smoking. The key will be in the door, you can come straight in.*

*We attach here the questions that will form the basis of our interview, so that you may think about them.*

*What does religious experience mean to you? Is that what you want for yourself? And to what degree? In what way?*

*Do you consider anguish a means of seeking a fulfilled existence? Do you think that your anguish must last for ever? Or do you hope to find forms of joy or mirth as offered by some mystical ecstasy? Or do you think that you can find joy, strength and overall achievement by means other than those offered by mysticism?*

*What do you imagine doing in order to obtain power? Power over yourself as well as real power over another person?*

*How far do you think you should go on the path of ascesis?*

[11 August 1938]

## PATRICK WALDBERG *The Image of Death* 58

*The image of Death is linked to the Passion. It can only appear with any power when total existence is at stake.*

*The image of Death, in the world around us, is everywhere distorted. It occurs, terrible and magnificent, when two lovers in that most intense moment when they are joined together, mutually give themselves up to death. Each lover has broken the bonds of habit that connect them to the world; even the bonds which connect them to the Other have disappeared. Each finds themself* alone*; and it is only at that moment that the image of Death has meaning.*

*We can only be worthy in the face of Death if we have mastered the ability to be alone, if we have ceased to exist 'as a function' of everything in order to exist at last as a World exists.*

*For us, as close as our world might seem to the world of Lovers, things are different: our existence and solitude are conquests, and not a reality from which there is no escape.*

*Once we have conquered the omnipotent hold a World has over itself, once we are alone — that is to say Masters — then we will have a Master's rights over Death; and of all these rights the greatest and most packed with meaning is the right to laugh at Death.*

30 August 1938

ROGER CAILLOIS

# *Introduction*

Present circumstances would seem to lend themselves particularly well to a *critical work* which is concerned with the mutual relations between man's way of *being* and society's: what man expects from society and what society demands of man.

Without question, in the last twenty years we have seen one of the most substantial intellectual *upheavals* it is possible to imagine. Yet nothing lasting, nothing solid, *nothing with any foundation*: already it is all crumbling apart and losing its shape, and time has still only moved on by a single step. But there is an extraordinary and almost inconceivable *degree of unrest*: the problems of the day before are every day being called into question, along with plenty of others that are new, extreme or misleading and are tirelessly being devised by minds that are prodigiously active but no less prodigiously incapable of patience or functioning without distraction. In simple terms, here is a source of production which is entirely overwhelming the market, and out of all proportion to its needs and even its capacity for consumption.

In fact, an abundance of riches and virgin territory has suddenly been opened up to exploration and even exploitation: dreams, the unconscious and all the various forms of the marvellous and of excess (the one defining the other). A frantic individualism, which made a virtue of *scandal*, gave it all a sort of emotional unity that was almost lyrical. True enough, this was somewhat beyond what had been intended, but in any case, for all the things thus given to society there is no pleasure as great as that of provoking it. Here perhaps should be found the seed of a contradiction that was to continue to grow until it came to dominate in a certain key the intellectual practice of our time, that is, writers awkwardly or arrogantly trying to take part in political struggles and realising that their personal concerns were so badly at variance with what was required by their cause that they must very quickly either give in or leave the field.

With regard to both of these contrasting objectives — research into the most profound of human phenomena and the attention we are obliged to give to social facts — neither of them can be abandoned without soon feeling a sense of regret. As for sacrificing one of them for the other, or hoping it might be possible to pursue them both at the same time, experience has always shown the serious mistakes that result from such false solutions. Salvation must come from somewhere else.

For half a century now the human sciences have developed at such a rate that we have still not become properly aware of the new possibilities they present, let alone had the time and the courage to apply them to the multiple problems posed by the working of the instincts and 'myths' that embody or animate them in today's society. From this deficiency stems the significant fact that one whole area of modern collective life, its most important aspect, being its deepest layers, eludes understanding. This situation not only has the effect of sending man back to the hollow potentiality of his dreams, but also of changing the way he perceives the whole range of social phenomena and of corrupting on principle the maxims of action which find within this understanding their reference and guarantee.

This concern with rediscovering the primordial urges and conflicts of the individual condition as they become transposed on the social scale is one of the key factors that led to the formation of the College of Sociology. Indeed it appeared as the conclusion of the text which announced the founding of the College and set out its programme, and must be restated here forthwith:

[Here the *NRF* text printed points 1 to 3 of the "Note", p.216 above.]

Man places the highest value on certain rare, fleeting and violent moments of his personal experience. The work of the College of Sociology begins with this given fact and endeavours to reveal various equivalent processes, at the very heart of social existence, in the elementary phenomena of attraction and repulsion which govern it as well as in its most prominent and important *formations*, such as churches, armies, brotherhoods and secret societies. There are three main problem areas which influence this study, to do with power, the sacred and myths. Resolving them depends not only on information and exegesis — beyond that, it must also embrace the *total* activity of being. Without question this requires that the work be undertaken collectively, with a seriousness, impartiality and critical rigour that will not only ensure any possible results will be generally endorsed but also that the research will command respect from the outset. However, it does conceal a hope of a quite different order, and one which gives the undertaking its whole meaning, namely the ambition that the community formed in this way will go beyond its original plan, moving from the will to knowledge to the will to power, and become the nucleus of a much larger conspiracy — the deliberate calculation that this body should find a soul.

MICHEL LEIRIS

# *The Sacred in Everyday Life* 60

What does the sacred mean for me? More specifically: of what does my sacred consist? What objects, places or circumstances awaken that mixture of fear and attachment in me, that ambiguous attitude which results when something that is at once attractive and dangerous, wondrous and cast aside draws near me, that combination of respect, desire and terror that together represents the psychological sign of the sacred?

There is no question here of defining my scale of values — with the one that is most important to me and most sacred, in the usual meaning of the word, at the top. Rather, it is a matter of searching through some fairly unassuming facts, extracted from everyday life and located outside of what is nowadays considered sacred in the official sense (religion, fatherland, morals), to reveal by means of certain minor details which aspects might allow me to make a qualitative assessment of my own sacred, and help establish the limit beyond which I know I am no longer moving in the plane of ordinary things (trivial or serious, pleasant or painful) but have instead entered a radically different world, as distinct from the profane world as fire is from water.

It seems clear that everything that captured our imagination during childhood, and left us with the memory of something that was just as disturbing, should be our first line of enquiry. For out of all the material available to us, this part extracted from the mists of childhood has some chance of being the least adulterated.

When I think back to my childhood, I remember first of all various idols, temples and, more generally, certain sacred places.

In the first instance, there were certain objects which belonged to my father,

Michel Leiris by Man Ray, *c.*1930.

symbols of his power and authority. His flat-brimmed top hat, that he hung on the coat rack every evening when he returned from the office. His revolver, a Smith and Wesson with its dangerous cylinder, just like all firearms, but more attractive to look at for being nickel-plated, a weapon he usually kept in a drawer of his writing-desk or his bedside table and which was the attribute *par excellence* of the person who, amongst other duties, was responsible for maintaining the household and protecting it against burglars. His purse, where he put his gold coins, a sort of miniature safe that was for a long time the exclusive property of the provider and which seemed to my brothers and me, right up until the time when we received one the same as a first communion gift, to be the mark of manhood.

Another idol was the "Radiant", a stove adorned with the effigy of a woman who resembled the woman in a bust of the Republic. A true spirit of the hearth, enthroned in the dining-room, it was attractive because of the heat it gave out and the way its coals glowed, but was something to be feared because we knew, my brothers and I, that if we touched it we would burn ourselves. It was next to this stove that I was placed, having been carried down during the night when I woke up in the grip of fits of nervous coughing, which are the symptoms of "false croup" and which gave me the feeling — having been attacked by some supernatural evil of the night, ravaged by a cough that had entered me like a foreign body — that all at once I had become someone of importance, like a tragic hero, surrounded as I was by my parents' loving care and concern.

As for places, first of all there was my parents' bedroom, which took on its full meaning only at night, when my father and mother were sleeping there — with the door open, the better for them to watch over their offspring — and where I could vaguely make out, by the glow of the night-light, the great bed, the epitome of the nocturnal world of nightmares that prowl through our sleep and are like the dark counterparts of erotic dreams.

The house's other sacred pole — the left pole, which inclined towards the illicit, as opposed to my parents' bedroom which was the right pole, corresponding to established authority and the sanctum where the clock and my grandparents' portraits were found — was the toilet, where every evening one of my brothers and I would lock ourselves in, out of natural necessity, but also to tell each other, from one day to the next, these sort of serial stories with animal characters which we took turns in making up. This was the place where we felt most like accomplices, as we cooked up our schemes and developed an entire, almost secret mythology, which we resumed every evening, sometimes copying it out into our school exercise-books, this sustenance of the most truly imaginative part of our lives. There were animal soldiers, jockeys, pilots for civil or military aviation, all pitched into contests of war or sport, or detective stories. Shadowy political intrigues with attempted *coups d'état*, murders and kidnappings. Draft constitutions before the setting up of an ideal government. Sentimental love-affairs played out in utter poverty, and which most often ended up in a happy marriage, followed by the birth of several children, but without necessarily excluding a final episode in which one of the parents died. The invention of war machines, underground passages, traps and snares (sometimes made using a simple pit covered with leaves, with sharp cutting blades set into its sides and bristling with stakes at the bottom, so that anyone who fell in would be chopped to pieces and impaled). Lots of battles and fierce struggles (on the battlefields or in the Roman circus). And after each battle, detailed statistics, noting the exact number of prisoners taken along with the dead and wounded on each of the opposing sides, the Cats versus the Dogs, for example, in which the former were royalists and the latter republicans. All of this duly recorded in our exercise-books, in the form of reports, pictures, maps and sketches, along with summary tables and genealogical trees.

Apart from all these legends we had made up and our pantheon of heroes, what was perhaps most clearly marked by the sacred in these long sessions we spent in the toilet was the very secrecy of our meetings. It goes without saying that the rest of the family knew we were in there, but, behind the closed door, no one knew what it was we were talking about. To a certain extent there was something forbidden in what we were doing, and in fact it was this that got us told off when we stayed shut in for too long. Just like in a "men's house" on some South Sea island — where the initiates gather and where, from mouth to mouth and from generation to generation, secrets and myths are passed on — in that room that served as our club-house, we endlessly worked on our mythology and never tired of trying to find answers to the various things that puzzled and obsessed us about sex. My brother was seated on the great throne, like a higher-ranking initiate, while I, the youngest, sat on an ordinary chamber-pot, which stood in for a neophyte's simple seat. The flushing mechanism and the hole were themselves mysterious things, and even quite dangerous (once it happened that while I was playing at running around the rim of the bowl pretending to be a circus horse, my foot slipped and got stuck in the hole, and my parents, summoned to the rescue, then had great difficulty getting it out again); had we been older and studied more, we would probably not have hesitated to see these elements as being in direct communication with the gods of the underworld.

Compared to the parlour — an Olympus that was closed to us on days when there were visitors — the lavatory seemed like a cavern, a cave that could be entered to seek inspiration by putting ourselves in touch with the most opaque and most subterranean powers. Here, in contrast to the right sacred of parental majesty, the ambiguous magic of a left sacred could take shape; here too we felt, in relation to everyone else, more cut off and marginalised, and yet, in the embryonic secret society we had formed as two brothers, we felt closest to each other and most in harmony. For us, in short, it was that eminently sacred thing that is the mark of any sort of pact — such as the bond of complicity that unites all the pupils in the same class against their teachers, a bond so firm and undeniable that, of all the moral imperatives that govern adult *consciences*, very few can be compared to the one according to which children forbid themselves to sneak on one another.

As far as outdoor places are concerned, I remember two that, with the benefit of hindsight and the knowledge I have since acquired, seem to have been permeated, for the pious child I was in all other respects, with a sacred character: the sort of bush country, or no-man's-land, that stretched between the old city fortifications and the racecourse at Auteuil, and also the track itself.

When our mother or our older sister took us for a walk, at times in the Bois de Boulogne or else in the public gardens adjoining the greenhouses of the city of Paris, it often happened that we would cross this ill-defined space (in contrast with the bourgeois world of houses, just as the village — for those belonging to so-called "savage" societies — can be contrasted with the bush, in other words the world of shadows, so well suited to all mythical adventures and strange encounters, that begins as soon as the precisely laid-out world of the village is left behind), this "zone" that in all likelihood was alive with cut-throats. So we were warned, if it should happen that we stopped there to play, to beware of strangers (in actual fact satyrs, I realise now) who might, under some false pretence or other, try to lead us off into the woods. It was a place apart, extremely taboo, an area strongly marked by the supernatural and the sacred, so different from the public gardens where everything was planned, organised and neatly raked over, and where the signs that told us not to walk on the grass, even though they too were symbols of taboos, could only endow it with a sacred that had grown very cold indeed!

The other outdoor place that fascinated one of my brothers and me was the racecourse at Auteuil. From a bridle-path that skirted part of the track, my brother and I could watch the jockeys — in their multicoloured silks on their horses with gleaming coats — as they jumped a hedge then climbed a grassy ridge beyond which they disappeared. We knew that it was here that people (the ones we could see gathered in the stands and who we could hear when they roared and shouted at the finish), on account of these riders in their dazzling finery, placed their bets and were ruined, like one of my father's former colleagues, who had once been a man with "horses and carriage", but had gambled away his entire fortune and now often tapped him for a hundred *sous* when they ran into each other at the stock exchange. It was the most marvellous of places, because of the spectacle that occurred there, and the large amounts of money that were won or lost; it was the most immoral of places, in so far as everything there depended on good luck or bad, and brought out my father's thunderous condemnation, since he was uneasy with the thought that when we were older we might become gamblers too.

One of our greatest joys was when the race was started near to the spot where we were standing. The starter, in his frock-coat and mounted on a horse that was muscled like a wrestler, a hefty beast beside the thoroughbreds that were taking part in the event; scraping at the ground like roosters or swaying like swans, the group of competing horses gathering for the start; then, after the always difficult task of getting them to line up, the sudden gallop of the pack and the noise of the horseshoes on the ground, the subtlest vibrations of which it seemed to us we could sense. Though I have never had much of a taste for sport, I have retained from this time an impression of wonder that makes me see any sporting spectacle as a sort of ritual display. The paraphernalia of the jockeys' saddles, the white ropes of boxing rings, and all the various preparations: the procession of the horses for each event, the presentation of opponents before the fight, the job of the starter or the referee; and all the things we picture going on behind the scenes, the rub-downs, massages and dopings, the special diets and meticulous planning. The protagonists seem to operate in a world apart, at once closer to the public and more isolated from it than, for example, actors on a stage. For here nothing is false: however important the stage performance, the sporting spectacle, with its theoretically unforeseeable outcome, is a real act and not a sham, all the eventualities of which duly unfold in accordance with what has been determined in advance. Because of this there is an infinitely greater participation and at the same time a much keener awareness of separation, since the individuals we are separated from here are not simple mannequins — approximate reflections of ourselves, yet with nothing essentially in common with us — but individuals like us, every bit as solid as we are, at least, and who could even be us.

During this whole time when we had a passion for the races, my brother and I often imagined that when we were older we would become jockeys — the way that so many boys from poorer neighbourhoods might dream of becoming racing cyclists or boxers. Just like the founders of religions, the great revolutionaries or conquerors, champions seemed to have a destiny, and their dizzying rise to success, for people who often came from the most deprived strata of society, was a sign of exceptional luck or magical power — a *mana* — which enabled them to jump right up the ladder and achieve a social standing that was, of course, somewhat marginal, but quite beyond anything ordinary people have any reasonable rights to expect, no matter what their status from birth. In certain respects, these figures remind us of shamans, who very often too started out as being simply deprived, but then took an astonishing revenge on destiny, owing to the fact that they, and they alone, to the exclusion of others, have certain connections with the spirits.

Doubtless my brother and I had a vague idea of this, when we pictured ourselves wearing our jockey silks like some sort of coat of arms or liturgical vestments, which would have distinguished us from others, whilst at the same time uniting us with them, in so far as we would have been focal points, supports for their collective effervescence, the points of convergence and repositories of their gaze, fixed on us like so many pins to attach their wonder to us. Better than father's top hat, revolver or purse, these thin silk tunics would have been the mark of our power, our *mana* that is the special reserve of people who leap every obstacle while clinging to the underside of their horses' bellies and expose themselves victoriously to all dangers when they land.

Alongside the objects, places and events that held such a special attraction for us (an attraction for everything that seemed cut off from the world we lived in, such as, for example, a brothel — with all its naked people and the musty smell of a bath-house — so far removed from the clothed world and fresh air of the street, even though it was only separated from it by a simple threshold, the taboo in concrete form imposed on this place of perdition), alongside these I discover circumstances, facts which are, so to speak, imponderable, that have given me the acute sense that there exists a separate realm, set to one side and quite different from anything else, being detached from the bulk of the profane with the same strange and dazzling crudeness as when, in a night-club with showgirls, the powdered and depilated bodies suddenly surge to within an inch of the tables and their sullen, sweating diners. I mean certain facts of language, words which themselves are open to several interpretations, or words misheard or misread that suddenly trigger a sort of vertigo when we realise they are not what we first thought they were. Such words often functioned, in my childhood, as keys, either because what they sounded like suggested various surprising lines of thought, or because, when I found out that up until that point I had always mangled them, then all of a sudden understood them fully, this somehow seemed like a revelation, like a veil being abruptly torn asunder or the detonation of a certain truth.

Some of these words, or expressions, are connected to places, circumstances or images which by their very nature explain the emotive power with which they were charged. For example, "The Empty House", the name my brothers and I gave to a pile of rocks, grouped together like a sort of natural dolmen, in the vicinity of Nemours, not far from the house where our parents, several years running, took us for our summer holidays. "The empty house": it sounds like how our voices sounded beneath the granite vault; it evokes the idea of the deserted home of some giant, or a temple of impressive proportions hewn from a single rock and left in a state of considerable ruin.

Likewise, a word that belongs strictly to the sacred is a proper noun such as the name Rebecca, learned in Religious Education, and for me evoking a typically biblical image: a woman with bronzed face and arms, in a long tunic with a full veil over her head, with a pitcher on her shoulder and her elbow resting on the well's edge. In this instance, the name itself worked in a specific way, making me think, on the one hand, of something sweet and full of flavour, like raisins or muscat grapes; on the other hand, something hard and unyielding, from the initial "R" and especially the "...cca", something of which I still find today in words such as "Mecca" or "impeccable".

Finally, another vocable was at one time for me endowed with the magical properties of a password or an abracadabra: the exclamation "Baoukta!", invented by my eldest brother as a war-cry for when we were playing Cowboys and Indians and he took the part of the brave and valiant chief. What struck me here, as with the name Rebecca, was in particular the word's exotic appeal, the strangeness it embodied; a word like this could have belonged to the Martian language or the language of demons, or again even been wrested from a special vocabulary, laden with hidden meaning, whose secret was known only to my eldest brother, the high priest.

Apart from these words which — if I can put it this way — spoke to me by themselves, there were other aspects of language that imparted the vague sense of that kind of displacement or deviation which still signifies for me the passage from a general state to a more privileged, crystalline and remarkable state, the gradual shift from a profane state to a sacred state. It is, in fact, a question of very tiny disclosures: corrections of hearing or reading which, by bringing two variants of the same word together, cause a special disorder to emerge from this divergence. It could be said that language has become twisted here and that in the tiny gap that separates the two words — both of which having become filled with strangeness at the moment, now, when I compared them to each other (as if each one was only the other in a mangled or twisted form) — a breach opened up sufficient to let in a world of revelations.

I remember that one day, when playing with my lead soldiers, I dropped one of them, picked it up and, seeing that it wasn't broken, exclaimed: "… *Reusement*!"[1] Whereupon someone who was there, my mother, sister or eldest brother, pointed out that it's not pronounced "*reusement*" but "*heureusement*", which seemed to me to be an astounding discovery. In the same way, from the moment I learned that the name *Moïse* [Moses] was not pronounced "*Moisse*", as I had always thought when, still only being able to read very badly, I was learning Religious Education, these two words took on a peculiarly disturbing resonance for me: "*Moïse*", "*Moisse*", the very image of his cradle, perhaps because of the word "osier" (which the first word resembles), or just because I had already heard, but without noticing it, certain cradles being called "*moïses*". Later, when learning the names of the French *départements*, I could never read the name Seine-et-Oise without a twinge of emotion, because that earlier reading error of a name in the Bible had for ever, in my mind, attached a certain special value to all the words that more or less resembled "*Moïse*" or "*Moisse*".

In a manner analogous to the way in which the word "*reusement*" was contrasted for me with its corrected form "*heureusement*", my brothers and I would make the distinction, in the area of countryside where we went on holiday with our parents, between the *sablonnière* [sand-pit] and the *sablière* [sand quarry], two sandy places that hardly differed from each other apart from the hugely greater size of the second. Later on, we enjoyed a pleasure similar to what could be gained from our so-called "Byzantine" discussions, by giving names to the two different types of paper aeroplanes we used to make, with one being the rectilinear kind and the other the curvilinear. In doing this we were acting as ritualists, for whom the sacred is ultimately resolved into a subtle system of fine distinctions, minutiae and points of etiquette.

If I compare these various things — the top hat, signifying my father's authority; the Smith and Wesson, signifying his courage and strength; the purse, signifying the wealth I attributed to him by way of the fact that he was the bread-winner for the household; the stove, that could burn you even though, in principle, it was the protective spirit of the hearth; my parents' bedroom, which was the epitome of the night; the toilet, in the secrecy of which we swapped our mythological stories and theories on various things to do with sex; the dangerous area, that extended out beyond the fortifications; the racecourse, where enormous sums of money were staked on the luck or skill of characters in special outfits with their marvellous gestures; the windows opened, by certain elements of language, on to a world where a person could easily lose their footing — if I gather together all these things taken from what was, for the time when I was a child, my everyday life, then bit by bit I can see an image taking shape of what, for me, is the sacred.

Something marvellous, like the different attributes of my father or the great house made of rocks. Something strange, like the clothes the jockeys wore for the race, or certain exotic-sounding words. Something dangerous, like the red-hot coals or the scrubland of bush and thickets scattered with prowlers. Something ambiguous, like the coughing fits that bring on rending pains but also transform the sufferer into a tragic hero. Something forbidden, like the parlour where the adults perform their rituals. Something secret, like the conventicles held amidst the stench of the lavatory. Something dizzying, like the leaps of galloping horses or the false-bottomed boxes of language. Something that, when all is said and done, I can scarcely conceive of otherwise unless it is marked, in some way or another, by the supernatural.

If one of the most "sacred" aims a man can set himself is to acquire as precise and intense an understanding of himself as is possible, then it seems desirable that each of us, by scrutinising our memories with the greatest possible honesty, should examine whether we can discover some sign amongst them that might enable us to discern for our part which *colour* holds the very notion of sacred.

GEORGES BATAILLE

# 61 *The Sorcerer's Apprentice*

This text is not exactly a sociological study as such, but rather it sets out to define a point of view so that sociological results may be obtained in response to more virile concerns than those which typically inform the specialised approach employed in science. In fact, it is difficult for sociology to avoid the criticisms applied to pure science, specifically that it is a phenomenon of dissociation. If the social fact alone is considered to represent the totality of existence, and if science is an activity that tends to fragment, then a science that contemplates the social fact is unable to achieve its objectives, since the action of attaining them would require the negation of its own principles. Sociological science must therefore operate under conditions different from those which prevail in scientific disciplines devoted to the study of dissociated aspects of nature. Its development, particularly in France, seems to have been directed by those who have in mind the coincidence of social and religious facts. Nevertheless, the results obtained by French sociology risk coming to naught if the question of *totality* is not posed in all its magnitude. [GB]

## I. ABSENCE OF NEED MORE REGRETTABLE THAN ABSENCE OF SATISFACTION

A man is burdened with a great many needs which must be satisfied so that he may avoid distress. At the same time he may be afflicted by some complaint and yet be unaware of any suffering. Misfortune may deprive him of the means of satisfying his needs, but he is no less affected when it is an elementary need itself that is denied him. The loss of virility generally entails neither suffering nor distress — it is not in this case his loss of satisfaction that diminishes such a man — yet even so, it is a deficiency widely dreaded as a calamity.

There is therefore an initial level of suffering, although not felt by those who are affected; it is painful only for those who must face the threat of some future mutilation.

Consumption, which destroys the lungs without causing suffering, is undeniably one of the most pernicious diseases;[1] the same may be said for all ailments that make their attacks surreptitiously so that there is no possibility of a person knowing they are affected. Perhaps the worst of all the ills afflicting mankind is the reduction of its existence to the condition of a servile organ. It is not generally acknowledged that becoming a politician, a writer or a scientist is akin to an act of despair, and that so doing also makes it impossible to remedy the inadequacy which is felt by those who have renounced any aim of becoming a whole man in order to become nothing more than a function[2] of human society.

## II. MAN DEPRIVED OF THE NEED TO BE MAN

The harm would be less widely felt if it affected only a limited number of unfortunate sufferers. The one who mistakes the fame of his literary works for the fulfilment of his destiny may thus delude himself without human life as a whole being dragged into a general decline. But outside of science, politics and art nothing is deemed to exist, and these moreover only in isolation, each for itself, like so many servants of a dead master.

With most activity subordinated to useful production, and with any substantial change seen as an impossibility, man is all too inclined to regard the slavery of work as a boundary he must not overstep. Nevertheless, the absurdity of such an empty existence obliges the slave to accomplish his production by means of a response which is faithful to what art, or politics or science asks him to be and to believe: and so he finds there everything he considers worthwhile in terms of human destiny. The 'great men' who practise in these areas thereby define a limit for everyone else, and even though they are half dead there is no hint of a wake-up call attached to this suffering, merely a slight sense of depression (which is almost agreeable if it is coexistent with the memory of tensions that in the end proved to be disappointing).

Man is free to love nothing, because the causeless and aimless universe that gave him life has not necessarily granted him an acceptable destiny. But the man who fears human destiny, who cannot tolerate its interlocking system of greed, crime and misery, cannot be virile either. If he turns away from himself, there is no justification for his endless, tiresome complaining. His existence is endurable only on condition that he forgets what it really consists of. Artists, politicians and scientists have been charged with lying to him; those who most dominate existence are almost always the ones who lie best to themselves, and consequently the ones who lie best to others. Under these conditions, virility declines, as too does our love for human destiny. All exercises in subterfuge are welcomed in order to distance us from the heroic and fascinating image our fate presents: in a world where the need to be a man does not apply, it is only the useful man who may exhibit his unappealing face.

But although this absence of need is the worst possible outcome, it is perceived as a blessing. Its harmfulness only becomes apparent if the persistence of his "*amor fati*" makes a man a stranger to the present world.

## III. THE MAN OF SCIENCE

The "man deprived by fear of the need to be a man" is the one who has put his greatest hopes in science. He has renounced the *totality* his actions possessed at the time when he aspired to live out his destiny. For scientific acts must be autonomous, and scientists exclude from their work any human interest besides the desire for knowledge. A man who shoulders the burden of science has exchanged an involvement with human destiny for one concerned only with discovering truth. He moves from the totality to the part, and serving this part requires that the rest counts for nothing. Science is a function that developed only after it took the place of the destiny it should have *served*. As long as it was a servant it lacked all power.

Paradoxically then, here is a function which could only be fulfilled by presuming to become an end in itself.

The body of knowledge that man has it his disposal is all the consequence of similar deceptions, and while it is true that the human realm has been enhanced, it has been for the benefit of an invalid existence.*

*It does not follow that science must be rejected... Only its *moral* depredations are criticised here, but it is not impossible to dispute them, and so far as sociology is concerned, the principle of knowledge even makes such a contravention a necessity. (cf. prefatory note, p.290)

## IV. THE MAN OF FICTION

The function assumed by art is more equivocal. It seems that the writer or artist does not always have to accept the renunciation of existence, and what they relinquish is more difficult to pinpoint than in the case of scientists. Compared with scientific laws, what art and literature express is less like a headless chicken running about; instead, the disturbing figures they concoct, so contrary to a methodically represented reality, only appear after having been tricked out in all their shocking seductiveness. What do they signify, these painted or written phantoms, which have been raised up in order to make the world in which we have awakened slightly less unworthy of being haunted by our idle existences? In the imagination, all images are *false*. False with a lie that no longer knows either hesitation or shame. The two essential elements of life thus find themselves strictly separated; truth as pursued by science is only true when emptied of meaning, and nothing possesses meaning unless it be fiction.

The servants of science have excluded human destiny from the realm of truth, while those who serve art have given up on fashioning a true world out of what an anxious destiny compels them to produce. But for all that, it is not easy to escape the necessity of attaining a real, rather than a fictive life. These servants of art can accept a fugitive and shadowy existence for the beings they create, but they themselves are obliged as living beings to enter the realm of truth, money, fame and social position. As a result it is impossible for them to live a life that is anything but lame. They frequently believe themselves possessed by what they imagine, but what has no true existence can possess nothing: they are only really possessed by their careers. In place of the gods, who could possess him from outside, Romanticism has substituted the miserable destiny of the poet, but he is left no less lame as a result. Romanticism has only made it possible for misery to become a new sort of career, and makes the lies of those it did not kill all the more excruciating.

## V. FICTION IN SERVICE TO ACTION

The hypocrisy associated with a career, and, more generally, with the *ego* of the artist or writer, prompts him to engage his creations in the service of some more solid reality. If it is true that art and literature do not constitute a world that is sufficient in and of itself, then they can at least be made a subject of the real world by contributing to the glory of Church or State, or, if this is a world divided by factions, to religious or political action and propaganda. In such a case, however, they amount to no more than a service or an adornment to something else. Were the institutions thus served themselves troubled by the contradictory flows of destiny, art might encounter the possibility of serving and expressing a more profound existence. However, when it is a question of organisations whose interests are linked to circumstance, to particular communities, then art introduces a confusion between profound existence and partisan action which sometimes shocks even the partisans.

Most often, human destiny can only be lived through fiction. Even so, the man of fiction suffers from not fulfilling in himself the destiny he describes; he suffers because he escapes fiction only to find himself bound by his career. Hence he attempts to bring the phantoms that haunt him into the real world. As soon as they belong to the world made real through action, however, or when the author links them to some particular truth, they lose their privileged quality of representing human existence as a whole: they are no longer anything but tedious reflections of a fragmented world.

## VI. THE MAN OF ACTION

If the truth revealed by science is stripped of human meaning, and if the *fictions* of the mind alone correspond to man's will in all its strangeness, then these fictions must be *made true* in order for this will to be fully realised. He who is possessed by a need to create is only feeling the need to be a man, but he forsakes this need if he forsakes the creation of anything apart from fantasies and lies. He remains virile only while seeking to make reality conform to what he thinks; all his strength urges him to subject to the vagaries of his dreams the disappointing world in which he finds himself.

However, this necessity most often appears only in an obscure form. It seems futile to be content with simply reflecting reality in the way science does, and equally futile to seek to escape it by means of fiction. Action alone proposes to transform the world, in other words, to make it resemble the dream. "Act": this word resounds in our ears like the trumpet-blasts before the walls of Jericho. No other imperative is more harshly effective, and the necessity to move to action is immediately and unconditionally imposed on whoever hears it. Yet if he expects his will to be realised quickly by his actions, he soon meets with unforeseen consequences. The novice discovers that the will whose action proves most effective is the will that limits itself to only dismal dreams. He accepts this, then gradually comes to understand that the only thing he has gained from action is the benefit of having acted. He believed he could transform the world in accordance with his dreams, but all he achieved was to transform his dreams in line with the most impoverished reality: all he can do is stifle his own will — *in order to be able TO ACT.*

## VII. POWERLESS TO CHANGE THE WORLD, ACTION IS CHANGED BY IT

The first renunciation that action requires of he who wishes to act is that he reduce his dream to the proportions dictated by science. Any concern with providing a field of action for human destiny outside of fiction is scorned by political theorists. Such a concern cannot be ruled out in the case of actions undertaken by extreme parties who expect their militants to put their lives at stake, but a man's destiny does not become real simply because he fights. It is also necessary for this destiny to merge with that of the forces within whose ranks he faces death. Yet the theoreticians, having this destiny at their disposal, reduce it to equal well-being for all. The language of action accepts only one formula as being in conformity with the rational principles that govern science, and this ensures it remains detached from human life. No one imagines that a political act can be defined and personified like those of the heroes of legend. For the theorists, only the fair division of material and cultural goods can assuage their fixation with avoiding anything resembling the human face and its expressions of either avid desire or joyful defiance in the face of death. They are fully convinced of how objectionable it would be to address the struggling masses as if they were a crowd of already dying heroes. Consequently they speak only using the language of self-interest to those who are, one way or another, even now streaming with the blood of their own wounds.

Men of action follow or serve *that which exists*. If their action is a revolt, they are still following *that which exists* when they get killed in the attempt to destroy it. Such individuals become possessed by human destiny during the act of destruction, but it is lost to them as soon as they are left with nothing but the will to order their faceless world. Scarcely has the destruction been accomplished than they find themselves, along with any who follow them, at the mercy of what they have destroyed, and which then begins to reconstruct itself. Dreams that science and reason have reduced to empty formulas, these amorphous dreams, cease to be anything more than the dust stirred up by ACTION as it passes by. Thus enslaved, and at the same time destroying everything that does not yield to a necessity to which they themselves submit before all others, men of action blindly abandon themselves to the current that sweeps them along and which is only hastened further by their futile agitation.

## VIII. DISSOCIATED EXISTENCE

Existence, when thus broken up into three parts, has ceased to be *existence*; it is only art or science or politics. Where once it was a primitive simplicity that made men dominant, now there are only scientists, politicians and artists, who have all subscribed to the same condition: they have renounced their existence in exchange for a function. Some scientists have artistic or political concerns, and certain politicians and artists are not entirely restricted to their own realms of interest, but three infirmities added together do not constitute a fully viable man. Such an assortment of abilities and areas of expertise has little to do with a totality of existence — which could no more be cut into independent parts than could a living body. Life is the virile unity of the elements of which it is composed. It has the simplicity of an axe-blow.

## IX. FULL EXISTENCE AND THE IMAGE OF THE BELOVED

Simple, solid existence, not yet destroyed by servility to function, is possible only to the extent that it ceases to be subordinated to some particular project, such as action, depiction or measurement: it depends on the *image of destiny*, and feels silently in accord with this seductive and dangerous myth. A human being becomes dissociated when *he devotes himself* to some useful work that is meaningless in itself: he cannot then discover the whole and seductive fullness of total existence. Virility is nothing less than the expression of this principle: that when a man no longer has the power to respond to an image of desirable nudity, he recognises his loss of virile integrity. And just as virility is linked to the attraction of a naked body, full existence is linked with any image which arouses hope and dread. In this world of dissolution, the BELOVED has become the only power that has retained the ability to return us to the warmth of life. If this world were not being endlessly criss-crossed by the convulsive movements of individuals in search of one another, were it not transfigured by the face 'whose absence brings pain', it would appear a joke to those who have been born here: human existence would resemble only a memory, or a documentary film about 'primitive' countries. We must dismiss fiction with a gesture of irritation. What remains in our innermost being as regards loss, tragedy and that 'blinding marvel', can only now be found in bed. It is true that the dust of complacency and the cares of the dissociated intrude upon bedrooms just as they do everywhere else; yet there are still bedrooms that are locked, and in the almost limitless void of the mind they are so many islands where images of life may be recomposed.

## X. ILLUSORY CHARACTER OF THE BELOVED

At first, the image of the beloved appears with an unstable brilliance. It illuminates and at the same time arouses fear in whoever holds it in view. If a man is primarily absorbed with his own function he puts the image from his mind and smiles at his childish excitement. A man who has become 'serious' believes that existence can be easily found anywhere else than in the response such an appeal requires of him. Yet even if some other, less plodding man should allow himself to be burned by this fearful seduction, he must nevertheless acknowledge that the image is only illusory.

Because living, on its own, is enough to oppose it. Eating, sleeping and speaking empty it of meaning. When a man meets a woman and it becomes evident to him that this is his destiny, what then seizes hold of him like some silent tragedy is incompatible with this woman's necessary daily activities. The image of the beloved in which destiny has, for a moment, been brought to life, has been projected into a world in which this daily disruption can play no part. The woman a man is drawn to as if towards the very incarnation of his human destiny does not belong to this realm where money exerts influence. Her sweetness eludes the real world she passes through, for she can be no more confined than a dream. Misfortune would ravage the spirit of anyone who let himself be possessed by the need to capture her. Her reality is as vacillating as a flickering light, but the dark inflames it.

However, the first uncertain appearance of these two lovers who join together on their night of destiny is not of the same order as the illusions seen in the theatre or in books. Theatre and literature cannot by themselves create *a world where beings find each other*. Even the most lacerating visions presented by art have never done more than create a fleeting link between those they have touched. If lovers meet in such a setting they must content themselves with expressing what they have felt in sentences, substituting comparison and analysis for communicable reactions. Real lovers, on the other hand, find common understanding even in the most profound silence, their every movement charged with a burning passion that has the power to bring ecstasy. It would be pointless to deny that the furnace thus lit constitutes a real world, the world in which lovers find one another as they had first appeared, when each assumed the thrilling form of the other's destiny. So it is that the tempestuous currents of love make true what at first was only an illusion.

The obstacle encountered by actions that are fragmentary and detached from others — actions that are oblivious to dream — is thus surmounted when two people unite their bodies in love. Shadows pursued to the point of embrace are every bit as marvellous as the far-flung creatures of legend. The sudden appearance of a woman belongs almost to the tumultuous world of dreams, but possession plunges this dream-figure, naked and drowning in pleasure, into the narrowly real world of the bed-chamber.

The happy act is 'sister to the dream' in the very bed where the secret of life is revealed to knowledge. And knowledge is the ecstatic discovery of human destiny in this protected space where science, just as much as art or practical action, has lost any possibility of offering even a fragmentary meaning to existence.*

*This description of the 'world of lovers' has, however, only a *demonstrative* value. It is a world that signifies one of the rare possibilities offered by daily life, and its realisation presents something far less distanced from the totality of existence than is the case with the worlds of art, politics or science. Even so, it does not complete human life. At the same time it would be erroneous to consider it as the prototypical form of society. The idea that the couple is the basic social unit has had to be abandoned and for reasons that would appear to be conclusive.

## XII. AGGREGATIONS OF CHANCE

Renouncing the dream, and the practical will of the man of action, are not the only ways to touch the real world. The world of lovers is no less *true* than the world of politics. The totality of existence is even absorbed by it, which politics is unable to do. Its essential qualities are not those of the fragmentary, empty world of practical action but those relating to *human life* before it has been reduced to servility: the world of lovers, like life itself, is constructed upon the *aggregation of chance events which provide the response anticipated by an avid and powerful will to be.*

What determines how the beloved is selected — so that even the logical acknowledgement that another choice might be possible fills one with horror — can in fact be reduced to *a series of chance events*. Simple coincidences arrange the encounter and mould the female figure of destiny so that a man feels bound to it, sometimes to the point of death. The value of this figure depends on long-standing and obsessive expectations which are so difficult to satisfy that they paint the beloved with the colours of the greatest good fortune. The fate of the stakes in a card-game is decided by a particular configuration of the cards; an unexpected encounter can rearrange existence in the same way as an unusually lucky hand. However, even the perfect hand is worthless unless it appears at a point in the game where it can be used to take possession of the pot. The winning hand is only an arbitrary combination; the desire to win, and winning itself, is what makes it real. Only *consequences* grant truth to a configuration of lucky circumstances that would otherwise be meaningless had they not been chosen according to some human caprice. The encounter with a woman would elicit no more than an aesthetically pleasing emotion devoid of the desire or will to possess her, or to make true what her appearance seemed to signify. Once won, or lost, the fugitive image of destiny ceases to be a random figure and instead enters into reality, that impediment to fate.

Truth is thus conditional upon there being an "avid and powerful will to be", but an *isolated individual* can never have the power to create a world (he makes the attempt only if he himself is in the grip of forces that *alienate* him, that make him mad); a coincidence of wills is just as necessary for the birth of human worlds as coincidences of chance. Only the agreement between lovers, like that between players at a gaming table, creates the living reality of what remain somewhat formless correspondences (if the agreement is missing then unhappiness, in which love nevertheless remains real, is the inevitable consequence of a first act of complicity). The accord between two, or many, adds to the general belief that validates the images and configurations I described earlier. The meaning of love is determined in legends that illustrate the fate of lovers in the minds of everyone.

This "avid will to be", precisely because it is *communal*, is not at all similar though to the will that contemplates or intervenes. It is a will that resembles a blind recklessness in the face of death and entrusts itself for the most part, like a man caught in a deadly shoot-out, to *chance*. Only a *random* act is capable of producing the response an undeclared passion hopes to obtain from the fortuitous appearance of 'aggregations'. An outstanding card-game counts for nothing if the cards were not shuffled and cut; had they been pre-arranged in a set order that would amount to *cheating*. The player's decisions too must be based on *chance*, and must be made in ignorance of the cards his partners are holding. The secret power possessed by *those who are loved* and the value that results when they join together must no longer follow from decisions or intentions that have been fixed in advance. It is true that, while disregarding the institutions of marriage and prostitution, the world of lovers is even more given to cheating than that of gambling. Between the ingenuous encounters of individuals incapable of ulterior motives, and the shameless flirtations of those relentlessly set on schemes and cheating, there are no precise boundaries, only a great number of nuanced degrees. Only the unselfconscious and the guileless have the power to conquer the miraculous world in which lovers find themselves.

Luck and chance — together competing for life against teleological determination and subjection to the rule of means and ends — thus win the conflict and, with divine ardour, appear to carry off the prize. Intelligent thought long ago ceased to imagine the universe as being in the power of some prescient reason; existence, when it measures itself against the starry sky or against death, recognises that it is at the mercy of chance. It recognises itself in all its magnificence, made in the image of a universe unsullied by the defilements of merit or intention.

## XIII. DESTINY AND MYTH

It is impossible to contemplate, without falling into considerable anguish, how the mass of people tend to recoil from the 'abominable' realm of chance, the same mass, in fact, who require that an *assured* life should depend only on calculation and appropriate decision-making. The life "that measures itself only against death" eludes those who have lost the taste for burning in "flames of hope and dread", in the way that lovers and gamblers do. Human destiny requires that capricious chance be in charge: reason would substitute for luck's luxuriant foliage, and in place of a great adventure to be lived, only a correct, but empty solution to the difficulties of existence. Actions undertaken with some rational end in mind are nothing more than slavish and submissive responses to necessity. Only actions undertaken in pursuit of chance's seductive images respond to the need to live like a flame. It is human to be on fire in this way, to be consumed to the point of suicide at the baccarat table, and although cards may well be only the tokens of an impoverished version of good or bad luck, what they depict, and what winning or losing money depends on, at least has the virtue of signifying destiny (the queen of spades sometimes signifies death). It is not human, on the other hand, to abandon existence in favour of a chain of useful acts, even though some part of our human abilities must inevitably be devoted to avoiding various sufferings, such as hunger, cold and social constraints. Life, the life which escapes servitude, gambles itself; in other words, it stakes itself on the luck it encounters.

*Life gambles itself*: destiny's project is realised. What was only a figure in a dream becomes myth. And a *living* myth, of the sort dusty intellects consider to be *dead*, or an amusing error based on simple ignorance; the myth-lie represents destiny and becomes *being*. Not the being that rational philosophy betrays by defining it as immutable, but the being who is described by both a fore- and a surname; then the double being, abandoned in its endless embraces; and finally, the collective being that "tortures, decapitates and goes to war".

The person who is incapable of being satisfied by art, science or politics still has *myth* at his disposal. Whilst love constitutes a world in itself, it leaves intact everything that is outside it. The experience of love even enhances the awareness of pain: it intensifies the unease and powerful sense of emptiness that result from contact with a society in disintegration. To one who has been broken by every such trial, myth alone returns the full and abundant image that may be extended to the community in which men gather together. Myth alone enters the bodies of those it binds together and asks of them the same expectation. It is the quickening of every dance; it brings existence 'to its boiling point'; it communicates the tragic emotion that makes its sacred intimacy accessible. For myth is not only the divine figure of destiny and the world in which this figure moves: it cannot be separated from the community to which it belongs and which ritually takes possession of its kingdom. It would be fiction if the *accord* a *people* manifests in the agitation of a festival were not thereby made the vital human reality. Myth is fable too perhaps, but this fable is situated in opposition to fiction, as can be seen by the people who dance it, act it, and for whom it is a living *truth*. A community that does not consummate the ritual possession of its myths only possesses a truth that is in decline: it is living to the extent that its will to be animates the mythical chances that represent its inner existence. A myth cannot then be compared to the scattered fragments of some whole that has broken apart. It is dependent on a *total* existence, and is its tangible expression.

Myth ritually lived reveals true being, no less: here life appears no less terrifying, and no less beautiful, than the *beloved woman* lying naked on the bed. The half-light of the sacred place that contains the real presence is more oppressive than the light in the room that encloses the lovers; what is offered to knowledge in the sacred place is just as removed from the science of laboratories as what takes place in the bedroom. Human existence when it is brought to the sacred place encounters the figure of destiny fixed by the whim of *chance*: the *determining laws* defined by science are the opposite of this game of fantasy that is life. This game turns away from science and intersects with the delirium that engenders images in art, but whereas art acknowledges the final reality and the superior character of the real world that constrains man, myth enters into human existence with a force that obliges *inferior* reality to submit to its rule.

## XIV. THE SORCERER'S APPRENTICE

It is true that returning to this old dwelling-place of mankind's is perhaps the most anxious moment in a life devoted to a succession of deceptive illusions. Even when approached by this unlikely route, the old dwelling-place of myth seems just as deserted as 'picturesque' temple ruins, because this idea of myth as an expression of the totality of existence is not based upon present-day experience. Only the past, or the civilisations of 'backward peoples', has made possible the knowledge, if not the possession, of a world that seems nowadays inaccessible. It might be that a total existence is now no more than a simple dream for us, nourished by historical descriptions and the secret urging of our passions. Human beings today may only be able to make themselves masters of the scrapheap of the ruins of existence. This acknowledged truth, however, seems immediately to be at the mercy of the lucidity that is invoked by the need to live. At the very least, a first experience will need to have resulted in failure before the denier of this 'truth' earns himself the right to *sleep* his denial guarantees. A methodical description of the experience to be attempted shows, moreover, that all it requires is realistic conditions. The 'sorcerer's apprentice', first of all, does not encounter demands which differ in any respect from those found on the difficult path of art. The inflexible figures of myth are not excluded from determined intention any more than the inconsequential figures of fiction; the requirements of mythological invention are simply more rigorous. They do not, as a rudimentary notion would have it, reflect some obscure faculties of collective invention; but they would decline to recognise any value in figures in which the part that is intentional had not been set aside with the rigour peculiar to the sense of the *sacred*. From start to finish, in fact, the 'sorcerer's apprentice' must become completely familiarised with this rigour (supposing that it does not correspond to his own most intimate imperative). Secrecy is no less essential, in this domain he is moving into, than it is to the transports of eroticism (the total world of myth, the world of *being*, is separated from the *dissociated* world by the same boundaries that separate the *sacred* from the *profane*). A 'secret society' is indeed the name of the social reality these initiatives create. However, this romantic expression should not be understood, as it usually is, in the vulgar sense of a "conspiracy society". For the secret relates to the seductive reality which constitutes existence, not some act that is contrary to the security of the State. Myth is born in ritual acts hidden from the static vulgarity of a disintegrated society, but the violent dynamic associated with it has no other object than the return to a lost totality: even though it is true that its repercussions are decisive and transform the face of the world (whereas party political action gets lost in the quicksand of contradictory words), its political repercussions cannot be other than the result of existence. The vagueness of such projects is only an expression of how disconcertingly new the direction is that is necessary at the paradoxical moment of despair.

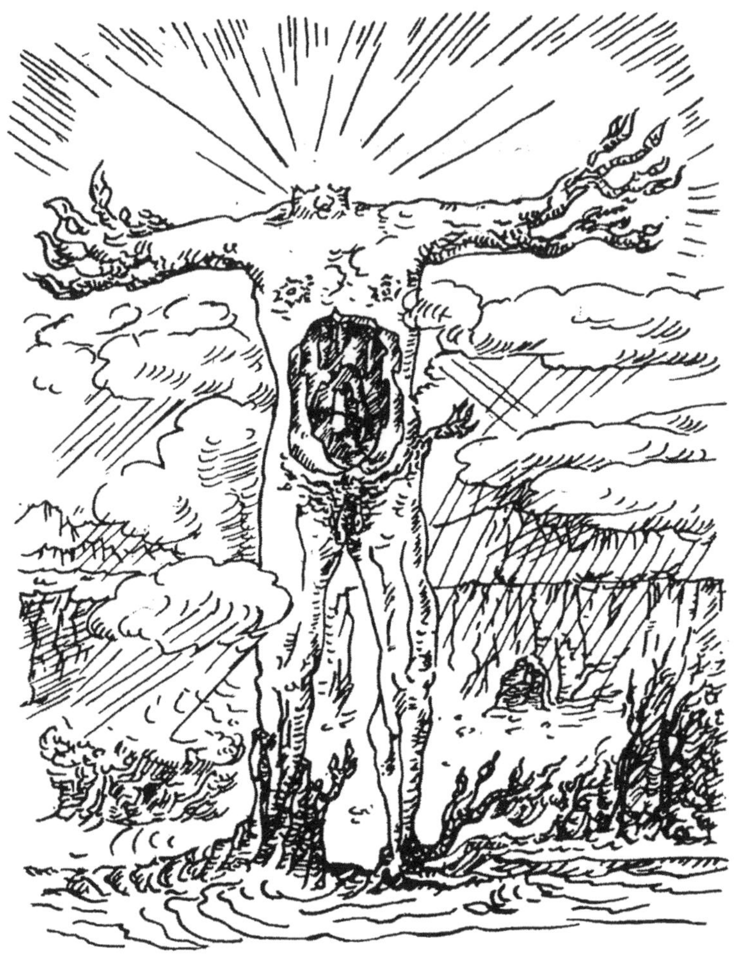

Drawing by André Masson found among
Laure's papers after her death.

THE SACRED CONSPIRACY

# VI

September 1938 – October 1938

# CHRONOLOGY

## 1938

**9 September.** Bataille and Ambrosino summon Chavy to an interview on the following day at 6.15 pm at the Café Le Firmament, on rue du Quatre-Septembre (a first interview had likely occurred at the Café Le Bouquet de Grenelle, Avenue de la Motte-Picquet). The topic is the same questionnaire given to Andler on 16 August, ●57.[1]

**17 September.** Chavy is summoned to the Café Le Firmament at 2.30 pm for a further interview.[2]

**18 September.** Daladier agrees to join Chamberlain in the appeasement policy over the threatened German annexation of German-speaking parts of Czechoslovakia, the so-called "Sudetenland", events which are reflected on in ●62.

**19 September.** The second stage of Waldberg's adeption takes place at 9 pm, at 39 rue Dauphine.

**24 September.** Ambrosino and Bataille arrange another interview with Andler, at the Café Le Firmament, at 2.30 pm.

**25 September.** Bataille sends Rollin two texts, one of which is "Twenty Propositions on the Death of God", a version of ●65. Andler's undated and unpublished text, "Propositions on the Death of God", is a response to Bataille's text that was circulated within the Society.

**28 September.** Waldberg's induction ceremony takes place at night in the forest of Marly, as described in ●68. The procedure for it by Bataille, ●67, is preceded by two texts: "Degrees", which outlines three stages of initiation with the secret names of *larva*, *mute* and *prodigal*; and Nietzsche's "Hard school", both in ●66.

**29 September.** A general meeting of Acéphale is held at 39 rue Dauphine, ●69. The question of the Society's position with regard to the war is discussed, and how it differed from that of the Surrealists.

Chamberlain, Daladier, Hitler and Mussolini sign the Munich Agreement, the treaty which permitted Nazi Germany's annexation of the Sudetenland. Opinion polls in France show the population overwhelmingly in favour of the settlement, while a Catholic demonstration in Vienna ends with the crowd chanting "Jesus is our Führer!" The Second World War is declared less than a year later.

**October.** Probable date of a letter from Laure to Bataille concerning a long-term affair he has been conducting with a woman (probably Dora Maar or Isabelle Farner) who had been involved with the meetings in the forest, which Laure has always avoided: "I know *everything* that you have been doing for more than a year, *everything*, before and after Sicily, everything that crystallised around someone who was the image of your dream, a shattering dream that can shatter everything, a dream that escapes all the everyday banalities [...]: a well-organised adultery, planned, careful and clever, and it burned because secret [...] Never, do you understand, will she be able to touch what we share between *us*. [...] I would come and help you organise these trysts. I will remain perfectly calm and happy, I will show you."[3]

**2 (or 11) October.** Andler requests an interview with Ambrosino and Kelemen.

**7 October.** Drafting of the "Declaration on the International Crisis", ○75, a text by the College which attacks the resigned attitude of the Western democracies to the Munich Agreement. Signed by Bataille, Caillois and Leiris, it appears in the *NRF* on 1 November. Bataille returns to the Czech crisis in his lecture "The Structure of the Democracies and the Crisis of September 1938", given to the College on 13 December.

Patrick Waldberg and Robert Folio* (Saint-Paul), *c.*1933.

**8 to 20 October.** Bataille addresses a "Note", ●71, to Ambrosino, Andler, Chavy, Chenon, Dussat, Kelemen and Waldberg which describes a critical moment within Acéphale. In order to combat the apathy he sees affecting the secret society, Bataille proposes that the members accept the concept of the "disagreeable". The debate within the Society on this point can be traced through texts by Andler and Dussat not included here but which are summarised in the *Commentary*.

**10 October.** Bataille's text to the members of Acéphale, "Instructions Concerning the Encounter of 10 October 1938", ●72, about what was probably Koch's first outing to the forest after he had signed the oath of silence in the Place de la Concorde. According to his memory of it, the light was "neither that of summer nor winter".

# COMMENTARIES

## ACÉPHALE [MG]

Acéphale's activities continued unabated, and the texts in this section very much follow on from those in the previous one. The idea of "a single sessional meeting, a long one, covering the period from July to September", as mentioned at the meeting of 25 July, ●51, was, however, abandoned. The need to go beyond the phase of a "still embryonic cohesion" meant activities had to be brought forward to the end of July so as to put the Society on a new, more urgent footing. Even so, there are very few texts by adepts from this time (only Andler), whereas the meetings, both individual (two interviews, likewise with Andler, one on 24 September, and the other requested by him on 2, or 11, October) and collective, followed in quick succession so that it appears it was in this autumn of 1938 that the community's "being for itself" attained its high point. This strengthening of communal unity though seems only to have emphasised its shortcomings. According to Bataille in his "Note" of 8 October, ●71, the group was being undermined from within by "inertia and complacency", but also by the persistent attraction of aestheticism, a danger Andler warned against in his "Certain lapses of taste...", ●74, while asserting the Society's adherence to the world of Heraclitus and Nietzsche. This text recalls Kierkegaard's "stages" (see p.153), which an earlier piece by Dussat, dated 25 March but not included here, had proposed to reformulate in order to situate Acéphale "beyond the Christian". In this text "Moving within Ethics", Dussat suggested this should be accomplished with "weapon in hand" by discounting sin in favour of using up existence "in fire and consuming", so that the individual may "assert his right to commit crimes."[1]

In September and October 1938, it was political events that exerted the greatest influence on the texts of this religious organisation and which contributed to the "arming of the figure" of the Acéphale. These texts begin with Andler's "The War", ●62, written on 18 September, three days after the start of the crisis which led to Hitler taking over Czechoslovakia. Andler develops the position of Acéphale in the expectation that conflict will break out in a world divided into two camps, a position which implies that adepts, who "have assumed the task of murderous sons giving a new face to the world", should have no illusions with regard to the democratic regimes. These are unable to oppose "doctrines of miserable aggression or class rationalisation", since they "have already, in times of war, embraced a militarised existence". He stresses, however, that the adepts should not avoid taking part in the war, since that is preferable to the "false inversion of all the values that has been introduced by doctrines of enslavement for social and national ends". This topic is also addressed by Bataille in his lecture on 13 December on "The Structure of the Democracies and the Crisis of September 1938", which Hollier referred to as "a highlight in the history of the College".[2] Bataille defends democracy by making the integrity of territory sacred, recalling that when faced with the defeat represented by the ratification of the Munich Agreement: "Man, even if he does not know whether essential values are involved in the struggle, will have to accept becoming on intimate terms with suffering and death, without knowing in advance what reality will emerge from it."[3]

The "Propositions on the Death of God",[4] ●65, sent by Bataille to Rollin on 25 September, were a rewriting of the nine "Propositions...", a manuscript conserved among Bataille's papers,[5] and a version of this text was published in *Acéphale* 2 following a first section entitled "Propositions on Fascism". This, at least, is what seems to be implied by the two versions of the text preserved in the papers donated by Dubief to the Bibliothèque Nationale. One of these has nine propositions, and its first page has been annotated: "first state / superseded by the following text"; the other version has twenty-one propositions (a copy of this, with further variants, was also in Andler's archive[6]) with the annotation, also present on Rollin's copy: "responses to be sent by the 18th at the latest". This rewriting affects not only the numbering as it appeared in the earlier version published in the journal, but also the content. New propositions are introduced (among them, 1 to 4 and 16 to 20), and earlier propositions are added to (proposition 6 from the journal becomes proposition 5 here, with the addition of a new sentence[7]); finally, certain of the earlier propositions are modified yet retain their original numbering (proposition 8, as it appears here and in the journal, has different endings), while others incorporate modifications from the manuscript in the BN.

The overall effect of the new "Propositions" is to accentuate the identification of Nietzsche's superman with the Acéphale. In the early version of the text in *Acéphale* this link was made through the unleashing of ecstatic time as produced by "puerile" chance, and then through the revolutionary putting to death of kings. However, in the version of "Propositions" that was promulgated within the Society, the link to the superman is made by means of a "'children's' conspiracy" that is able to reject "those who do not have the strength to desire their unwavering destiny — the violent tragedy of human life". In this way it will be open to universality, far from the sovereignty of God and the sovereignty of the state, "in free and purposeless expenditure, [and] in non-servile religious activity". The new proposition 17 makes this explicit: "In universal terms, religion only means to us the act of laughing (or tears, or erotic stimulation) in the precise sense that laughter (like tears or erotic stimulation) represents the defeat of everything that had sought to impose its permanence."

The 21st proposition, included in both Andler's and Dubief's copies of the text, returns to the image of the "leaderless crowd" first introduced by Bataille in ●14, but here expressing something of the "acephalic universe", ●65: "The identification of the participants with the myth of the Acéphale represents the first attempt to form a leaderless 'crowd' (with the 'crowd' existing as an emotional, which amounts to saying a mythological whole)".

The 'strong moment' of Acéphale's communal life was nevertheless most significantly marked in the texts to do with Patrick Waldberg's initiation. Beginning soon after his arrival in Paris, with an oath of silence taken facing east on the balcony of the building where Bataille lived, it was completed in two further stages. In the version given many years later by Waldberg himself in his "Acéphalogram", ●68, a different dating is introduced, and he describes only the first and third stages of his initiation. The texts in Andler's files, on the other hand, refer to the last two stages, namely the trial of "adeption", ●63, which took place at 9 pm on 19 September at 39 rue Dauphine, Dussat's address since December 1937;[8] and the induction in the forest of Marly, ●67, on 28 September.

This ceremony was enacted on an embankment to the north of the deep hollow of the ruins of Montjoie in order to set up a correspondence with the two poles of the sacred, the pure and the impure, a distinction made by both Durkheim and Mauss. This polarity was explored in several lectures at the College in 1938: by Leiris in "The Sacred in Everyday Life", ○60, by Bataille in his two lectures on "Attraction and Repulsion" and by Caillois in "The Ambiguity of the Sacred" in which he specified that: "The East and South seem to be the seat of the qualities of growth, which cause the sun to rise and become warmer. The West and North are the habitat of the powers of perdition and ruin, which cause the star of life to descend and become extinguished."[9] In this same lecture Caillois also discussed Robert Hertz's studies on the religious meanings of the supremacy of the right hand[10] in primitive societies and its persistence in contemporary society. Hertz's essay contains this passage: "It is the right side of man that is consecrated to the god of war; it is the *mana* of the right shoulder which guides the spear to its target; it is therefore the right hand alone that carries and handles weapons."[11] The text on the encounter of 28 September, ●67, and the first extract from Waldberg's "Acéphalogram", ●68, show the central role of this passage from Hertz in the ritual of induction into

Acéphale, in particular, in the handling of the knife with the right hand by Ambrosino at the moment he cuts Waldberg's forearm — like the drawn sword of the Rex Nemorensis who stands guard day and night at the tree in the sacred grove of the goddess Diana, awaiting he "who was sooner or later to murder him and hold the priesthood in his stead".[12] Other details relating to the ritual emphasise the role of the left hand or the left side in general, which represents those things that partake of "the underworld and the earth", as opposed to the right which "represents the uplands, higher things, the heavens"; such were the connections Hertz noted[13] between the two sides of the body and the regions of the world and the universe. Thus in Waldberg's induction ceremony the knife is held in the right hand, but the arm to be cut is the left, and the "Memento", ●16, which is read aloud after the incision is made, is then placed in Waldberg's left pocket. The establishing of a communal link by the rite of a sacrificial wound, accompanied by the formula read by Bataille, "This is the text that we offer to you to sign and to seal with your blood", ●67, refers to the sacred nature of bodily emissions, and the positive and vivifying qualities attributed in many primitive rites to the shedding of blood, a subject studied by Konrad Preuss[14] and cited by both Bataille and Caillois in the College.[15] Waldberg informs us that the "cut" also formed a part of the initiation of Okamoto, and Rollin told me it was the same for him, before then denying it, while mischievously adding, "since we were bound to keep this a secret, maybe I have repressed it all".[16] The nocturnal ceremony was conducted in a deep silence by the light of a sulphurous fire which illuminated a complicated arrangement, whose full significance remains obscure: the adepts end up positioned around Bataille with Waldberg facing him, having traced enigmatic paths around the embankment from a place "to the north of the deepest point of the excavation" to a tree with a sign at the entry to the ruins, and then to the path leading to the Étoile Mourante (see pp.57 and 60). They then return to their original positions.

Before Waldberg's induction each of the adepts had received certain texts, copies of which were later found among Chavy's papers. "Degrees", ●66, marks the establishment of three initiatory ranks within the Society (see p.45), an arrangement that was intended to bolster the "fundamental secret which surrounds the society as a whole, and the secrecy that gradually comes to protect its deepest and most essential nucleus."[17] This text concludes with a passage from Nietzsche, "Hard school", taken from volume II of *The Will to Power*.[18]

The sessional meeting of 29 September, ●69, at 39 rue Dauphine, in keeping with the "Rules as of 24 September 1937", ●38, represents in many respects a culmination of the meeting in July devoted to the arming of the figure of Acéphale. The first part of the programme for the September meeting is concerned with "The Eleven Aggressions", a "more exact and developed form" of the seven aggressions of July, ●52, and in the same way those things previously proposed in the agenda for the internal activities of the group in July have now become established projects. "The Eleven Aggressions" introduces the formula of "joy in the face of death" while the second part of the programme supersedes that of July with seventeen points which chiefly propose creating an autonomous force opposed to all established political positions, by "Breaking with those who reject the struggle, and with those who accept it but join the ranks of certain parties which then demand that they give up their position", as well as by bringing into play the notion of expenditure. This latter finds its formulation in paragraph X: "a human being is not simply a stomach to fill, but an excess of energy to be squandered." The question of the class struggle, meanwhile, is reformulated in paragraph XI: "The essential problem of existence is not a problem of production and the distribution of products. The intensity of the class struggle does not change simply according to the working wage: the excess energy of the workers is also a factor in their constant unrest." This is an assertion Rollin returned to in a letter to Bataille of December 1938, ●82, and it also reappears as a paraphrasing of the Gospel in a fragment from 1939 included in the *Anti-Christian's Manual*: "Man does not live by bread alone, but by every open wound that puts human existence at stake".[19]

Bataille's "Message", ●70, is another text that is probably related to this meeting, and announces the encounter in the forest with Koch, which had to take place before the expiry of two weeks following a sessional meeting, as stated in the "Rules of 24 September 1937", ●38. A brief document that is omitted here indicates that Koch probably took part in the encounter of 10 October,[20] shortly after "the return of Chenon and Dussat"[21] (whose names are among those to have received Bataille's "Note", ●71), and, according to Waldberg's copy of this text, with the active participation of Ambrosino and Kelemen. The protocols associated with this encounter are given in ●72, and include, besides the role of the right hand previously seen in Waldberg's induction ritual, the rite of sulphurous fire, and passing the hand through a flame, which Koch also mentioned in one of his conversations with me.

## THE COLLEGE OF SOCIOLOGY

The "Declaration on the International Crisis", ○75, was the only overtly political statement published by the College, and one which quickly returns the argument to its own territory. It was occasioned by the build-up to and signing of the Munich Agreement on 30 September 1938 by Chamberlain for Great Britain, Daladier for France, Hitler for Germany and Mussolini for Italy. This was the "peace for our time" agreement that Chamberlain triumphantly brought back to Britain and which legitimised the Nazi takeover of German-speaking areas of Czechoslovakia, the prelude to the invasion of the country as a whole. This act of appeasement is nowadays seen as making the Second World War an inevitability, and was also the death-blow to the Spanish Republic, which had been hoping for a European anti-Fascist alliance.

The College's declaration was dated 7 October, and published at the beginning of November in three journals, the *NRF*, *Esprit* and *Volontés*, and was the only one of its joint statements to be signed by Leiris, who signed it reluctantly at that. He explained later: "I'll tell you frankly, I was very pleased that the spectre of war had been averted. But I shared the view, perhaps a little hypocritically, that the democracies and certainly France had not provided people with the myths which would have enabled them to confront the war."[22]

A second declaration in response to a statement by Paulhan was proposed at this time but came to nothing initially, presumably because it coincided with the last days of Laure's illness, and her death on 7 November.[23] However, although Bataille was still referring to this declaration the following January in a letter to Paulhan,[24] it was then abandoned in favour of a personal declaration, as covered in the next commentary.

# TEXTS

September 1938 — October 1938

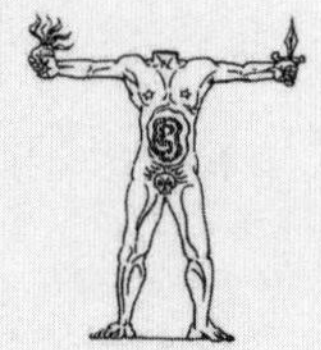

Les quinze jours qui suivent la session compteront à partir du 29 septembre 1938. Ils prendront fin exactement le 14 octobre à minuit.

Tous ceux d'entre nous qui ne participeront pas à la rencontre qui aura lieu avec Koch, si possible au retour de Chenon et de Dussat devront se rendre dans la forêt seuls. Dans ce cas, <u>ils devront répondre à la présente communication en précisant le jour qu'ils choisiront auquel ils devront se tenir</u>.

70. Georges Bataille, *Message*.

## PIERRE ANDLER *The War* 62

*We, who live in a world that wants to be punished, are not obliged to make the same choice as everyone else. For this world is not, for us, an empty frame, an abstraction, or the simple manifestation of an appearance. And if the world is real, if that reality was just a joke, we are still a part of it, because we are doomed to this tragic reality and because tragedy insists on the irony of circumstances. We are thus brought to accept the world, if not the punishments specific to it. This also means accepting the war.*

*The war that will break out tomorrow*[1] *will have no meaning for us, apart from the danger involved in transforming not so much the world as only the balance of power between politics and the police. What is at stake in the war as it is presented to us is almost nothing in our eyes: in fact, anything is preferable to this corpselike rigidity, and this false inversion of all the values that has been introduced by doctrines of enslavement for social and national ends. We have become entrenched just like those same individuals who died believing they recognised a tragic existence in the wretchedness of social or national conflicts, or in the appalled contemplation of a god on a cross. What separates us from the old democracies in which we live is just as burning a subject; but we have assumed the task of murderous sons giving a new face to the world. And thus our primary hatred is directed at those who have perpetrated the false inversion of those values, our near-triumphant rivals whose duplicity cannot but sicken us, even more so than the lack of ambition on the part of the rest. The reality that connects us in this way to societies of which we are members only by chance is extremely fragile, but it does not leave us indifferent. Even so, we must be permitted to indulge no illusions: it is not a matter of putting our trust in the democratic societies which have already, in times of war, embraced a militarised existence, but which lack that inner quality of inflexibility that would defend them against being invaded by doctrines of miserable aggression or class rationalisation. We will thus have taken it upon ourselves to participate in a war whose outcome, in any case, is merely a decoy. Nothing indicates to us that the internal transformation of the forces in operation will empty war of the only meaning it can have in the eyes of politicians and pitch us into a totally different position, the most likely seeming be that of a third camp. The responsibility that we have taken on ourselves — of giving a new face to the world — will thus at no point have ceased to play its part. The turmoil courted today by a world duly divided into two camps, one of which pretends to be the successor of the other, whilst the latter may at any moment supersede itself, incites us as much as our own aggression. It is possible that in their misfortune men today aspire as much to war as to deliverance, to a tension that is so incredible that it will liberate them from a tension that is merely extreme. We must seek in such a war only what is actually ours, by turning away from every other image. We may take part in it on condition that we are who we want to be, that we continue to love and hate in war the things we chose and rejected in peace, and that we remember what unites us and what must unite so many others, all others.* 18.IX.[19]38

63 GEORGES BATAILLE *Procedure for Patrick Waldberg's Adeption*[2]

*The adeption procedure for* PATRICK WALDBERG *will take place on Monday 19 September 1938 at 9 pm, at 39 rue Dauphine.*

*Please think through in advance a brief response to the question that will be asked during this procedure, as there will be no general discussion beforehand.*

[September 1938]

64 GEORGES BATAILLE AND GEORGES AMBROSINO *To Pierre Andler, Interview of Saturday 24 September [1938]*

*We request another interview with you in accordance with the rules that have been followed previously. It will take place on Saturday 24 September at 2.30 pm at the Café Le Firmament (take the Métro to 4 Septembre).*

*We enclose a list of questions that will explain the purpose of this interview.*

*G. Bataille*

*G. Ambrosino*

*Right:* Patrick Waldberg's adeption "notification", with the sign of the labyrinth in Bataille's hand.

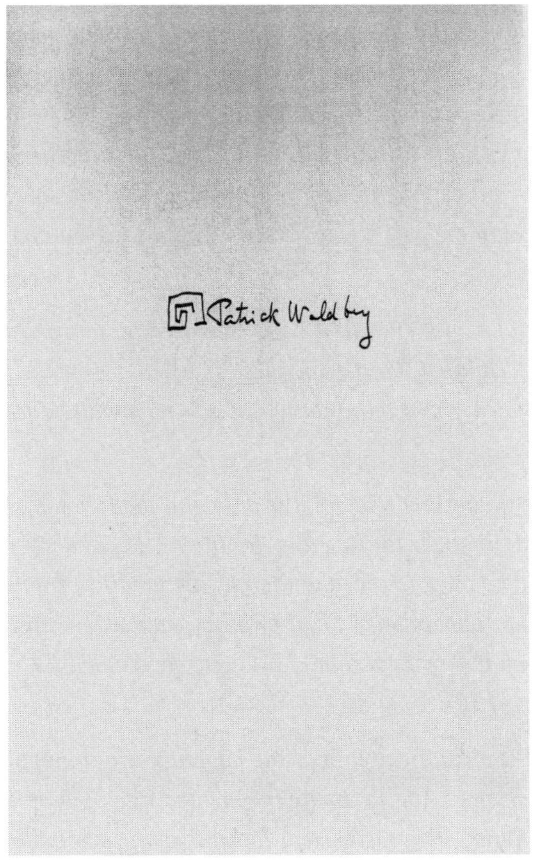
Patrick Waldberg

*1. The myth of the superman can only transform reality in the form of emotional identification. Identification with the superman unavoidably has the opposite meaning of the Christian's identification with God or Jesus. It excludes both the sovereignty of the father and the submission of the son. The superman demands identification with a mode of human existence in which the attitude of insubordination, or rather of total unconditionality, is also an exalted acceptance of tragic destruction. The will sovereignty can call upon to escape time is not only the object of a clearly marked exclusion but of an aggression that cannot tolerate release.*

*2. Identification cannot be achieved in a vague and individual way, but only by means of a formal conspiracy, a 'children's' conspiracy, that is to say by means of an order that exists to reject inconsistency and renunciation as acts resembling a betrayal for the benefit of 'important people'.*

*3. The Profane, these 'important people', the wise and the rational, are those who do not have the strength to desire their unwavering destiny — the violent tragedy of human life. "Let us then have the courage to consider man as the product of simple chance, like a defenceless nothing [and] abandoned to all forms of damnation: this notion is as well suited to breaking human will as is that of a divine government" (Nietzsche,* Posthumous Fragments, *138).*

*4. The death of God straight away throws the largest part of human existence back into meaninglessness, aimlessness and existence fragmented into each of its specialised functions. The superhuman necessarily steps forward as the emotional identification in a world where God is dead and he alone steps forward. The superhuman is at once the requirement, the fulfilment and the consequence of the death of God.*

*5. The* Acéphale *expresses in mythological terms the sovereignty that is dedicated to destruction, to the death of God, and in this respect its identification with the headless man corresponds to and mingles with an identification with the superhuman, who IS entirely 'the death of God'. Once revealed, the stubborn course of life's hunger for death (as is present in every type of game or dream) will no longer appear as a desire for annihilation, but as the pure hunger to be* me, *death or the void being nothing but the domain in which there rises up again and again — owing to its very failure — an empire of* me *whose form must be represented as an abyss.*

*6. The myth of the superman is no different from God except in the respect that it is the criminal negation of God, and also because it expresses a possible way for man (as subject) to be more than simply the object of his emotional existence. In this sense the myth is also different from the Acéphale, who is more immediately object than subject (hence the myth of the Acéphale does not require its subject to renounce his cerebral faculties, still less to underrate their practical value; it is only to the extent that these faculties become, for man, an object which can be invested in the name of Reason with the strongest emotional charge, that the decapitation of the Acéphale will be offered as an imperative requirement).*

*7. The Similarity between the superman and the Acéphale resides in the fact that they are linked by a flash of lightning that is equivalent to time's role as the imperative object of life. In both cases time becomes the ultimate object of ecstasy, and it is only of secondary importance that it appears as the "eternal return" in Nietzsche's ecstasy at Surlej, or as "catastrophe" in the vision in* Sacrifices; *it is thus as different from the time of the philosophers (or even Heideggerian time) as the God of erotic saints is to the God of the Greek philosophers. Movement that is directed towards time enters directly into the world of concrete existence, while movement inclined towards God immediately turns away from it.*

*8. Ecstatic time can only occur in the sight of things that puerile chance introduces into the field of appearances: corpses, nakedness, explosions, pools of blood, abysses, lightning and the sun.*

*9. War — to the extent that it is born out of the desire to secure a nation's permanence, the nation being sovereignty and absolute resistance to change, the authority of divine right and God himself — represents man's desperate stubbornness to confront the exuberant power of time and find security in a fixed structure that is close to the most sterile slumber. National and military existence live on in the world in order to attempt to deny death by reducing it to the level of a constituent part of a moment of glory untouched by anguish. Nation and army drive a deep divide between man and a universe given over to unconditional exuberance and to wayward expenditure squandered amid man's laughter and tears… deep, at least in so far as the uncertain victories of human avarice can be said to be deep…*

*10. The Revolution should not be considered only in terms of its supporters and successes that are widely known and acknowledged, but also in its raw appearance, whether it is waged by puritans, encyclopaedists, Russian Marxists or Spanish followers of Bakunin. The Revolution in its relevant historical situation at the summit of today's civilisation appears before the eyes of a world struck dumb with astonishment like the arrival centre stage of a multitude of regicides. The divine authority of the fact of the Revolution ceases to be the foundation of power; authority no longer belongs to God but to the time whose unbridled exuberance puts God to death, the time embodied today in the tumult of that multitude of regicides. In Fascism too, authority has been reduced to something founded on a would-be Revolution, a homage that is hypocritical and subject to the only enduring majesty, that of revolutionary catastrophe.*

*11. God, kings and all their gang stand between men and the Earth — in the same way that the father before the son is an obstacle to his rape and possession of the Mother. The economic history of modern times is dominated by the enormous but shockingly disappointing attempts made by stubborn men to claim ownership of the Earth's resources. The Earth has been disembowelled, but what men have dug up from within its belly is mostly iron and fire, which they then use to continue disembowelling each other. The incandescence deep within the Earth is not only brought up to the surface by way of volcanic craters: it turns red and spits death with its fumes in the smelting of all nations.*

*12. The burning reality of the maternal belly of the Earth cannot be touched or owned by those who fail to recognise it. It is ignorance of the Earth, ignorance of the heavenly body on which they live, ignorance of the nature of its resources, in other words of the fire contained within this wandering star, which puts man's existence at the mercy of the goods he produces, the most significant part of which are devoted to death. As long as men forget the true nature of life on Earth, which demands ecstatic and effusive intoxication, this nature will not be able to recapture the attention of accountants and economists of every stripe except by abandoning them to the most dismal results of their accounting and their economics.*

*13. Men do not know how to enjoy the Earth and its products freely and lavishly: the Earth and its products are only lavish and inexhaustibly free in order that they may destroy men. The prosaic warfare of the kind demanded by modern economics also teaches the meaning of the Earth, but teaches it to apostates whose heads are full of calculations and short-term considerations, which is why it teaches that it should be waged with heartlessness and depressing fury. Within the disproportionate and lacerating approach of the aimless catastrophe that is warfare today, it is still possible for us to recognise the unbridled immensity of time which has remained the mother of men; and so too in the chaos breaking out all around us with its unprecedented clamour — the limitless annihilation of God.*

*14. War's absence of outcome and purpose is what leads men from different nations to recognise their kinship with both the blind outbursts of Earth and the absence of God. But they do not understand in the first place that their misery and death are, alongside the misery and death of God, the inevitable revenge exacted by Earth against those who have disowned it in favour of affirming God's sovereign power (that is to say to damp down the violent convulsions of all those things that hurl themselves, and freely demand to be hurled, into time).*

*15. The search for God, for absence of movement, for* tranquillity*, is the fear that wrecks all attempts at universal existence. The heart of man is untroubled only until the moment when it comes to rest in God: the universality of God still remains a source of anxiety for him, and relief comes only if God remains locked away in isolation and within the deeply steadfast permanence of a group organised along military lines. For universal existence is unlimited and thus restless; it does not close life in upon itself but opens it up and casts it back into the anxiety of the infinite. The eternally unrealised universal existence, Acéphale, a world that resembles a bleeding wound, sets itself against beings that are strangely complete; in this way universality is the death of God who in essence is nothing but a limited and fixed form of sovereignty.*

*16. Human universality either will or will not be a religious movement. It cannot attain true and living existence in abstract forms that are not able, in universal terms, to survive the disappearance of the specific, concrete existences of those states they have proposed to destroy. Revolutionary parties cannot preserve their universal character once they have assumed, as a result of their success, the task of organising the material resources of a given territory; their mode of existence then begins to resemble that of any other particular mode of existence, and the revolutionary state becomes a state like any other. Furthermore, the universal mode excludes all possibility of state sovereignty: it is necessarily limited to that part of existence which excludes all subordinate and functional usage, in other words universal existence cannot be manifested in acquisition and conservation, but only in free and purposeless expenditure, in non-servile religious activity. Every limited undertaking makes itself distinct from everything else and loses out on universal life that cannot offer any secondary purpose unless it is strictly subordinate to the conflagration that consumes men's shared existence in the world. There is thus for ever and ever an annihilation of God and the explosion of time: nothing is stable in the universe any more, which is just one huge mockery of everything that seeks to establish eternal domination.*

*17. In universal terms, religion only means to us the act of laughing (or tears, or erotic stimulation) in the precise sense that laughter (like tears or erotic stimulation) represents the defeat of everything that had sought to impose its permanence.*

*18. The movement that pits the individual against a particular society is not at first any different from the movement that pits open (universal) existence against closed (national) existence. But if it does not reach fruition, if it lingers at the moment of individual egotistical existence, it is the worst misery the life it fragments can undergo. For the fragment does not resign itself to existing* per se, *but absurdly takes itself to be the totality to which it lends its insufficient form, which is even more risible by far than the form of the nation from which it has escaped. Only with the unconditional gift of the sickly head rescued from the acephalic existence of the universe, and from the catastrophe of time, will being cease trying to put out the spark of free life.*

*19. Everything that was previously linked to the concern with guaranteeing the integrity of some particular existence must be rejected and instead a resolute and sometimes violent effort must be made to recover a childlike freedom. The clearly marked oppositions between the different modalities of life are irreducible, and the return to freedom must be made in such a way that it is profoundly different from the freedom of primitive life, but above all men must live in tune with their baseness. The negation of base things is what has resulted in a reality that dominates the fall into time: in affirming this fall we rediscover all the naïve freedom associated with such dangerous matters.*

*20. It would be futile to want to eliminate from the world one of the successful modalities of existence. If these modalities can indeed undergo profound change, then a form of existence as fundamental as a particular society with its territorial limits and the infrastructure to organise its own resources can under no circumstances disappear. But another form of shared existence remains possible, as shown by the examples of Buddhist and Christian churches that have advanced to a certain stage in the direction of the universal. It is therefore a question of knowing which new modifications made to closed (national) existences might result in the development of a 'conspiracy' that is much more radical than the previous ones that were put in place in opposition to forms of divine sovereignty. However, it is necessary to establish the existence of such a 'conspiracy' over and above those nations that are more and more closed off, and to establish it in such a way that it is neither less concrete nor less alive in the eyes of its participants than a nation or a Church.*

*21. The identification of the participants with the myth of the Acéphale represents the first attempt to form a leaderless "crowd" (with the "crowd" existing as an emotional, which amounts to saying a mythological whole).*

## GEORGES BATAILLE *Degrees* 66

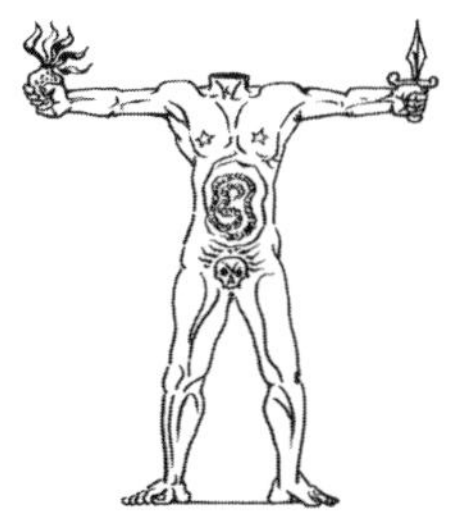

*This text is to be given to each of the adepts in the same way as the papers handed out during meetings.*

*Each of us has the secret name* larva*: in so far as he is an adept ("he who has attained"), he has in fact only attained the first degree. Compared to what is represented by the objective we have chosen, he is what a* larva *is to the* imago*, no more than the rudimentary form of the insect is to its final form.*

*Those amongst us who attain the second degree have the secret name* mute*; and those who attain the final stage have the secret name* prodigal.

*There is no question of* any *of us going beyond the degree of* larva *until a long period of time has elapsed. The word refers, etymologically, to phantom skeletons and masks. However, the sense of "cutting" which it inevitably has for us relates to Nietzsche's* fundamental text *on the "hard school", an unabridged copy of which is appended to this letter.*

*The designation of one of us to a degree above that of* larva *may only be carried out according to the principles of secrecy and of decisions made without discussion which regulate everything concerning our ritual activity. Even so, the* degrees *must not be confused with the function of decision-making or with the ritual functions themselves.*

*The* modalities *of this organisation are not planned in advance and will not be decided unless there is felt to be a tacit and deep-seated agreement between each of us.*

*The* secret names *must be subject to the same rigour as everything else that remains secret between us, that is to say they may not be uttered owing to the fact that they refer to the degrees, and there can be no question of this happening except in interviews between adepts; interviews may be* called on this subject *if any two of us agree to do so, in conformity with the rule that has already been set in place. However, an adept of a given degree may not know who the adepts are of a higher degree or even if there actually are any.* [28 September 1938]

*Hard school*

*"I absolutely cannot see how anyone can make up for having missed going to a* good school *at the proper time. Such a man does not know himself; he walks through life without ever having learned to walk; his flabby muscles betray him at every step. Sometimes life is merciful enough to help a man recover the hard schooling he has missed; through long periods of sickness perhaps that demand, over several years, the utmost will-power and self-sufficiency; or sudden poverty, that also affects his wife and children, forcing him to such activity that restores energy to his slackened fibres and* toughens *his will to live. The most desirable thing is under all circumstances to have had a hard discipline* at the proper time, *i.e. at the age when we take pride that great things are expected of us. This is what distinguishes the hard school from all the schools that are merely good — that much is demanded of us, and sternly demanded; that the good, even the exceptional, is demanded as the norm; that praise is rare, and indulgence non-existent; that blame is cutting and precise without regard for ability or parentage. Such a school is an absolute necessity both for the body and for the soul; and it would be catastrophic to draw distinctions here. The same discipline makes both the good soldier and the good scholar; and, if his character is examined more closely, it will be seen that no good scholar lacks the instincts of a good soldier. He must have the ability to command and also to obey with pride; to take his place in the ranks, but also to be capable at any moment of leadership; to prefer danger to comfort; not to weigh up too carefully what is permitted and what is forbidden; to be the enemy of the petty, sly and parasitic, rather than the ill-behaved. —* What does one learn *in a hard school? To* obey *and to* command."

*Nietzsche,* The Will to Power, *vol. II*

GEORGES BATAILLE *Encounter of 28 September 1938*

*Second Part*

*Leaving the station at S.N.[3] at 8.45 pm, Andler, Ambrosino (carrying with him four* mementos*), Chavy and Kelemen are to meet at Montjoie where they will arrive at*

*9.45 pm. A-o immediately hands over a* memento *to each of the other three and keeps one for himself.*

*A-o accompanies A-r and C-y to a point beyond the excavation where, after moving ten steps away from each other (they must avoid making the slightest noise), they must wait.*

*A-o then returns to K-n who is waiting at the near end of the path to M-e; he fixes a notice to the tree with a sign on it,*[4] *then with K-n starts off down the path leading to the Étoile Mourante, where they wait some way down the path and a good distance apart from one another.*

*Bataille and Waldberg, having left S.G. at 9 pm, arrive at M-e at 10 pm and make their way to the embankment alongside it (to the north of the deepest point of the excavation).*

*B-e leaves W-g on the embankment and walks towards A-o and K-n, and then stops and waits not far from them.*

*After a quarter of an hour, both A-o and K-n light their torches, A-o takes the unsheathed knife in his right hand and B-e lights some sulphur: they then make their way towards the embankment.*

*A-r and C-y begin to walk towards the embankment as soon as they see the torches coming closer, just slowly enough to arrive at the same time as the others.*

*B-e rolls up W-g's left sleeve and A-o immediately makes an incision on his arm.*

*B-e reads the text, after having said: "This is the text that we offer to you to sign and to seal with your blood."*

*B-e unfolds the* memento *he is to hand over to W-g and reads out the formula on it before slipping it into W-g's left pocket.*

*During this time W-g must stand between A-o (on W-g's left) and K-n (on his right). B-e stands in front of W-g, A-r and C-y stand behind.*

The spot occupied by B-e and W-g is what determines where the others stand.

*A-o, while he is making the incision, gives his torch to one of those who are standing behind him and takes it back once he has finished.*

*Once the* memento *has been read by B-e and handed over to W-g,* straight away *A-o and K-n leave, leading W-g by one arm while making the sign to him.*[5] *C-y and A-r follow. B-e makes sure to close the bag and follows on last of all. The torches are put out when they arrive back at the path.*

*The return is via S.G., on the 11.25 train.*

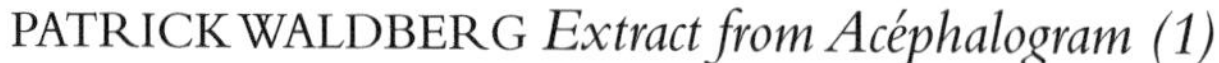

## 68 PATRICK WALDBERG *Extract from Acéphalogram (1)*

*As soon as I arrived in Paris I was taken by Bataille up to the balcony of the building where he was living, at 76* bis *rue de Rennes. It was dusk. He turned me to face the east, in other words towards the night, and made me take an oath of silence. The initiation I was to undergo was due to take place a few days later. To this end he gave me a timetable and the drawing of a map. On the appointed date, the night of the new moon, I was told to take the train from Saint-Lazare station to Saint-Nom-la-Bretèche. If in the course of the journey I happened to come across any people I knew, I was advised to ignore them, just as, after we got off the train and while we were following the path through the forest, if the same people were also on that path our instructions were to keep our distance and remain silent. The long silent walk along sunken paths, steeped in the damp smell of the trees, took us in pitch darkness to the foot of an oak that had been struck by lightning, on the edge of an* étoile, *where soon enough there gathered a dozen still and silent shadows. After a short while someone lit a torch. Bataille, standing at the foot of the tree, took an enamelled dish out of a bag and put a few pieces of sulphur on it, which he then set alight. As the blue flame sputtered, smoke rose up and wafted towards us in suffocating gusts. The person holding the torch came and stood on my right as one of the other officiants walked towards me, face on. He was holding a dagger identical to the one brandished by the headless man in the effigy of* Acéphale. *Bataille took my left hand and rolled my jacket and shirt sleeves up to the elbow. The person holding the dagger pressed its tip into my forearm and made a cut several centimetres long, although I did not feel the slightest pain. The scar is still visible today. Someone then tied a handkerchief around the wound, my shirt and jacket sleeves were rolled back down again and the torch was put out. Another moment passed, which seemed long to me, and during which, still in complete silence, we stood around the tree, nervous yet impassive, with our faces softly illuminated in the blue sulphurous light. Then someone gave the signal to leave and we set off in the ever-darkening night, in single file and at some distance from one another, not towards Saint-Nom-la-Bretèche this time but in the direction of Saint-Germain-en-Laye. As on the outward journey, the instructions made it very clear that it was forbidden on the train back to Paris to exchange even the least sign of recognition.*

*The encounters at the foot of the tree struck by lightning took place every month on the night of the new moon, come wind or rain. The 'communional unity' we thus achieved led by implication to the establishment of new rules for living. Time was divided into periods of tension and periods of licence. During the former, members of the community were required to observe silence and a certain ascesis, and had to avoid even seeing one another unless it was absolutely necessary. By contrast, during the periods of licence every excess was sanctioned, including those that involved promiscuity.*

## GEORGES BATAILLE *Sessional Meeting of 29 September 1938* 69

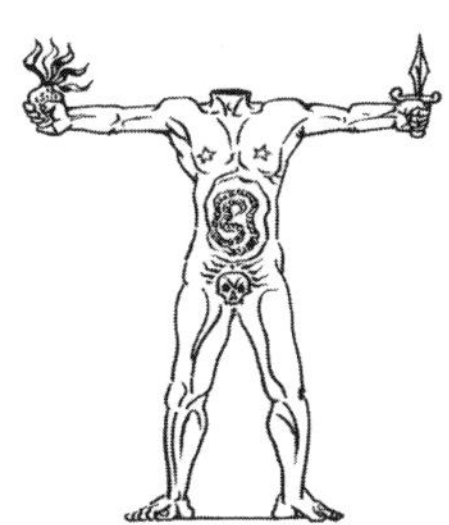

*Our internal movement leads us to it, external circumstances hurry us along: our organisation, discipline and aggression culminate in the composition of the armed figure which, in the night to come, will sustain us against antagonistic forces of all kinds as they join together in their desire to drag man down.*

*We propose to define this figure in a* programme *to be assembled from the following texts (the first part of which consists simply of a more exact and developed form of the* aggressions *which have already appeared on the agenda of the July sessional meeting).*

### First Part
### *The Eleven Aggressions:*

1. *CHANCE*
   *against the mass*

2. *COMMUNIONAL UNITY*
   *against the impostures of the individual*

3. *AN ELECTIVE COMMUNITY*
   *against all communities based on blood, land or business interests*

*4. THE RELIGIOUS POWER OF THE TRAGIC GIFT OF THE SELF*
*against military power based on avarice and coercion*

*5. THE UNCERTAIN FUTURE, DESTROYER OF LIMITS,*
*against the desire for fixity in the past*

*6. THE TRAGIC TRANSGRESSOR OF THE LAW*
*against the humble victims*

*7. THE INEXORABLE CRUELTY OF NATURE*
*against the debasing image of a pleasant god*

*8. FREE AND LIMITLESS LAUGHTER*
*against all reasonable explanations of an absurd universe*

*9. THE 'LOVE OF DESTINY',*[6] *EVEN THE HARSHEST,*
*against the resignations of pessimism or anguish*

*10. THE ABSENCE OF GROUND AND ALL FOUNDATIONS*
*against the appearance of stability*

*11. JOY IN THE FACE OF DEATH*
*against all forms of immortality*

## Second Part

*I. First and foremost, we denounce all present-day undertakings, positions and programmes, whether they are revolutionary, democratic or national, as the work of liars bent on concealing a failure which is plain for all to see; silence is the only response to the incontinence of these garrulous people who promise happiness.*

*II. We do not promise any happiness, we speak of* virility. *The violent* joy *we bring is found as much in death as in success or power.*

*III. We break with all forms of servility: we shall assemble an autonomous force by bringing together all those hoping for a human destiny and not simply some useful and lucrative function.*

*IV. We are structuring this force by taking into account proven methods — such as Freemasonry or the Jesuits soon after they had formed — but although we are employing the experience of those who came before us and whom we detest, it is only their rigour we retain and their understanding of laws that are based on power.*

*V. The force we are putting together is that of human* virility *which does not admit any concession even in the face of necessity. This is no longer a matter of some lacklustre pursuit of happiness, whether through a God, a political party or a fatherland, it is MAN who speaks now; from this stems the intransigence we are ready to apply in our tragic support of the autonomy of this force, in the face of all those powers who wish to subject human life to the principle of servile necessity.*

*VI. We place lucidity, self-control, indiscriminate stubbornness and precise, rigorous and* predictive *science in the service of this force, in such a way that a mere handful of men may keep it intangible amidst a world in which only blind forces have been judged capable of power.*

*VII. We shall denounce cowardice and scourge the shame and fear that is in men by their nature; we shall compel people to recognise in* avidity *— in the fact that every force grows or even endures only by destroying and absorbing all it can of the other forces it encounters — the law of all earthly existence. We shall cut short the words of the emasculated and the hypocrites.*

*VIII. On the other hand, we shall demonstrate that the energies accumulated by this natural avidity must be* expended *and squandered without limit. Acquisition can have no objective other than expenditure; production must not be the purpose of work, nor must consumption be necessary for production, but rather it must be* inutilious *consumption (as practised by primitive peoples, who are more human than economists). The only things that give meaning to existence are the sun, which lavishes its strength, endlessly indulging in a loss of blazing energy, and man, who loses his seed through orgasm, and who, for his beliefs, offers the tragic gift of his life.*

*IX. We shall learn to consider as* slaves *those who accept that man is put on the Earth to work, and who confine human existence within a horizon of* slaves, *while making* useful work *the only measure of value. We shall support an inexpiable struggle against the ethics of work, being fully aware that what is at stake is human destiny: the whole of humanity is threatened by being reduced to one vast system in which all are enslaved.*

*X. We affirm — and shall treat this affirmation as an unyielding denunciation of all those who capitulate — that man must not be valued according to the useful work he provides, but according to the infectious strength he can apply to drawing others into a* free *expenditure of their energy, their joy and their life: a human being is not simply a stomach to fill, but an excess of energy to be squandered.*

*XI. We remind all those economic sages, whatever faction they speak for, of their profound ignorance of the facts concerning the problems they claim to have resolved. And we remind everyone else that men who have done nothing more than exchange the constraints of a capitalist economy for the constraints of militarised labour deserve only ridicule and hatred. The essential problem of existence is not a problem of production and the distribution of products. The intensity of the class struggle does not change simply according to the working wage: the excess energy of the workers is also a factor in their constant unrest. Men need, above all, the* faith *to allow them to squander the energy available to them to expend.*

*XII. We are not proposing* bread *or riches like those liars who live by the unsustainable promises they make to others: we bring men a* faith.

*XIII. Men have wasted their lives on a God who emasculates them, on fatherlands that militarise them and on revolutions that have militarised them every bit as much as their fatherlands; all the forces to which they have given their energy and countless lives are now dragging them towards a ruin of dead-ends. All that is wasted merely in the service of God, revolutions and fatherlands, we propose to give back to* MAN*: the* VIRILITY *that yields to nothing is the* FAITH *that we bring to those who have sufficient lucid resolution of purpose to discover a splendour, strength and blazing joy* in the ineluctably tragic destiny of man.

*XIV.* VIRILITY *and* MAN *represent a reality whose demands are no less rigorous than those of the God of dead creeds. Only one thing counts, that human existence should attain degrees of boldness, science, joy and brilliance that still remain out of reach; everything must be sacrificed to the tragic splendour that* MAN *may hope to attain. Death and the renunciation of happiness can only be joys on a path that is also* human.

*XV. Buffoons and faint-hearted idlers imagine man's splendour to be a treasure they might* possess *for themselves and which would allow them to look down on those following more simple paths. But human splendour would have no meaning if it did not demand from the person seeking it a tragic gift of his strength and life. It can be found only in unrestrained lavishness and is mere comedy whenever it strives to become the particular splendour of some conceited individual rather than the impersonal splendour of MAN.*

*XVI. Dilettantes and lovers of tranquillity and proud but hollow words believe they can sustain their virility even in isolation or in flight. But virility belongs only to those who* struggle. *How could a person who is not prepared to give his blood and his life in order to sustain* what he is *be regarded as anything other than a mockery of man?*

*XVII. Breaking with those who reject the struggle, and with those who accept it but join the ranks of certain parties which then demand that they give up their position, we lay claim to and shall maintain, with all necessary aggression, the rule of violent opposition to all those powers that thrive on man's diminished circumstances. We rule out all negative methods which have only opened up the field to a military domination that is even more stifling than all the old authorities that have been destroyed; we shall create an* order *that practises, through discipline and through the incontrovertible authority of a 'tragic gift of the self', a religious* power *that is both more real and more intangible than any that have gone before; we shall be the force that gives MAN's voice an emphasis that will shatter the ears of the deaf.*

*AGENDA*
*of the Sessional Meeting of 29 September 1938,*
*to be held at 39 rue Dauphine, at 9 o'clock sharp.*

First Part

*ANNUAL SUMMATION*

Second Part

*PROPOSALS*

I. Internal activity

*Additions to the list of names and update on the results of conversations conducted with various people.*

*Update on the planned founding of a* Society of Acéphale Publications.

*Update on the planned teaching programme.*

*Forms of personal participation in the organisation's activities; each of us must set out his interests regarding this point, those who are not in Paris doing so in their letter of solidarity.*

II. PUBLICATIONS and definition of Acéphale's position

*General update on publication projects.*

*Discussion of the programme (all proposed modifications or additions must be received in writing; they may be sent together with the letter of solidarity).*

*Definition of Acéphale's autonomous position in the event of war and the proposed publication of this position.*

*Definition of Acéphale's stance with regard to the* International Federation of Independent Revolutionary Art.

Third Part

TALK:

*Bataille:* What religious experience might mean for us.

## 70 GEORGES BATAILLE *Message*

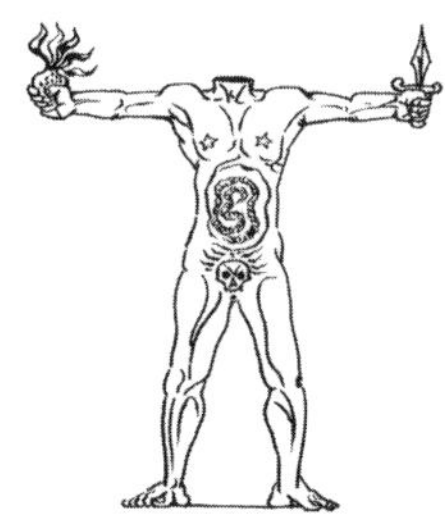

*The two-week period that follows the sessional meeting will begin on 29 September 1938. It will end on 14 October at exactly midnight.*

*All those of us who are not participating in the encounter to take place with Koch, if possible after the return of Chenon and Dussat, must make their way to the forest alone. In such a case* they must reply to this message and specify what day they have chosen, and then keep to it.

[September 1938]

## GEORGES BATAILLE *Note to the Members of Acéphale* 71

*I have spoken several times about what we have achieved. I do not know if I have done so with enough clarity. I am aware that if some of us do not change, then what we have undertaken must be regarded in exactly the same way as anything else that deserves our most angry contempt. And it is with anguish, a sometimes incapacitating anguish, that I reflect upon the following: if within us we had the kind of emotion that leaves us breathless and permits no peace of mind, if within us we had the kind of faith that makes us aware that there is an empire to build, then even the most unpleasant means, even misguided means, would not make us hesitate and might then be accepted with joy. It is time for* all *of us to understand that if we are not capable of seeing through something that is* disagreeable, *we will quickly join the very misfits we have not been afraid to mock. It is not a matter of knowing if such a method is flawed or not — on the question of means, if it is unacceptable for us to shirk, then it is certainly vital to speak out — but I categorically reject inertia and complacency: for these things I feel there is such a cry and such suffering waiting to burst out of me that their noise will be heard for ever. If we carry inside us the power we hope to use against other people's inertia, how can we bear the humiliation, the wounds we suffer when we compare ourselves with those who have put themselves in service to God or to some Germany?*

*I address this note to the following individuals in person: Ambrosino, Andler, Chavy, Chenon, Dussat, Kelemen and Waldberg, with the request that it is included in the* Book of Adepts,[7] *along with any responses that are forthcoming.* 8-X-[19]38

## GEORGES BATAILLE *Instructions Concerning the Encounter of 10 October 1938* 72

*Purchase a single ticket for Saint-Nom-la-Bretèche. Take the 8.39 pm train and do not get off until the final stop.*

*Find a seat in the carriage away from anyone else and open the enclosed envelope.*

*At Saint-Nom station, follow Ambrosino whilst observing the silence that must not be broken except in the event of something drastic happening, and then only if it is absolutely unavoidable.*

*Stop every time Ambrosino stops and holds up his right hand but without turning round. If Ambrosino walks on again without making a sign, wait until one of us has turned round and made a sign.*

*When Ambrosino walks on the grass beside the road, do the same, in order to avoid as far as possible the sound of footsteps.*

*Once you have arrived at the site for the encounter, upon a direct and very obvious sign from one of us, go alone right up to the burning flame, pass your hand through it (or as close as you can) and then return to take your place with the others.*

*Keep your silence on the return journey just as on the outward one.*

*Upon arrival at the station, purchase a single ticket for Paris,* wait alone *on the platform and do the same on board the train. At Saint-Lazare station, leave on your own.*

*These instructions must be* remembered *as precisely as possible.*

73 PIERRE ANDLER *To Ambrosino and Kelemen, Interview*

*I would like to request an interview with Ambrosino and Kelemen. I do not know if it makes any sense from their point of view to ask to speak to them together, but I hope they would agree to do so. I suggest Thursday, Friday or Saturday at 7.15, at the café on the corner of rue Dauphine near the river. Hoping A and K can find a day that will suit them both and that one of them will call me to say which day they have chosen.*

*Andler* II.X.38

74 PIERRE ANDLER *Certain lapses of taste…*

*Certain lapses of taste have reminded me how much our activities stray perilously close to aesthetics. I have never stopped being alert to this. I know that aesthetic research and concerns have led certain men to rediscover the living truth and madness too, and the fate of these men is what has interested me about them above all else. I know that aesthetics has often played a dominant role in shaping every one of us, and I realise that we will never completely reject it. I am the first to accept this direct relationship, and with a lightness of heart, because aesthetics is by definition unconcerned with anything servile or that can be brought under control. But by way of such obvious and persuasive reasoning, today I feel deep misgivings and a nagging pain. We know the world we belong to: the world of Heraclitus and Nietzsche. And as for the sense of belonging, we have affirmed that for us this means total engagement. In this world we have taken the most ardent symbols and given them a face that is appealing but still terrifying. (In science we have even found the elements of a doctrine.) We have since built a community around this face. In this way we have brought together all the constituent elements of a myth. We have devised and performed rites of clear efficacy.* Nothing indicates that we have not already succeeded in creating this myth. *In fact, for it to become a genuine mythical figure only one element is missing:* the right or the determination to make demands in its name. *This element must be a part of it from now on: our myth demands of us some sort of action.*

*But this is precisely where the question of aesthetics comes into it. So that our myth is not an aesthetic creation, and that our love of religion should mean religion and our adherence to faith should mean faith, these demands made in the name of myth must be categorical. But is it enough that we know it must be categorical for it to be so in practice? Do the demands themselves depend on aesthetics? Is it enough to make the demands right now so that we can finally escape aesthetics?*

*Giving up one's life is so much easier.* 12.X.[19]38

THE COLLEGE OF SOCIOLOGY

# 75 *Declaration on the International Crisis*

The College of Sociology views the recent international crisis as a most important experience in several respects. We have neither the opportunity nor the time to examine all the aspects of this matter. In particular, we do not presume to have the competence to interpret one way or another the diplomatic developments which have led to the current state of peace, still less to declare how much they were foreseeable and how much unexpected, what parts were agreed to and what was imposed, and where appropriate what was play-acting and what sincere. We are also aware how facile and tenuous such interpretations may be; by exercising caution we hope that our example will be followed by those whose competence does not exceed our own. That is the first point.

The College of Sociology sees its own role in the objective appraisal of the collective psychological reactions aroused by the prospect of war and which, as the threat of danger passes, then sink into an oblivion that should rightly be seen as *an atonement*, or else become quickly transformed in the collective memory into pleasant and almost comforting recollections. The most hopeless individuals end up thinking they have become heroes. Already the public believes in the fairy story that they have conducted themselves with composure, dignity and resolve; was the prime minister somehow incapable of thanking them for that? And it must be said here that the words used to describe these sentiments are much too nice when up until now the only ones that were appropriate were consternation, resignation and fear. The performance we witnessed was one of mute and spellbound confusion, woefully at the mercy of events; this was the reaction of a population that was bound to be frightened and aware of its inferiority, when its politics refuses to admit the possibility of war when confronted by a nation whose own politics are entirely based upon war. That is the second point.

To this state of moral panic was added the absurdity of the current political positions. Right from the beginning, the situation was already marked by paradox: dictatorships apparently concerned for the right of the people to self-determination, and democracies backing the principle of natural borders and the vital interests of nations. In due course, these positions will become more and more extreme. We see the heir and successor of the Joseph Chamberlain who used to talk quite openly about England's global dominion, and on which its empire was built, going to plead with Mr. Hitler to agree to any settlement whatsoever, *provided that it was peaceful.* A Communist daily newspaper recently drew a parallel between this "messenger of peace" and Lord Kitchener, with the latter coming out on top in every respect. Without having seen it with our own eyes we would have refused to believe that the Communists should one day be congratulating the man who commanded the war in the Transvaal — with its systematic destruction of the civilian population and its concentration camps — for having secured a large area of land for his country (true enough, they made no mention of the gold and diamond mines gained for City traders). We should also bear in mind the state of public opinion in America which, from the other side of the ocean, and hence some distance away, has demonstrated its capacity for lack of awareness, self-righteous hypocrisy and a sort of impractical, Platonic idealism which seems to be more and more characteristic of the democracies. This is the third and final point, before the conclusion.

The College of Sociology is not a political organisation. Its members have their own opinions. Nor do we feel obliged to consider France's special interests in this business. Our role is exclusively to learn the lessons that must be gleaned from these events, and to do that while there is still time, that is to say before everyone becomes absolutely convinced that they have in all truth shown composure, dignity and resolve throughout the ordeal. The College of Sociology regards the general absence of any spirited reaction to the war as a sign of man's *devirilisation.* We feel certain that the cause of this is to be found in the loosening of the bonds that currently hold society together, indeed in their near non-existence, on account of the development of bourgeois individualism. We decry its effects without any show of emotion: men who are so alone, *so bereft of destiny* that they have absolutely no resources when faced with the possibility of death; men who, lacking any deep-seated reasons to join the struggle, inevitably turn into cowards when it comes to conflict, any kind of conflict, like some sort of sentient sheep resigned to the slaughterhouse.

The College of Sociology has essentially defined itself as an organisation for study and research. This continues to be the case. But we reserved for ourselves, at the time the college was founded, the possibility of being something else, if it could be done: this was to be a focus of energy. Yesterday's events suggest to us, perhaps even demand of us, that we concentrate on this aspect of our self-appointed activity. This is the reason we are taking the initiative of issuing this public statement. And it is for this reason that we invite those who have found that the only result of anguish is that it creates a vital bond between men, to join us, with no other condition except their awareness of the *utter deceit* of all present forms of politics and the need to reconstruct on principle a collective mode of existence which takes no account of any geographical or social constraints and which will allow us to show a little dignity when death approaches.

Paris, 7 October 1938

BATAILLE, CAILLOIS, LEIRIS

THE SACRED CONSPIRACY

# VII

## October 1938 – May 1939

# CHRONOLOGY

## 1938

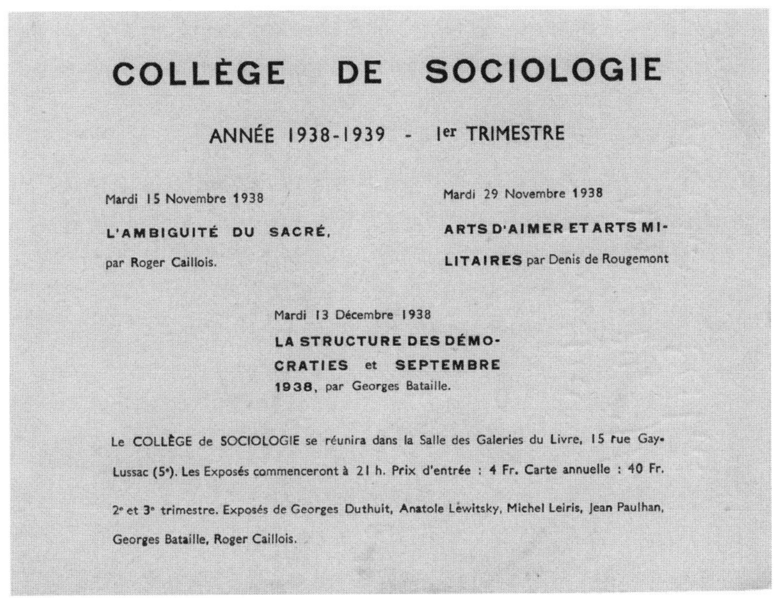
COLLÈGE DE SOCIOLOGIE

ANNÉE 1938-1939 - Ier TRIMESTRE

Mardi 15 Novembre 1938
L'AMBIGUITÉ DU SACRÉ,
par Roger Caillois.

Mardi 29 Novembre 1938
ARTS D'AIMER ET ARTS MILITAIRES par Denis de Rougemont

Mardi 13 Décembre 1938
LA STRUCTURE DES DÉMOCRATIES et SEPTEMBRE 1938, par Georges Bataille.

Le COLLÈGE de SOCIOLOGIE se réunira dans la Salle des Galeries du Livre, 15 rue Gay-Lussac (5e). Les Exposés commenceront à 21 h. Prix d'entrée : 4 Fr. Carte annuelle : 40 Fr.

2e et 3e trimestre. Exposés de Georges Duthuit, Anatole Lewitsky, Michel Leiris, Jean Paulhan, Georges Bataille, Roger Caillois.

**10 October.** An open meeting is held at the Critérion at 6.30 pm. Koch recalled Lacan being present at certain of these meetings.

**Before 15 October.** Bataille writes two questionnaires for members, labelled A (lost, apart from its supplement) and B, ●76. This latter is a set of rules concerning the activities of members, and is at the origin of a dispute with Kelemen.

**15 October.** Andler writes his response, "On Bataille's Questionnaire and Note", ●78.

**1 November.** The Popular Front government is dissolved as a result of the Communist refusal to endorse the Munich Agreement.

**2 November.** Bataille replies to Kelemen's objections to "Questionnaire B" by emphasising the urgency of the struggle against Christianity, Socialism and Fascism. This is the

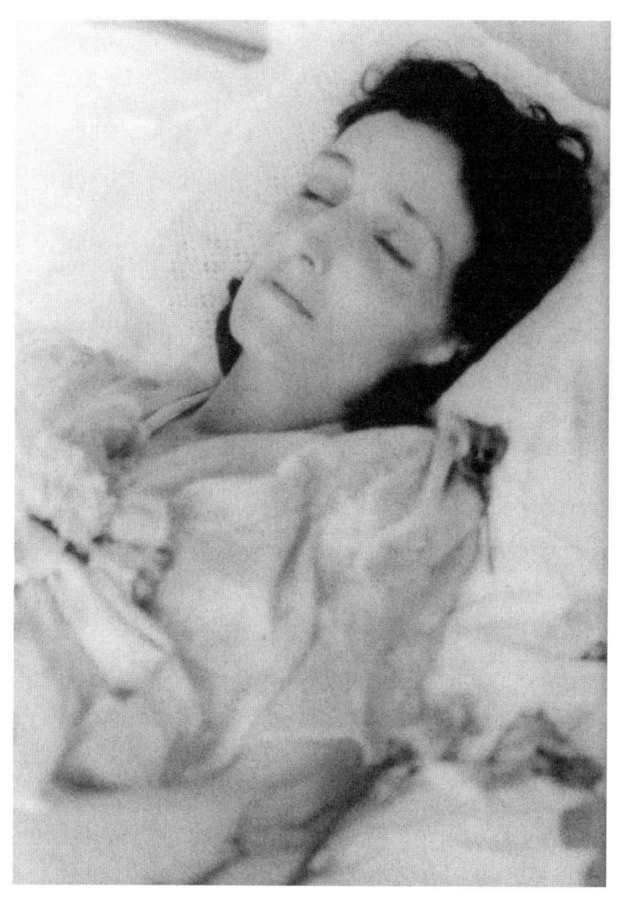

The last photograph of Laure,
taken on 7 November 1938.

subject of "The Tricephalous Monster", ●80. In the letter to Kelemen accompanying this text, Bataille sketches out the similarities he sees between the will for festival and the will for death which later informs the lecture "Joy in the Face of Death", ○95, he delivers to the College in June 1939.

Later the same day Laure's illness reaches its final crisis. A year afterwards Bataille recalled: "I tried to speak to her but she did not respond [...] I understood that everything was coming to the end, and that I would never speak to her again, that she was going to die like this in a few hours and that we would never again speak to each other [...] The world crumbled pitilessly."[1]

**7 November.** The death of Laure in Saint-Germain-en-Laye after an agony lasting four days. Bataille, Leiris, Moré and her mother and sister are present. The family are devout Catholics and request a priest, but Bataille refuses to allow one in his house.[2] Laure's last words: "It's ravishing", of a rose Bataille had given her. He places a translation of Blake's *The Marriage of Heaven and Hell* in her coffin. His grief is exacerbated when he discovers her writings; one text in particular, "The Sacred", overwhelms him because of its similarities with what he himself had recently written. Against the wishes of her family, in 1939 he and Leiris publish a private edition of her writings, under the name of Laure, with this same title, *The Sacred*. He later wrote: "Pain, terror, tears, delirium, orgy, fever, then death, this was the daily bread that Laure shared with me and this bread left me with the memory of a powerful but intense sweetness; it was the form taken by a love eager to exceed the limits of things and yet how many times did we find moments of impossible happiness, starry nights, flowing streams [...]."[3]

**9 November.** The attacks of Kristallnacht take place across Germany. Hundreds of Jews are killed and thousands are arrested and sent to camps, while countless synagogues and Jewish businesses are destroyed.

**During the second term of 1938,** Georges Duthuit* and Camille Schuwer lecture to the Society of Group Psychology on "Representations of Death".[4]

**10 November.** Bataille writes to Caillois, probably referring to Laure: "Do not say a word about what you know", before moving on to problems concerning the publication of the College "Declaration" in the *NRF*.

**15 November.** Bataille continues to organise the activities of the College of Sociology, which resume with a lecture by Caillois, "The Ambiguity of the Sacred".

**29 November.** Denis de Rougemont lectures to the College on "Arts of Love and Arts of War". Also in November, Bataille's article "Chance" appears in *Verve* I, 4.

**13 December.** Bataille lectures to the College on "The Structure of Democracies and the Crisis of September 1938", the text of which is lost. Victoria Ocampo, the publisher of *Sur*, attends the lecture and she and Caillois soon begin a relationship.

**17 December.** Bataille writes to Caillois proposing a programme for the College for 1939, most of which was carried out.[5] A printed version is produced for the second "trimester" (*overleaf*). Around this time Farner and Waldberg move in with Bataille at Saint-Germain-en-Laye, and the three of them share this house until autumn 1939.

**Late December.** Rollin, who was the original point of contact between the Spanish anarchist Miguel González Inestal and Acéphale, writes to Bataille from Barcelona, ●81, concerning the sessional meeting of 29 September, ●69. He appends his text "The Acéphale", ●82, a commentary on Bataille's "Propositions on the Death of God," ●65, and probably his translation of a text by González Inestal that commented on Acéphale. Kelemen's "We live on the surface of the Earth...", ●83, likely also dates from this time.

**Late December/early 1939.** Probable date of Bataille's "Propositions," ●85, in which he

# COLLÈGE DE SOCIOLOGIE

## ANNÉE 1938-1939 — 2[me] TRIMESTRE

Mardi 10 Janvier 1939

**LA NAISSANCE DE LA LITTÉRATURE**, par René Guastalla

Mardi 24 Janvier 1939

**HITLER ET L'ORDRE TEUTONIQUE**, par Georges Bataille

Mardi 7 Février 1939

**LE MARQUIS DE SADE ET LA RÉVOLUTION**, par Pierre Klossowski

Mardi 21 février 1939

**COMMÉMORATION DU MARDI GRAS**, par Georges Bataille

Les Mardi 7 et 21 Mars 1939

**QUELQUES ASPECTS DU CHAMANISME**, par Anatole Levitsky

Les réunions ont lieu dans la Salle des Galeries du Livre, 15, rue Gay-Lussac (5e), à 21 h.

Prix d'entrée : 4 fr. Abonnement trimestriel : 15 fr.

# COLLÈGE DE SOCIOLOGIE

## ANNÉE 1938-1939 — 3[me] TRIMESTRE

Mardi 18 Avril 1939

**LES RITES DES ASSOCIATIONS POLITIQUES DANS L'ALLEMAGNE ROMANTIQUE**, par Hans Mayer

Mardi 2 Mai 1939

**THÉORIE DE LA FÊTE**, par Roger Caillois

Mardi 16 Mai 1939

**LE LANGAGE SACRÉ**, par Jean Paulhan

Mardi 6 Juin 1939

**LA JOIE DEVANT LA MORT**, par Georges Bataille

Mardi 20 Juin 1939

**LE MYTHE DE LA MONARCHIE ANGLAISE**, par Georges Duthuit

Mardi 4 Juillet 1939

**LE COLLÈGE DE SOCIOLOGIE**, par Georges Bataille, Roger Caillois et Michel Leiris

Les réunions ont lieu dans la Salle des Galeries du Livre, 15, rue Gay-Lussac (5e), à 21 h.

Prix d'entrée : 4 fr. Abonnement trimestriel : 15 fr.

introduces "joy in the face of death" as the fundamental principle of the Society.

## 1939

**3 January.** Bataille writes the first part of "The Madness of Nietzsche" for *Acéphale* 5.

**10 January.** René Guastalla lectures to the College on "The Birth of Literature".

**24 January.** Bataille lectures to the College on "Hitler and the Teutonic Order". The text is lost.

**25 January.** Bataille writes to Caillois to criticise his comments about Communism in an article he has not yet published. He claims it not only demonstrates Caillois's self-confessed "total political incompetence" but could be mistaken for the views of the College.

**26 January.** Andler signs his "Personal Commitment" to the secret society.

**7 February.** Klossowski lectures to the College on "The Marquis de Sade and the Revolution".

**21 February.** Bataille's lecture to the College on "The Commemoration of the Mardi Gras" stresses the revolutionary significance of the carnival within a democracy (the text is lost). On this date too Caillois probably reads his lecture "Sociology of the Executioner", which puts forward an opposite thesis. It is published in the autumn in the *NRF*.

**27 February.** The French Chamber of Deputies recognises Franco's government in Spain. Madrid alone remains in the hands of the Republic but falls to the Fascists on 28 March, and the new government declares a complete victory on 1 April. In this period nearly one million refugees cross over into France.

**February.** Monnerot publishes a questionnaire on "spiritual advisers" in *Volontés*, a journal edited by Georges Pelorson. The responses, published in June, include one from the College of Sociology. In the February issue Queneau objects to the mythomania in intellectual circles, insisting that myths cannot be invented, but can only exist as the emanation of a community.[6]

**7 March.** Anatole Lewitsky* gives the first of a two-part lecture to the College, "On Certain Aspects of Shamanism". He gives the second part on 21 March.

**15 March.** Invasion of Czechoslovakia by Nazi Germany.

**17 March.** In a letter to Caillois, Bataille discusses possibilities for the next series of lectures. He also announces that he will speak on the Nazi incursion after the second lecture by Lewitsky at the College on 21 March. Bataille's speech was to be called "The New Defenestration of Prague" and redefines the College by emphasising "two political principles of sacred sociology".[7] His own summary is given on pp.360-1.

**Probably 21 March.** A private meeting is held at Bataille's flat to resolve the immediate programme of the College. No lecture has been scheduled for late April, and Bataille asks Walter Benjamin and Hans Mayer* if they would speak. Benjamin proposes a lecture on the meaning of fashion, Mayer on the rites of German nationalism. Bataille chooses the latter, but accepts Benjamin's proposal for the next series. Mayer later writes, "The College had reached a point of terrible uncertainty".[8]

**22 March.** Bataille writes to Caillois summarising the previous day's meeting, and includes the programme for the third term, which now includes Mayer's lecture.

**23 and 24 March.** France and Britain issue decrees promising to intervene in the case of a German attack on Belgium, the Netherlands, Switzerland or Poland. This is extended on 13 April, after Italy's invasion of Albania on 7 April, to include Romania and Greece.

**25 March.** Dussat, in Toulon, writes for Acéphale "The Role of Irony in Tragedy" (not included here).

**Spring.** Bataille and Waldberg take Duthuit into the forest of Marly in the hope that he will join

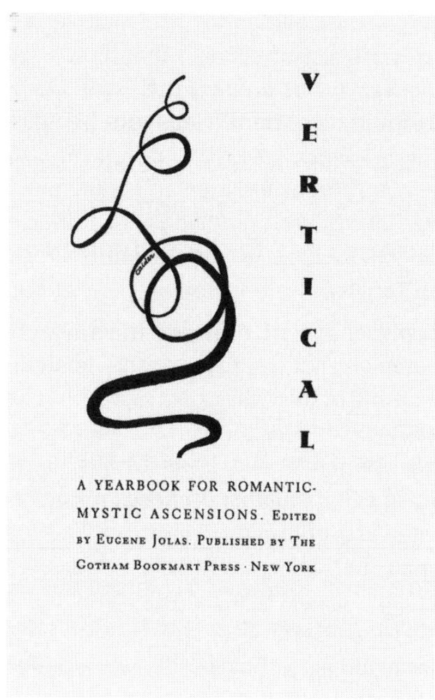

VERTICAL
A YEARBOOK FOR ROMANTIC-MYSTIC ASCENSIONS. EDITED BY EUGENE JOLAS. PUBLISHED BY THE GOTHAM BOOKMART PRESS · NEW YORK


The title-page of *Vertical*, published in New York in 1941, which featured a selection of texts relating to the College, "The Sacred Ritual", and which was edited by Georges Duthuit.

the Society, but Duthuit later writes that he was never invited to Acéphale's meetings.[9]

Publication of *The Sacred* by "Laure", edited and annotated anonymously by Bataille and Leiris. In spring 1943 they edit a second book of hers, *Histoire d'une petite fille* (*Story of a Little Girl*).

**April.** Caillois publishes the article Bataille had criticised in January in the journal *Les Volontaires*: "The Hierarchy of Beings: relations and oppositions between democracy, Fascism and the notion of order".

**7 April.** Possible date for the encounter in the forest described in the text "In Search of Joy in the Face of Death", ●86.

**18 April.** Mayer lectures to the College on "Rites of Political Associations in Germany during the Romantic Period".

**Late April.** Duthuit edits a section in *Cahiers d'art* 1-4, consisting of texts by Bataille ("The Sacred"), Caillois ("The Polycrates Complex, after the Tyrant of Samos") and Duthuit himself ("Representations of Death").

**2 May.** Caillois lectures to the College on "Theory of the Festival", ○91, a text which appears in the *NRF* in December 1939 and January 1940 and then in *Man and the Sacred* (1940), the foreword of which is dated March 1939.[10]

**16 May.** Paulhan lectures to the College on "Sacred Language".

**17 May.** Bataille sends a letter, ●87, with instructions for the encounter in the forest, the first stage of the initiation ritual into the secret society, to Louis Couturier.[11]

**31 May.** Bataille addresses a text to the members of Acéphale urging the secret society to strengthen its communal unity by abandoning all half measures and carelessness, ●90.

# COMMENTARIES

## ACÉPHALE [MG]

The first texts in this section, dating from October, would have benefited from being read with a document that has not been found, "Questionnaire A". We have also omitted another document, the "Supplement to Questionnaire A", since it lists "subjects of interest to the organisation"[1] that turn out to be very close to those studied by the College. This closeness raises the question of how far Acéphale influenced what topics were to be lectured upon at the College. Another document omitted here, Dussat's "Debate on the Problem of War", returned to one of the main preoccupations of both Acéphale and the College since the Sudeten crisis: the threat of war. This concern, introduced by Andler's text "The War" (as noted on pp.311-12), explained the urgency to define the group's political position at the sessional meeting of 29 September, ●69. Dussat's contribution engaged with the debate on a more philosophical level, in terms of the incompatibility of the "death offered in warfare" with "death as the supreme object [...] of the joy of existing".[2] This was close to the distinction made by Bataille during the lecture on brotherhoods, on 19 March 1938 at the College, between, on the one hand, "the armed brute" for whom "death is more than anything [...] what he has in store for the enemy", and the "man of law and discourse" who "rejects tragedy in so far as it is an expression of crime", and on the other hand, the man of tragedy who alone "knows he is a victim of human absurdity, and the absurdity of nature, but accepts this reality which has left him no other outlet but crime".[3] It also resembles the "tragic gift of the self" in §XVII of the programme announced at the meeting of 29 September, ●69, and the last of the "Eleven Aggressions" in the same document. This latter formula was also the likely source for Andler's "Meditation on Joy in the Face of Death", ●77, at the end of which he returns to the taste for aestheticism among the adepts he had first criticised in ●74.

"Questionnaire B", ●76, Bataille's follow-up to his text of 28 September 1938, "Degrees", ●66, specified the different types of activities expected of adepts. Andler's "On Bataille's Questionnaire and Note", ●78, of 15 October, concerns the upheaval within the Society caused by Bataille's "Note", ●71, of the week before, and his "Questionnaire

B". Andler wrote: "... it is not possible to appeal *to almost everything* that unites us so deeply." In fact, he says, "nothing *essential* is at stake in the questionnaire" and, as regards the notion of the *disagreeable* put forward by Bataille in his "Note", that too is meaningless because the adepts will not "refuse *the most challenging sacrifices* demanded by the community". The upheaval became an outright dispute on Kelemen's part, according to two documents which he later gave to Andler: Bataille's letter of 2 November, ●79, and his "The Tricephalous Monster", ●80. This text meant that the community was now implementing the programme of 29 September, ●69, in which Bataille called upon the members to match the semi-divine heroes of Hesiod's *Works and Days* by forming an aggressive force to oppose the "three hostile heads: Christianity, Socialism and Fascism". Since the age of iron had passed, however, it was no longer a matter of sharpening Hesiod's "weapons made of metal", but rather "words we must sharpen". Henceforth, application to this task would be the condition for adepts to reach the second degree, that of "the man who has attained the fullness of power and virility", ●80.

Both Rollin's letter, ●81, responding to the "Eleven Aggressions" and programme of 29 September, and his text "The Acéphale", ●82, a commentary on the "Propositions on the Death of God", ●65, which accompanied his letter, bear witness for the period of late December 1938 or January 1939 to even more profound objections than those expressed by Andler. Rollin pointed out that awareness of the tragedy of existence cannot lead to redemptive action, and so a contradiction lay at the heart of the secret society: "*The will to power asserted tragically is a will to loss; asserted in practice, it is domination, the creation of a form of power*." This explained his refusal to subscribe to the second, fourth and ninth aggressions and to the "fullness of power" at the heart of Acéphale's programme, virility, which he suggested be replaced by the affective reality of human solidarity as a proper means of achieving the liberation of man. From this followed a reflection on the identification of the Acéphale with the superman who can only be "the requirement, the fulfilment and above all the consequence of the death of God", if the will to power is conceived of not "as an existing force or entity, to which it fails to correspond, but as an indeterminate quality through which it is a question, in the course of its creation, of *revealing* and affirming existence", ●82. Finally Rollin opposed any move towards individualism by means of a new "*egotism*", whose "quality and intensity" was a gift opposed to "charity or pity". An unpublished text by Kelemen, of uncertain date but preserved amongst Andler's papers, is likewise linked to ●65. "We live on the surface of the Earth...", ●83, which followed a meditation at the acephalous tree, denounces "the voice [...] *at the surface*", which is allied to "the forms taken by man's cowardice" and which provokes man's "headlong flight in the face of death" into the arms of "*God, infinite* and *eternal*". Only "the ecstasy of love" can provide the necessary "violent and magnificent negation of the eternal and infinite God".

Although few in number, the last texts in this section, which all probably date from early in 1939, suggest other ways for harnessing the Society's aggressive force, ●85 §5, to create "a world that will break free from all prevailing laws relating to necessity and fear". This is the text in which "joy in the face of death" becomes the Society's fundamental principle and links it to the power the group "is determined to use". Furthermore, breaking with its previous positions on the question of war, the Society is henceforth urged by "Propositions" to agree to participate in military operations only on condition that all moral bonds between the soldier and his flag are severed. Andler's "Personal Commitment" of 26 January, ●84, is symptomatic of this new climate within the group. It took the form of a "trial" setting out the number of hours to be devoted to Acéphale during the coming year, and the consequences of falling short by the time the new period was inaugurated with the sessional meeting in September.

"In Search of Joy in the Face of Death", ●86, a brief text found in the papers of Andler, Chavy and Waldberg, refers to a nocturnal encounter at the oak tree in the forest of Marly. Andler's copy has a pencilled note attached: "Andler / 7-4-39" followed by "Gare S[aint-] L[azare] 20h. / go there first / return via Saint-Nom", and similar instructions preceded the first encounter in the forest of Louis Couturier, and his experience of the communal rite of the sulphur fire before the tree. In a letter of 17 May 1939, ●87, Bataille explained: "The sulphur we use calls to mind volcanoes. Lightning and volcanoes are connected for us with 'joy in the face of death'."[4] Was Couturier only a "participant" in the Society, or had he acquired the title of "larva" (see ●66), following a rite of initiation? The absence of any documentation relating to the sessional meetings of 1939 means this question cannot be answered, but his relations with Bataille appear warm and extended beyond the disbanding of Acéphale. In a letter to him on 10 November 1938, Bataille wrote: "It seems to me that the task we are engaged in must of necessity be difficult. In particular, everything connected with the mystical experience seems fraught with real dangers. [...] For my part, I have tried to find what connects mystical and erotic states, not excluding those that are the most abject. I do not want to suggest in the least though that they may be confused with one another [...] But once the deep connection is laid bare, the object of mystical ecstasy can be apprehended with a boldness that has been all but lost and by forces that until now were inconceivable."[5] Whatever the case, Couturier's involvement in the Society was important enough for the walk to the stricken tree to appear in the first chapter of his novel *Les Portes dauphines*, published in 1954 (see ●88), a few years after he had been excluded from any involvement with Surrealism.

Matters were otherwise, however, with regard to Duthuit. Waldberg recounts their long walk in the forest of Marly to the tree with Bataille in spring 1939,[6] just before Duthuit gave his lecture to the College on "The Myth of the English Monarchy", the text of which is lost. According to Waldberg, "he was greatly interested in the recent ideas of Bataille", but he "never went so far as initiation",[7] a decision he reached only after some hesitation. Duthuit confirmed his position in a letter to Breton of 18 November 1943, published in February 1944 in *VVV* in the section "Towards a New Myth? Premonitions and Challenges", and in fact the numerous references to Bataille in his works mainly concern the College.[8] While in New York in 1941, he put together some texts from the College under the title "The Sacred Ritual" for Eugene Jolas's *Vertical* anthology, and linked the College and Acéphale by including Masson's drawing of Dionysus. These first texts collected together in English consisted of Caillois's "Introduction", ○59, and "The Ambiguity of the Sacred", Bataille's "The Sacred Conspiracy", ●1, and his own "For a Sacred Art".

The final text here, from Bataille to the members of Acéphale, ●90, was one of the few to be found among the papers of Isabelle Waldberg and is another call for the Society to strengthen its communal unity a few days before Bataille lectured to the College on "Joy in the Face of Death".

## THE COLLEGE OF SOCIOLOGY [AB]

The lectures in the first year of the College had been delivered only by those who had contributed to its formation. In the second year they included a number by lecturers who had not, amongst them Duthuit, Guastalla, Lewitsky, Mayer, Paulhan and Rougemont. Benjamin's presentation was postponed until the following year, by which time he had died while attempting to cross the Spanish border. None of these lectures are summarised here.

In the first year, Bataille and Caillois had expounded a preliminary thesis describing aspects of the structure of the sacred and it seems they now hoped that the "community" of the College would be strong enough for lecturers from outside the initial group to contribute to elaborating these ideas. However, the speakers' lack of familiarity with the discussions about "active" sociology which had informed the setting up of the College led, on occasion, to a certain loss of intensity, and some of these lectures also failed to engage adequately with the precepts laid out by Bataille and Caillois in the previous year. Perhaps if abstracts or complete texts had been distributed to participants either before or after the lectures, then the coherence of the programme might have been more sustainable. Notes by Bataille from 1937 show he had explored the possibility of creating a College journal, which might have performed the same function, but concluded that it was not affordable.[9]

Having communicated his ideas and intentions from "The Sacred Conspiracy" to "The Sorcerer's Apprentice", and in the lectures that fell between, Bataille must now have felt that the real arena for his activities should be Acéphale. The death of Laure had also affected him deeply, and he may have hoped that the College could function on its own to some extent, and serve as a means for recruiting new members to the Society.

The second year's lectures moved from Saturdays to Tuesdays, and began with "The Ambiguity of the Sacred" by Caillois, who had not actually spoken at the College since April. He returned to its central concern, the sacred, but the sacred considered primarily within an ethnographic and anthropological context rather than the contemporary one envisaged by Bataille in ○29. The text is known because it later appeared, in April 1939, in *Mesures*, and formed a chapter in Caillois's book *Man and the Sacred*, in November the following year (although presumably revised for publication).

Caillois's presentation is elegantly precise and has a rhetorical clarity that Bataille's writing often lacked. Conversely, his decision to consider this topic historically meant it lacked Bataille's sense of urgency, while its chief aim appeared to be recapitulative and it added little to Bataille's interpretation of Durkheim. Caillois describes a world in which the profane everyday is bounded by two abysses that are in fact one, a realm of ambiguity in which the awe felt before sanctity finds its equivalent in the fear of defilement,[10] where fascination and aversion are hard to distinguish, a confusion that almost always signifies the presence of the sacred. He cast the explorers of this realm in a heroic light, but whether he imagined himself in this role is left unstated:

> He who dares to unleash subterranean forces, to abandon himself to the powers of the underworld, will be unsatisfied with his lot, perhaps because he has been unable to sway the heavens. He is nevertheless qualified to try and force entry. The pact with the devil is just as much a consecration as is divine grace. He who has signed the pact, or is burdened by grace, is for ever separated from the common fate, and the prestige of his destiny disturbs the dreams of the timid and the jaded who have never been tempted by any abyss.[11]

Bataille's lecture on "The Structure of the Democracies and the Crisis of September 1938" is lost, and this is particularly regrettable since, according to an account of the evening by Bertrand d'Astorg, it was the only lecture to the College that specifically addressed the immediate political situation. Presumably it would have built upon the "Declaration", ○75, published the previous month, which was likewise prompted by the Munich Agreement of September. D'Astorg makes it clear that the lecture was no defence of the democracies, and Bataille's claim that they were on the verge of expiring provoked a heated discussion with Paulhan and Julien Benda. D'Astorg observed that: "we could not tell whether these orators were treacherous anti-democrats, or if they were defending a personal conception of an ideal democracy".[12]

The prospectus issued by the College for 1938-9 was published on three small cards rather than as the single sheet of the previous year. This allowed the programme to be announced in parts rather than in full at the start of the year, and is likely symptomatic of the difficulty of finding suitable lecturers. Shortly after Bataille's lecture on the democracies, a letter to Caillois on 17 December considered the options for the rest of the year. Apart from the lectures by these two, most of those discussed came to pass as planned, with the exception of the lecture proposed by Duthuit. He had been supposed to speak on "Representations of Death" in art, but instead gave this presentation at the Society of Group Psychology. However, the lecture was still placed within the orbit of the College by being published together with texts by Bataille and Caillois in *Cahiers d'art* in April 1939, around the time Bataille and Waldberg were interested in Duthuit joining Acéphale. The schedule of lectures was soon confirmed though and the new programme rapidly printed (see p.348), since the first lecture by Guastalla on "the miseries of literature",[13] took place on 10 January.

Bataille's lecture on "Hitler and the Teutonic Order" followed two weeks later, but no description of it survives apart from Bataille's own in the same letter to Caillois from 17 December (the Teutonic Knights were German, the Knights Templar French in origin):

> It is a question of starting from the opposition between the Teutonic Knights and the Knights Templar as presented by those involved in occultism, and allow that Hitler's affiliation to the Teutonic Order is probably "mythical", whereas that is not the case for the Ordensburgen, the schools for future leaders which are constituted along the same lines as those of military orders; furthermore, a response to the Ordensburgen is required from those of us who are unwilling to submit to the domination of a power which we do not recognise, etc.[14]

The Ordensburgen were of course the military schools about which Caillois later recalled his enthusiasm (pp.77-78).

On 7 February Klossowski spoke on "The Marquis de Sade and the Revolution", in which he expressed points of view that Bataille and Caillois must have found problematic. Klossowski had been involved with Contre-Attaque and was a great exegete of Nietzsche and Sade, and somehow reconciled these inclinations with his Catholic faith. This perhaps explains his ambiguous status at the College, where he was involved in its inner workings but held slightly at arm's length (alongside his friend Benjamin). He was also involved with Acéphale from its beginnings, but in the "Annual Summation" of September 1937, as we have seen, Bataille wrote that "Klossowski has gone so far as to interpose God between himself and us", ●39. Klossowski seems then to have ceased his participation with the Society, although the following July the group considered reconnecting with him, ●52.

Klossowski, however, remained active in the College, despite his ideas being at odds with Bataille's, and in this lecture he defended his earlier position. He set out —in that year of the 150th anniversary of the French Revolution — to distinguish between the Sadean revolution of the sublime perversity of the "complete man", and that of the "Incorruptible" Robespierre and his "natural man". Klossowski viewed the latter only as an idealisation of banal man, whom he shows to be just as much a criminal. He suggests that free-thinking and libertine nobles such as Sade are essential precursors of revolution, and are "complete" because they are sufficiently lucid to be able to objectify "the contents of their guilty *conscience*".[15] A sort of unholy example then, but when the revolution comes they find that they have no place in the Republic it creates because their existence was based upon their being an opposition which was only meaningful within the prohibitions of the old society. Sade and his like (if there was such a like) undermine this old society and in revealing the criminality of its overlords, "will provide the incentive for perpetrating regicide so as to adopt a republican government".[16] This, however, will be carried out by "natural" men who will thus have assumed some of the attributes of "complete" men, by killing the earthly representative of God.

At this point Klossowski expands upon the points in his text for Acéphale that contributed to the rift between him and the group two years previously, "On the Master and the Slave", ●25 (see pp.152-153 for Marina Galletti's discussion of other possible points of contention). He asserts that it was the Church's grouping "of social forces into an order that granted moral significance to each",[17] in other words a hierarchy of power, that put an "end to the law of the jungle" and substituted for the ancient Master and Slave relationship one of master and servant, a supposedly superior arrangement. This is obviously contrary to ideas previously expressed at the College, for example, in the lecture on "Power" (pp.257-258). So for Klossowski, the crime celebrated by Bataille and Acéphale leads only to a vicious circle of more and more crime. The revolutionary reinstatement of the pre-Christian situation means each person in turn becomes master and is murdered by his slave, in a sort of profane replication of the killing of the King of the Woods. Thus, in effect, Robespierre's Republic "can never begin".[18] Klossowski cites in support of his argument the same passage from Sade that Bataille had used at the start of "The Sacred Conspiracy", ●1: "A nation that is already old and corrupt, that bravely shakes off the yoke of its monarchical government so as to adopt a republican one instead, can only survive by committing countless criminal acts; this is because it already exists in a state of crime...". The "inexpiable" crime of the killing of the king condemns the new society, and in his lecture Klossowski repeats a sentence from ●25, almost word for word: "Henceforth everything you undertake will bear the mark of murder".[19] Such a statement in this context carries an opposite inflection to Bataille's notion of society as being founded on crime, and even if this argument were accepted, it ignores the fact that Christian morality shares the same mythical foundation, the killing of the God/King. To that extent then, and within this schema, the revolutionary outcome will be no different, and that would be its only failure. The question should rather be, what morality will the new society put in the place of the one founded on Christianity?

Bataille's "Commemoration of the Mardi Gras" followed on 21 February. It is probable that Caillois read his "Sociology of the Executioner" on the same evening, and although this lecture does not appear on any of the College programmes it was certainly given there (in his introduction Hollier cites various witnesses who recalled it). Bataille's lecture is again lost; Boissonnas spoke a little about it in the passage cited in the introduction (p.86), and her notes are the only record of it.[20] She wrote: "The strangeness of M. Bataille's presentation seduced me, even though it seemed rather more devastating than at all constructive. It troubles me that I cannot remember all the points of his lecture..." Her diary records that after the lecture Caillois spoke to disagree with Bataille, a public disagreement that followed a private one (p.349, *25 January*). The substance of Caillois's objection to the lecture was mentioned in a letter from Paulhan to Boissonnas,[21] namely that the "Mardi Gras might be more of a safety valve, less likely to precipitate revolution (as Bataille hoped) than to delay it indefinitely."

There was more at stake here for the College than at first appears. Hollier in his introduction[22] pointed out that Bataille saw in carnival a cohesive force associated with expenditure that could match that of military cohesion (for which read Fascist cohesion), but in which a revolutionary potential yet seemed a possibility. Caillois, for his part, had already associated such festivals with political upheaval when he wrote that "Dionysism coincided with the revolt of rural elements against the urban nobility", ●28, yet in his lecture on the sociology of the state executioner he drew a distinction between the killing of the king in societies in which this is a regular (if often symbolic) occurrence, and a society where it "occurs in the course of a crisis within a regime or dynasty. It then has only a strictly political significance, even if it quite understandably arouses *within certain individuals* reactions of a clearly religious nature." This interpretation appears to suggest a fundamental disagreement with Bataille in which the notion of expenditure that lay behind all his thought could in fact have a diffusing effect within a collective, rather than concentrating effervescence so as to provide a revolutionary potential. The College had been founded, at least in part, as a means of surpassing politics by revivifying the sacred as a virulent effervescence that would radically change the society it infected, but Caillois now seemed to be suggesting it would be a safety valve that had the opposite effect, and actively maintain a society's present state.

The first section of Caillois's lecture considered the huge press interest in the recent death of the state executioner, Anatole Deibler, which Caillois claimed was a demonstration that the power of myth and "the realities giving birth to it"[23] were far from absent in present-day society. He then described the complex mythical interplay between the figures of the king and the executioner. For example, while the king has power over life and death, it is the abject person of the executioner who takes upon himself the crime of actually carrying out the sentence. These two represent in their persons the pure and impure sacred respectively, so that when the latter kills the former in a powerful moment of sacrifice and sacrilege it appears as a sort of culmination, a vivid representation of the overturning of the established order, and a point of no return. Yet Caillois, as we have seen, argued that this was not a social fact, while also stating that "*in the popular conscience* the decapitation of the king appears as the pinnacle of the revolution" which, one would have thought, makes it indistinguishable from a collective representation, and thus indeed a social fact.

Also in February 1939, Monnerot published in *Volontés* an article that examined the notion of spiritual or moral authority, and the interplay between the two, and which began with two questions: "There have always been directors of *conscience* in the West: popes, priests, reformers, pastors; do you think such spiritual direction is an organic function of human society? Or, on the contrary, do you believe that the society in which we live, as members of a historical community, has attained a sort of adulthood that allows us to do without directors of *conscience*?"

The French expression "*directeur de conscience*" would usually be translated as "spiritual adviser", but in this context a more literal translation has been adopted, since this was evidently not an enquiry about parish priests. Monnerot's questions were sent out to some 150 people, and their answers were published in June. There were separate responses from various individuals associated with the College, including Duthuit, Guastalla, Klossowski, Moré, Paulhan and Wahl, and also from the College itself, one of the briefest published:

> The problems raised by your inquiry are precisely those which, for the past two years, the College of Sociology has endeavoured to understand and resolve. All our labours, all our initiatives and all our public events are aimed specifically

towards this end. Such can be no surprise to the author of this questionnaire, for he participated in the discussions which led to the College of Sociology, his signature is on the declaration that announced its foundation and the association even owes its name to him.

Be that as it may, the College of Sociology cannot summarise in a few incomplete and empty lines what constitutes the essential part of its activity. Here we should only recall that we consider our sole task to be that of *answering* the questions posed by your inquiry and that we aspire, as far as we are able, to *be* that answer.

The two lectures in March were given by Lewitsky on shamanism. In a letter to Caillois on the 17th, Bataille informs him that several of those who attended Lewitsky's first lecture were "bored in the extreme".[24] Paulhan too complained of Lewitsky's lifeless delivery,[25] but Boissonnas was delighted by Bataille's summing up, recording in her diary:

> Bataille brought the lecture to a close with a wonderful ease, clarity and authority. His mouth is the most animated part of his face, his eyes are small. He is a big man, and carries himself so that he appears strong, Olympian. His chin is slightly receding. His eloquence is quite remarkable, and comes very naturally to him. He follows the argument effortlessly, and always finds the striking image.[26]

In fact, Lewitsky's mode of presentation seemed to improve somewhat with his second lecture, and Bataille was not alone in saying that it only partially detracted from its content.

Between these two lectures there was a sudden deterioration in the international situation. On 15 March, Germany used its bridgehead in the Sudetenland to occupy Czechoslovakia. The "peace for our time" had lasted less than six months. The College was plunged into a period of "terrible uncertainty" according to Mayer.

One of many German Jewish intellectuals then exiled in Paris, Mayer had first met Bataille late in 1938. Impressed by the "Declaration on the International Crisis", ○75, he had written to the College and a meeting was arranged in a café. Bataille, Caillois and Leiris all arrived together (which somewhat contradicts the idea that Leiris was playing little part in the College by this time). Mayer became close to Bataille and left an account of these few months when they met on a regular basis.

Bataille and Caillois now had extreme doubts about the relevance of their enterprise in the face of unfolding events. In a letter to Caillois, Bataille proposed that he should speak on the crisis after the second lecture by Lewitsky on 21 March. His speech, based upon the second "abandoned" declaration of the College, was to be called "The New Defenestration of Prague",[27] but this is lost and nor is it known if it was actually read at the College, although Bataille summed up its content in his letter to Caillois:

> Our role is to insert into the heads of our fellow men the conviction that they are nothing.
>
> I would thus like to highlight two political principles of sacred sociology:
>
> I. That if everyone who feels the need to serve a sacred cause is cast out to the extremes (right or left), then society will waste away. Sometimes it is necessary for the life of society that such scattered forces should be concentrated. This, in my opinion, is what is required now and can only be done by people like us.
>
> II. Whether the development of economic institutions gives rise to slavery or whether it simply tends towards slavery, it is pointless to co-operate on any development based upon the necessity of things, which it would also be mad to oppose, instead we should create an organisation which cannot be enslaved, an irreducible nucleus resistant to any eventualities, and around which existence can be recomposed in all its wholeness.
>
> I would like to end by saying that there is no place in the world for disordered mobs, that a place must be made for that which alone possesses the power to order life, which is to say the sacred, and for whatever enters its orbit and thereby grows and becomes concentrated, organically, like a storm.

Needless to say, the notion that sacred sociology must have political principles was not something that had been accepted in the early days of the College, but events were causing previous certainties to collapse. The programme for the final term was settled, at a meeting that probably took place on 21 March, and it was at this particularly ominous moment that Bataille must have chosen the topics for his own lectures, which appear designed to bring down the supposed barrier between the College and Acéphale. The first of them, for 6 June, would now be "Joy in the Face of Death", which Bataille proposed as the fundamental principle of Acéphale at around this time, ●85 §3 (although it had first appeared within Acéphale as the 6th "aggression" in July of the previous year, ●52). The final lecture was to be on the College itself; Bataille, Caillois and Leiris would each have half an hour to express their opinion of what it was, its aims and its methods. Bataille wrote to Caillois with these proposals on 22 March, and the last lines of his letter are both defensive and cautionary:

> What I said to you yesterday about the intellectual integrity associated with the mystical experience is a position that I have thought through. I do not think you yourself can avoid taking a stance. Rigour will necessarily demand that you choose,

one way or the other. I confess that I often feel great impatience when I see the huge intellectual laxness which is the rule, so that essential problems are not asked in people's minds.[28]

Also in March 1939, Caillois wrote the foreword to his book *Man and the Sacred* which would appear in 1940. This book is profoundly informed by the work of the College, yet Caillois never mentions it, nor Bataille, apart from once in the foreword: "I must express my gratitude to Georges Bataille: it seems to me that on this question [the sacred] we established between us an intellectual osmosis, which after so many discussions does not allow me, on my part, to distinguish with certainty his contribution from mine in the work we pursued in common." In a text from the early 1950s[29] Bataille described this as an exaggeration, especially in regard to two of its chapters that had been given as lectures, "The Ambiguity of the Sacred" and "Theory of the Festival", ○91, before distancing himself from them by describing them as Caillois's most "personal" statements to the College.

On 18 April, Mayer lectured on the "Rites of Political Associations in Germany during the Romantic Period" in which, according to Mayer himself, he showed that the entire vocabulary of the Waffen-SS could be found in German Romanticism.[30] This was followed on 2 May by Caillois's "Theory of the Festival", which returned to the subject he and Bataille had already disagreed upon after the latter's lecture on the Mardi Gras. Perhaps it was for this reason that Caillois, as in "The Ambiguity of the Sacred", primarily considered the festival in the context of archaic societies. He avoided the issue of its meaning in the present day until the very end of his lecture, and then considered it only superficially.

When *Man and the Sacred* was republished in 1951, Bataille wrote a long review of it for *Critique*.[31] Essentially he suggested that Caillois had written a strictly sociological account, scientific rather than sacred sociology. He disagreed with Caillois's interpretation of the sacred, which too often lacked aspects of prohibition or crime. With regard to festivals, Bataille thought Caillois ascribed too utilious a function to them. In his text, Caillois variously describes the festival as a means of regenerating societies, or of waste disposal, or even as a sort of potlatch conducted with fate itself in which "destiny is obligated to return with compound interest what it has received" (p.401). For Bataille these outcomes, these "concerns for the future",[32] had less meaning in the context of the festival than the festival *itself*. He concluded: "It is remarkable that such a book, in order for it to be written, had to be the work of a man who wanted totality but who renounced it [...] and chose as its object [the sacred] something which is not an object, which is in fact the destruction of all objects".[33]

At the end of May Bataille issued his edict to the members of Acéphale that there must henceforth be no half measures.

# TEXTS

October 1938 — May 1939

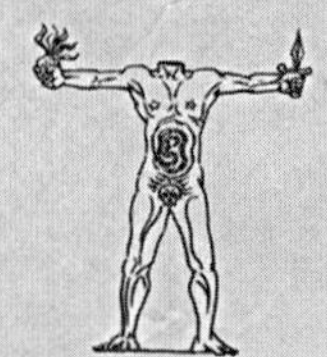

31 mai 1939,

Je ne pense pas que le pacte conclu entre nous ait eu jusqu'ici autre chose qu'une existence larvée et souffreteuse.

Je demande qu'il soit mis fin à toutes les demi-mesures. Je rappelle la sanction devant laquelle nous nous sommes placés : une défaillance définitive nous ferait relever du mépris, pour ne pas dire du dégoût, que nous avons en nous-mêmes pour d'autres prétentions injustifiées.

S'il est parmi nous quelqu'un qui pense que ce qui a été convenu entre nous ne sera pas <u>réel</u>, qu'il y aura des échappatoires, que le laisser-aller ne sera supprimé que dans les conventions écrites, non dans les actes, il est temps qu'il s'éloigne de lui-même : il doit se rendre compte que ce qui existe entre nous est <u>inflexible</u> et que c'est quelque chose qui <u>sévira</u>, qui pourrait devenir un charme, qui ne peut en aucun cas se terminer en comédie.

Je prend sur moi d'observer les règles des jours fermés, non seulement dans les limites convenues mais aussi tous les jours neutres — et, s'il le fallait, même tous les jours.

Je n'ajouterai rien à cette lettre. Je ne ferai allusion à rien. Mais chacun d'entre nous doit savoir que, la prochaine fois qu'il me rencontrera, il se trouvera en présence d'un homme changé. — G.B.

90. Georges Bataille, *To the Members of Acéphale.*

### GEORGES BATAILLE *Questionnaire B* 76

*Written responses to the following proposals:*

*1. An adept may only attain the second degree if he devotes all his time to the organisation, apart from what is socially or physically unavoidable and during certain permitted periods (in which case it is advisable to give equal time to studies, conversations and work materially related to Acéphale and essential general information).*

*2. Each adept of the first degree shall devote to the organisation, symbolically and in a strict and formal manner, a part, even a minimal part of his time, to be determined by him according to his availability and his wants (in which case the only things that may be considered are careful reflection, meditation or the very precise study of questions which most closely concern Acéphale).*

*3. Each adept shall report in letters to be written at set intervals (without name and address or other formal phrases) the different activities he has taken occasion to devote to the organisation (of equal relevance here are meditations, periods of time spent in the forest, study or reading, letters or written texts, conversations, discussions or verbal reports, material work etc.).* [October 1938]

### PIERRE ANDLER *Meditation on Joy in the Face of Death* 77

*The meditation on joy in the face of death, and joy in the face of death itself, even though they are deeply anchored in being are not* by their nature *beyond aesthetics.*

*What criterion could indicate to us that we are beyond aesthetics? No raised voices, no* way of behaving *could be enough here to establish* the difference.

*Shall we one day simply lay claim to the will to power, a 'secular' will to power? Will our demand, at that moment, stripped of all its religious associations, not be more coldly, more exclusively,* whole*?*

*I can commit myself entirely to all the games. I am as capable as anyone else, for the sake of a cause I have made my own, of turning my DESIRE TO BELIEVE into actual BELIEVING. I want it to be known that if I announce in public what it is that dwells within me like an obsession, it is not because I cannot bear the tension of a very difficult game, but because I feel all of a sudden openly provoked by what I feel* in spite of myself *to be* aesthetic.

14.X.38

## 78 PIERRE ANDLER *On Bataille's Questionnaire and Note*[1]

*Briefly, I would like to say this: I would have preferred not to have been asked today to have to answer Bataille's note and questionnaire. I am preparing my response to the latter and my delay is explained by certain* fundamental *difficulties and not by any concern for making myself clear in a careful manner as regards the direction my research has been taking. As for Bataille's Note, I am sure that the notion of the* disagreeable[2] *— which he introduces — has no meaning for any of us. I believe that it is already clear that no one here will refuse* the most challenging sacrifices *demanded by the community; there is something humiliating about seeing doubt cast on our capacity to submit with joy to the disagreeable. But it is not possible to appeal* to almost everything *that unites us so deeply. If one or more of us considers this or that initiative to be* vexatious *(but not disagreeable), they have the right and even the duty to take note of it from the moment when what is* essential *is not at stake. I maintain that nothing* essential *is at stake in the questionnaire, and if I am applying myself to responding to it that is because I consider [?] it to be both excellent and* absurd, *and thus altogether acceptable. I have nothing further to add, and would prefer it if any explanations, if they are really necessary, are only asked of me after a certain amount of time has elapsed.*

15.X.38

## 79 GEORGES BATAILLE *To Imre Kelemen*

2-XI-[19]38

*My dear Kelemen,*

*I am sending you these few notes today rather than giving them to you next Tuesday — the only reason being that notes 2 and 3 include a response to what you said on the subject of questionnaire B.*

*Of course, we should arrange to meet up, but I confess that I do not really understand*

J'ai à dire brièvement ceci : j'aurais voulu ne pas être mis aujourd'hui en demeure de répondre au questionnaire et à la note de Bataille. Je prépare ma réponse au premier, et ma lenteur s'explique par des difficultés de fond et non par le souci de préciser d'une manière approfondie l'orientation de mes recherches.

En ce qui concerne la note de Bataille, je suis convaincu que la notion de désagréable — qu'il met en jeu — n'a de signification pour aucun d'entre nous. Je crois que d'ores et déjà personne ici ne se refusera aux plus durs sacrifices demandés par la communauté ; il y a donc quelque chose d'humiliant à voir mise en doute notre aptitude à nous soumettre joyeusement au désagréable. Mais il n'est pas possible d'en appeler à propos de tout à ce qui nous unit profondément. Si l'un de nous ou si plusieurs d'entre nous considèrent telle ou telle initiative comme contraire (et non désagréable), ils ont le droit et même le devoir d'en faire état, tout en [illegible] que l'essentiel n'est pas en jeu. J'estime que l'essentiel n'est pas en jeu dans le questionnaire, et si je me prépare à y répondre, c'est parce que je le considère à la fois excellent et absurde, et somme toute acceptable. Je n'ai rien à ajouter, et je voudrais que des explications, si elles sont jugées nécessaires, ne me soient demandées que dans quelque temps.

15 X 38.

78. Pierre Andler, *On Bataille's Questionnaire and Note.*

your attitude. What can it hope to achieve? You talk about "insisting". From an individual perspective, you are constantly insisting on all sorts of things that could slow us down. Do you think we are moving too quickly? I realise that this dispute could all too easily be reduced to something quite intangible, but can you imagine a single moment when the primacy we have accorded to the will to be is so little threatened that it's because the very thing we experience is what cruelly marks out the distance between being and inertia? Ultimately, will the concrete proposals that you should have brought to the meeting, which you called, a few days ago all boil down to this purely negative response?

All the deep reasons for friendship and discretion cannot prevent us from getting to the bottom of this. What sense could there be in my concealing from you that after the relief I felt on the day you called this meeting, I then had to return to a judgement of your character which, to make matters difficult, requires nothing less than recognising the incompatibility of your current attitude with our undertaking. I do not think, and let me be quite clear about this, that what is bothering you so deeply might be seen as something we need to rule out, perhaps it is just the opposite, but nothing is possible if this peculiar attraction we undoubtedly all feel is not seen for what it is. I think more and more that in the festival, the will to celebrate is a profound will for death, but life can only consist in this contradictory alternation between action and celebration. What we carry inside us is precisely the possibility of demonstrating that actions result in failure, that is to say celebration, but that failure already requires fulfilment and the only real form of celebration is heroes, in other words those who have triumphed before dying tragically.

In any case, do realise that our argument here cannot be allowed to develop into some kind of commonplace disagreement and that my affection towards you remains intact.

Georges Bataille

## 80 GEORGES BATAILLE *The Tricephalous Monster*

1

The life we wish to lead can only have a heroic meaning for us, that is to say the 'works' we choose to undertake are unavoidably like those of 'heroes'. The 'monster' we must defeat has three heads, three hostile heads: Christianity, Socialism and Fascism. The heroes of ancient legend fought with the wisdom and cunning of an armed peasant. We belong to an urban reality and the tricephalous monster we are fighting is an urban monster. The basic weapons of this monster are not teeth or fire but knowledge, forthright

80. Georges Bataille, *The Tricephalous Monster.*

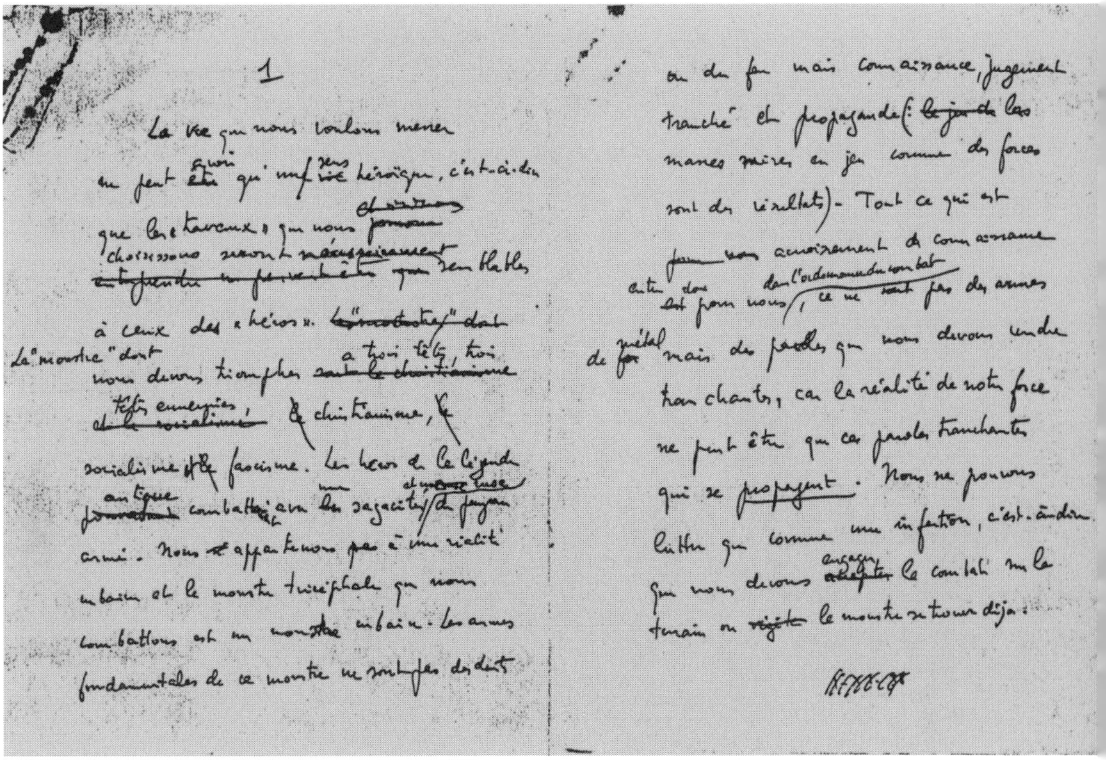

*judgements and propaganda (with the result that the masses are recruited as their forces). Everything that qualifies as an increase in knowledge therefore becomes a weapon we can use in the fight, and not weapons made of metal but of words we must sharpen, for in reality our strength can only be found in these sharp-edged words that* propagate *by themselves. We can only do battle as an infection, in other words we must engage in combat on the monster's own ground.*

2

*As a group we have made sure to insist on being. However, our activities have just been systematically called into question. What is Kelemen objecting to with his "insisting* again *on BEING". I do not understand. If we were overly busy with our activities... But the situation is the exact opposite. If things do become too busy, then it will be time for us to take stock. All these objections against action, whatever form they take, only cause* delays.

*What must be done now is to continue right to the end: this BEING we are supposed to keep insisting on again is not action, since Kelemen specifically locates it in opposition to action, and neither is it contemplation or knowledge (Kelemen is hostile to both of these). This BEING is thus NOTHINGNESS. We cannot be surprised to encounter in our midst this profound will to NOTHINGNESS. It has opened up inside us like a wound and not one of us can consider it alien to his person. We can have the strength to live with pride with this open wound, but first of all we must recognise it as a wound.*

3

*"The actions of an adept should in no way contribute to his accession to a higher category."*[3] *This is Kelemen's proposal but it seems to me the opposite of* common sense, *for it also implies that we should ask what ought be contributing to this accession. It would seem, however, quite sufficient to have understood that for there to have been no actions at all in certain cases might not be considered an obstacle. On the other hand, I would suggest that in actual fact such cases will be extremely rare: the second degree should unequivocally indicate the man who has attained the fullness of power and virility. It is almost out of the question for this power and virility to show themselves other than through some form of action that meets its set objectives without the slightest deviation.*

*I am sure that Kelemen's proposal does not really imply anything that runs counter to what I have just written, but I am struck by a certain contrary-to-common-sense method used in expressing it. It is clear that in practice it is time for us to become common sense itself, and the most vulgar common sense at that. Anything which, in practical existence, is not 'night is black, snow is white', will always be in danger of becoming mere beating about the bush. I intend no bias here in favour of what is obvious but rather of what is clear-cut, since every cure involves cutting with a knife, with no argument.*

[November 1938]

JEAN ROLLIN *To Georges Bataille* 81

[Barcelona, December 1938–January 1939]

*The slowness of my reply*[4] *is not because of any lack of interest, but on the contrary, the result of multiple concerns and questions which have occurred to me since reading the general letter. The events that have taken place, and what I have experienced here, have only intensified my reactions.*

*On reflection, I cannot wholly subscribe to the communications I have received.*[5] *I can recognise most of my aspirations in them, I am willing to support them, but I feel it is difficult to commit to them fully because of the way in which they are presented and defined, and the way the phrasing condenses their meanings.*

*I am reading the eleven aggressions. Apart from the second and the fourth, they all correspond very accurately to my way of thinking.*

*In order to respond to the programme that you have sent me, I cannot do better than to express my thoughts as they come to mind.*

*The point here is knowing* exactly *what action must be undertaken, or more accurately in fact, whether or not to undertake any action at all. To create a force involves some sort of action — religious or political,* every action carried out upon reality *involves a compromise with it.*

*It is necessary, or not, to create using existence itself. The tragic awareness of destiny is born out of the awareness and experience of human reality. It cannot, without risk of losing its meaning and surrendering its value, lead to a* redemptive *action, which seems to me to be inherent in the affirmations presented.*

*The true nature of human resolve implies that perfection does not exist in human terms, and that it is ridiculous to assign an unlimited objective to human activities, since death, or extinction, are present in each one. Awareness of the actual nature of this resolve is the real tragedy here, which is not an awareness of the ineluctability of divine law but of the limit within every achievement that is opposed to human power.*

*This power, ultimately, is not shaped from aspirations. It finds its precise measure and value in its contact with reality.*

*Stirring up human power, or stirring up avidity, leads, we must not forget, to exhaustion and death. Strength in the service of this power must either* rebel, *in other words* be sacrificed *to reality, or become reconciled with it.*

*If we want to establish a force that will bring us to practical action, we cannot assert, unless we acknowledge that we also want to be mistaken, that it might develop from a tragic* opposition. *The assertion that will become apparent will necessarily be a function of the connection [between this] tragic opposition and reality.*

*If we wish to act in a certain way, we will be led, so that we might feed and nourish* hunger, *to define the means of action. We pass from* opposition *to* imposition. *The energy accumulated by this natural hunger will not be spent and squandered uselessly,*[6] *but will serve to enable it to become established, that is to say out of necessity to capture the forces that act according to the principle of servile necessity.*

*Duly fed by these captured and devoured forces, the tragic force's hunger is of necessity transformed, as water puts out a fire.*

*It seems to me that the main contradiction resides in the fact that we are asserting the inutility of existence, which rightly speaking should be located on a religious level, by giving a tragic value to this assertion, and that we are also asserting the necessity of some sort of* redemptive action, *which cannot be considered inutilious since utility is the very basis of action, both in terms of its necessity and its reality.*

*"A human being is not simply a stomach to fill, but an excess of energy to be squandered."*[7] *Yet if our strength develops in the direction suggested, this human being will become above all else an excess of energy, capable of exerting control and domination.*

The will to power asserted tragically is a will to loss; asserted in practice, it is domination, the creation of a form of power.

*It is vital to clarify this point and to highlight its implications. They explain, for example, why I do not hold with the ninth aggression.*[8] *They even suggest that our communional unity may take on bogus forms.*

*We cannot fail to stress that calling upon man's* virility[9] *is just as vague, and as much a part of man's enslavement to tragic and liberating aspirations, as appealing to liberty, or to authority. God, the fatherland and happiness are at one and the same time abstract entities and living realities.*

*Personally, I am unable to resolve the contradictions that present themselves each time I endeavour to understand what might be called the liberation of man. I am not yet in a position to put forward any objections. All the same, these objections would seem sufficiently well established for me to be unable to agree, in anticipation of this liberation, with the proposed programme.*

*The organisation of any aggressive force only seems possible to me if we take these essentials as our starting point, and seek to build against them.*

*The question we are asking concerning 'a human religion' remains unanswered.*[10]

*For my part, I am not giving up. But the principles upon which the programme bases this religion, and the means it proposes to use, do not appear to be at all effective in terms of avoiding fakery and illusion, which, it seems to me, we have always fought against and wish to escape.*

*Rather than turning to virility, if it is indeed necessary to call upon a notion or power principle, I would consider* human solidarity *an effective emotional reality for organising man's liberation, which is what I am hoping for.*

*These are my thoughts, though I would have wanted them to be both fuller and more profound. I cannot hide the fact that they are, unfortunately, in the main rather negative. But I did want to reply to your communication and most of all to dismiss any impression that I am losing interest. More than ever, albeit not with all the attendant conditions, I am trying to understand what problems have arisen and in what manner.*

*If the thoughts I pass on here do not seem to be entirely at variance with your ideas I would earnestly request that you have faith in my complete commitment, and keep me informed of your activities.*

*Yours truly, Jean Rollin*

### JEAN ROLLIN *The Acéphale* 82

*Identification with the myth of the superman*[11] *can only signify a practical adherence to a form of life that has at once the* form *and the* force *of life. It means deliberately, in spite of and in the face of all constraints, establishing oneself in the zone where life and its consequences take on a value different from all other values, burned away and stripped bare as those values are by the furnace that is their source.*

*This adherence is distinguished at a fundamental level from the* pursuit *of an ideal — it can no longer be identified with the search for perfection.*

*All sense of finality is expressly foreign to it — it seeks not to exhaust the world's resources by means of a set form of words or a regulated process, but on the contrary to bring forth or raise high the unexpected result of its action, which is the only thing fit to transform and create the world beneath its feet. It strives to obtain* a revelation of the world by the world.

*Far from finding in constraint the justification to accept life with all its constraints, as ordained by sages and saints, it finds in this constraint the necessity that is the basis of a total liberation which simultaneously affirms and denies existence. It alights on this affirmation and negation — the crux of this contradiction, and this contrast — as* though on a taut rope that cuts right through it.

Both lost and won at every moment, life must thus appear to be solely and entirely responsible for itself and its end — in other words death. God disappears at the moment the extra-temporal existence and demands of eternity are implicated.

The raw existence of life is its only value.

To live the myth of the superman it is thus necessary to be at once the prey, the game and the instrument. The will to power, in order for it not to be a value that is simply explained or offset, must not be perceived as an existing force or entity, to which it fails to correspond, but as an indeterminate quality through which it is a question, in the course of its creation, of revealing and affirming existence. Hence the superman will be at once the requirement, the fulfilment and above all the consequence of the death of God.[12]

It is not individualism that can account for this attitude but, in terms of being, a new egotism, the gift of which would best express its quality and intensity, as opposed to charity or pity.

This egotism may act on being to the point of making it the acephalic will so as to affirm God's will to death, his fulfilment and its consequences.

Contemplation is to ecstasy what God is to the superman — the affirmation that only eternity understands life, because from the beginning it extends infinitely beyond it. Chance is no more than an arrangement of providence, and those things that are immutably fixed depend upon chance alone.[13] Acéphale re-establishes the game of the world — it is the mythological sign for the power of encounters in which the force of chance is fully reinstated, within the possibility it contains for total transformation or destruction.[14]

Things conjured up do not come to us because they are foretold or summoned — but because they are provoked. They rise up out of man's footprint, "the product of ordinary chance, a defenceless nothing abandoned to all perdition."

The fact that being is at once prey, game and instrument of the myth of the superman is contained and affirmed in this act of provoking. It accounts for its demands and attends to its fulfilment.

[December 1938-January 1939]

## IMRE KELEMEN *We live on the surface of the Earth…*

I. We live on the surface of the Earth — whoever else lives here, together with all his fellows, is not me any more than the surface of the Earth is the Earth itself. And yet, this *surface is definable — it is the tension of what exists inside.*

*The path that takes me away from this surface, that leads into its depths, is dark and dangerous. It is only my* movement along it *that brings it into existence, that* is *my existence, shorn of glittering memories and deathly, empty associations.*

*This depth is not a state of excitation, but a state in which the bond between beings is freedom, in which freedom is the bond between beings, the source of all freedom.*

*II. In the train, returning from Saint-Nom-la-Bretèche to Paris, a voice inside me asks: "Were we just behaving like idiots back there?" The voice asking this question is* at the surface *— it does not correspond to anything within me that would be the 'victim' of the surface, but rather to something that loves the surface and is attracted to it. I know that I am the world and that settles the question: all science, all myths and all rites may be formed within me.*

God, infinite *and* eternal*: these are the forms taken by man's cowardice and his headlong flight in the face of death, a futile flight from the imprisoned skeleton that* exists *beneath the surface of his own body. Faced with the presence of such cowardice, it would be pointless and childish to expect any kind of* courage*:* the point is to allow no room inside for it.

*The ecstasy of love that opens up this surface and penetrates into the depths has been relegated in vain to the surface of the epidermis and subdued by this cowardice — it is both freedom and the bond with the other being; it is also the violent and magnificent negation of the eternal and infinite God.*

*III. When it is a question of considering what I am, what I was and what my life is, I run up against the system's natural resistance which is created by the surface in order to deny the tension it brings into being itself. Locked inside this system, my life would be emptied of all its meaning, would become past, present and future, and become no more than something to serve as the subject of a biography.*

*Time does not hold back, does not signify any 'progression', is not 'making its way' towards any value.*

*My eyes are sometimes closed and sometimes wide open, but* I *recognise* myself *in my victories and in my defeats, my catastrophes and ecstasies; so too in the blows aimed at the blind man but received with open, seeing eyes. None of that would belong to what is called* the past, *because it all still lashes me with its strict demands. It would be virtually impossible to find one moment in my life that was more decisive than any other.*

*IV. I know what the old religious teaching signifies; I know that it is true that the person who rebels against God finds himself face to face with his own death.*

[December 1938-January 1939]

## PIERRE ANDLER *Personal Commitment of 26 January 1939*

Timetable

*From 1 February until the summer (leave for Copenhagen):*
*Monday, Wednesday, Thursday: 8.30–11.30, making 9 hours*
*Friday to Sunday: 6 hours*

*Tuesday evening is either for the College, or for* x.
*Sessional or other meetings are also included.*

*A total of 15 hours shall be allocated to make up for time spent working at the office in the evening and for trips to Brussels.*

Dispensation

*Every dispensation, whether granted for serious reasons or otherwise, must be made up in the week following. Every dispensation that is not made up in due course will be considered a default. In the event of a second default a summons to an interview will be issued.*

*A new period shall be understood to begin the day after the September sessional meeting.*

*The purpose of this commitment is not to increase my knowledge but so that I may undergo a test. It corresponds therefore to a ritual.*

Je m'engage.*

*Discretion, or discreet affirmation, are mandatory.*

**I pledge my commitment.*

*1. The principle that participants are free to make up their own minds is clearly upheld for all of us. The organisation reserves the right only to define attitudes which conform to the spirit that inspires it and to oppose others that do not.*

*2. Since the fundamental principle of the organisation is* JOY IN THE FACE OF DEATH, *and since the power it has determined to use can only be linked to the virtue of this principle and to the authority it must confer upon those who carry it into effect, then a deliberate act by one of us intended to shield him from a situation where the vast majority of the others accept the risk, cannot be considered as responding to the spirit of the organisation.*

*3. The fact of behaving in a particular situation in a manner that does not respond to the spirit of the organisation cannot be considered as proof that a participant is not in fact responding to that spirit; but if it occurs that a participant is keen to bind his life closely to the life of the organisation, the onus will be upon him to prove that he is possessed by the spirit of* JOY IN THE FACE OF DEATH.

*4. The organisation is considering the* formal *repudiation of the moral bonds that claim to join the soldier to his flag as the fundamental condition of any participation in a military operation.*

*5. When the organisation is obliged to consider the question of war, alongside other questions of general interest, it will do so regardless of its established positions, with a radically new state of mind and bringing to bear as much irony as brutality in the face of other people's terror (just as if it was the terror that can always arise amongst its own participants). It is essential to remember that the organisation means to create a world that will break free from all prevailing laws regarding necessity and fear.*

[1939?]

86 GEORGES BATAILLE[15] *In Search of Joy in the Face of Death*

*Once more our steps lead us*
*into the forest and into the night*
*— in search of joy in the face of death,*

*in search of*
*JOY*
*in the face of*
*DEATH*

87 GEORGES BATAILLE *To Louis Couturier*

17 May 1939
59 *bis* rue de Mareil
Saint-Germain, 13-23

*My dear friend,*
*Your train leaves Saint-Lazare station at 8.38. You should buy a single ticket for Saint-Nom-la-Bretèche (a small suburb). The platform is the first on the left.*

*At the station at Saint-Nom, please follow the person from our group who will lead you, keeping about fifty paces behind him. When he leaves the small road you have been following (after forty minutes), continue going straight: a few minutes later you will be at the end of your walk, with a clearing in front of you. You won't see anybody there because we will be standing in the darkness, all you will see will be a fire at the foot of a tree.*

*The tree we meet at is an ancient oak that has been struck by lightning. The sulphur we use calls to mind volcanoes. Lightning and volcanoes are connected for us with 'joy in*

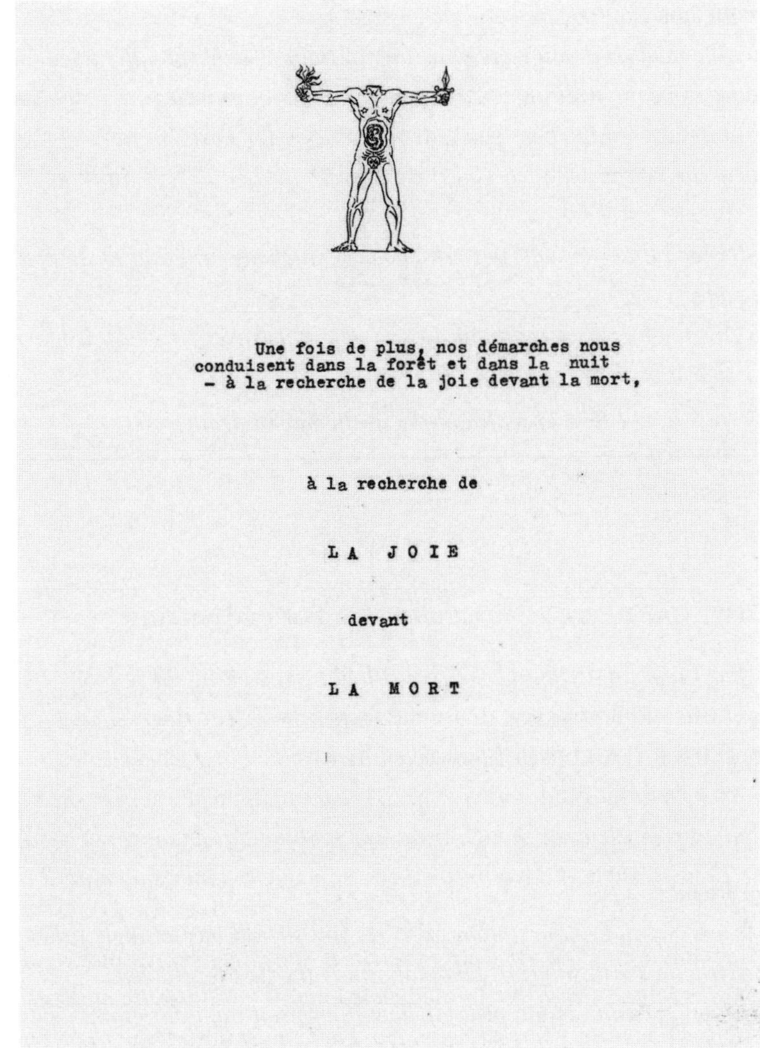
Une fois de plus, nos démarches nous
conduisent dans la forêt et dans la nuit
- à la recherche de la joie devant la mort,

à la recherche de

L A J O I E

devant

L A M O R T

86. Georges Bataille, *In Search of Joy in the Face of Death.*

*the face of death'.*

*You will stay as long as you think necessary, and before you leave you will walk towards the fire and the tree.*

*Leave by the road as if you were returning to Saint-Nom and after a few minutes you will notice someone walking ahead of you. Follow him until you arrive back at the station at Saint-Germain, where you will buy a ticket for Paris. In front of the station you will allow the person who led you there to walk away and will think no more about him.*

*It is understood that you will not acknowledge anybody and that at no point will you speak to anyone.*

*Perhaps this might all seem complicated to you, but if you re-read this letter carefully you will see that it is all very simple.*

*The 'encounter' will take place whatever the weather.*

*With best wishes,*
*Georges Bataille*

## 88 MICHEL CARROUGES *Extract from* Les Portes dauphines

*I was sure that I had finally found the path I had been seeking for so long.*

*The night was still and warm. Above me soared the Great Bear. Shadows lurked everywhere. The forest grew deeper and cooler. As I walked, my footsteps felt sure and steady, born of something I did not recognise. A wave of apprehension washed over me slowly, building up inside even though there was nothing for me to worry about. From time to time I caught sight of a gap in the trees, or a single clambering vine, a clearing or a logging site.*

*I walked on and came to a dried-up tree, which must have been struck by lightning a long time ago, the largest tree I saw in the whole forest. The silhouette of the figure up ahead had slowed down, so I slowed down too. There must have been a torch just below the level of the embankment, lit by some unknown hand and set out of sight in a ditch, which illuminated the bark of the tree, for it seemed strangely bright in the darkness. I stood there for several moments, until I realised that the lantern had gone.*

*It was at the beginning of spring 1939 that I first had the opportunity to spend a little more time with Georges Duthuit. He came to visit us in Saint-Germain-en-Laye, in the house where we were living, Bataille and I, on rue de Mareil towards the bottom of the hill, almost on the outskirts of Le Vésinet. It was an attractive rural house, which according to tradition was once connected to the château by an underground passage that had long since been blocked up, and had been the hunting lodge of the exiled king James II.*[16] *The house opened on to a high-walled garden that we looked after by ourselves with the hesitance and awkwardness of confirmed city-dwellers suddenly confronted by the mysteries of the earth. The house itself consisted of a ground floor that was almost entirely taken up by one large room that was both kitchen and communal area, which we used as dining-room, reading-room and a place where we could entertain friends. Nothing on the walls, other than the shelves groaning with books that covered the whole of one wall, and a drawing of Dionysus by André Masson. Upstairs there were a few comfortable and spacious rooms: in his, Bataille had brought in various pieces of furniture he had inherited from his family; mine, at the back of the house, was simply furnished with just a small bed, a work table made of planks resting on trestles and two garden chairs of painted wood. The almost monastic austerity of the décor was not at all gloomy, since the light played cheerfully on the bare white walls, but instead inspired contemplation and study.*

*Most of those who knew the house in Saint-Germain — there were only a few — were struck by the atmosphere of the rooms themselves and the strange rhythm of spiritual respiration whose mark had been left there by Bataille. Georges Duthuit told me years later that few human habitations had made such a strong impression on him. At the time of his visit we took him for a walk in the forest of Marly and came to the edge of it after walking for several kilometres, having left Saint-Germain and headed south, towards Pontoise, then turning off to the left, towards Saint-Nom-la-Bretèche. In those days the forest was usually deserted and nothing detracted from the majesty of its ancient trees, the secret of its lost paths and copses, the pure geometry of its straight walks and the* étoiles *where they crossed. We walked in a silence that remained unbroken until we returned to the town. Bataille, who was walking a few steps ahead of us, went down a track and signalled to us to stop in front of a huge beech tree to the trunk of which someone had nailed a crow. We stood there for a few moments looking at this victim of ancestral fears, before leaving by way of a more difficult path through thick undergrowth, which took us to the wall that surrounded the Retz estate, where collapses in the stonework had opened up large gaps here and there. We were thus able to look around the great abandoned park, and in the distance glimpsed some fake ruins smothered in ivy. After a detour that took us to the foot of an oak tree struck by lightning, where we briefly stopped once more, we returned to the house as night fell.*

## 90 GEORGES BATAILLE *To the Members of Acéphale*

31 May 1939

*I do not think that the pact agreed between us has up until now had anything other than a larval and sickly existence.*

*I ask that we put an end to all half measures. I am reminded of the sanction that applies to us: ultimate failure would heap on us the same contempt, not to mention the disgust, we ourselves have felt for other unwarranted and vain attempts.*

*If there is anyone among us who thinks that what has been agreed between us will not be* real, *that there will be ways out of it, that any slackness will only be suppressed in our written agreements, and not in our actions, then it is time for him to withdraw; he must realise that what exists between us is* inflexible *and that it is something that will make an impact; it might become a tragedy, but it will not in any circumstances end in comedy.*

*I hereby take it upon myself to observe our rules for 'closed days', not only within the appointed limits but also on all neutral days — and even, if necessary, on every day.*

*I shall add nothing more to this letter. I shall not refer to anything in particular. But each of you must know that the next time you meet me you will find yourself in the presence of a changed man.*

G.B.

ROGER CAILLOIS

# *Theory of the Festival* 91

The exhilaration of the festival[1] is opposed to ordinary life, occupied as the latter is with daily tasks and hemmed in with a system of taboos and precautions in which the maxim *quieta non movere*[2] maintains the order of the universe. If only its external aspects are considered, the festival demonstrates identical characteristics on all levels of civilisation. It connotes a large conglomeration of moving and boisterous people. These massed gatherings eminently favour the creation and contagion of an exalted state that exhausts itself in cries and movement and that is incited to abandon itself uncontrollably to the most irrational impulses. Even today, when attenuated and infrequent festivals grow out of the grey background symbolising the monotony of contemporary existence and seem scattered, crumbling and almost submerged, there can still be distinguished in these festivals some miserable vestiges of the collective euphoria that characterised the ancient celebrations. In fact, the disguises and audacious acts permitted at carnival time, the drinking and dancing in the streets on 14 July, attest to the same and continuing social necessity. There is no festival, even on a sad occasion, that does not imply at least a tendency toward excesses and good cheer. The burial feast in rural areas is an example. In times past or at present, the festival is always characterised by dancing, singing, eating, and drinking. It is necessary to eat to the point of exhaustion or illness. That is the very law of the festival.

## I. THE FESTIVAL, RESORT TO THE SACRED

In civilisations described as primitive, the contrast is much more evident. The festival lasts several weeks, or several months, punctuated by rest periods of four or five days. It often takes several years to re-amass the amount of food and wealth ostentatiously consumed or spent, and even destroyed and wasted, for destruction and waste, as forms of excess, are at the heart of the festival.

The festival ends voluntarily, in a frenetic and orgiastic way, with nocturnal debauchery involving noise and movement while the crudest instruments are beaten as a rhythmic accompaniment to the dance. According to the description of an observer, the human mass, swarming, undulating and stamping the ground, pivots and sways about a centre pole. The movement increases as a result of many stimuli. It is augmented and intensified by whatever enhances it — the clash of spears on shields, guttural chants of a rhythmic nature, the jerking and promiscuity of the dance. Violence erupts spontaneously. From time to time quarrels break out. The combatants are separated, lifted up by strong arms and rocked rhythmically until calmed. The dance is not interrupted. Couples suddenly leave the dance to have sexual relations in the surrounding woods, returning to take their place in the frenzy that continues until morning.

It is understood that the festival, being such a paroxysm of life and cutting so violently into the anxious routine of everyday life, seems to the individual like another world in which he feels sustained and transformed by powers that are beyond him. His daily activity — food gathering, hunting, fishing or cattle-raising — can only occupy his time and provide for his immediate needs. Doubtless it requires his attention, patience and skill, but more profoundly, he lives by recalling the festival and awaiting another, since the festival signifies for him, in memory and desire, a time of intense emotion and a metamorphosis of his being.

*Advent of the Sacred*

It is to Durkheim's honour that he recognised the splendid illustration of the distinction between the sacred and profane that festivals afford, in contrast to working days. In effect, they oppose an intermittent explosion to a dull continuity, an exalting frenzy to the daily repetition of the same material preoccupations, the powerful inspiration of the communal effervescence to the calm labours with which each busies himself separately, social concentration to social dispersion, and the fever of climactic moments to the tranquil labour of the debilitating phases of existence. In addition, the religious ceremonies forming part of the festival agitate the souls of the believers. If the festival is the time of joy, it is also the time of anguish. Fasting and silence are required before the festival starts. Habitual taboos are reinforced, and new restrictions are imposed. Debauchery and excess of all kinds, the solemnity of the ritual and the severity of the previous restrictions are equally united to make the environment of the festival an exceptional world.

In reality, the festival is often regarded as the dominion of the sacred. The day of the festival, the Sabbath, is first of all a day consecrated to the divine, on which work is forbidden, on which one must rest, rejoice and praise God. In societies in which festivals are not diffused throughout one's working life but grouped into a true *festival season*, the point at which the latter in fact constitutes the period of sacred pre-eminence can be seen even better.

Mauss's study of Eskimo society provides the best examples of the violent contrast between the two kinds of life, always meaningful for peoples where climate or the nature of their economic organisation condemns them to prolonged inactivity for part of the year. In winter, Eskimo society contracts. Everything is done or takes place communally, as against the summer when each family, isolated in its tent in an almost desert-like vastness, finds its food separately with nothing intervening to reduce the role of individual initiative. In contrast to the summertime, almost entirely secular, winter seems a time "of continuous religious exaltation", a protracted festival. Among the American Indians of the far north, social organisation varies no less seasonally. There also, the concentration of winter succeeds the dispersion of summer. Clans disappear and give way to religious brotherhoods, which then perform the great ritual dances and organise tribal ceremonies. It is the time for the transmission of myths and rites, a time in which spirits appear to novices and initiate them. The Kwakiutl have a saying: "In summer, the sacred is on the bottom, and the profane is on top; in winter, the sacred is on top, the profane on the bottom." It could not be phrased more clearly.

It has been demonstrated that the sacred, in ordinary life, is expressed almost exclusively through taboos. It is defined as "the guarded" or "the separate". It is placed outside common usage, protected by restrictions intended to prevent any attack upon the order of the universe, any risk of upsetting it or introducing any source of disturbance into it. It seems essentially *negative*. This is, in fact, one of its basic characteristics, one most often observed in ritual taboos. Hence, the sacred period of social life is precisely that in which rules are suspended, and licence is in order. Without doubt, a ritualistic meaning can be denied to the excesses of the festival, and they can be considered merely as *discharges of energy*. "In this way, one is outside the restraints of the ordinary conditions of existence," writes Durkheim, "and one is so adjusted to it that he places himself beyond the bounds of ordinary morality." To be sure, the unrestrained movement and exuberance of the festival corresponds to a kind of detumescent impulse. Confucius took this into account when he said, in justifying the merrymaking of Chinese peasants, that it is unnecessary "to always keep the bow taut, without ever unbending it, or always unbent without ever stretching it". The excesses of collective ecstasy certainly also fulfil this function. They arise as a sudden explosion after long and strict repression. But this is only one of their characteristics, less an assurance of their reason for being than their physiological mechanism. This characteristic must be cathartic. In fact, the native people see in them the magical efficacy of their festivals. They attest, in advance, to the success of the ritual and thus indirectly give promise of fertile women, rich harvests, brave warriors, abundant game and good fishing.

### *Excess, Remedy for Attrition*

Excess constantly accompanies the festival. It is not merely epiphenomenal to the excitement that it engenders. It is necessary to the success of the ceremonies that are celebrated, shares in their holy quality, and like them contributes to the renewal of nature or society. In reality, this seems to be the goal of festivals. Time passes and is spent. It causes one to age and die, it is that which *uses one up*. The Greek and Iranian root from which the word is derived has the same meaning. Each year vegetation and social life are renewed as nature inaugurates a new cycle. All living things must be rejuvenated. The world must be created anew.

The latter comprises a *cosmos* ruled by universal order and functioning according to a regular rhythm. A sense of proportion and a rule maintain it. Its law is that everything has *its own* place, that every event happens in *its due* time. This explains the fact that the sole manifestations of the sacred may be in the form of taboos, which protect against anything capable of threatening the cosmic regularity, or of expiations and reparations for all that can disturb it. It tends toward immobility, for any change or innovation may be perilous to the stability of the universe, whose development one wishes to control so as to destroy the chance of death. But the seeds of its destruction reside in its very functioning, which accumulates waste and induces the erosion of its mechanism.

There is nothing that this law may not subsume, defined and confirmed as it is by all experience. The very health of the human body requires the regular evacuation of its "defilement", urine and faeces, and menstrual blood for the female.

In the end, however, old age weakens and paralyses it. In the same fashion, nature each year passes through a cycle of growth and decline.

Social institutions are not exempt from this alternation. They must also be periodically regenerated and purified of the poisonous waste matter that represents the ill-omened residue left by each act performed for the good of the community. Necessary as it may be, it is evident that it involves some defilement for the officiator who assumes responsibility for it, and by extension, for the entire society. Thus, the gods of the Vedic pantheon seek a creature to which they can transfer the impurity they contract by spilling blood in the course of the sacrifice. This type of purging is generally effected by expelling or putting to death a scapegoat charged with all the sins that have been committed, or a personification of the old year which must be replaced. It is necessary to expel evil, weakness and erosion, notions that more or less coincide. In Tonkin, rites are performed with the explicit goal of eliminating the impure residue from each event, particularly from acts of authority. One seeks to neutralise the irritation and the malevolence of those whom the government has condemned to death for treason, rebellion or conspiracy. In China, they pile up tip refuse, the daily waste matter of domestic living, near the door of the house, and it is carefully disposed of during the New Year's festivals. Like all defilement, it contains an active principle that results in prosperity when properly utilised.

The elimination of the waste matter accumulated by every organism's functioning, the annual liquidation of sins and the expulsion of the old year are not sufficient. They only serve to bury a dying and sullied past, *which has had its day*, and which must give way to a virgin world whose festival is destined to hasten its arrival. Taboos are demonstrably powerless to maintain the integration of nature and society. They are unable to restore it to its early youth. Rules do not possess any inherent principle capable of reinvigorating it. It is necessary to invoke the creative quality of the gods, to return to the beginning of the world, and to resort to the powers which at that time transformed chaos into cosmos.

### *The Primordial Chaos*

In fact, the festival is presented as a re-enactment of the first days of the universe, the *Urzeit*, the eminently creative era that saw all objects, creatures and institutions become fixed in their traditional and definitive form. This epoch is none other than the one in which the divine ancestors, whose story is told in mythology, lived and moved. The myths of the Tsimshian of North America are precisely distinguished from other legendary tales by the fact that they take place in this time long past, when the world had not yet assumed its present form.

The character of this mythical dream-time has been the subject of an excellent study by Lévy-Bruhl, with special reference to the Australians and Papuans. Each tribe has a special term to designate it. It is the *altjiva* of the Aranda, the *djugur* of the Aluridia, the *bugari* of the Karadjeri, the *ungud* of the peoples of north-west Australia etc. These words often designate, at the same time, dreams and, in a general way, anything that seems unusual or miraculous. They serve to define a time in which "the exception was the rule". The expressions used by observers all seem to illustrate this aspect of the primordial age. According to Fortune, this mythical time is one in which "life and natural history begin". It is located simultaneously at the *beginning* and *outside* of evolution. Elkin remarks that it is no less present or future than past. "It is a state as well as a period," he significantly writes.

Basically, the mythical time is the origin of the other and continuously re-emerges by causing everything that is manifestly disconcerting or inexplicable. The supernatural is always discovered lurking behind the natural, and it ceaselessly tends to manifest itself in this sphere. The primordial age is described with singular unanimity in the most diverse areas. It is the ideal place for metamorphoses and miracles as nothing has yet been stabilised, no rule pronounced, and no form fixed. Whatever has long been impossible, was then feasible. Objects would disappear, canoes would fly through the air, men would be transformed into animals, and *vice versa*. They shed their skins instead of growing old and dying. The entire universe was plastic, fluid and inexhaustible. Crops grew spontaneously, and the flesh was replaced on animals soon after it was cut off.

*Creation of the Cosmos*

Finally, the ancestors imposed an appearance upon the world, which has not changed much since that time, and enacted laws that are still in force. They created man out of earth or by transforming pre-existing indeterminate creatures or half-animals. At the same time, they created or formed the various species of animals and plants. In fashioning a single individual, they arranged for his descendants to resemble him so that all would benefit from the mutation of the archetype with no further intervention necessary. They also established the sea, dry land, islands and mountains. They separated the tribes and instituted civilisation, ceremonies, ceremonial details, rites, customs and laws for each.

But by the fact that they contained each thing and each being within given limits, *natural* limits from that point on, they deprived them of all the magic powers that would permit them to gratify their wishes instantly and to become immediately anything they pleased, without encountering any obstacle. Order is, in fact, incompatible with the simultaneous existence of all possibilities, with the absence of all rules. The world thus learns the unbreakable bonds that confine each species to its own being and prevent its escape. Everything became immobilised, and taboos were established in order that the new organisation and legality should not be disturbed.

Lastly, death was introduced into the world by the disobedience of the first man, more frequently by the first woman, by the error of the "trickster" ancestor, who, very commonly, clumsily tries to imitate the gestures of the Creator and whose imbecilic obstinacy leads to both comic and catastrophic consequences. In every way, with death as a worm in the fruit, the *cosmos* emerges from *chaos*. The era of chaos is closed, natural history begins, the rule of normal cause-and-effect is instituted. The burst of creative activity is succeeded by the vigilance necessary to maintain the universe that has been created in good order.

*Chaos and the Golden Age*

It is evident that the mythical time seems clothed in a basic ambiguity. Indeed, it is described as having the antithetical quality of chaos and the golden age. The absence of a dividing line attracts, as much as it repels, disorder and instability. Man looks nostalgically towards a world in which all he has to do to pick luscious and ever-ripe fruits is merely to reach out his hand; a world in which obliging crops are stored in his barn without him working, planting or harvesting; a world that does not know the hard necessity of labour; in which desires are realised as soon as conceived without becoming mutilated, reduced or annihilated by a material obstacle or social taboo.

The golden age, the childhood of the world akin to the childhood of man, corresponds to this conception of an earthly paradise in which at first everything is provided, and upon leaving there man has to earn his bread by the sweat of his brow. It is the reign of Saturn and Cronus, without war, commerce, slavery or private property. But this world of light, tranquil pleasure, and easy, happy living is at the same time a world of darkness and horror. The time of Saturn is one of human sacrifice, and Cronus ate his children. The spontaneous fertility of the soil cannot be free of disaster. The first age is presented as the era of exuberant and disordered creation, of monstrous and excessive childbirths.

Soon, the two antagonistic conceptions become inextricably blended, then logically separated, then mythologically distinguished and opposed, chaos and golden age in succession. These seem like the two aspects of the same imaginary reality, that of a world without rules from which is derived the regulated world in which men now live. The opposition is like that of the world of myth to the world of history, which begins when the former ends. The contrast is even more like that of the world of dreams, as it is aptly called, to that of wakefulness. Lastly, it seems like a time of idleness, abandon and prodigality, for the return of which man vainly hopes while seeing himself condemned to work, penury and frugality.

At the same time, more or less obscurely, he doubtless thinks of his childhood. To establish it, there is no need of recalling the heartfelt regret and the trick of memory that cause the adult to much embellish the recollection of his youth, which now suddenly seems to have been devoted to play and exempt from care. He regards it as a time of eternal festivity in a garden of Eden. Moreover, he does not doubt that the two conceptions of the first age of the world and the *vert paradis des amours enfantines*[3] shade into one another.

Also, it is a fact that, before the initiation ceremonies that introduce him into the social organisation, the youth's activity is not governed by the taboos limiting the adult's behaviour. For example, before marriage, in many cultures, the adolescent's sex life is generally the freest imaginable. It seems that then the individual is not yet part of the order of the universe, and as a result there is no risk of disturbing it by transgressing laws that do not concern him. He lives on the margins, so to speak, of the regulated universe, just as he lives on the border of organised society. Only half of him belongs to the cosmos, for he has not yet broken all his ties to the mythical universe, the beyond, where his ancestors have extracted his soul and caused it to be reborn in his mother's bosom.

In opposition to order and "natural history", the first age of the world represents a time of universal confusion that cannot be visualised without anxiety. Among the Eskimo, the contradictory aspects of the primordial era appear intimately intermingled. It has the characteristics of undifferentiated chaos. All was darkness, and there was no light on earth. Neither continents nor seas could be distinguished. Men and animals did not differ from one another. They spoke the same language, lived in similar houses, hunted in the same way. In the description of this time are also recognised the traits that usually portray the golden age. Talismans then had considerable power, for one could be transformed into an animal, plant or pebble. The flesh of the caribou was replaced on its skeleton after it was eaten. Snow shovels moved about by themselves, so that they did not have to be carried.

But this last possibility already manifests, significantly, a mixture of regret and fear. It illustrates the desire for a world in which everything is achieved without effort, and causes fear of the shovels coming alive again and suddenly escaping from their owner. They can never be stuck into the snow, therefore, without being watched.

## II. THE RE-CREATION OF THE WORLD

Simultaneously nightmare and paradise, the primordial age seems like the period or the state of creative vigour from which the present world escaped, with its vicissitudes of wear and tear and the threat of death. Consequently, it is by being reborn, by reinvigorating himself in this ever-present eternity, as in a fountain of youth with continuously running water, in which he has the chance to rejuvenate himself and to rediscover the plenitude and robustness of life, that the celebrant will be able to brave a new cycle of time.

This is the function fulfilled by the festival. It has already been defined as a re-enactment of the creative period. To use again Dumézil's apt formulation, it constitutes a passage to the great age, the moment when men stop their activity in order to gain access to the reservoir of all-powerful and ever elemental forces represented by the primordial age. It takes place in churches and shrines, which similarly are thought of as passages to the great void in which the divine ancestors evolved, and whose sites or consecrated mountain peaks are the visible landmarks associated with the decisive acts of the Creators.

Then one proceeds to the ceremony that is a critical phase of the seasonal cycle. It is when nature seems to renew itself — when it visibly changes, as at the beginning or end of winter in arctic or temperate climates, and at the beginning or end of the rainy season in the tropical zone. With intense emotion, simultaneously reflecting anxiety and hope, a pilgrimage is made to the places that once were frequented by mythical ancestors. The Australian aborigines piously retrace their itinerary, stopping everywhere that they did and carefully repeating their actions.

Elkin has forcefully stressed this vital and religious bond, much more than merely geographic, that exists between the native and his country. The latter, he writes, appears to him as the pathway to the invisible world. It puts him in contact with "the powers that bestow life, to the advantage of man and nature". If he has to leave his native land or if it is over-run by colonisation, he believes that he must die. He can no longer maintain contact with the sources of his periodic reinvigoration.

*Incarnation of the Ancestor-Creators*

The festival is thus celebrated in the context of myth and assumes the function of regenerating the real world. The time when vegetation renews itself and, the situation permitting, the place in which the totemic animal is abundant, are chosen for this purpose. It is the place where the mythical ancestor created the living species from which the group is descended. The ritual of creation that has been handed down, and which alone is capable of leading to success, is repeated.

Actors imitate the heroic deeds and gestures. They wear masks that identify them with this ancestor, half-man and half-animal. Often these accessories are equipped with shutters that, at the desired moment, suddenly reveal a second face, thus allowing the wearer to reproduce the instantaneous transformations that took place in the first age. It is, in fact, important to conjure up the active presence of the beings from the creative period, who alone have the magic quality that can confer the desired efficacy upon the rite. Besides, no clear-cut distinction can be made between "the mythical base and the actual ceremony". Daryll Forde has explicitly shown this for the Yuma of Colorado. His informants continuously confused the rite they were accustomed to celebrate with the act through which their ancestors instituted it originally.

Various procedures are employed concurrently to recreate the fecund time of the powerful ancestors. Sometimes the recital of the myths suffices. By definition, these are secret and powerful narratives that retell the creation of a species or the founding of an institution. They are as exciting as passwords. To recite them is sufficient to provoke the repetition of the act that they commemorate.

Another way of conjuring up the mythical period consists in retracing on rocks and in remote caves the paintings that represent their ancestors. In colouring and retouching them periodically (it must not be completely finished on one occasion for continuity would be broken), the beings that they depict are recalled to life or *actualised*, so that they can assure the return of the rainy season, the multiplication of edible plants and animals, and the increase of spirit-children that make women pregnant and guarantee the prosperity of the tribe.

Sometimes a truly dramatic representation is encountered. In Australia, the Warramunga pantomime the life of the mythical ancestor of each clan, for example, for the people of the black snake, the life of the hero Thalaualla from the moment that he leaves the ground to the moment he returns. The actors have their skin covered with down, which falls off as they move. Thus they depict the dispersion of the seeds of life emitted from the ancestor's body. Having done this, they assure the multiplication of black snakes. Then men in their turn are restored, regenerated and confirmed in their intimate being by consuming the sacred animal.

It has been seen that the latter is sacrilegious and taboo, when it is a question of respecting the order of the universe and not renewing it. But presently, the members of the clan are identified with the beings of the mythical period who do not know the taboos, and who instituted them when they came into being. During the preceding period, the officiants are, in effect, sanctified by a vigorous fast and many taboos, which cause them to pass gradually from the profane world to the domain of the sacred. They have become ancestors. The masks and ornaments that they wear are the sign of their metamorphosis. They can then kill and consume the animal, gather and eat the plant of which they mystically partake. Thus, they realise their communion with the principle from which they derive their power and their life. With it they absorb a new influx of vigour. Then they abandon to people of other clans the species that they happened to resurrect and deconsecrate, by making first use of this holy nourishment, identical with themselves, and that they need to taste periodically in an act of animating cannibalism, of strengthening theophagy. From this moment on, they will no longer eat freely of it. The festival is ended, and order is once again established.

*Fertility and Initiation Rites*

Fertility ceremonies are not the only ones. Others have as their goal to make youths enter the society of men and thus add them to the collectivity. These are initiation rites. They seem exactly comparable to the preceding rites and like them are founded on the representation of myths related to the origins of things and institutions.

The parallelism is absolute. Fertility ceremonies assure the rebirth of nature, and initiation ceremonies assure the rebirth of society. Whether they coincide or are celebrated separately, they consist equally of making the mythical part real and present, in order to make a rejuvenated world emerge.

In the Madia cult of New Guinea, novices enter the sacred place acting as if newly born. They feign to be ignorant of everything, not to know the use of any utensil, to encounter for the first time the food they are given to eat. Then for their instruction, actors incarnating their divine ancestors present each thing in the order in which myths tell of its creation through their intervention. There is no good way of noting at what point the ceremony signifies the return to primordial chaos and, especially, the establishment of cosmic law. The coming of order into the world did not happen at one stroke, but was itself accomplished in orderly fashion.

According to Wirz, the Madia fertility and initiation ceremonies are identical. They only differ in their goals. In fact, society is always paired with nature. The novice is similar to the seeds in the ground, to soil that has not yet been cultivated. Their ancestors originally transformed the monstrous creatures of the Great Time into men and completed them by giving them sexual organs, the sources of life and fertility. Initiation similarly makes true men out of the neophytes. Circumcision *perfects* their phalluses. The entire ceremony confers various virile qualities upon them, particularly bravery, invincibility, and in addition, the right and power of procreation. It leads the new generation of men to maturity, just as rites performed for the reproduction of the totemic species assure the growth of the new crop or the new animal generation.

After initiation, the novices learn the myths, the mysterious and sacred tribal heritage. They assist in performing ceremonies that they will celebrate in their turn, the success of which will prove the excellence of their adult qualities. The ritual dances of North America are tied to magic gifts, which are themselves related to the secret narratives that explain how their ancestors acquired them. Knowledge of the story and performance of the dance confer, for example, 'possession' of the magic harpoon indispensable to the success of the otter hunt, of the brandy that revives the dead, and the burning fire that consumes from a distance. The dance is nothing else for the Kwakiutl, writes Boas, than "the dramatic representation of the myth related to the acquisition of the spirit", and as a consequence the gift that it personifies.

It has been revealed by the spirit itself to the novice who, in order to authenticate his initiation, repeats the dance while wearing the mask and emblems of the ancestor-protector who has taught it to him. In dancing, he incarnates it in animal form, for the ceremony was, as always, established in the mythical era before the Creator had fixed all things in their definitive forms. The spirits only appear in winter, that is, between two periods of profane labour, outside of ordinary times. Winter is the season for festivals, for dances in which youths incarnate spirits and by identifying with them acquire the gifts that they dispense and appropriate the powers they possess.

In mythical times, the two kinds of ceremonies (initiation and fertility) had become only one. Strehlow confirms this especially for Australia, where, moreover, they are most clearly distinguished in ritual. Ancestors frequent the great void with their novices and teach them, through performance, the rites by which they created beings or established them in a stable structure. Thus they initiated them, not by a "pale" ceremony, but by direct and effective demonstration, by the gift of their creative activity.

*Suspension of the Recording of Time*

In every way, the primordial age must first be actualised. The festival is chaos rediscovered and newly created. In China, the leather bottle that symbolises chaos is considered transformed when it has been pierced seven times by lightning. Again, man has seven apertures in his face, and a man who is well-born has seven in his heart. Outer chaos is symbolised by a stupid man, "without openings", without a face or eyes. At the end of a feast, lightning strikes seven times, not to kill, emphasises Granet, but to cause rebirth and patterning to a higher existence. Shooting arrows into the leather bottle appears to be connected ritualistically with a winter festival, with drinking bouts all night long. This takes place during the last twelve days of the year.

This is a widely diffused custom. The festival recalls the time of creative licence, preceding and engendering order, form and taboo (the three notions are related and, together, are the opposite of chaos). This period has a fixed place in the calendar. In fact, when months are counted by the time between new moons and a year by the Earth's rotation about the sun, twelve days remain in suspense at the end of the solar cycle. They permit the two ways of measuring time to coincide. These interpolated days do not belong to any month or year. They are outside recorded time and simultaneously seem designated for the periodic return and recreation of the great age.

These days are the exact equivalent of the entire year, its "replica", as expressed in the Rigveda with regard to the sacred days of mid-winter in ancient India. Each day corresponds to a month, and what happens in the first foreshadows what will happen in the second. Their names are identical and in the same sequence. If they are counted in two-and-a-half year cycles as in the Celtic calendar of Coligni,[4] the interpolated period comprises thirty days, equivalent to a twelve-month sequence repeated two and a half times.

### *The Presence of Ghosts*

Whatever its duration, time is confused in both the beyond and this world. Ancestors or gods, incarnated by the masked dancers, mingle with men and violently interrupt the course of natural history. They are present at the Australian totemic festivals, the New Caledonian *pilou*, and the Papuan and North American initiation ceremonies.

In addition, the dead leave their abode and invade the world of the living. All barriers are broken and nothing any longer prevents the trespassers from visiting their descendants during this suspension of universal order that the change from old to new year connotes. In Thailand, an infernal being opens the doors of the abyss and the dead emerge into the sunlight for three days. A temporary king governs the country, with all the prerogatives of a true sovereign, while the people are given to games of chance (a typical activity involving risk and waste, directly opposed to the slow and sure accumulation of wealth through work). Among the Eskimo, at the time of the winter festivals, the spirits are reincarnated in the members of the group, thus affirming its solidarity and the continuity of the generations. Then they are solemnly dismissed so that the normal conditions of life can resume their course.

When the festival season is parcelled out and distributed over the entire year, a period is always observed in which the dead are permitted to be diffused into the society of the living.

At the end of the time allotted for their annual invasion, they are sent back to their own domain by explicit entreaties. In Rome, on fixed dates, the stone that closes the *mundus* is raised. This is a hole in the Palatine Hill that is regarded as the passage to the infernal world, as a contraction of this world, and, as its name indicates, as the exact counterpart of the world of the living, to which it is symmetrical. It represents the epitome of the great void in contrast to the area of the profane and enables them to communicate. The souls wander at large in the city for three days in May, after which each family head chases them out of his house by spitting out berries which discharges him and his family from incursion until the following year. The return of the dead is often linked to times of change. In all Europe, it is mainly during St. Sylvester's Eve, that is, during the last night of the year, that ghosts, spectres and phantoms are permitted to be rampant among the living.

## III. THE FUNCTION OF DEBAUCHERY

This interlude of general confusion that the festival connotes appears to be a time in which the order of the universe is suspended. That is why excesses are then permitted. It is a matter of contradicting the rules. Everything is done in reverse. In the mythical age, the course of time was reversed. One was born an old man and died a child. Two reasons coincide in these circumstances to make debauchery and extravagance appropriate. To be more certain of recapitulating the conditions of existence in the mythical past, one tries to do the opposite of what is customarily done. Also, all exuberance signifies an increase in strength that can bring nothing but abundance and prosperity in the coming spring.

Either reason leads to the violation of taboos and immoderate behaviour, in order to profit by the suspension of the cosmic order so that the forbidden act may be performed, and so that the order may be permissibly and unrestrainedly abused. Also, all the prescriptions that protect the natural and social welfare are systematically violated. However, these transgressions are still deemed sacrilegious. They are an attack upon the traditional rules that on the morrow will become holiest and most inviolate. They truly involve major sacrilege.

In a general way, every circumstance in which the existence of society and the world seems to be threatened, and to require renewal through the influx of youthful and excessive vigour, is assimilated into the emotionally charged moment when time changes. Under such conditions, it is not surprising that licence is resorted to and which is analogous or identical to that of intercalary days, so as to ward off the effects of plague as one Australian tribe is reported to do when threatened by epidemics, or another during displays of the *aurora australis* that is seen as a celestial fire that threatened to consume them. On that occasion, the elders ordered wives to be exchanged.

It cannot be doubted how strongly native peoples feel about restoring the universe that has been attacked in its very essence, when it is observed that the Fijians, whenever there is a crop failure and starvation is feared, have a ceremony called "creation of the Earth". In fact, this demonstrates the exhaustion of the soil. It is celebrated in order to rejuvenate, and to bring rebirth, to conjure away the ruin that lies in wait for men and the world.

*Social Sacrileges upon a King's Death*

When the life of society and nature is symbolised by the sacred person of a king, the hour of his death determines the critical moment that unleashes ritual licence. This assumes a character corresponding strictly to the catastrophe that has occurred. The sacrilege is against social order. It is perpetrated at the expense of majesty, hierarchy and power. There is no case confirming that the unleashing of long-repressed passions is due to the forced weakness of government or the temporary absence of authority. (The latter has never in the least resisted popular frenzy.) It is considered just as necessary as was obedience to the deceased monarch. In the Hawaiian Islands, the populace upon learning of the king's death commits every act ordinarily regarded as criminal. It burns, pillages and kills, and the women are required to prostitute themselves publicly. On the Guinea Coast, reports Bosman, as soon as the people learn of the king's death, "each robs his neighbour, who in turn robs another", and these robberies continue until a successor is proclaimed. In the Fiji Islands, the facts are even clearer. The death of the chief is a signal for pillage, the subject tribes invade the capital and commit all types of brigandage and degradation. To avoid these acts, the king's demise was often kept secret, and when the tribes came to ask if the chief was dead, in the hope of devastating and sacking the community, they were told that his body was already decomposed. They then withdrew, disappointed but docile, for they had arrived too late.

This example shows that the time of licence is exactly that in which the king's body decomposes, that is, of the period of acute infection and defilement that death represents. In this time of full and open virulence that is very potent and contagious, society must protect itself by showing its vitality. The danger ends only with the complete elimination of the putrescent substance of the royal cadaver, when nothing more is left of the remains but a hard, sound and incorruptible skeleton. Then the dangerous phase is deemed to be over. The habitual pattern of things can be re-established. A new reign commences after this time of uncertainty and confusion during which the flesh of the guardian had melted away.

In fact, the king is a guardian whose role consists in keeping order, moderation and rules — principles that wear out, grow old and die with him, that lose their power and efficacy at the same time as his physical strength decreases. Also, his death inaugurates a kind of interregnum of inverted efficacy, a rule of the principles of disorder and excess generating an effervescence out of which is born a new and reinvigorated order.

### *Dietary and Sexual Sacrilege*

In the same fashion, dietary and sexual sacrilege in totemic societies has as its goal to assure the group of subsistence and fertility for an additional period. Licence is tied to the ceremonies in which the sacred animal is renewed or in which youths are integrated into the society of men.

In fact, these rites inaugurate a new vital cycle and, consequently, play the precise role of the changing seasons in the more differentiated civilisations. Thus they constitute a return to chaos, a phase in which the existence of the universe and law is suddenly questioned. Taboos that ordinarily assure the proper functioning of institutions, the predictable progress of the universe, by separating the spheres of the permitted and the forbidden, are then violated. The revered species is killed and eaten by the group, and parallel to the great dietary crime, the great sexual crime is committed. The law of exogamy is violated.

Under cover of the dance and the night, and in defiance of kinship ties, men of the clan have sexual relations with the wives of the complementary clan, who are originally from their clan and, therefore, are taboo. Among the Warramunga, the evening after the men of the Uluura moiety celebrate their initiation ceremony they lead their wives to the men of the Kingilli moiety, who, it is recalled, have made all the preparations for the Uluura festival. The latter have relations with the women who belong to their own moiety. Ordinarily, these incestuous unions cause a chill of terror and abomination, and the guilty are condemned to the most vigorous punishments. Yet in the course of the festival, they are permitted and obligatory.

It must be stressed that these sacrilegious acts are regarded as just as ritualistic and holy as the very taboos they violate. Like the taboos, they free man from the *sacred*. In the course of the *pilou*, the great New Caledonian festival, writes Leenliardt, a masked character arrives who contradicts all the rules. He does everything that is forbidden to others. Reincarnating the ancestor whose mask identifies him, he pantomimes and repeats the actions of his mythical patron who "pursues pregnant women and reverses emotional and social concepts".

### *Myth and Incest*

It is important to conform exactly to the legendary example of the divine ancestors who practised incest. The original act of incest was most often between brother and sister. That is the case for numerous Oceanic, African and American tribes. In Egypt, Nut, the sky goddess, each night comes to have sexual relations with her brother Geb, the earth god. In Greece, Cronus and Rhea are also brother and sister, and if Deucalion and Pyrrha, who repopulate the world after a flood, are not brother and sister, they are at least cousins, whom the law of exogamy separates. More emphatically, incest is characteristic of chaos. They are mutually inclusive. Chaos is the time of mythical incest, and incest currently takes place in order to loose cosmic catastrophes. Among the African Ashanti, if the one who couples with a forbidden woman and thus compromises the universal order has not received his just punishment, hunters can no longer kill in the forests, crops stop growing, women no longer give birth and clans intermingle and cease existing. "All is now chaos in the universe," clearly concludes the observer.

Among the Eskimo, sexual licence clearly manifests a return to the mythical period. Orgies take place at the time of the festival of the extinguishing of the lamps, which is celebrated at the winter solstice. All lamps are simultaneously extinguished and later relit. Thus the changing year is recognised, localised and honoured. During the darkness symbolising chaos, couples have sexual relations at the bottom of the deep embankment that runs along the walls of the winter house. All wives are then exchanged. Sometimes the principle that determines these temporary unions is enacted. In Alaska and Cumberland Sound, a masked actor who personifies the goddess Sedna matches men and women according to their names, just as their legendary ancestors were, after whom they are named. Thus, the suspension of the ordinary rules of sexual behaviour signifies nothing else than a temporary ascent to the beginning of the ancient time of creation.

Myths of incest are myths of creation. They generally explain the origin of the human race. The quality of the forbidden union and the characteristics of the dream-time are added to the normal fertility of sexual union. Erotic practices are particularly important among the Kiwai and Marindanim of Papua. They merely reproduce those practices that enabled their ancestors to create edible plants. In the festival, as Lévy-Bruhl has remarked, debauchery is equivalent to sympathetic magic and to participation in the creative power of the primordial beings.

### *The Value of Sexual Licence*

The sexual act already inherently possesses a fecundating power. It is *hot*, as the Thonga say, in that it generates a power capable of increasing and exciting everything in nature that manifests it. The orgy of virility occasioned by the festival thus assists this function by the sole fact that it encourages and revives the cosmic forces. But this can result as well from any other kind of excess or debauchery. Anything may play its role in the festival.

Just as order, which preserves but is used up, is founded on proportion and distinction, so disorder, which regenerates, implies excess and confusion. In China, a continuous barrier of taboos separates the sexes in all manifestations of public or private life. Man and woman work separately in distinct occupations. Moreover, nothing pertaining to one may come in contact with anything belonging to the other. But each time that festivals are created, the joint action of both sexes is required for sacrifices, ritual labour and the casting of metals. "The collaboration of the sexes," writes Granet, "was as efficacious when reserved for sacred moments, as it was sacrilegious at normal times." The winter festivals ended in an orgy in which men and women fought and tore off their clothing. Doubtless, this was not so much to strip themselves naked as to re-clothe themselves in the clothing of victors.

In fact, the exchange of clothing seems like the very mark of the state of chaos, as the symbol of the reversal of values. It took place at the time of the Babylonian Sacaea, and among the Jews, at the orgiastic festival of Purim, in direct violation of the law of Moses. It is doubtless necessary to connect rites of this type with the dual disguise of Hercules and Omphale. In Greece in any case, the Argive festival in which boys and girls exchange clothing bears the significant name of *hubristika*. For *hubris* represents an attack upon the cosmic and social order, or disproportionate excess. The texts present it as a characteristic of the centaurs, monstrous half-men and half-animals of mythology, ravishers of women and eaters of raw meat, reincarnated, as Dumézil has recognised, in the masked members of initiation brotherhoods, violently intruding at the time of the new year, and like their legendary prototypes, typical violators of all the taboos.

### *Excesses in Fertility Rites*

Fertility is born of excess. To the sexual orgy, the festival adds the monstrous ingestion of food and drink. The 'primitive' festivals, prepared long in advance, manifest to a high degree this character that is maintained in striking fashion in more advanced civilisations. At the Athenian Anthesteria, everyone is given a bottle of wine. Then ensues a kind of tournament, in which the victor is the one who is the first to empty his bottle. At Purim, the Talmud indicates that one must drink until it is impossible to distinguish the two cries specific to the festival, "May Haman be accursed" and "May Moredecai be blessed". In China, if the texts can be believed, food is stocked "in piles as high as hills", troughs are dug and filled with wine, on which boats could sail, just as a chariot race could be run across the accumulation of food.

Everyone must stuff himself with as much food as possible and become bloated like a distended leather bottle. The exaggeration of traditional descriptions manifests another aspect of ritual excess. This is the competition in boasting and bragging that accompanies the waste and sacrifice of accumulated wealth. The role of boasting duels in the festivals and drinking bouts of the Germans, Celts and other peoples is well known. The prosperity of the next harvest must be assured, by recklessly dispensing the contents of the granaries. In a sort of wager with destiny, ruinous consequences are courted in the attempt to be the one who will give away the most, so that destiny is obligated to return with compound interest what it has received.

Each one thinks that he will receive, concludes Granet in commenting on the Chinese data, "a better remuneration and a greater return for his future labour". The Eskimo reckons in the same way. These exchanges and the distribution of presents that accompany the festival of Sedna, or the return of spirits to the beyond, possess a mystic efficacy. They make the hunt successful. "Not by motives of generosity or chance," Mauss emphasises, "gift exchange results in producing an abundance of wealth." What is still practised in Europe, specifically on New Year's Day, seems like the meagre vestige of an intense circulation of wealth, once destined to reinvigorate cosmic existence and restore the cohesion of social life. Economy, accumulation and moderation define the rhythm of profane life, while prodigality and excess define the rhythm of the festival, of the periodic and exalting interlude of sacred life that intervenes and restores youth and health.

Similarly, the frenzied agitation of the celebration at which they are devoured is in contrast to the established routine of work that permits food supplies to be amassed. In fact, the festival not only involves debauches of eating, drinking and sex, but also those of expression — words and gestures. Cries, ridicule and insults, the give and take of crude pleasantries (obscene or sacrilegious) between the public and a procession that crosses through it (as on the second day of the Anthesteria, at the Lenaean rites, at the Great Mysteries, at the carnival, or at the medieval Festival of Fools), jesting tourneys between groups of women and men (as at the shrine of the Mysian Demeter near Pellana in Achaia) constitute the major verbal excesses.

Movements, such as erotic pantomime, violent gesticulations and simulated and real conflict, do not lag behind. The obscene contortions of Baubo, by making Demeter laugh, reveal the nature of her lethargy, and make her fertile. One dances until exhausted and whirls about until dizzy. Atrocities are quickly provoked by the dance. At the fire ceremony of the Warramunga, twelve of the participants seize flaming torches. One, using his firebrand as a weapon, charges his opposite. Soon there is a general mêlée in which they strike and crack their heads with torches, and the bodies of the combatants are showered with burning sparks.

*Parody of Power and Sanctity*

Forbidden and extravagant behaviour does not seem to emphasise sufficiently the difference between the time of release and the time of control. Contrary acts are added to them. One tries to act in a way exactly the opposite of normal behaviour. The inversion of all relationships seems manifest proof of the return to chaos, the time of fluidity and confusion.

Also, the festivals that endeavour to revive the primordial era, the Greek Cronia or the Roman Saturnalia, imply the reversal of the social order. Slaves eat at their master's table, ordering them about and mocking them, while the latter serve and obey them, submitting to their affronts and reprimands. In each house, a state in miniature is established. The high functions, the roles of priests and consuls, are confined to slaves, who then exercise a power that is ephemeral and a parody of real power. In Babylon, roles were equally reversed at the time of the Sacaean festival. In each family, a slave, dressed as a king, ruled over the household. An analogous phenomenon occurred with the hierarchy of the state. In Rome, a monarch was chosen for a day, issuing ridiculous orders to his subjects, such as to make the rounds of the house while carrying a flute-player on one's shoulders.

Certain data lead us to think that the false king met a tragic fate. Every debauchery and excess was allowed him, but he was put to death on the altar of the god-king, Saturn, whom he had reincarnated for thirty days. The king of chaos being dead, order was restored, and the regular government again directed an organised universe or a cosmos. On Rhodes, at the end of the Cronia, a prisoner was made drunk and sacrificed. At the Babylonian Sacaea,[5] a slave was hanged or sacrificed, who, during festival time, had fulfilled the king's role in the city, using the latter's concubines, giving orders in his place, affording the populace an occasion for orgies and luxury. Doubtless it is necessary to bring together these false kings — doomed to death after having shown themselves, during the annual suspension of regular power, to be extreme tyrants, committing excesses and debauchery — with Nahusha (equally given to excess, outrage and debauchery), who rules over the sky and earth during the retreat of Indra, "across forty-three yards of water" after the murder ofVritra. This is also related to Mithotyn, the usurping magician who governs the universe after the retreat of Odin, when the latter goes into exile in order to purify himself of the defilement contracted because of his wife, Frigg. More generally, one thinks of the temporary sovereigns, notably in Indo-European myths, who take the place of the true ruler of the gods when he leaves to do penance for the sins with which he has been charged by the very exercise of his authority.

Everything suggests that the modern carnival be viewed as a sort of moribund echo of ancient festivals of the Saturnalia type. In fact, a cardboard effigy depicting an enormous king, coloured and comical, is shot, burnt or drowned at the end of the period of licence. The rite no longer has religious validity, but the reason for it appears clear. As soon as an effigy is substituted for a human victim, the rite tends to lose its expiatory and fecundating value, its double aspect of liquidating past defilements and creating a new world. It takes on the character of parody, which is already implicit in the Roman festival and which plays an essential role in the medieval Festival of Fools or of the Holy Innocents.

The lower clergy celebrates the Festival of the Holy Innocents during the period of rejoicing that begins about Christmas-time. They proceed to elect a pope, a bishop or a mock abbot, who occupies the throne until the Eve of Epiphany. These clerics wear feminine garb, intone obscene or grotesque refrains to the airs of liturgical chants, transform the altar into a tavern table at which they feast, burn the remains of old shoes in the censer and, in a word, devote themselves to every imaginable impropriety. Finally, an ass clad in a rich chasuble is led into the church with great pomp, and prayers are offered in its honour.

At the heart of these burlesqued and sacrilegious parodies, the ancient preoccupation with the annual reversal of the order of things is recognised. Perhaps it is even more evident in the exchange of roles between nuns and school-girls in the great convent of the Congregation of Notre-Dame, in Paris, on Holy Innocents Day. The pupils are clothed in the nuns' habits, and take charge of the class, while their teachers take their place on the benches, and make believe that they are paying attention. The same festival was celebrated at the Franciscan Monastery of Antibes, where the roles of priests and laity were reversed. The clergy replaced the lay brothers in the kitchen and garden, and the latter said Mass. They were clothed for the occasion in sacerdotal vestments, ragged and turned inside out. They read the holy books while holding them upside-down.

### *Regulations and Infractions*

No doubt, in these latter-day manifestations, no more should be seen than the automatic application in a new environment of a kind of atavism, a heritage of the times in which it was felt vitally necessary to reverse everything or commit excesses at the time of the new year. Only the principle behind the rite and the idea of temporarily substituting the power of comedy for a regular power have been retained.

The festival represents a complex totality in other respects. It implies a farewell to time past, to the year that has ended, and at the same time it implies the elimination of the waste-material produced by the functioning of every economy and the defilement associated with the exercise of all power. In addition, one returns to the creative chaos, to the *rudis indigestaque moles*,[6] from which the organised universe was born and reborn. It inaugurates a period of licence during the absence of the regular authorities.

At Tonkin, the great seal of justice is enclosed in a small box, symbolising that the law is dormant. The courts are closed, and of all offences, only murder is still recognised. But the punishment of those guilty of murder is postponed until the rule of law is restored. In the mean time power is entrusted to a monarch charged with violating all taboos, and indulging in every excess. He personifies the mythical sovereign of the golden age of chaos. General debauchery rejuvenates the world, and strengthens the animating powers of nature that are threatened by death.

When it becomes necessary to re-establish order, to fashion the universe anew, the temporary king is dethroned, expelled and sacrificed. This eventually facilitates his identification with the symbol of the primordial age, when it was reincarnated in a scape-goat, who was hunted or put to death. The spirits of the dead are again dismissed. The ancestral gods leave the world of men. The dancers, who depicted them, bury their masks, and erase their pictures. Barriers between men and women are again erected, and sexual and dietary taboos are again in force.

The restoration achieved, the forces of excess necessary to reinvigoration must give way to the spirit of moderation and docility, to discretion which is the beginning of wisdom, and to everything that maintains and preserves. Frenzy is succeeded by work, and excess by respect. The sacred as regulation, as taboos, organises creation, conquered by the sacred as infraction, and makes it endure. One governs the normal course of social life, the other governs its paroxysm.

### *Expenditures and Paroxysms*

In fact, in its pure form, the festival must be defined as the paroxysm of society, purifying and renewing it simultaneously. The paroxysm is not only its climax from a religious, but also from an economic point of view. It is the occasion for the circulation of wealth, of the most important trading, of prestige gained through the distribution of accumulated reserves. It seems to be a summation, manifesting the glory of the collectivity, which imbues its very being. The group then celebrates births to come, which assure its prosperity and future welfare. It takes to its bosom newly initiated members upon whom its vigour is based. It takes leave of its dead and solemnly affirms its loyalty to them. At the same time, it is the occasion on which, in stratified societies, the different social classes approach and fraternise with each other. And in societies with moieties, it is the occasion for antagonistic groups to blend. They thus attest their solidarity, and cause the mystic principles incarnate in them, which ordinarily are carefully segregated, to collaborate in the work of creation.

"Our festivals," explains a Kanaka, "mark the movement of the awl that is used to join the parts of the thatched roof, a single word for a single roof." Leenhardt does not hesitate to comment on this declaration: "The summit of Kanaka society is not the head of the hierarchy, the chief, but rather the *pilou* itself. It is the moment in which the allied clans, stimulated by discussions and dances, together exalt the gods, totems and invisible beings, who are the source of life, the support of power, and the very condition of society."

In fact, when these exhausting and ruinous festivals are abandoned, under the influence of colonisation, society loses its bonds and becomes divided. As varied as imaginable, all taking place in a single season, or spread over the course of the year, festivals everywhere still fulfil an analogous function. They constitute an interruption in the obligation to work, a release from the limitations and servitude of the human condition. It is the moment in which the myth or dream comes alive. One exists in a time in which one's only obligation is to spend and be spent in it. Acquisitive motives are no longer admissible, for each one must squander and waste his wealth, food and sexual and muscular vigour in competition with others. But it seems that in the course of their evolution, societies tend toward indifference, uniformity, equalisation of status and relaxation of tensions. The complexity of the social organism, to the degree that it is admitted, is less tolerant of interruption of the ordinary course of life. Everything must continue today the same as yesterday, and tomorrow as today.

General turbulence is no longer possible. It no longer occurs at fixed times or on a vast scale. It is as if it were diluted in the calendar and necessarily absorbed in monotony and regularity. The festival is then succeeded by the vacation. To be sure, it is always a time of free activity, of interruption in the pattern of work, but it is a phase of relaxation, not paroxysm. The values are found to be completely reversed. In one case, each part is in its place, and in the other, everything is gathered at the same point. Vacations (as the very term indicates) appear as a void, or at least an easing of social activity. By the same token, they are powerless to satisfy the individual. They are deprived of all positive character. The happiness they bring is primarily due to freedom from the boredom of which they are a distraction, from the obligations of which one has been freed. To go on vacation is first of all to flee care, to enjoy a 'well-earned' rest. In addition, one is isolated from the group, instead of entering into communion with it, at a time of exuberance and jollity. Also, unlike the festival, vacations constitute not the flow of collective life but its ebb.

It therefore must be asked what brew of similar potency liberates the instincts of the individual, repressed by the exigencies of organised living, and at the same time leads to a collective effervescence of comparable magnitude. It seems that, with the rise of firmly established states, more and more strictly regulated as their structure affirms, the traditional alternation of merry-making and work, of ecstasy and restraint, that periodically cause order to be reborn from chaos, wealth from prodigality and stability from disorder, is replaced by an alternation of a very different order, that, in the modern world, alone represents something comparable. It is the alternation of peace and war, prosperity and the destruction of the fruits of prosperity, regulated tranquillity and obligatory violence.

THE SACRED CONSPIRACY

# VIII

. . . . . . . . . . . . . . . . . . . . . . . . . . . . . . . . . . . .

June 1939 – October 1939

*Chronology*
*Commentaries*

## ACÉPHALE 5

●92. Georges Bataille *The Madness of Nietzsche*
●93. Georges Bataille *The Threat of War*
●94. Georges Bataille *The Practice of Joy in the Face of Death*

## THE COLLEGE OF SOCIOLOGY

○95. Georges Bataille *Joy in the Face of Death*
○96. Georges Bataille *The College of Sociology*

## THE SECRET SOCIETY OF ACÉPHALE

●97. Georges Bataille *The Star Alcohol*
●98. Georges Bataille *Joy in the Face of Death (Meditation Text)*
●99. Georges Bataille *Heraclitean Meditation*
●100. Georges Bataille *To Saint-Paul*
●101. Patrick Waldberg *Extract from Acéphalogram (2)*
●102. Georges Bataille *To Patrick Waldberg*
●103. Georges Bataille *To the Members of Acéphale*
●104. Georges Bataille *To the Members of Acéphale*

# CHRONOLOGY

## 1939

**6 June.** Bataille lectures to the College on "Joy in the Face of Death", ○95. This precipitates an immediate crisis, with Caillois, Paulhan and Wahl objecting to Bataille's embracing of mysticism. A further text on the subject, ●94, appears in *Acéphale* 5, published the same month. This final issue of *Acéphale* has a smaller format, lacks adverts or any of the other paraphernalia of a 'journal', and has the title *Madness, War and Death*. No author's name appears either but it is written by Bataille alone. It appears here in its entirety.

"The Practice of Joy in the Face of Death", ●94, includes a series of mystical meditation exercises which Bataille described, writing in *Guilty*, as a method that was "similar in technique to sacrifice. The moment of ecstasy is laid bare if I inwardly shatter the particularity that encloses me within myself."[1] The exercises resemble those in undated texts for meditations to be used by members of Acéphale: "The Star Alcohol", ●97, addressed to Isabelle Farner, "Joy in the Face of Death (Meditation Text)", ●98, and the "Heraclitean Meditation", ●99.

**15 June.** Gallimard publishes Leiris's *Manhood*. So merciless is the self-exposure in this book that Picasso remarked that his worst enemy would have been hard pressed to portray his personality in a more negative light.[2]

**20 June.** Duthuit lectures on "The Myth of the English Monarchy".

**23 June.** Caillois sails from Cherbourg with Victoria Ocampo for Buenos Aires. His return to France, scheduled for late September, is deferred until the end of the war in August 1945.

**1 July.** A few of the members of Acéphale, Ambrosino, Chavy, Farner and Waldberg, form a group to study Nietzsche's *The Gay Science*.

**4 July.** At the final gathering of the College, Bataille's lecture "The College of Sociology" makes plain his disagreements with other members of the group, in particular Caillois and Leiris (who refuses to speak).

**11 July.** Caillois arrives in Buenos Aires, where the Spanish version of *Le Mythe et l'homme* has just been published by Ediciones Sur, and between July and early August he gives a series of lectures on "Themes of the Great Myths".[3]

**20 July.** In a long letter to Caillois, Bataille goes over their disagreements from the final evening of the College, but also seeks a reconciliation and requests contributions for a new journal.

**July-August.** Discussions take place with the aim of rebuilding the College around Bataille, Moré and Wahl. In Buenos Aires, Caillois, in association with Ocampo's *Sur*, initiates what is intended to be an Argentine branch of the College. A number of sociological debates take place, with others following until 1942.[4]

**14 August.** A collective project is initiated by Chavy, to assemble a collection of Nietzsche's aphorisms as the possible prelude to a new morality within Acéphale.

**23 August.** Nazi-Soviet non-aggression pact.

**24 August.** In France, mobilisation of army reservists begins. All Communist newspapers are banned a few days later.

**26 August.** Bataille writes to Couturier stressing the necessity to maintain links between a small group of people: "I think war need not be an impediment [...] On the contrary, I think it might represent the decisive moment, since the physical barriers to the burning contagion I want to set in motion are so enormous [...]. What is at stake is the birth of the sort of man who rises above the worst, who is able to see the worst as a reality and be equal to it."[5]

**1 September.** Germany and Slovakia attack Poland, with the result that France and Britain, allies of Poland, declare war on Germany. The beginning of the "phoney war", that ends on 10 May 1940 with the German invasion of the Netherlands, Belgium, Luxembourg and France. Leiris is mobilised.

**5 September.** Bataille begins the diary that is published in 1944 as *Guilty*. He writes: "This book is violently dominated by tears, as it is violently dominated by death".[6] He is reading *The Book of Visions* of Angela of Foligno.[7]

**8 September.** The evening before he joins his unit at Beni Ounif in Algeria, Leiris dines with Bataille, who leaves this description of him: "His lined face, shaped by a distant sense of reserve, was at once tense, feverish and assailed by the constant rending of an impossible internal agitation, combined with his shaven head (of an almost uniform colour as if made of wood or stone), form perhaps the most contradictory impression I have ever encountered: an obvious cowardice (more obvious than my own) but marked with so much seriousness, so far beyond saving, that nothing could be more distressing to look upon; this was a naughty little boy and a venerable elder, an ordinary sailor on shore-leave and a foolish god whose stone head is lost in the darkness of the clouds..."[8]

**9 September.** Bataille's diary confirms that his debauchery and libertinage continues unabated: "The orgy I went to (participated in) last night was of the most vulgar sort. Yet my unaffected nature quickly put me on a par with the worst of them. I remained quiet and sensitive, not at all hostile amidst the shrieks and howls and the tumbling bodies."[9]

**14 September.** In *Guilty*, Bataille recounts his night-time ritual since Colette's death, when he would go from the house in Saint-Germain-en-Laye to the little cemetery in Fourqueux to visit her grave, which he had requested be "covered in vegetation" and marked with neither stone nor inscription: "Yesterday I went to Laure's grave and as soon as I had stepped out of my door the night was so black that I wondered whether it was going to be possible to find my way [...] When I arrived there I wrapped my arms around myself in pain, no longer knowing or feeling anything, and at that moment it was as if I had split myself in two in some obscure way and that I was holding her in my arms again [...] A terrible sweetness came over me and this happened exactly as it did when we would find each other, all of a sudden; when the barriers that separate two beings fall away."[10]

**21 September.** From *Guilty*: "In a moment of acute calmness in the presence of the starry black sky, the hill and the black trees, I found the thing that reduced my heart to a pit full of ashes [...] I became a soaring flight out of myself, as if my life was flowing past in slow rivers across the ink of the sky."[11]

**1 October.** Bataille returns to the theme of joy in the face of death in a letter to Saint-Paul. He writes: "It relates to a joy felt when facing the certainty of death and to the foundation of a religious existence that is quite distinct from Christianity." ●100.

**2 October.** In *Guilty*, Bataille notes that this was the date he first met Denise Rollin Le Gentil, his future partner.[12]

**3 October.** Bataille writes in *Guilty*: "In the 'desert' I am travelling through there is a total solitude that is made yet more empty by Laure's being dead."[13]

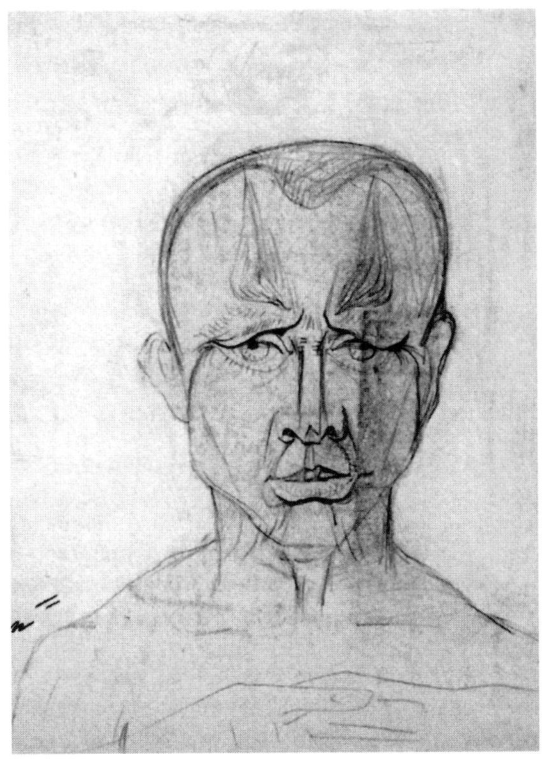

Portrait of Michel Leiris by André Masson, 1939.

**16 October.** In *Guilty* again, Bataille reveals that he is practising meditational exercises, some of which involve the overwhelming images of Chinese torture he had first been shown by Borel in 1925 (*see above*).[14]

He described his method: "On the wall of appearances, I projected images of explosion and laceration. First I had to establish absolute silence within myself. With time, I managed to achieve this almost whenever I wanted. In this silence, which was often boring, I called to mind every possible laceration. One obscene, or laughable or lugubrious representation followed another. I pictured the depths of a volcano, war or my own death. [...] On the first day the wall fell, I found myself in the forest at night..."[15]

**20 October.** Faced with obvious apathy within the group, Bataille, after discussing the situation with Patrick Waldberg, writes him a letter, ●102; it contains another letter addressed to Waldberg and to Ambrosino, Andler, Chavy, Chenon and Farner, ●103: this text marks the disbanding of the Society. In ●102, however, Bataille confirms he will be at the meetings at the Café Ruc for the day after and on the 25th. "On receiving this text, Andler wrote to him, as did Chavy, asking for clarifications the following Wednesday, in place of the usual meeting."[16] In a further letter the same day to the same addressees Bataille reiterates his "unshaken, even [...] increased confidence in the movement", ●104.

**21 October.** There is no entry in *Guilty* for 20 October, the day on which the last of these three great projects of Bataille's came to an end. The next day, considering how wrong he had been to attach himself to this group "as a possibility for life", despite Laure's violent objections, he writes: "So, I am abandoned, abandoned with inexplicable brutishness. I expected it. I did not protest. I even felt the necessity of it..."[17] However, shortly before his death, he returned to the subject of Acéphale, and firmly associated his writings with this crucial experience: "It was a monstrous mistake, but my writings as a whole will demonstrate both the error and the value of its monstrous intent."[18]

# COMMENTARIES

## THE COLLEGE OF SOCIOLOGY [AB]

The subject matter of the last two lectures by Bataille had been decided upon in a moment of crisis, and they had the effect of bringing the various tensions within the College out into the open. Some of these were inherent to its initial formulation, others more recent, and all were only heightened by the inevitability of war.

Although Bataille attempted to situate his lecture of 6 June within the continuum of the College's previous lectures it self-evidently expressed concerns that were more closely associated with Acéphale than with the College, while he abandoned all pretence of following a sociological method in favour of an explanation of what had become the central tenet of Acéphale's "religion". The lecture more or less coincided with the final, anonymous issue of *Acéphale*, which came out the same month, its editorial address now the same as that of the College.

Ten years earlier *Documents* had collapsed because the heterogeneous elements dear to Bataille began to escape the section of the magazine intended to contain them (the "Critical Dictionary"). The same process appeared to be repeating itself here. It was one thing to accept that an active sociology might encompass lived experience if it were bolstered by a proper sociological methodology, but it was another thing altogether for it to consist of lived experience alone. "Joy in the face of death" was effectively a mystical method of meditation which Bataille had begun to practise soon after the death of Laure, and perhaps because of it, Hollier suggests.[1] Such a method appears to exist outside of the realm of social facts. Although Bataille had already defended the mystical position in his letter to Caillois cited earlier (p.361), on the morning of the lecture, at 9.35, he wrote him another letter (that would have arrived before midday), justifying his plans:

> My dear friend,
>
> Please excuse the delay. My statement will start from this principle: that society revolves around nuclei formed by strong emotional ties — these I shall represent as the fundamental principle of the College. Speaking then for my own part, I shall

try to show that these nuclei are formed by "men of death", men who give meaning to death. Describing the various attitudes to death that have been inflicted upon men, I will show that only joy is appropriate to those who are lucid. Finally, I will try to establish a relation between the various forms of accumulation and expenditure, on the one hand, and attitudes to death, on the other (an economy of salvation = an economy of accumulation; "joy in the face of death" being linked to a *conscious* will to expenditure, and resulting in a struggle between the forces of expenditure and those of accumulation). Overall I shall endeavour to emphasise that the problem of death is the essential problem of man.

Until tonight, in friendship,

Georges Bataille[2]

This meeting of the College was described by the literary critic Georges Blin as "demoralising", and according to Hollier[3] it was "interrupted by groups from both the extreme right and the Communists. A scrummage ensued so that the bookseller feared for his stock, Caillois began stammering horribly and Bataille, his voice quite hoarse, struggled to make himself heard." Afterwards, according to Bataille in his next lecture, Caillois, Paulhan and Wahl had voiced their objections to the lecture's content.

The text given here, ○95, seems to be the (incomplete) transcript of Bataille's lecture, but parts of it are difficult to understand outside the context of another text of his from the same period, "Sacrifice", in particular its final section:[4]

*"Joy in the Face of Death" as a Sacrificial Act*

The human spirit is dominated by a need that makes bliss unbearable. Bliss gives rise all of a sudden to a greater and more exacting desire than the desire to be happy — the desire to blight and destroy bliss itself. It is this impulse, which presupposes his happiness and strength, that enables man to complete within himself "that which makes him a man". The greatest and worst serenity may naturally serve as an avenue to "joy in the face of death". The Romantic imagination supplies an erroneous idea of this impulse, which necessarily denudes man and sends him naked into the desert. In the desert there is a great simplicity which collapses the objections of those who say: "it is a fraud, since we do not actually die, to talk of 'joy in the face of death'". It is not a matter of dying but of being transported "to the pinnacle of death". A sense of light-headedness and laughter without bitterness, a sort of growing power, but one that sadly disappears into itself and becomes a supplicating hardness, this is what is accomplished in a great silence.

The penultimate lecture to the College, on 20 June, was by Duthuit on "The Myth of the English Monarchy", the text of which is now lost.

In retrospect the final manifestation of the College, dedicated to the College itself, is a sort of culmination, almost an execution. Its tone would guarantee that the College could not continue under Bataille's direction alone, and indeed, some sort of congress to discuss its future work had already been mooted for September, in which a more collective leadership appears to have been envisaged.[5] The irony of the College collapsing as a result of the actions of its "head" is all too obvious, but in the event it proved impractical to continue, both because of its internal contradictions, and the outbreak of war.

It had been agreed at the end of March that Bataille, Caillois and Leiris would each speak for around half an hour on the College,[6] and the lecture was scheduled for 4 July, but on 23 June Caillois embarked for Buenos Aires with Victoria Ocampo, intending to return in September. It is not known if he discussed this departure with Bataille beforehand. Meanwhile, Leiris assembled some notes for his talk.[7] He was always a reluctant public speaker, and the lack of enthusiasm in these pages is palpable. The day before the lecture he decided he was unable to participate.

Bataille took to the podium alone, and read the defiantly uncompromising text that follows. It is an astonishing statement, and one which, it should be noted, does not much address the intended topic, the aims or methods of the College, except to overwhelm them. Even amidst this deluge, however, Bataille manages to return to his disagreement with Caillois by restating the problem of the festival in terms that take neither side, a remarkable olive branch: "… it is difficult to know to what extent the community is only the propitious occasion for the festival and sacrifice, or if the festival and sacrifice is the measure of the love offered to the community." He also stresses the importance of the distinction: "this question, which might be thought a little quaint, represents the ultimate question for man, even more so, the ultimate question of being", ○96.

The correspondence exchanged between Bataille, Leiris and Caillois at this time can only be briefly summarised here. Both Leiris and Bataille wrote to each other independently on the day before the final lecture took place. Leiris pointed out, rather belatedly as he admitted, that he had serious disagreements with certain aspects of the College's sociological methods (disagreements that could only have been aggravated by these final two lectures of Bataille's). He later summarised his objection to the fact that Bataille "over-exaggerated the Sacred" and that this contradicted Mauss's idea of the "total phenomenon" by which he meant that all phenomena also have religious, economic and moral aspects: "The Sacred wasn't necessarily dominant."[8]

Leiris took this letter to Bataille rather than posting it, and according to the latter, their discussion "made it possible to say that we remained in essential agreement".[9]

Bataille in his turn had written to Leiris to communicate a text received from Caillois called "An Examination of Conscience" which he had asked Bataille to read out after he had spoken. Bataille had severe reservations about doing so, and in the event did not read the text, which is now lost (likewise, at the end of his lecture Bataille refers to "practical proposals", and we have no idea what these were). The day after the lecture Bataille wrote to Leiris to defend a new form of sociology that might include personal experience, based, one presumes, upon what had occurred within Acéphale: "The experience of the sacred is such that it cannot leave anyone indifferent: anyone who encounters the sacred can no longer remain estranged from it."[10] A reply from Leiris on the 6th began by noting that "you can be sure that I was happy to hear that it [Bataille's lecture] had been judged — by many, at least, it seems — to have been the most significant session at the College of Sociology".[11]

On 20 July, Bataille wrote to Caillois. His letter concerns Caillois's ideas about spiritual power and the means to acquire it and Bataille goes to great lengths to be constructive, despite what he perceived as the "hostility" of certain of Caillois's criticisms of him. All could be resolved in the congress they were planning for later in the year, but in the event Caillois did not return to France and Leiris, soon enlisted, was sent to North Africa. Apart from a pale version of it established by Caillois in Buenos Aires, the College ceased to exist.

These events, and the correspondence associated with them, coincide with a hiatus in the activities of Acéphale, or at least we have no reliably datable documents between ●90 at the end of May and ●100 from 1 October, but after July only the secret society remained.

## ACÉPHALE [MG]

These last two commentaries must be something of an epilogue for both Acéphale and the College. As far as the history of Acéphale is concerned, this section is the least complete: we have no documents relating to sessional meetings, nor any recollections from two of the best informants. Rollin could not recall taking part in the secret society on his return from Madrid after the end of the Spanish Civil War, and Koch ended his participation in the group's activities in April or May 1939. It was a long while before he again met up with Andler, who told me that he, Chavy and Chenon had kept in contact with Ambrosino. This was more probably to do with the methodical study of Nietzsche begun by some of the adepts in July, since Ambrosino was no longer in Paris.[12] Having gone on vacation in July 1939, after failing his "*agrégation*", Koch stayed in the south of France until he was called up at the end of August.

Everything included in this last section, however — the texts from the final issue of *Acéphale* together with those of the Society and the last lectures by Bataille to the College — is linked by a single theme: joy in the face of death.

The June 1939 issue of *Acéphale* begins with "The Madness of Nietzsche", ●92, written by Bataille at Saint-Germain-en-Laye on 3 January 1939[13] in commemoration of the fiftieth anniversary of the tragic event when the philosopher, on the Piazza Carlo Alberto in Turin, made his self-identification with Dionysus or the crucified Christ, thus fulfilling the words of Zarathustra: "When a living thing commands itself, it must atone for its commanding and become the judge, avenger and VICTIM of its own laws". This was a necessary event which "leads to the realisation — without there being any possibility to avoid it — that the 'embodied man' must *also* go mad," as Bataille comments, following Blake's proverb, "*If others had not been foolish, we should be so*".[14] He went on to affirm, contrary to those who delight in the "simulated deliriums of art" or literature (certainly a reference to the Surrealists), that: "Madness cannot be cast out or excluded from human *wholeness*, which cannot be fully accomplished without it", ●92. According to Klossowski, the punishment suffered by Nietzsche was a "privilege", a "*delirium that transformed the executioner into the victim*", and he recalled that Nietzsche, "in the sense that no man had more faith [...] and in accepting that he was guilty of the 'Death of God' — accused himself in the name of all men, while also seeing himself in the crucified Christ".[15]

The other two texts by Bataille in this issue are undated. "The Threat of War", ●93, introduces the necessity for a Church to claim "spiritual power" and constitute "a force that can be developed and is capable of influencing others" whose values — equally opposed to military Fascism, national interests or the bombastic sloganeering of the democracies — must "put Tragedy at the apex". In other words, this is the opposite of the "Church militant" of Caillois's "Sociology of the Intellectuals", published in the *NRF* on 1 August 1939. Here he described a rigorously hierarchical and "strong community" of intellectuals — modelled on the Jesuits, in that they "project outside the Order what is triumphant within"[16] — and endeavoured to elaborate new values which respond to the "necessities of the moment" in which "action is permeated by contemplation".

The central text in *Acéphale* 5, however, is "The Practice of Joy in the Face of Death", ●94, a description of a state in which "ecstatic contemplation and lucid knowledge" are achieved by an activity that "cannot fail to be dangerous", and which is thus quite unlike the Christian's "bliss that is satisfying in and of itself" and grants a "foretaste of eternity". According to Bataille, the word "mystical" is no longer applicable to the religious practices of Europe or Asia, since only joy in the face of death is proper to those for whom there is no life beyond, because its "shameless, immodest holiness can lead to a sufficiently happy *loss of self"*. The six variations of what Bataille hesitated to call "exercises" allow us some appreciation of the "mystical training" he had begun to undertake by, in the words of Jean Bruno,[17] "closely associating [...] eroticism and other intense feelings with the more ethereal drunkenness of illumination, subtly slipping from one register to another and rejecting the mutilations of asceticism". Bruno likewise points out that the essence of Bataille's method, founded on silence and dramatisation, had already been referred to in his article "Friendship", begun in the summer of 1939 and published in April 1940 in *Mesures*. This later became a part of the first section of *Guilty* (cited on p.412, *16 October*), where Bataille concluded: "I no longer doubted that ecstasy could dispense with a representation of God."[18]

Although Bataille's text does not constitute a systematic explanation of his technique, according to Bruno, the six meditations reflect the successive stages of an inner research Bataille continued to pursue ever more intensively in the following years. The "lucid somnolence" induced by the first one, the "meditation on peace", dates from the end of May 1938, Bruno tells us. This was followed, in the second meditation, by joy in the face of death, which "while lacking the peace of the first" retains its method through being based upon "concentration on a poem with an insistent rhythm", which then leads to the third meditation, in which "visual representations of annihilation take on cosmic perspectives" intended to provoke "a kind of incandescence".[19] The fourth introduces a further method, in which silence and dramatisation are augmented by a "polarisation [whereby he is] alternately oriented towards interiority and the outside".[20] In this way Bataille "projects beyond himself a point on which his desire to burn is concentrated",[21] in order to access, in the fifth stage, the place where death is confused with the "grey light" of the "haze of the sky" and "appears to be of the same nature as the illuminating light", a state Bruno calls "volatilisation". Finally, in the sixth meditation, he returns to the paroxysmal images of the Heraclitean meditation on war so as to provoke — as with the the contemplation of Chinese torture Bataille described in *Guilty* and in *Inner Experience* — a violent tearing capable of opening "a breach in the psyche".[22]

Three texts from within the Society are connected to these meditations. The first, preserved among Isabelle Waldberg's papers, is "The Star Alcohol", ●97, written on crossed-out headed paper for the College of Sociology. Its title may refer to the poetry collection *Alcools* by Apollinaire, whose name appears in the margin of the manuscript for "The Sacred" from the previous year, accompanied by a note: "a sacred consisting of privileged moments and no longer of substance."[23] The first part of the text describes how to achieve silence by refraining from conscious thinking and by paying attention to breathing, and then proceeds to the method of the meditation: "You must not read the text but slowly recall it from memory", in order to bring on an "actual stupor". The second part, the meditation itself, echoes both a "Meditation on Alcohol" found among Chenon's papers,[24] which is evidently a first version of this text, and the third meditation from "The Practice of Joy in the Face of Death" as it appeared in *Acéphale*, ●94, which appears to be the definitive version of this text. The second text, "Joy in the Face of Death (Meditation Text)", ●98, was among the papers of Chavy and Andler. It begins in the same manner as "The Star Alcohol", but differs in its expression of the acephalous. The third meditation — found among Andler's papers and Waldberg's, though in his lacking its first page — the "Heraclitean Meditation" on war, ●99, expands upon the sixth meditation in ●94. The consumption that results from the "hunger to endure" of all human beings responds to the same double image that had expressed the "composite ontology" developed by Bataille in his text "Celestial bodies":[25] the burning sun, which "lavishes its energy on space" in an ecstatic gift of itself, and the cold earth, whose surface particles are "no longer expending but on the contrary devouring energy", and thus appear to be dedicated to "useful" acquisition.

Bataille also wrote on joy in the face of death in his letter to Saint-Paul, ●100. His aim here was to dissociate it not only from Christianity but also from "military courage" in order to clarify that it was "not a searching for death since that would be a condemnation of life" but rather it was something whose outcome can only be "death submitted to with joy as the fulfilment of a life". This is the last text we have from the secret society of Acéphale.

On 20 October, Bataille sent a letter to Patrick Waldberg, ●102, following a "decisive discussion"[26] and "an excess of language", that included another, ●103, addressed to Ambrosino, Andler, Chavy, Chenon, Isabelle Farner and Waldberg, in which, confronted with "such a solid consensus" within the group "against he who was its foundation", to inform them of the disbanding of Acéphale. After Andler and Chavy requested clarification, a further letter followed, ●104, on the same day. On 25 October, the group formally came to an end in a final meeting with Andler and Chavy at the Café Ruc.

This end seemed almost inevitable, given the succession of crises within the group. Bataille, however, was surprised by the ensuing silence. While in his second letter he stressed the members' lack of confidence in the group and refused to participate in any "discussion or general conversation", having acknowledged only the "consecration of this state of affairs", namely the gulf that had opened between him and the members, he still affirmed his certainty that "a prospective collaboration should be possible to achieve one day or another". In fact, as Ambrosino wrote to Waldberg, the denouement was "a 'definitive' separation despite various appeals"[27] on Bataille's part, that in the event went unanswered, despite Chavy and Andler's attempts to broker discussions. The lack of any further documents here mean the ending of this communal experience remains to some extent indecipherable.

In his "Autobiographical Note" written many years later, Bataille indicated that his disagreement with the adepts was brought about because of their apprehension at "the imminence of war".[28] However, not all the adepts saw it that way. In 1944, Waldberg was invited by Breton to open a public debate on Acéphale and the question of the current status of myth as posed by his *Prolegomena to a Third Surrealist Manifesto or Not*. Waldberg then openly distanced himself from Bataille by publishing in *VVV*[29] (February 1944) a long excerpt from a letter to his wife dated 19 September 1943. Here he denounced the purely literary character of Acéphale, and the artificial nature of the rituals that marked out the existence of the secret society which in his opinion was undermined by the absence of any pre-existing myth. Waldberg took Breton's position to argue that the nature of myth implied the necessity "first of all of founding an order, and then of letting it develop by improvising according to its needs", because a cult's "object of worship could be just about anything at all". However, he later withdrew these objections, and in a renewed adherence to the state of incandescence to which Acéphale had aspired, he recalled that "for some of us, including me, the expression 'life-changing' was not at all just an empty catchphrase", ●101. Despite this though, and remembering the "internal strife and dissension" that had undermined the group towards the end together with "the awareness of its incongruous position in the midst of global disaster", he then revealed the impossibility encountered in its final act when Bataille attempted to ensure the survival of the community by definitively situating it in the realm of tragedy and crime (also ●101).

More recently, Koch, returning to the "profound, unalloyed" failure of Acéphale, nevertheless pointed out that this attempt — "unique" in the modern world — to create a " 'sacred' without God or gods, [...] inspired by a will that was aimed exclusively towards the future", was necessitated by the "paradoxical character [...] of a society from which the sacred was totally absent."[30] It was there that he discovered the seeds of a new modernity, in which might be attempted, however weakly or imperceptibly, a going "beyond the desacralisation" entailed by the death of God: "The strange hold Georges Bataille exerted in person, [...] the light brought to bear on what was being concocted at the College of Sociology, the thrilling beauty of its secret, nocturnal rites and even the lacunae that ran like a thread through the interviews I had with their associates, the acute feeling of inadequacy, the sustained *longueurs* of silence — all these aspects have left such a strong impression in my memory because such a ferment was laid down then that it has never ceased to work on me."[31]

# TEXTS

June 1939 — October 1939

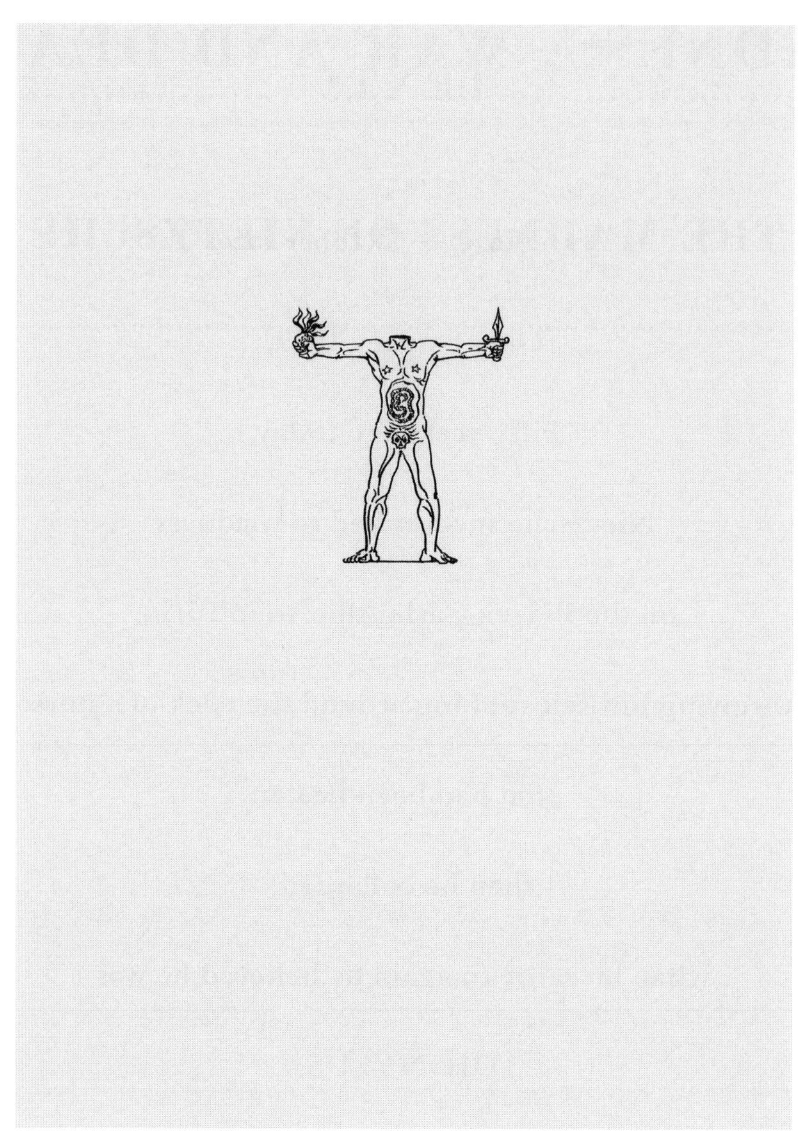

# MADNESS, WAR AND DEATH

## THE MADNESS OF NIETZSCHE 92

**On 3 January 1889,**

**Fifty years ago today,**

**Nietzsche succumbed to madness**

**on the Piazza Carlo Alberto in Turin,**

**throwing himself sobbing around the neck of a horse**

**that had been beaten,**

**then he collapsed;**

**when he came to again he believed he was**

**DIONYSUS**

**Or**

**CHRIST CRUCIFIED.**

**This occurrence**

**should be commemorated**

**as a tragedy.**

**"When a living thing,"**

**said Zarathustra,**

**"commands itself,**

**it must atone for its commanding**

**and become**

**the judge, avenger and**

**VICTIM**

**of its own laws."** [1]

# I

We wish to commemorate a tragic occurrence and are present here today, with life's full backing. The starry sky stretches out above our heads and the Earth turns beneath our feet. Life is in our bodies, but in our bodies too death is on the march (even from afar a man can always sense his last gasps as they draw near). Above us, day follows night, and night day. Yet we speak, and we speak loudly, without even knowing what sort of living beings we are. And if someone does not speak according to the rules of language, then the rational men that we are declare that he is *mad*.

We too are afraid of going *mad*, and stick to these rules with a considerable sense of uneasiness. Furthermore, the various types of derangement of the mad have been documented and recur with such monotony that they tend only to elicit a sense of extreme boredom. The harshness and seriousness of this logic is borne out by the fact that demented people offer little that is attractive. However, a philosopher holding forth is perhaps a more untrustworthy "mirror of the empty heavens" than someone who is insane, and in that case, shouldn't we just discard these categories?

This argument should not be taken *seriously*, on the basis that it reads well, or it would at once cease to have any meaning. However, there is absolutely no part of it that could be seen to be joking. For it is essential that we too should know what it is like to sweat with anxiety. What excuse can there be for not allowing yourself to struggle until you break out in a sweat? The absence of sweat is far more untrustworthy than the pranks of someone who does sweat. A philosopher is someone who is referred to as being wise, but he does not exist independently from a social group. This group is composed of a few philosophers who tear each other apart and a larger mass, variously indifferent or stirred up, which ignores them.

At this point, those who sweat are colliding *in the dark* with those who see the movement of history as what makes sense of human life. For it is true that throughout history the masses bent on destroying one another attribute the consequences to the inconsistencies of various philosophies — with their dialogues taking the form of acts of carnage. But completion is as much of a struggle as birth and, beyond completion and struggle, what else is there apart from death? Beyond words that endlessly destroy each other, what else is there other than a silence that will make people mad with sweat and laughter?

But if all people — or more simply their whole existence — were EMBODIED in one being — obviously just as alone and forsaken as they were before — then the head of this EMBODIED being would be torn apart by a conflict that could never be appeased — and so violent that sooner or later it would explode. For it is difficult to appreciate quite how powerful the storms or outbursts would be as met with in the visions of this embodied being, who must see God but at the same instant kill him, then become God himself, but only so as to be pitched at once into nothingness: he would then find he was a man again as insignificant as the first person who happened to pass by but deprived of any possibility of peace.

He could not, in fact, be satisfied with thinking and speaking, because some inner necessity would compel him to live what he thought and said. Such an embodied being would thus have a freedom that was so extensive that no language would be sufficient to reproduce all its movements (nor any other languages its dialectic). Only human thought, embodied in this way, could become a festival where intoxication and uninhibited behaviour would be just as unfettered as feelings of tragedy and dread. This leads to the realisation — without there being any possibility to avoid it — that the "embodied man" must *also* go mad.

How many times would the Earth spin violently round in his head! At what point would he be crucified! At what point would he be the bacchanalia (and behind him, all those who would be afraid to see his...)! But since he would become all alone, like Caesar, all-powerful and most sacred, so a man could not look upon him without bursting into tears. Assuming that... how could God not become distraught on discovering there in front of him the evidence of his rational inability to know madness?

**3 January 1939**

## II

Yet it is not enough to express a violent outburst in this way: words would betray the initial impulse if they were not linked to the desires and decisions that are the reason for them to come into being in the first place. It is easy to see that a representation of madness at its peak cannot also suffer its direct outcome: no one can choose to destroy within themselves the system of expression that connects them to their fellow men — as one bone is connected to the other bones.

A proverb of Blake's says that *if others had not been foolish, we should be so.* Madness cannot be cast out or excluded from human *wholeness*, which cannot be fully accomplished without it. Thus Nietzsche becoming mad — in place of us — made this wholeness possible; and those who went mad and lost their reason before him did not manage to do so with anything like as much brilliance. But can the gift a man makes of his madness to his fellows be accepted without it being repaid with interest? And if this is not irrationality on the part of someone receiving madness from someone else as a royal gift, what could its opposite be?

There is another proverb: *He who desires, but acts not, breeds pestilence.*

Without any doubt, the highest level of pestilence is reached when the desire that is expressed becomes confused with acting it out.

For if a man begins to follow some violent impulse, the fact that he is expressing it means that he forgoes following it at least for the time it is being expressed. Such expression requires us to substitute for its passion the external symbol that describes it. The man expressing himself must therefore pass from the burning sphere of the passions to the relatively cold and listless sphere of symbols. When in the presence of the thing that has been expressed, it is therefore always essential to ask whether the one who is expressing it is not getting ready for a deep sleep. Any such examination must be carried out with unfailing rigour.

Whoever has once understood that only madness can be the full realisation of man is thus led to choose with all lucidity — not between madness and reason — but between the imposture of "a nightmare that vindicates snoring" and the will to take orders from oneself and to conquer. No betrayal of the flashes and lacerations discovered at its peak shall seem more hateful to him than the simulated deliriums of art. For if it is true that he must become *the victim of his own laws*, if it is true that the fulfilment of his destiny requires that he be used up — and accordingly if madness or death have for him the brilliance of a festival — then his very love of life and destiny prompts him right away to commit within himself the crime of authority he will later atone for. Herein lies the thing required of him by the fate he is bound to by a feeling of extreme chance.

Proceeding in this way directly from powerless delirium to power — just as at the culmination of his life he must proceed in reverse from power to some sort of collapse, whether slow or sudden — his years could no longer pass in the quest — quite impersonal — for strength. At the moment when the wholeness of life appeared to him in all its connections to the tragedy that fulfilled it, he could see how much this revelation risked making it weaker. All around him he could see the ones who were getting closer to the secret — who thus represent the true 'salt' or 'meaning' of the earth — as they surrendered themselves to the dissolute sleep of literature or art. The fate of human existence thus appeared to him to be bound up with a small number of individuals deprived of any possibility of power. For some men, in their moral decay, bear much more within themselves than they believe: as when the masses around them, together with those who represent them, make everything they come into contact with subservient to necessity. Whoever has been formed as far as possible in the meditation of tragedy must therefore — instead of revelling in the 'symbolic expression' of these lacerating forces — demonstrate the consequences to those who resemble him. With persistence and strength of mind he must show them how to organise themselves and how to stop being, in contrast with Fascists and Christians, the despised rag-dolls of their enemies. For the onus falls on them to impose chance on the mass of those who require all men to accept a servile way of life: chance, which is to say what they already are but have given up through lack of will.

93

# THE THREAT OF WAR

Circumstances are only difficult for those who shrink from the tomb.
SAINT-JUST

It is useful here to present a few counter-arguments to the repudiations voiced by some people and the evasions of others, by means of a small number of unequivocal assertions.

1. Conflict and life are one and the same thing. A man's value depends on his aggressive strength.

2. A 'living' man sees death as the fulfilment of life; he does not regard it as a misfortune. On the other hand, a man who does not have the strength to find something bracing in his death is already somewhat 'dead'.

3. If the intention is to discover the limits of human destiny then it is impossible to remain alone and a veritable Church must be formed, laying claims to a 'spiritual power' and at the same time establishing a force that can be developed and is capable of influencing others. In the present circumstances, such a Church would have to accept and even seek out the conflict within which it would assert its existence. But in terms of essentials, this Church would need to bring the conflict in line with its own interests, in other words with the conditions of a 'fulfilment' of human potential.

4. War cannot be reduced to an expression or a means to develop an ideology, even one founded on military aggression: on the contrary, it is ideologies that become reduced to being just another weapon in the conflict. In every respect war exceeds the contradictory 'words' that are spoken on these occasions.

5. Fascism subordinates all values to the service of its struggle and its work. The fate of the Church we are attempting to define here must be linked to values that are neither military nor economic: there should be no difference as far as it is concerned between existing and opposing a closed system of servitude. At the same time it should maintain its distance from the national interest or the fine words of the democracies.

6. The values of this Church should be of the same order as the traditional considerations which put Tragedy at the apex; independently of political results, however, it is impossible to see any descent from our human universe to the various domains of Hell as something that has no meaning. But as regards the infernal, it ought to be possible only to speak about it in a modest manner, without either lowering our voices or shouting about it.

# THE PRACTICE OF JOY IN THE FACE OF DEATH

94

All this I am, and wish to be: at the same time dove, serpent and pig.
NIETZSCHE

When a human being finds himself situated in such a way that the world is reflected happily within him and there is no chance of it leading to destruction or suffering — as on a beautiful spring morning — he can allow himself to go along with the enchantment or the simple joy that result. But at the same moment he may also notice the dullness and the inconsequential concerns of empty repose which such bliss actually signifies. At this point, what rises up in him so bitterly is like a bird of prey ready to tear out the throat of a small bird in a blue sky that seems peaceful and clear. He sees that he cannot fulfil his life without giving in to some inexorable impulse, and feels its violence going to work in the most inaccessible part of his being with a rigour he finds frightening. If he looks back at others, who do not go any further than this state of bliss, he feels no hatred; on the contrary, he feels sympathy for such necessary happiness: he is only at odds with those who claim to be fulfilling their lives and who act out their risk-free charade so that they become known for having reached fulfilment, when all they have done is talk about fulfilment. But it is much to be preferred if all this does not end up making him feel light-headed. For his light-headedness exhausts him and puts him in danger of being quickly flung into a new concern that he is happy in his leisure time, or failing that, finds a painless existence. Or, if he does not give in but continues in his fearful haste to tear himself apart right to the end, he enters into death in such a way that nothing could be more horrible. The only one who can be truly happy here is the one who, having felt light-headed until the point where all his bones were shaking and it was no longer possible to gauge how far he had fallen, suddenly regains the unexpected power to be able to change his last gasp into a joy powerful enough to freeze and transfigure any who come into contact with it. Yet the only ambition that can take hold of a man who, with calm and even temper, sees his life reach its fulfilment in this tearing apart, cannot lay claim to greatness when it depends entirely on chance for its power to take effect. This kind of violent resolution, which bars him from finding any peace, does not necessarily entail either his light-headedness or a fall into sudden death. It may instead become in him the action and power by means of which he dedicates himself to that rigour whose workings tirelessly snap shut as sharply as the beak of a bird of prey. Contemplation is no more than the expanse, sometimes calm and sometimes stormy, across which the swift force of his action must be put to the test at one time or another. The mystical existence of the one whose "joy in the face of death" has become an inner violence cannot under any circumstances arrive at a bliss that is satisfying in and of itself, such as the bliss of Christians which grants a foretaste of eternity. The mystic who contemplates joy in the face of death cannot be regarded as trapped owing to the fact of his amused laughter at everything a human being is able to do and because he knows every spell it is possible to know; yet the totality of life — ecstatic contemplation and lucid knowledge *being fulfilled in a process* which cannot fail to be dangerous — is just as inexorably his lot as death is for the condemned man.

★

The texts that follow cannot by themselves constitute an initiation into the *exercising* of a mystical understanding of "joy in the face of death". If we accept that such a method might indeed exist, these texts do not even represent a part of it. While verbal initiation is itself difficult, it is impossible in the space of a few pages to give anything but the vaguest outline of something that is by its nature so difficult to comprehend. Taken as a whole, these writings are, furthermore, not so much *exercises* in the proper sense of the word as simple descriptions of a contemplative state or of ecstatic contemplation. These descriptions might not even be acceptable if they were not given for what they are, in other words freely. Only the text that appears first could, at a stretch, be seen as an *exercise*.

★

While there is a case for using the word *mystical* with reference to "joy in the face of death" and its practice, this indicates no more than an affective similarity between this practice and those of the religious peoples of Asia or Europe. There is no reason to associate this joy, which has no other object than the life at hand, with a certain presupposition concerning some other supposedly profound reality. "Joy in the face of death" belongs only to the one for whom it is not from *beyond*; it is the only intellectually honest path that the search for ecstasy may follow.

Moreover, how could a *beyond*, or God, or anything at all like God still be considered acceptable? No words are sufficiently clear to express the happy contempt of the one who "dances with the time that kills him" for those who find refuge in the anticipation of eternal bliss. This kind of timorous holiness, which right from the start had to be shielded from erotic excesses, has now lost all its power: the only reaction can be to laugh at a sacred intoxication which sought to make itself consistent with a 'holy' horror of debauchery. Prudery is perhaps a wholesome thing for the misguided; yet whoever would be afraid of naked girls and whisky would have very little time for "joy in the face of death".

Only a shameless, immodest holiness can lead to a sufficiently happy *loss of self*. "Joy in the face of death" means that life can be glorified from its roots to its summit. It deprives of all meaning anything that is an intellectual or moral beyond, whether substance, God, immutable order or salvation. It is an apotheosis of the perishable, an apotheosis of the flesh and of alcohol as well as the trance states of mysticism. The religious forms it rediscovers are the primitive forms that preceded the intrusion of servile morality; it revives that type of tragic jubilation that man 'is' once he ceases to behave like a cripple, taking pride in necessary work and allowing himself to be emasculated by the fear of tomorrow.

★

1

I give myself up to peace until my annihilation.

The sounds of struggle are lost in death like rivers in the sea, like the brilliance of stars in the night.
The power of conflict is fulfilled in the silence of all action.

I enter into peace as into a dark unknown.
I fall into this dark unknown.
I myself become this dark unknown.

2

I AM joy in the face of death.

Joy in the face of death upholds me.
Joy in the face of death casts me down.
Joy in the face of death annihilates me.

I remain in this annihilation and, from there, imagine nature as a play of forces expressed in a multiple and never-ending death agony.
In this way I slowly become lost in meaningless and endless space.

I reach the end of worlds.
I am gnawed at by death.
I am gnawed at by fever.
I am absorbed into the darkness of space.
I am annihilated in joy in the face of death.

## 3

**I AM joy in the face of death.**

**The depths of the sky, the emptiness of space, this is joy in the face of death: everything is deeply cracked.**

**I picture the Earth spinning giddily in the heavens.**
**I picture the heavens themselves slipping, spinning and becoming used up.**
**The sun, like an alcohol, spinning and exploding until out of breath.**
**The depths of the sky like a debauch of icy light becoming lost.**
**All that exists destroying itself, consuming itself and dying, each moment only bringing itself forth in the annihilation of the one that came before and itself only existing with fatal wounds.**
**I too destroying and consuming myself endlessly within myself in a great festival of blood.**

**I picture the frozen moment of my own death.***

***One night, in a dream, X feels he has been pierced by lightning: he understands that he is dying and is at once miraculously dazzled and transfigured; at this moment in his dream, he reaches the unexpected, but then wakes up.**

## 4

I fix a point in front of me, and picture this point as the locus of all existence and all unity, all separation and all anguish, all unsatisfied desire and all death that is possible.

I cling to this point, and a deep love for what is in this point burns away at me until I refuse to continue living for any other reason than for what is there, for that point which, being together the life and death of the beloved being, thunders like a cataract.

And at the same time it is essential that all external representations are stripped away from what is there, until it is nothing but pure violence, an interiority, a pure inner fall into a limitless abyss; this point endlessly absorbing the whole cataract of the nothingness within it, in other words what is vanished, 'past', and in the same movement endlessly prostituting a sudden apparition to the love that seeks in vain to grasp what will cease to be.

The impossibility of being satisfied in love is a *guide* for the *leap to fulfilment* at the same time as being the nullification of all possible illusion.

## 5

If I picture myself in a vision, within a circle of light that transfigures the ecstatic and exhausted face of a dying being, what radiates from this face of necessity lights up the clouds in the sky, whose glimmering greyness thereby becomes more penetrating than the light of the sun itself. In this representation, death appears to be of the same nature as the illuminating light, in so far as the latter fades away after leaving its source; it appears that no less a loss than death is needed for the spark of life to journey through and transfigure dull existence, since only its wrenching free can *become in me* the power of life and time. And so I cease to be anything except the mirror of death, just as the universe is only the mirror of light.

## 6. *Heraclitean Meditation*

AND I AM WAR.

I picture a human movement and rebellion which are limitless in their potential; this movement and this rebellion can only be *appeased* by *war*.

I picture the gift of an infinite suffering, of blood and bodies opened up, in the image of an ejaculation, knocking down the one it shakes and leaving him to an exhaustion racked with nausea.

I picture the Earth projected into space, like a woman screaming with her head on fire.

Before the terrestrial world, whose summer and winter regulate the death agony of everything that is alive, before the universe formed of countless spinning stars that fade away and consume themselves beyond measure, all I can see is a succession of cruel splendours whose movement alone is enough to require my death; this death is merely an *explosive* consumption of all that was, the joy of existing felt by everything that comes into the world; up until my own life requires that everything that is, and in all places, endlessly gives itself up and disappears into nothingness.

I picture myself covered with blood, broken but transfigured and in harmony with the world, at the same time a victim and one of the jaws of TIME, which is constantly killing and constantly killed.

Almost everywhere there are explosives and it will perhaps not be too long before they put out my eyes. I laugh when I think that these eyes continue to ask for objects that cannot destroy them.

GEORGES BATAILLE

# 95 *Joy in the Face of Death*

1

On the one hand, a fearless respect for death elicits the ironic and impassioned sensation that there is a fundamental absurdity in human affairs: the solidarity that exists between one man and his fellows can often appear laughable to the one who takes his place "at the pinnacle of death". But on the other hand, it is unquestionable that solidarity and devotion to a cause are as a rule necessities for those who pit themselves against death on an equal footing. Joy in the face of death is not some commonplace nostalgia born out of weariness and so cannot serve as a pretext any longer for those who would prefer not to put their lives at risk. It would be easy to say, "I belong to death. Why should I be killed?" There isn't anybody who would not shrink in revulsion from the likes of those who would contrive such a farce. Joy in the face of death assumes, in the first place, the sense of the *greatness* inherent in human life: it would be a nonsense if life were not driven by an insurmountable desire for greatness. It is for this reason that those who experience it do not need to seek out at random — for indeed that is what it must be — the cause that will actually allow them to pit themselves against death. What requires and guarantees the *greatness* of these individuals is the cause to which they are dedicated. And whatever requires and guarantees insignificance and pettiness in turn represents what they must discredit and bring to ruin — since it is true that the air they breathe, the sun and the smiles of young women must be the things their pride rests on. As a matter of fact, they are condemned (to dominate other men) to sustain this intractable pride, assuming they do not agree to disappear. But it is not only the joy they have of knowing that they will perish, and which they associate with the physical destruction they will meet, that situates them directly at the level of domination (right from the start it is obvious that no force, in a human nature that will not look them in the face, could withstand or overcome them) — another element contributes to providing them with a destiny that responds to the deepest needs of social cohesion.

2

I have said before that the nuclei around which society revolves were "formed out of small numbers of men bound together by emotional bonds". I have attempted to define these "nuclei of social gravitation" further as so many geometrical loci where attitudes towards death were determined. These representations, I suggested, can only be coherent if the "emotional bonds", around which discordant human reality forms, are consistently integrated into a necessary relationship with death. Elsewhere I put forward this paradox, "that the human heart beats for nothing so hard as it does for death": it seems that a kind of strange and powerful communication is established between men whenever the violence of death is close by. It may well be that they are joined together by a simple sense of common danger: even when one of them is overcome by death while at the same moment the people nearby are not threatened, this reminder of their fragility prompts those who have survived to seek consolation in communication. But the meeting with death has yet another meaning which cannot be reduced to simple fear. For when fear is absent, the 'domain' of death does not become a matter of indifference. It has an attraction to which the ordinary bystander is just as susceptible as the man who is threatened by death. The momentous and decisive change brought about by death is such a blow to the spirit that it is — far from the world it has been used to — cast out and transported, gasping for breath, somewhere between earth and sky; it is as if it suddenly noticed the dizzying and endless movement that has taken control of it. This movement then appears partly horrifying and partly hostile, yet in a way that is *external* to the person threatened with death or indeed the one who is dying; it is all that remains, cutting off from reality the one who looks upon his dying no less than the one who is dying. So it is that, in the presence of death, what there remains of life can only subsist *outside of itself.*

There is a moment suspended in time when everything is swept away, when everything wavers: the sure and deeply rooted reality claimed by the individual has disappeared, and all that remains are much more energetic presences, altogether mobile, violent and inexorable. The disconcerted mind can hardly make out the furious churning of this hell, having been drawn here by its intoxication and left to flounder: the extreme emotion it feels is translated into the murky diversity of phantoms and nightmares with which it peoples the place. All that thrives here are forces possessed of a violence that can be compared to the might of a storm when it breaks. Our puerile attachments to trivial matters in normal times — the little diversions that order our everyday stupidity — are duly borne away in the roar of a great wind: existence, having been hunted down, is called out in its entirety to greatness. The lone individual driven from the 'pettiness' of his own person becomes indistinguishable within the community of men, but his disappearance would be meaningless if this community was not capable of responding to the situation. What human destiny describes as 'unappeased', or 'unappeasable' — that incredible thirst for glory that prevents sleep and allows no rest — represent the only possible options that are sufficiently energetic to meet the need that arises each time existence wavers when confronting death.

3

Taking into account this shift outside the self, which inevitably occurs when death comes into play, it is easier to see why the army and religion alone are capable of satisfying man's most significant aspirations. The first of these makes it its job to confront death in real terms, while the other alone knows the language stamped with dread and stormy majesty which befits those on the threshold of the tomb. An attitude that is neither military nor religious becomes untenable in principle from the moment death intervenes. It is impossible to be placed in proximity with death and at the same time to communicate with men whose attitude is grossly profane. The shift outside the self which occurs in the face of death requires a sacred world such that, at the moment we are lost, there would appear some vaster reality as well as forces that are capable of confronting the terror involved. There is nothing of this sort in a café, a department store or a bank: the necessary silences, solemnities and acts of violence are found, in essence, only with armies and churches.

4

What I have shown here is that, in the first place, communities based on emotional bonds have been essential to human life; then, that these emotional bonds were to be found in those who were approaching death in full awareness of the fact, and who were thus shaping the common attitudes to our common fate. In this way I have introduced, in connection with the ancient reality of sacrifice, a representation of joy in the face of death through which the intimate agreement between life and its violent destruction is asserted. But it is not only the formation of emotional bonds that demands an answer to the fundamental question of death, nor is it important alone that this answer does not avoid the problem: it appears that the very fact of coming into contact with the destruction of life involves a community of the heart which unites those spirits that are also situated "at the pinnacle of death". I shall now return to my initial argument and show that joy in the face of death would be an imposture if it was not also tied in with the turmoil of that union. The one who looks upon death and rejoices is already no longer the individual whose future is given over only to the rotting of the flesh, since the simple action of involving himself with death had already projected him outside of himself, right into the glorious community that laughs at all the misery of his fellow men, with each moment chasing and annihilating the one that went before, so that the triumph of time seems connected with the progression of his own conquests. Not that he thinks as a result that he can escape his fate by substituting a more stable community for his own person. On the contrary, the community is necessary for him to feel a proper awareness of the glory inherent in the moment when he sees himself torn from his own being. The sense of cohesion he feels with regard to those who have chosen to share their great intoxication is, at most, only a means of perceiving everything that loss signifies in terms of splendour and conquest, everything the dead person's fall means in terms of renewed life, springing back and "alleluia". There is a connection here that is not easily reduced to analytic formulas. This excess of joy must be experienced at least once in order to know how much the rich prodigality of sacrifice is expressed in it, and how much it can only be a progressive conquest, an overwhelming need to subject man to those [...]

GEORGES BATAILLE

# 96 *The College of Sociology*

The subject of this meeting was to have been the College of Sociology itself. Since the College of Sociology is to some extent a unique undertaking, and one that is difficult to classify according to usual forms of activity, there appeared good reason to clarify its meaning and intentions, and all the more so as its unconventional nature may perhaps have given rise to misunderstandings and confusion in the minds of those who watched us in our work. To tell the truth, circumstances are such that relations have become so strained between those of us who have striven this far to carry things to a successful conclusion that I have grounds more for speaking of a crisis than the general development of an organisation. The talk I am now embarking on will, therefore, only give expression to the profound disagreement which has already opened up a crack in our structure. It was understood that three of us would be speaking this evening, Caillois, Leiris and I; but I am here on my own. It is not without sadness that I acknowledge this. Caillois left for Argentina a few days ago; his absence is obviously unavoidable, but that does not make it any less relevant. The few notes I have received from him since he left are, in any case, of a sort that would bring an end to the fellow feeling that existed between us. I shall not discuss them today because it seems not impossible that a verbal explanation — Caillois is to return in September — would resolve the difference of opinion they have created between us. I prefer, for the moment, to talk on the basis of a disagreement, rather than on terms that accuse him, and possibly through misunderstanding. Now, by elevating the debate, and moving it on to a point where love and death alone are at stake, it may be that I am doing nothing more than ruling out the possibility of a reconciliation at a later date. Though this may seem to be the case, I remain convinced that at this moment I am acting in the opposite manner, but even were I aware that in doing so I was destroying what possibilities there are left, I would do no differently because there are other things more important than a College of Sociology. If I have come here this evening, if I have been coming here for the past two years, it is, in fact, less with the intention of establishing an influential organisation, than with the will to create a force out of an awareness of the misery and greatness of this perishable existence that is our lot. CONFRONTING DESTINY remains, in my view, the very essence of knowledge. Having realised that the results put forward by science with regard to the sacred were taking away from man the means he possesses to escape from what he is, I felt it was the right time to found an association which would examine this science in particular. No one is more eager than I am to discover the virtues this association may have, none more fearful than I of the imposture which is the basis of individual isolation; however, the *love of human destiny* is strong enough in me to allow me to give only secondary importance to the forms through which it may come forward.

It seems to me that the interest aroused by the College of Sociology, both inside and outside, resulted from the vehemence with which it called everything into question. The intentions of its various members perhaps differed, but I did not mean to imply, in speaking of my own reasons, that they were not specifically my own. Nevertheless, it goes without saying that it is only our long-term intentions and our ability to redefine crucial problems that have justified our existence. To the extent that the College of Sociology is not a door opening on to that chaos in which each life-form makes its first stirrings, grows up and dies, and on to the upheavals of festivals, of power and the deaths of human beings — it offers only emptiness to truth. That is why it hurts me to see Leiris, who has declined to speak here today because of his doubts regarding the soundness of our activities, it hurts me to see Leiris reproaching us for not modelling ourselves more on those scholars and teachers we claim as our inspiration. Leiris thinks we are not abiding by the rules of Durkheim's sociological method and that the role we have assigned to the sacred does not conform to Mauss's doctrine of the total fact. To these reasons he adds his fear of seeing our efforts only end up creating the worst sort of literary clique. I said before that I would elevate this debate which has arisen because of the crisis already mentioned. And I shall elevate it as high as I can. I believe that works by Caillois, or my own, when they are published, will attract criticism but also command respect. But that is not at all the issue. The real point here is, above all, to discover whether it is still possible to ask fundamental questions, whether we can agree to continue as far as is possible with our arguments on the subject of life, in order to demand of ourselves *everything* of which our remaining virtue is still capable. Specific points of method and doctrine, the inevitable obstacles and inevitable risk of failure, all of that is certainly important, but it is also possible to fix our gaze beyond such unavoidable difficulties.

That there is something beyond, I mean a terrestrial beyond that belongs to the man of today, is a truth it is difficult to dispute. It is no less disputable that access to this beyond must present itself initially in the form of combat and danger. And no one doubts that the *inner* dangers, the dangers within every impulse, are formidable, and even more than that, demoralising.

The disagreement referred to by Leiris, it should be added, does not at all exclude the possibility of collaboration later on, once the various aims and limits have been well defined, and especially once it has been possible to make clear the modes of freedom necessary for the development of a venture that is still unsure of itself. The questions posed by the differences that have arisen between Caillois and me are doubtless more serious, at least in the sense that they have to do more with the foundations than the methods of our activities. But since, as I say, they touch upon its actual foundations, you will allow me to speak about them in a round-about way, and by avoiding discussing any specifics I shall limit myself to speaking about the profound reality this dispute calls into question. The fact that Caillois is not here, moreover, seems to make any other way of proceeding impossible. It is enough for me to point out, by way of beginning, that the roles I allocate to mysticism, drama, madness and death seem to Caillois to be difficult to reconcile with our original principles. I will add that Caillois is not the only one to be troubled by this sense of incompatibility. Paulhan and Wahl have also expressed similar feelings to me.[1] So, I have every reason to present today an attempt at clarification, as one of the consequences of this state of crisis. I shall therefore try to show how the development of the College of Sociology contained within itself the necessity of the present crisis. I am also more than happy to have had this opportunity to go right down into the foundations of my own thinking, and not in the calm of solitary reflection, but in the disorder of contention.

As such I have been led to develop a general representation of things that should be classed in the category of philosophical representations. And only when I have laid this out will it be possible for me to show how the communional unity, that is to say power itself, is formed, along with this sort of mental disturbance that operates somewhere between mysticism and madness. I would not, however, want you to become concerned at seeing me step into the dreary undergrowth of philosophical reflection. While I must take on the central problem of metaphysics, I think I can still be clear: in any case, I am sure that I shall be speaking of matters that directly concern every human being, or at least those who are averse to torpor.

One of the best-established results of man's efforts to discover what he really is would doubtless be his lack of unity as an individual. In olden times men saw themselves as one indivisible reality. There are certain animals that can be cut into two pieces, and then, after some time has passed, these pieces become complete animals that are quite distinct from each other. Yet nothing could be more shocking than if such a thing happened to a man, from the point of view of those who hold with the classical image of the human soul. Habits of thought are so well established that it is difficult for any of us to picture ourselves divided into two, with one half seeing the other, loving the other, or fleeing from it. In truth, the surgery performed on human beings or the higher animals is still far from such brutal possibilities. Indeed, it has only reached the stage of producing cross-breeds which leave the essence of the resulting creature intact. At the most we may glimpse some distant future in which certain truly disturbing possibilities could occur, such as switching over the cerebral hemispheres of two great apes... I mention this not out of any interest that such an experiment could take place but so as to introduce a maximum of disorder into our usual viewpoints. I suspect that the idea of a composite being, as the result of linking together the brains of any two of us, is likely to make people feel very uneasy and light-headed. However, this might also be an idea we could become used to. It is no more than a banal suggestion nowadays to imagine a human being as an ill-assembled collection of parts, some of which are distant from the body, poorly attached or even ignored. It is generally acknowledged that an individual is no more than incomplete assemblage: an animal, or a human being, is simply seen as a well-defined and stable compound, whereas a society is united only by bonds that are very loose and easily broken. At the same time it is understood that neither the individual nor the society is an exception, and that every element in nature is a combination of parts, at least until we get down to the simplest level, with the electron. Science categorises atoms, in spite of their name,[2] as collections of elementary particles, molecules as collections of atoms, and continues step by step until it arrives at the individual as a collection of cells and then finally society (which, in fact, it holds back from recognising — though it is hard to see why — as a simple case of a unified compound composed of multiple elements).

I don't wish to dwell on any of this, which is merely a scientific introduction to the essence of what I would like to put to you today. I am in haste to press on, and my haste is perhaps understandable because of the need to find descriptions that are less external with regard to the reality of what we are. I can only speak directly about something each of us may experience, and shall first of all discuss an aspect of our lives that would appear to be as remote as possible from our union with the social group, namely the erotic behaviour that most of us indulge in with one or, successively, with several of our fellow beings. This digression has the advantage of bringing us face to face with realities that are not only the most unclear but also the most familiar. Indeed, no image can be more vivid in our minds than that of the union between two individuals of opposite sex. Yet as commonplace and vivid as it is, its meaning none the less remains concealed: all that can be said is that each of these beings is blindly obeying its instincts. This is not so much a means of avoiding the difficulty but more a way of giving a name to this instinct, making it the expression of a will to reproduce that is entirely down to nature. For in fact, other needs besides that of procreation are satisfied in the course of copulation.

The introduction of a sociological point of view casts an unexpected light on this natural obscurity.

If I consider the reproduction of a simple asexual cell, the birth of a new cell seems to result from an inability on the part of the whole to maintain its integrity: a split, a wound is produced. The growth of this tiny entity creates an overflow, together with a laceration and a loss of substance. Sexual reproduction amongst animals and amongst human beings is divided into two phases, each of which presents the same characteristic overflow, laceration and loss of substance. In the first phase, two individuals communicate with each other by way of their concealed lacerations. No communication is more profound, and the two individuals are lost in a convulsion that ties them together. But they can only communicate by losing a part of themselves. Communication binds them together through their wounds or their unity, while their integrity dissipates in their fervour.

Two beings of opposite sex lose themselves in one another, and together form a new being that is different from both of them. The precarious state of this new being is obvious: it is never such that its parts can be distinctly its own; and in its brief moments of darkness there is nothing more than a tendency to lose consciousness. Yet if it is true that the unity of the individual stands out far more obviously, it is also just as precarious. Without a doubt, there is only a difference of degree between the two cases.

Love expresses a need for sacrifice: every unity must lose itself in some other unity which exceeds it. Yet these joyous movements of the flesh work in two directions. Just because passing through the flesh — passing to the point at which the unity of the person is torn apart in it — is necessary if we wish in losing ourselves to find ourselves again in the unity of love, it does not follow that the moment when that tearing apart occurs is itself meaningless in terms of the existence that is torn apart. It is difficult to know what part is played during copulation by the feeling of passion for another being, the part played by erotic frenzy; so too the extent to which this individual is seeking life and power, the extent to which he is led to tear himself apart, to lose himself, at the same time as tearing apart and losing the other person (and of course, the more beautiful the woman and the more she has been torn apart, the more desirable is her loss or simply her being stripped bare). Beyond the will to leave our narrow being for one that is vaster, and very often mixed in with this first will to loss, there is a will to loss that reaches a limit for its enormous urges only in fear, and furthermore, that can use this fear it has generated to make itself still more ablaze and delirious.

To this picture of the first forms of being revealed by love there must be added the union that results from marriage. There are many possible stages between the basic passionate urge and that sort of oppressive conjugal life in which the heart is not involved. At the extreme limit, self-interest and the law establish a joyless union between individuals for whom physical love is nothing but a concession to nature. If we now turn to the various social groupings that correspond to the different and contrasting forms of sexual union, we can see that a judicial and administrative society bears a close resemblance to the conjugal union based on self-interest, whereas communities formed by emotional bonds call to mind the passionate union of lovers; other forms are not lacking which show — in common with erotic perversions — that the loss of self within a vaster being results in a loss of self in a formless universe and in death.

I realise there is an element of paradox here, since these comparisons will inevitably seem very arbitrary. However, I am only suggesting them because I intend to explain their meaning more precisely. I propose that we accept as an unstated law that human beings are only ever united with one another by means of these tearings or wounds; there is a certain logical force to this idea. If elements are arranged to create a whole, this may occur easily when each one loses a part of its own being through a tear in its integrity for the benefit of the collective being. Initiations, sacrifices and festivals are examples of just such moments of loss and communication between individuals. Circumcision and orgies are sufficient examples to show that there is more than one connection between sexual and ritual tearing; we can add to this that the realm of erotic activity itself specifically refers to the act in which it reaches its fulfilment as a sacrifice, and likewise refers to the conclusion of this act as a "little death". However, one of these two areas spills over into the other: the social tears that coincide with sexual ones acquire a different, richer meaning, and the multiplicity of forms involved stretches from war to the bloody cross of Christ; putting a king to death and the sexual act have nothing more in common than that they unite through a loss of substance. And where they resemble each other is in the creation or maintenance of a new unity of being: it would be a waste of time to try and claim that the one just like the other was simply the effect of some obscure biological instinct, which accounts through its actions for all human forms of being.

I am therefore given to say of the 'sacred' that it is communication between beings and in consequence of that, the formation of new beings. The idea developed by sociologists, according to which it is possible to describe how the sacred works by comparing it to electrical currents and charges, at least allows me to introduce an image to explain my proposition. The wounds or tears I have been speaking of would intervene to open up so many eruptions of accumulated force; but this eruption of force out of oneself, which is produced for the benefit of social power, whether in religious sacrifice or in war, is not at all produced in the same way as the well-understood expenditures of money that must be made to obtain some desirable or necessary object. While sacrifices and festivals are generally useful, they have an intrinsically attractive quality independent of the conscious or unconscious results they give rise to. People gathered together for a sacrifice or festival are satisfying the need they have to expend a vital superfluity. The sacrificial laceration that opens the festival is also a liberating one. The individual who takes part in the loss has a vague awareness that it is this loss which engenders the community that sustains him. But for the man who is making love a desirable woman is necessary, although it is not always easy to know whether he is making love because he is attracted to this woman or if he is using the woman because of a need to make love. In the same way, it is difficult to know to what extent the community is only the propitious occasion for the festival and sacrifice, or if the festival and sacrifice is the measure of the love offered to the community.[3]

In fact it appears that this question, which might be thought a little quaint, represents the ultimate question for man, even more so, the ultimate question of being. For indeed, being is constantly drawn in two directions, one of which leads to the creation of lasting regulations and conquering armies, while the other leads by means of expenditures of force and increasing excess to destruction and death. We encounter these inducements even in the most trivial circumstances of our lives; any discussion about how advisable a useful or tempting expenditure may be is played out against the balance between the principles of acquisition and loss. But in everyday situations these extremes have disappeared so far as to become almost unrecognisable. The meaning of this interplay reappears when we consider sexual commerce. The union between lovers is confronted with this open-ended question: suppose the unified being they form together counts more for them than love, and they are then condemned to the slow stagnation of their relations. The empty horror of regular conjugal intercourse already closes about them. But if the need to love and to lose themselves is stronger in them than the wish to find themselves, then the only possible outcome is for them to be torn apart, with all the perversities of a tumultuous passion, drama, and if it be all-consuming — death. I would add that eroticism constitutes a sort of flight from the harshness of this dilemma. But I only mention that now so as to pass on to a more general consideration.

When a man and a woman are united by love, together they form an association, a being that is completely closed in on itself, but when the initial equilibrium is compromised a strictly erotic search may be added to or substituted for the lovers' search — which had no other object from the start but the two of them. The need to lose themselves exceeds their need to find themselves. At this point the presence of a third person is not necessarily the worst obstacle, as it would have been at the beginning of their love. More than the common being they encounter in their embrace, they seek an immeasurable annihilation in a violent expenditure in which the possession of a new object, a new woman or new man, is simply the pretext for an even more annihilating expenditure. In the same way, those who are more religious than others stop feeling so closely concerned about the community for which sacrifices are performed. They no longer live for the community, they live only for the sacrifice. So it is that gradually they become possessed by the desire to spread their sacrificial frenzy through contagion. Just as eroticism slips easily into orgy, the sacrifice that becomes an end in itself lays claim beyond the narrow needs of the community to a universal value.

In the case of social life, however, the first movements can only expand as far as the aspiration for sacrifice is able to find a suitable god. Just as in its enclosed forms, in other words in its simplest forms, the community was for some an occasion for sacrifice, it was necessary to find the equivalent of the community in the form of a universal god, so as to extend the sacrificial orgy indefinitely. Dionysus and the Crucified Christ thus launched a whole tragic procession of Bacchants and martyrs. But it turns out that the tear that was opened up when the universal god burst forth from the old local community will close over in the long run. The god of the

Christians is in turn reduced to the status of a guarantor of social order. But he also becomes the wall against which love's rage for love is smashed. And it is doubtless at this point that the ultimate question of being takes shape. The eternal reach of God serves in the beginning as the object of loss for each being who in losing himself then finds himself again in God. But what is missing there is the satisfaction for those who only aspire to lose themselves without any wish to find themselves again. When Teresa of Ávila cried out "I die because I do not die",[4] her passion opened a breach beyond any possible closing into a universe in which, perhaps, structure, form and being no longer exist, and in which death seems to roam from world to world. For the organised structure of different beings is apparently emptied of all meaning when it comes to the totality of things: totality cannot be the counterpart of composite beings who are driven by one single impulse that we know.

I suppose at this point my purpose will seem puzzling. However, I only wished to outline the full extent of the problem whose dangers are thrust upon us from the moment man agrees to answer the questions set by the sphinx of sociology. It seems to me that the encounter with this sphinx has increased the thoroughness and the bluntness of metaphysical enquiry to a remarkable degree. Essentially, what I wanted to say is that a College of Sociology, in the form in which we conceived it, was inevitably going to open up this endless enquiry. It may be that I sometimes give the impression of having a somewhat sullen predilection for considering the impossible. I could answer that with a single sentence. But I shall not do so today. Today I will be content with introducing a few practical proposals in line with the means available to the College of Sociology.

[Text of Caillois's letter][5]

GEORGES BATAILLE *The Star Alcohol* 97

(To Isabelle Farner)

*This is a meditation text. You must shut yourself away somewhere as quiet as possible, empty yourself of everything and completely let go; remain seated but do not let your body slouch, empty your mind and to begin with breathe deeply whilst attempting to let yourself fall under the spell of silence. You may fall into an actual stupor. You must not read the text but slowly recall it from memory.*

*There should be a long period of time between the first three sentences and the rest. And also a little time between each sentence in the second part.*

*THE STAR ALCOHOL*

*I take Acéphale for violence.*
*I take its sulphur fire for violence.*
*I take the tree and the wind of death for violence.*

*I AM JOY IN THE FACE OF DEATH*

*The depths of space are joy in the face of death.*
*I imagine — until it nauseates me — that the Earth is spinning in the heavens at a dizzying rate.*
*I imagine the sky itself turning and exploding.*
*Sun, flame, alcohol, blinding light all turning eyes closed and so dazzling that you lose your breath.*
*The whole depth of the sky like an orgy of frozen light, fading, fleeing.*
*Everything that is real destroying itself, consuming itself and dying like a*

COLLÈGE DE SOCIOLOGIE

15, RUE GAY-LUSSAC, 5e

Voici un texte de méditation. Il faudrait s'enfermer aussi tranquillement que possible, faire le vide en soi, s'abandonner complètement, en demeurant assis mais le corps non affaissé, s'abstenir et tout d'abord respirer profondément en tâchant de se laisser emporter par le silence. Cela peut devenir une vraie torpeur. Il ne faudrait pas lire le texte mais se le remémorer lentement.

Il devrait y avoir beaucoup de temps entre les trois premières phrases et les autres. Et aussi un peu de temps entre chaque phrase de la seconde partie.

L'ETOILE ALCOOL

Je prends l'acéphale pour violence
Je prends son feu de soufre pour violence
Je prends l'arbre et le vent de la mort pour violence

JE SUIS LA JOIE DEVANT LA MORT
La profondeur de l'espace est joie devant la mort
Je me représente ~~enfoncé~~ – projeté à la nausée – que la terre tourne vertigineusement dans le ciel
Je me représente le ciel lui-même tournant et explosant, étant ivre
Je le soleil, brasier, alcool, lumière aveuglante tournant les yeux clos et éclatant à perdre la respiration
Toute la profondeur du ciel comme une orgie de lumière glacée, se perdant, fuyant
Tout ce qui est réel se détruisant, se consumant et mourant comme de feu incandescent
Moi-même me détruisant, me consumant et m'égorgeant ~~moi~~ de ma propre avidité comme du feu
Riant et mourant comme tout ce qui tourne, vacille, brûle et éclate
Je me représente l'instant glacial de ma propre mort dans un ciel glacé et parfaitement brillant ~~sous~~ la lueur de l'étoile Alcool / se révélant ~~comme~~ aussi subite qu'un trait de foudre et aiguisant jusqu'aux dents.

97. Georges Bataille, *The Star Alcohol.*

*glowing fire.*
*I am destroying myself, consuming myself and cutting my throat with my own hunger like the fire.*
*Laughing and dying like everything that turns, wavers, burns and flashes.*
*I imagine the ice-cold moment of my death in an icy and perfectly bright sky, in the glow of the star Alcohol revealing itself as suddenly as a flash of lightning and hugely intoxicating.*

[1939]

## GEORGES BATAILLE *Joy in the Face of Death* (Meditation Text) 98

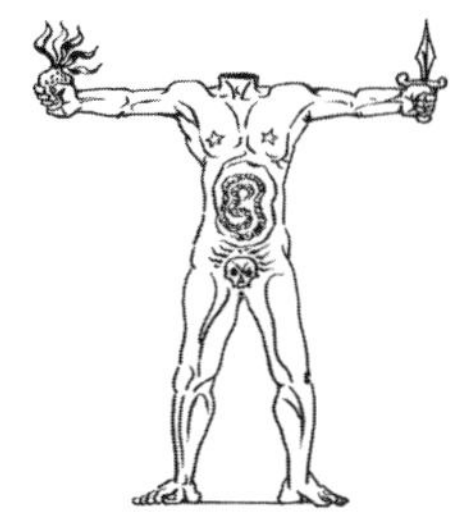

*Text on joy in the face of death,*
*offered for a renewed and searching reflection*

*I take Acéphale for violence.*
*I take its sulphur fire for violence.*
*I take the tree and the wind of death for violence.*

*I AM JOY IN THE FACE OF DEATH*

*The depths of the galaxy are joy in the face of death.*
*I imagine myself carried away in the giddily spinning explosion.*
*My head bursts into pieces. My body is standing upright in a world of violent acts.*
*My laughter echoes back from the depths of the galaxy in festival.*
*I imagine the silence of my death in the wasted silence of the galaxy.*

*The violence of Acéphale transports my death to the unimaginable festival of the galaxy.*

[1939?]

99 GEORGES BATAILLE *Heraclitean Meditation*

*I AM THE WAR*
*I AM JOY IN THE FACE OF DEATH*

*I imagine the inexorable movement and the intense excitement — the possibilities for which are limitless — which only quieten down in war.*

*I imagine some female divinity dancing in the night, with a muffled violence, greedy for blood, mutilated bodies and death.*

*I imagine the gift of an infinite suffering, of blood and bodies opened up to the image of an almost painful sexual ejaculation.*

*I imagine this gift as a burning catastrophe demanded by a limitless hunger like that of the fire which only devours in order to consume itself and to give of itself without measure, just as the dazzling sun or the most distant stars give of themselves without measure by radiating their unimaginable heat and light.*

*I imagine the Earth launched into space, like a woman shrieking in horror, with her hair in flames.*

*I hate the need for sustained foolishness that sets itself against the freedom of this great cry — but not the need for the gift of the lost self that results in this cry.*

*Taken to the extreme of the principle that governs it, relieved of the unbearable mask of stupidity (whether ideological or with some other meaning) of military exercises — the inexorable hunger demanding this cry becomes ME, and merges with the flame of life that consumes me right up until my death.*

*With all my strength, and going beyond the nausea I feel, I take on all that I can of the woeful hunger for being and enduring that makes the free gift of self an impossibility and delivers every existence to anguish.*

*With all my strength, I consume my own hunger to endure, and the hunger to endure of my fellow men, in my joy in the face of death, and, being thus consumed, I burn with mirth, following the example of the sun.*

*In this world of summer and winter, which constitutes the dying flame of everything that lives, in this universe that is spinning and fading away with stars which only consume themselves with a fury, I recognise a cruel hunger that makes violent demands for my death: it demands it for the sake of its boundless appetite, and for its dazzling joy at existing; everywhere it demands that everything that has been should be annihilated incessantly.*

*The only image of the reality within which man moves that is not entirely illusory is that of a cannibal deity who would split himself right in two and eat himself, showing no less glee or enthusiasm for dying and feeding upon himself than for simple killing and eating.*

*Through these representations, somewhat breathless or too human, I already hear a muted dance exploding and already begin to glimpse through my laughter what will blind these eyes that still wanted things to look at that would not lacerate them.*

[1939?]

## GEORGES BATAILLE *To Saint-Paul* 100

1 October 1939

*Originally, joy in the face of death was a formula for mystical meditation. It relates to a joy felt when facing the certainty of death and to the foundation of a religious existence that is quite distinct from Christianity. A man can apprehend the representation of his own death (and not the representation of God) as an object of meditation and ecstasy.*

*The desired outcome of such a practice can only be a death submitted to with joy as the fulfilment of a life, but not a searching for death since that would be a condemnation of life. There is nothing in death that makes it a sovereign virtue. Life is what can be loved, but life is what is used up in death and it is this possibility of being used up that can be loved to the point of ecstasy.*

*However, if it is pointless or even despicable to seek out death intentionally, it goes without saying that any costly or painful action by which the risk of death may be avoided renders the mystical attitude I have just described a laughable pretension. What emerges from these principles is a straightforward, virile attitude, which cannot be avoided but which does not look for opportunities. No virtue is more commonplace than military courage and that is not what this is about: what would make more sense would be for no question to be asked on this subject.*

*From the moment the battle waged by an army is seen as being favourable to interests that are deemed to be essential, it is inevitable that those who are part of that army accept its discipline.*

*As for those who are outside it, it would have been better, had it been possible, instead of leaving matters to personal decisions to judge them according to principles that have been clearly agreed upon, in a cold and rational manner, without glorifying them, and offering no opportunity for internal laceration neither in the one direction nor the other.*

## 101 PATRICK WALDBERG *Extract from Acéphalogram (2)*

*After war had broken out Acéphale faltered, undermined by internal strife and dissension, perhaps demoralised by the awareness of its incongruous position in the midst of global disaster. There were just four of us at the last encounter in the forest, when Bataille solemnly asked the other three if they would kindly put him to death, so that this sacrifice, which would establish the myth, would ensure the survival of the community. This request was declined. A few months later the real war began, sweeping away any last remnants of hope.*

*All of what had happened earlier, as I set it down here in writing, seems to me like relating a dream, or the kind of fiction a writer such as Villiers de l'Isle-Adam might have imagined. Never before, perhaps, had such an utter seriousness been combined with such immense puerility, with the purpose of raising life to a certain degree of incandescence and experiencing the kind of 'privileged moments' we have yearned for since childhood. Those who laughed had it easy — and will carry on doing so — and failure was inevitable. However, for some of us, including me, the expression "life-changing" was not at all just an empty catchphrase.*

## 102 GEORGES BATAILLE *To Patrick Waldberg*

20-X-[19]39

*My dear Patrick,*

*I no doubt used an excess of language but it is too late to regret that. At least things are clear now and you can breathe again. You will realise, I suppose, that it had all become impossible. Now it seems to me that nothing remains unclear. I ask only for a retraction of the last thing I said to you.*[1]

*Included with this letter is a text addressed to you, as well as to Isabelle, Ambrosino, Andler, Chavy and Chenon. I would be most grateful if you could forward it to each of them.*

*Regards,*

*Georges Bataille*

*I am sending this to you via pneumatic post;*[2] *I will be going to the Ruc tomorrow, Saturday, as usual (I will also be there on Wednesday); but in the event you are planning to go tomorrow, I am anxious that you should already have received this letter.*

### GEORGES BATAILLE *To the Members of Acéphale* 103

20-X-[19]39

*I ask you to consider yourselves freed of all ties with me. I will remain alone: I am convinced this position is preferable to taking sides. It must be rare to encounter such a solid consensus within a particular group against he who was its foundation. Finding myself in this situation, I shall not sin by indulgence — no more against others than against myself. But I would not wish to dwell at length on anything. I would simply like to add that I am not equivocating, that I feel neither weariness nor bitterness: if any of you still expect anything of me (you would not be wrong because* I am not abandoning anything*), you will see that I am not dead and nor do I bear a grudge.*

*I have arrived at the consecration of this state of affairs: I do not think much has changed in the little life that still remains between us. Perhaps you will argue that it is unlikely you will ever agree with me? But what is the use of arguing? There would be so much to argue about, on every side. Silence is preferable.*

*Georges Bataille*

*To Ambrosino, Andler, Chavy, Chenon, Isabelle Farner and Waldberg*

### GEORGES BATAILLE *To the Members of Acéphale* 104

20-X-[19]39

*There will be no discussion or general conversation with me. I will explain myself as briefly as I can. I waited but certainty did not come to me. Now I am aware that a gulf has opened up. Who has given any thought to helping me sustain even an appearance of cohesion? Waldberg had nothing to say to me when I presented him with a fact: that some of you had* abandoned *me. What hurt me about this abandonment was the way it was so abrupt and hushed up. I am not sorry about the abandonment itself. It is true, I must admit, that I am now very distant from you: none of you has followed me to the point where I am now; it wasn't even possible for me to speak. It is also true that present events are of interest to me in terms of their possible consequences and not so much in their moral implications; I differ from you on this point in the sense that I am living in another world. I would add that I have maintained an unshaken, even an increased confidence in the movement to which I have devoted my efforts: to my surprise, some of you seem to have ended up with a very different conviction.*

*I do not think that in bringing a certain class of things to a close it would be impossible for us to keep on good terms at a distance. On an external level, a prospective collaboration should be possible to achieve one day or another. I feel that the ties that continue to bind you all should not be broken; this should have a lot of meaning, if you do not succumb to presumption and shadowy isolation.*

*I will not enter into conversation about what I am trying to bring to a conclusion today because it would be a pity to aggravate what is already painful; it will be easier, in the first instance, to write, and then, whenever it is useful, to resolve specific questions without digressions.*

*Georges Bataille*

*To Ambrosino, Andler, Chavy, Chenon, Isabelle Farner and Waldberg*

The path from the ruins of Montjoie to the Étoile Mourante .>

## NOTES

By the respective editors unless stated otherwise.

***Preface* (pages 15-17)**

1. Bataille OC7, p.461.
2. See Galletti (e).
3. Respectively in *Le Collège de Sociologie*, Gallimard, 1979 and 1995, and *L'Apprenti Sorcier*, La Différence, 1999.

***The Secret Society of Acéphale: "A Community of the Heart"* (pp.19-49)**

1. Blanchot, p.27.
2. Camus, p.I.
3. Caillois (g), p.93.
4. MG, conversation with Fardoulis-Lagrange, Paris, 1987.
5. MG, conversation with Leiris in 1976; see also Leiris (b) pp.173-187.
6. Masson (b), p.29.
7. Bataille's *Œuvres complètes* includes only a brief section entitled "En marge d'Acéphale" (vol. 2), containing three texts, and in the notes to volume 11, a transcription of a manuscript (pp. 559-563) which is presumed to relate to Acéphale and the College:"What we undertook a few months ago..." (○29).
8. OC7, p.461.
9. OC7, p.462.
10. OC6, p.369.
11. MG, conversation in the company of Fardoulis-Lagrange shortly before her death in April 1990. See also [Waldberg, Isabelle], p.10.
12. Cf. Galletti (b).
13. Hollier (a), p.76 and Hollier (b), p.XXI.
14. Cf. Dumézil (c); and on Bataille's Middle Ages, Galletti (f).
15. OC11, pp.502-518.
16. Cohen, p.145.
17. OC6, p.369.
18. On Bataille and Surrealism, see Galletti (n), especially pp.30-31, 33.
19. Nadeau, p.369.
20. Monnerot (b), pp.72-73.
21. Bataille (e), pp.546-550.
22. Cf. Jean-Luc Nancy (b), pp.86, 101.
23. Camus, p.II.
24. Cf. Tourrès.
25. *Europe* 859-860, Nov-Dec 2000, Caillois issue.
26. *Revue des deux mondes*, May 2012, Georges Bataille issue.
27. This date must be incorrect, however, since Waldberg himself was only inducted into the Society in September 1938.
28. Waldberg (c), p.112; see also the statement by "X", in Frank (a), p.280.
29. MG, conversation with Koch, Paris, 19 February 1995. He was no doubt agreeing to become a "participant", before becoming an actual member of the Society.
30. Caillois (g), p.59.
31. Cf. Galletti (d), p.125.
32. Leiris (c), pp.26-27.
33. Détienne, pp.198, 203.
34. Jeanmaire, pp.124-125; cf. also Leiris (f), p.924, note 4.
35. Armel, p.220.
36. See Charbonnier, p.36.
37. Bataille (j), p.232.
38. OC8, p.640.
39. Cf. Galletti (h).
40. OC1, pp.220-226.
41. OC2, p.25.
42. Artaud, p.61.
43. Will-Levaillant, p.62; see also Masson (b), p.24.
44. AS, p.303; OC2, p.407.
45. OC1, p.92.
46. Clébert (b), p.37.
47. Clébert (a), p.67.
48. OC1, p.94.
49. Dussat (a).
50. MG, conversation with Barell, 1994.
51. Klossowski (e), p.188.
52. A letter from Claudine Frank. Cf. also Frank (b), "Introduction" and "Appendices" 3, 9 and *passim*.
53. OC7, p.484.
54. Mauss, p.151.
55. OC1, p.309.
56. Mauss, p.148.
57. OC1, pp.318-319.
58. OC1, p.305.
59. OC1, p.306.
60. Unpublished letter from Dussat to Chavy of 13 June 1936. (Claudine Frank archives)
61. Bataille (d), p.52.
62. The expression is from Henri Hubert, one of Durkheim's pupils, cited in Caillois (d), p.18.
63. CdeS3, p.827.
64. AS, p.313.

65. Caillois (b), pp.11-12, 13.
66. Béhar, p.14.
67. Bataille (d), p.55.
68. Dated the same day as the cancelled dinner at the Place du Tertre, a subject to which Ambrosino returns by proposing another "banquet". From the Andler archive and Claudine Frank in Caillois (j), p.69.
69. MG, conversation with Dubief, Cachan, October 1994, and Galletti (c).
70. OC7, p.462.
71. Waldberg (e), pp.157-158.
72. Waldberg (c), pp.102, 108.
73. Caillois (g), p.94.
74. Masson (c), p.331; Masson (a), p.290.
75. See pp.51-61.
76. Frank (a), p.279.
77. Simmel, p.85.
78. CdeS3, p.232.
79. CdeS3, p.185.
80. Dumézil (b), p.42.
81. CdeS3, p.183
82. CdeS3, p.192.
83. [Waldberg, Isabelle], p.10; MG, conversation with Koch, spring 1995.
84. CdeS3, pp.234, 235.
85. Waldberg (c), pp.110-111.
86. *Acéphale* 3/4, p.8.
87. OC1, p.488.
88. Monnerot (a), p.14, the phrase is from Nietzsche, *Twilight of the Gods*, VII, 45. Catiline was a senator who twice tried to seize power in Rome by means of a coup.
89. Klossowski (a), pp.27, 29.
90. *Acéphale* 3/4, p.6.
91. OC1, p.436.
92. OC1, p.435.
93. OC1, pp.435, 439.
94. OC1, p.441; on Bataille and laughter, cf. Galletti (i).
95. Hollier (a), p.129.
96. Simmel, p.96.
97. Hollier in CdeS3, p.26.
98. See p.479 for details of the Atlas Press edition.
99. MG, conversation with Koch.
100. OC1, p.356.
101. Klossowski (b), p.168.
102. CdeS3, pp.158-159; see Galletti (d) on the importance of the idea of the secret society to Leiris.
103. Cf. CdeS3, pp.833-39; Bataille (a); and Galletti (l) and (a).
104. OC11, respectively pp.63, 59, 61, 63.
105. CdeS3, pp.27, 17, 27.
106. Klossowski (c).
107. Eliade, pp.163-164.
108. Cf. Galletti (g).
109. CdeS3, pp.237, 240, 241.
110. CdeS3, pp.235-236, 849.
111. Cf. Dumézil (a), especially "Les Lupercalia et le pouvoir", pp.219-222.
112. Leiris (a), p.12 and IX.
113. Cf. in CdeS3, Hans Mayer's lecture, "Rites of Political Associations in Germany during the Romantic Period"; also Mayer.
114. Hollier in CdeS3, p.219.
115. CdeS3, pp.229, 238.
116. This would usually be translated as "the masses", but the French does not have the class meaning that it has in English. In French it is more expansive, meaning something more like "the general population". [Trans.]
117. Hollier in CdeS3, p.329.
118. Simmel, p.97.
119. Hollier in CdeS3, p.200.
120. Nietzsche, from "Immaculate perception", in *Thus Spake Zarathustra*.
121. Boissonnas, pp.114, 112; cf. also Hollier in CdeS3, pp.535-542.
122. OC2, p.395.
123. OC2, p.391.
124. OC2, pp.393, 395.
125. OC2, p.397.
126. OC2, pp.398-399.
127. Bataille (d), p.100.
128. OC2, p.388.
129. Cf. CdeS3, pp.737-738.
130. CdeS3, p.740.
131. Bataille (d), p 107.
132. Dussat (b).
133. Unpublished letter to Chavy. (Claudine Frank archives)
134. OC5, p.80.
135. Waldberg (d), p.85.
136. Bruno (b), p.710.
137. *Ibid*.
138. *Ibid*.
139. Bataille (d), p.108.
140. OC7, p.462.
141. According to Andler, but see Panné, p.43.

142. OC7, p.462.
143. Bruno (b), p.720.
144. See the Atlas Press edition of this collaborative work in *Encyclopædia Acephalica*, 1995.
145. According to Andler.
146. "Ambrosino insisted on his rejection of Bataille," said Esther Ambrosino in an interview in 1997, during which her sister Olga Tabakman remarked: "Ambrosino could not accept that Acéphale was not dead." Among those who took part in the "Saturdays" were the philosophers Allan Bloom and Eugene Fleischmann; Joseph Frank, the specialist in Dostoevsky; the ethnologist Eric de Dampierre; Pierre Hassner, the political theorist; and philosopher and composer Betsy Jolas (MG, interviews with: Catherine Roux Lanier, autumn 2014, who gave two presentations on Spinoza; and with Esther Ambrosino, Pauline Roux and Michel Waldberg). See also Frank (b), "Introduction".
147. Andler recalled his own expulsion, and Esther Ambrosino those of Louis Dumont and Charles Duits.

***Marly, Montjoie and the Oak Tree Struck by Lightning* (pp.51-61)**

1. The earliest map in the BN to name the *étoiles* is from 1726: Alexandre le Moine, *Plan des jardins et forest de Marly*.
2. AS, p.58; see also Galletti (b).
3. Pintoin, pp.755-757, Berthon, p.83.
4. Silvestre de Sacy, p.27; Anonymous, p.3.
5. Bachman, p.2.
6. Frank (a), p.279.

***The College of Sociology: a Paradoxical Institution* (pp.63-86)**

1. Durkheim (d), 18.
2. Durkheim (b), p.31.
3. Durkheim (d), p.314.
4. Durkheim (d), p.71.
5. Durkheim (d), p.312.
6. Durkheim (d), p.46.
7. Durkheim (d), pp.249, 256.
8. Durkheim (d), p.170.
9. Durkheim (d), p.257.
10. Durkheim (e), p.159, my additions in square brackets.
11. Durkheim (d), p.258.
12. Durkheim (d), p.309.
13. Durkheim (c), p.38.
14. Durkheim (a), p.52.
15. Durkheim (a), p.46.
16. Durkheim cited in Lukes, p.115.
17. OC11, p.62.
18. Frazer, p.13.
19. Frazer, p.364.
20. OC12, pp.575, 577, 585, 598.
21. Frazer, p.706.
22. OC5, p.272.
23. OC1, p.563.
24. Masson (b), p.25.
25. In Bataille (c).
26. OC1, p.91.
27. OC1, p.92.
28. *Ibid.*
29. OC1, p.305.
30. OC1, p.314.
31. OC1, p.308.
32. OC1, p.317.
33. CdeS2, p.xix.
34. OC12, p.48.
35. Caillois (f), pp.6-7.
36. Caillois (a), p.106; and CdeS3, p.882.
37. *Theses on Feuerbach*, p.11.
38. CdeS3, p.572.
39. Caillois (g), p.58.
40. Bataille (d), p.63.
41. CdeS2, p.161.
42. CdeS3, p.873.
43. Pic, p.88.
44. Bataille (d), pp.67-68.
45. Caillois (g), p.92.
46. Caillois (g), p.93.
47. Caillois (g), p.58.
48. Caillois (g), p.58.
49. Caillois (g), pp.59, 93.
50. Caillois (j), p.30; Frank (a), pp.279-280.
51. AS, p.112.
52. OC11, p.56.
53. OC11, pp.58-59.
54. OC7, p.461.
55. AS, p.314.
56. Caillois (a), unpaginated.
57. Caillois (a), unpaginated.
58. Caillois (f), pp.6-7.
59. AS, pp.320-321.
60. MG, conversation with Andler.
61. [Benjamin], p.101.

62. Lévy, p.195.
63. Caillois (a), unpaginated.
64. See his reply to Monnerot's questionnaire on "Spiritual Directors", CdeS3, pp.777-785.
65. Masson (b), p.29.
66. CdeS3, p.884.
67. Bataille (d), pp.64-65.
68. Duthuit cited in Kleiber, p.128.
69. Duthuit, p.138.
70. Waldberg (c), pp.98-99.
71. According to Pearce, although he also lists Adorno and Horkheimer (as does Lévy, p.209), who could have attended the first few lectures before leaving for the USA early in 1938, and Lévi-Strauss, who does not seem to have been in Paris at this time.
72. Boissonnas p.111.

**Chronology I (pp.89-105)**

1. Bataille (g), pp.15-16.
2. Leiris (c), p.159.
3. Leiris (c), p.166; Bataille (g), p.248.
4. Leiris (g), p.20.
5. See also Galletti (n).
6. OC11, p.572.
7. OC2, p.130.
8. Leiris (h), p.1006; Armel, p.299.
9. OC2, pp.61, 66.
10. *SASDLR* 1, pp.45-48.
11. Cf. Le Bouler, p.65.
12. OC6, p.278.
13. Bataille (e), p.69, note 4.
14. See also Galletti (g), pp.21-56.
15. Felgine, p. 87; Bataille (d), p.8; Caillois (a), p.93.
16. Armel, p.348.
17. Cf. Bruno (a).
18. OC5, p.90; see also Galletti (e), pp.xcv, cxvi.
19. OC6, p.278.
20. Masson (b), p.23.
21. OC2, p.258.
22. Surya, p.639.
23. OC5, p.90; Bataille (g), p.107.
24. CdeS3, p.741; see also Galletti (g), p.74.
25. Bataille (e), pp. 81-83; see also Galletti (j), p.226.
26. OC5, pp.90-91; cf. also Bataille (e), p.85.
27. OC6, p.278.
28. OC5, p.90.
29. Masson (c), p.210, note 1.
30. Laure (a), p.250.
31. Leiris (c), p.285.
32. Laure (a), p.306; Laure (b), p.162.
33. OC5, p.91.
34. Laure (a), p.306; Laure (b), p.162.
35. Laure (a), p.248; see also Laure (b), p.47.
36. OC3, p.395; OC6, pp.126-127, 409.
37. Barillé, p.261; Laure (b), p.162.
38. Laure (b), p.162.
39. Beaumelle, Bernadac, Hollier, p.144.
40. Bataille (e), p.98.
41. Bataille (h), p.102; see also Laure (a), p.307; Barillé, p.270.
42. Galletti (e), p.cvi.
43. OC6, p.416.
44. Caillois (a), unpaginated.
45. AS, pp.119-122.
46. AS, pp.119-120.
47. Laure (b), pp.125, 164.
48. AS, p.127.
49. Queneau, pp.319, 395.
50. OC5, p.514.
51. Combalia, p.55.
52. No. 8, 1936, pp.50-53, reprinted with changes in *Inner Experience*.
53. Cerenza, p.83.
54. Surya, p.640; see also OC2, pp.268-270.
55. Masson (c), p.261; Armel, p.370.
56. Bataille (d), pp.43-44.
57. Leperlier, pp.200-201.
58. See also Galletti (g).
59. Armel, p.392.
60. Felgine, p.112, Caillois (i), p.30.
61. AS, p.161.
62. AS, p.166.
63. AS, pp.178-179, n.13; see also Short pp.152, 174.
64. AS, pp.189-193.
65. See AS, pp.198, 201-202, 203, 225-226, 238-239, 249-250.
66. AS, pp.203, 225-26; see also Short, p.156; Dubief (b), p.53.
67. AS, p.113, note 3.
68. Frank (a), p.263.
69. Unpublished letters from Dussat to Chavy of 3 and 7 March 1936, courtesy of Claudine Frank.
70. Pierre, p.506.
71. Frank (a), p.263.

**Chronology II (pp.109-114)**

1. OC7, p.461.

2. This text, preserved in the archives of Andler, Chavy, Dubief and Kaan, was also sent to Chenon and Dussat according to an unpublished letter from the latter dated 15 April 1936, courtesy of Claudine Frank.
3. See Dubief (b), p.57; Pierre, p.506.
4. Barillé, pp.285, 287.
5. Laure (a), p.78; this and a fragment of the project from a later date, "Libertinage. Stages of 'Laure'", appears in the same volume.
6. See Masson (c), p.315.
7. Assouline, pp.457, 701, note 14; see also Masson's letter to Bataille on this film in AS, p.303.
8. Caillois (j), p.142.
9. Claudine Frank archives.
10. Bataille (g), pp.117-118.
11. Armel, pp.372-373; Leiris (c), p.889, note 1.
12. AS, p.313.
13. Bataille (d), p.55.
14. AS, p.314.
15. Caillois (b), pp.11, 6-14.
16. AS, p.340.
17. Ambrosino, pp.88-89; see also Galletti (c), pp.82-87.
18. OC5, p.503.
19. AS, p.593; Waldberg (e), pp. 257-258.
20. AS, p.322.
21. AS, pp.320-321.
22. AS, p.349.

**Commentaries II (pp.115-119)**

1. MG, conversation with Rollin.
2. As in the early lectures to the College, e.g. that on "Power", CdeS3, pp.183-185, summarised here on pp.257-258.
3. MG, conversations with Koch and Rollin.
4. Besnier, p.119.
5. Cf. Nancy (a).
6. OC6, p.14.
7. OC8, p.433.
8. OC1, p.451.
9. OC1, pp.452-453.
10. OC8, p.416.
11. *Acéphale* 2, p.28.
12. *Acéphale* 2, p.22.
13. *Acéphale* 2, p.27.
14. OC2, p.443.
15. Claudine Frank archives.
16. OC1, pp.541, 543.
17. CdeS3, pp.241, 240.
18. AS, pp.295-297.
19. See Dubief (b), p.57, who attributes the neologism "surfascism"to Dautry; and Pierre, p.506.
20. See Andler.

***Acéphale* 1: "The Monster" (pp.127-129)**

1. Re "time the destroyer" see the citation from Nietzsche in the preface to the text by him on Heraclitus (p.133).

***Acéphale* 2: "Heraclitus" (pp.133-136)**

1. I.e. Heraclitus. [Trans.]

**The Secret Society of Acéphale, ●6-12 (pp.137-144)**

1. An obvious reference to the Surrealists.
2. And here to leftist politics.
3. A distortion of Descartes's *"cogito ergo sum"*, I think therefore I am. Here: if I should die, therefore I am.
4. Pseudonym of Pierre Andler.

**Chronology III (pp.147-150)**

1. AS, p.323.
2. Caillois (a), unpaginated.
3. AS, p.343.
4. Caillois (f), p.7; Caillois (g), p.58.
5. Armel, pp.382-383; Leiris (c), p.133 (13.10.1940).
6. Cf. article II of its statutes, OC2, p.444.
7. [Benjamin], p.100; Pic, p.88.
8. Caillois (c), p.58.
9. Bataille (d), p.58.
10. Cf. on this journey, Galletti (j) & (m).
11. AS, p.420.
12. OC5, p.500.
13. Claudine Frank archives.
14. In Laure (a), p.122; cf. also Galletti (m).
15. Bataille (d), p.63.
16. Leiris (e), pp.134-135; Armel, p.376.

**Commentaries III (pp.151-158)**

1. Masson (c), p.331.
2. OC2, p.391.
3. Caillois (g), p.58.
4. Unpublished letter from Dussat to Chavy, 24.7.1937. (Claudine Frank archives)
5. Klossowski (e), p.177.
6. *Acéphale* 2, p.29.
7. Klossowski (b), p.175.

8. Klossowski (b), p.163.
9. Klossowski (b), pp.176, 178.
10. Klossowski (b), pp.177, 179.
11. *Acéphale* 3/4, p.8.
12. *Acéphale* 3/4, p.6.
13. *Acéphale* 3/4, p.8.
14. *Acéphale* 3/4, p.8.
15. *Acéphale* 3/4, p.31.
16. *Acéphale* 3/4, p.10.
17. *Acéphale* 3/4, p.30.
18. *Acéphale* 3/4, p.31.
19. *Acéphale* 3/4, p.20.
20. Caillois (g), p.58.
21. [Benjamin], p.104.
22. Kropotkin's text "Anarchism" appeared in the ninth edition of the *Encyclopedia Britannica*.

**The Secret Society of Acéphale, ● 13-26 (pp.161-185)**

1. *The Marriage of Heaven and Hell*.
2. Nikolai, brother of the philosopher Mikhail.
3. The SFIO was the French Section of the Workers' International, the Socialist party led by Jean Jaurès; in 1925 Maurice Maurin created *Étincelle socialiste* (Socialist Spark), a magazine as well as a faction in favour of a common front with the Communists.
4. E.G. Boulenger, *Searchlight on Animals*, Hale, London, 1936. [Author's note]
5. The title of this text is in Latin, and refers to the two prayers at the beginning of the Catholic Mass that commemorate the living and the dead. [Trans.] Note that the roneoed version of the "Memento" on p.176 shows that the last word of line 8, "*vois*" (see) was originally "*sais*" (know).
6. Power, prestige etc. in aboriginal languages. [Trans.]

***Acéphale* 3/4: "Dionysian Virtues" (pp.193-195)**

1. I.e. Olympian.

**The College of Sociology: "What we undertook a few months ago…" (pp.196-202)**

1. *Acéphale* journal.
2. We have been unable to trace this citation.

**The College of Sociology: "The Winter Wind" (pp.203-215)**

1. "Outside the Church there is no salvation", a maxim of Origen's cited by Nietzsche in *The Will to Power*: "The Christian with his formula *Extra ecclesiam nulla salus* reveals his *cruelty* towards the enemies of his band of Christians".
2. The hill upon which Remus failed to found the city of Rome. [Trans.]
3. Rimbaud [Author's note]. From "Bad Blood" in *A Season in Hell*.
4. Caillois here appears to be deliberately misinterpreting Stirner, who is not using the word "sacred" in the Durkheimian sense, but in reference to the Catholic Church.
5. Caillois's interpretation of attraction and repulsion here is very different from Bataille's in his lectures on the subject.
6. This process would apply equally to a harnessing of right-wing prejudices.
7. The Jesuit oath includes this line: "I do further promise and declare, that I will have no opinion or will of my own, or any mental reservation whatever, even as a corpse or cadaver (*perinde ac cadaver*), but will unhesitatingly obey each and every command that I may receive from my superiors in the Militia of the Pope and of Jesus Christ."
8. Cf. Balzac's *History of the Thirteen*, already cited, and Baudelaire's *The Painter of Modern Life*, chapter 9. [Author's note]
9. The argument that follows offers a distinctly different interpretation of these categories from Bataille's in "The Notion of Expenditure".
10. Paul Valéry. [Author's note]

**Chronology IV (pp.219-220)**

1. Cf. Caillois (i), p.55.
2. Armel, p.376; see also p.479 below.
3. Frank (a), pp.279-280.
4. Unpublished letter from Dussat to Chavy, 11 November 1937, courtesy of Claudine Frank.
5. OC5, p.525; Bataille in Laure (a), pp.308-309.
6. Bataille (d), pp.24-25, 72-73, 77; cf. also Koch's statement on p.41.

**Commentaries IV (pp.221-226)**

1. Klossowski (e), p.176.
2. Klossowski (b), p.155.
3. Klossowski (e), pp.177-178.
4. Cf. Galletti (e), p. XCVI.
5. MG, conversation with Andler.
6. See pp.40-41.
7. According to Dubief, he quit the Society when "it launched itself into dubious activities". (MG,

conversation with Dubief, Cachan, 1994)
8. See Lévy, pp.194-197.
9. The resignation of Puyo is mentioned in ●15; see also René Puyo in the Biographies.
10. MG, conversation with Andler.
11. OC1, pp.332-336.
12. CdeS3, p.56.
13. CdeS3, pp.56-57.
14. Bataille (d), pp.67-69.
15. CdeS3, p.123.
16. [Benjamin], p.99.
17. Caillois (f), p.7.
18. Bataille (d), p.72.
19. CdeS3, p.93.

**The Secret Society of Acéphale, ●32-46 (pp.229-244)**

1. Rollin had left for Spain in December 1936, where he remained for the duration of the Civil War.
2. This is probably a reference to Dautry, who had been called up for military service.
3. "Love of one's fate", which according to Nietzsche was "the highest state a philosopher can attain" (*Will to Power*, 1041).
4. I.e. the mark on the stomach of the Acéphale, also separately reproduced on the cover of the journal.

**Chronology V (pp.247-252)**

1. Laure (a), p.130.
2. Bataille (d), pp.83-84.
3. Bataille (d), p.83.
4. OC5, p.526.
5. OC5, pp.525-526.
6. Laure (a), p.136.
7. CdeS3, p.95.
8. Caillois (i), p.82.
9. CdeS3, p.252.
10. Bataille (d), p.87.
11. Martin, p.129.
12. Caillois (g), pp.58, 92, note 1.
13. OC5, pp.502, 515, 523.
14. Unpublished letter from Dussat to Chavy, 8 August 1938, courtesy of Claudine Frank.
15. OC1, p.683.
16. OC5, p.526; the lines are from Laure's poem "The Crow" of January 1936, cf. Laure (a), pp.96-98.

**Commentaries V (pp.253-261)**

1. See p.44.
2. Simmel, p.96.
3. Morando, p.67; see also Waldberg (c); and Klossowski (d).
4. See pp.39-40.
5. Hollier (a), p.115.
6. Hollier (a), p.116.
7. *Acéphale* 3/4, p.6.
8. CdeS3, pp.93, 130; see also pp.256-257.
9. OC2, pp.385-386.
10. OC6, pp.31, 228.
11. MG, conversation with Rollin; AS, pp.462, 506.
12. OC2, p.389.
13. CdeS3, p.124.
14. CdeS3, p.128.
15. CdeS3, p.178.
16. CdeS3, p.164.
17. CdeS3, p.168.
18. CdeS3, p.167.
19. CdeS3, pp.167-8.
20. CdeS, p.184.
21. CdeS3, p.192.
22. CdeS, p.193.
23. CdeS, p.197.
24. CdeS3, p.223.
25. CdeS3, p.229.
26. CdeS3, p.225.
27. CdeS3, p.228.
28. CdeS3, p.242.
29. CdeS3, p.243.
30. Bataille (f), p.167.
31. Bataille (f), p.175.
32. Bataille (d), p.83.

**The Secret Society of Acéphale, ●47-58 (pp.265-276)**

1. The date is incorrect, "38" should read "37".
2. Mass here means something like "crowd", but see note 116 on p.461 above.
3. This Nietzschean aphorism comes from "Discipline and Breeding" in *The Will to Power*, II.
4. Cf. ●53.

**The College of Socology: "The Sacred in Everyday Life" (pp.279-289)**

1. I.e. short for "*heureusement*", as follows, and in this context meaning "That was lucky!"

**The College of Socology: "The Sorcerer's Apprentice" (pp.290-305)**

1. Here Bataille must surely be referring to Laure's illness. [Trans.]
2. Bataille employs this word in a general sense here and below, but it is worth noting that a civil servant in France is a *fonctionnaire* (i.e. a "functionary"). [Trans.]

**Chronology VI (pp.309-310)**

1. Claudine Frank archives.
2. Claudine Frank archives.
3. Laure (a), p.262.

**Commentaries VI (pp.311-316)**

1. AS, p.436.
2. Hollier in CdeS3, p.449.
3. CdeS3, p.457.
4. First published by Dominique Rabourdin in *Nulle Part* 3, April 1984, under the title "Twenty Propositions on the Death of God", and reprinted under that title in AS.
5. Bibliothèque Nationale, box 6D, ff.124-133.
6. We have translated Rollin's version here, since it is the most complete.
7. Taken, in fact, from the fifth proposition in box 6D (see note 5 above).
8. According to the chronology compiled by Dussat dating from the death of his mother on 29 December 1912 to January 1942 (Michèle Boucheix Bergstrasser archive).
9. CdeS3, pp.380-381; translation by Meyer Barash from Caillois (e).
10. Cf. Hertz, and Granet, whom Bataille proposed as a lecturer to the College (Bataille (d), pp.94 and 103).
11. Hertz, p.123.
12. Frazer, p.11.
13. Hertz, p.114.
14. Cf. Preuss.
15. In Bataille's "Attraction and Repulsion" II and Caillois's "The Ambiguity of the Sacred".
16. Waldberg (c), p.109; MG, conversations with Rollin.
17. Simmel, p.96. The dating of "Degrees" is somewhat hypothetical, and is based on a handwritten note at the bottom of the first page of Andler's copy: "Text of the second part of the meeting of 28-IX".
18. The dating of this document from Chavy's papers is also difficult. In Chenon's archives it was pinned to Bataille's "What we undertook a few months ago..." of spring 1937 (letter from Claudine Frank). In Andler's archive, it was placed with "Degrees", just after the texts of 24 September 1937. However, Dussat's "On the 'Hard School'", which is not included here, is dated 20 October 1938 and concerns the Nietzsche text cited by Bataille (cf. AS, pp.501-503) and thus provides a certain date.
19. OC2, p.395.
20. AS, p.495.
21. Dussat and Chenon were probably mobilised at the same time.
22. Lévy, p.204.
23. Bataille (d), pp.89-91 and note 1.
24. Bataille (e), p.148.

**The Secret Society of Acéphale, ● 62-74 (pp.319-339)**

1. An allusion to the invasion of the Sudetenland.
2. Bataille employs an equivalent word in the French. [Trans.]
3. The abbreviations, in order of appearance, signify as follows: S.N. = Saint-Nom-la-Bretèche, A-o = Ambrosino, A-r = Andler, C-y = Chavy, K-n = Kelemen, M-e = Montjoie, S.G. = Saint-Germain-en-Laye, B-e = Bataille, W-g = Waldberg.
4. See p.51; *étoiles* were identified by a sign on the nearest tree, thus this probably indicates the Étoile de la Montjoie, immediately south of the ruins. The "notice" may have been Acéphale's sign of the labyrinth.
5. Again, presumably the "sign" of the labyrinth.
6. I.e. *Amor fati*, see note 3 to p.240 above.
7. According to Andler this was the "Internal Journal".

**Chronology VII (pp.345-350)**

1. OC5, pp.506-507.
2. Moré in Laure (a), p.284.
3. OC5, p.501.
4. Bataille (d), p.96, note 12.
5. Bataille (d), pp.93-94.
6. CdeS2, p.161.
7. Bataille (d), p.100.
8. Mayer, p.86
9. AS, pp.577-578; Kleiber, p.128.
10. Hollier in CdeS3, p.642.
11. Galletti (k), p.130.

**Commentaries VII (pp.351-362)**

1. AS, pp.507-508.
2. AS, p.505.
3. CdeS3, pp.225-226.
4. Fonds Carrouges, Manuscript Department of the Bibliothèque Nationale, also Galletti (k). In 1970, Carrouges sent a "strictly personal and confidential" photocopy of this letter to Jean Bruno, now held in the Bruno papers in the same institution.
5. Bataille in Galletti (k), p.131.
6. AS, pp.577-582; and ●89.
7. AS, p.581.
8. Cf. especially "Union et distance", *Cahiers d'art*, 1939.
9. CdeS1, pp.539-540.
10. CdeS3, p.371.
11. CdeS3, p.402.
12. CdeS3, p.456.
13. Bataille (d), p.94.
14. Bataille (d), p.93.
15. CdeS3, p.506.
16. CdeS3, p.513.
17. CdeS3, p.514.
18. CdeS3, p.517.
19. CdeS3, p.522.
20. Boissonnas, pp.111-115.
21. Boissonnas, p.114.
22. CdeS3, pp.535-536.
23. CdeS3, p.568.
24. Bataille (d), p.99.
25. Boissonnas, p.117.
26. Boissonnas, p.118.
27. In the first "defenestration", various town councillors were thrown to their deaths from the windows of the town hall by Hussites, an event that marked the start of the Hussite Wars that lasted for 37 years. The second defenestration was of two Catholic lords and their secretary who survived the 70-foot fall from a tower by the intercession either of the Virgin Mary or a dung heap. This was the start of the Thirty Years' War.
28. Bataille (d), p.103.
29. OC8, p.250.
30. Mayer, p.82.
31. OC12, pp.47-57.
32. OC12, p.53.
33. OC12, p.54.

**The Secret Society of Acéphale, ●76-90 (pp.365-382)**

1. The latter part of the MS. of this text becomes increasingly illegible.
2. I.e. a response to ●71 and 76.
3. Presumably meaning "degree", as in the adept's position within the group, cf. ●66.
4. I.e. in replying to ●56, and a second letter from Bataille sent on 25 October 1938.
5. Probably ●65 and 69.
6. Here and below Rollin is criticising §VIII of ●69.
7. From §X of ●69.
8. ●69 §II, XIII and XIV.
9. See ●69 §XIII and XIV.
10. See the talk in the third and final part of ●69.
11. See the opening paragraph of ●65.
12. A more or less direct citation from ●65 §4.
13. See ●65 §8.
14. See ●65 §7.
15. Another "note" for an encounter, dated, according to Andler's copy, 7.4.[19]39.
16. James II, King of England (1633-1701), who died in exile in France and is buried in Saint-Germain-en-Laye. [Trans.]

**The College of Sociology: "Theory of the Festival" (pp.383-406)**

1. It is pointless to emphasise that this theory of the festival is far from an exhaustive account of its different aspects. In particular, it would have to be correlated with a theory of sacrifice. In fact, the sacrificial victim seems to be a kind of privileged character at the festival. It is akin to the inner mechanism that sums it up and gives it meaning. They seem united in the same relationship as soul and body. For want of being able to stress this intimate connection (a choice had to be made), I tried to indicate the sacrificial atmosphere of the festival in the hope that it would thus become meaningful to the reader, just as the dual dialectic of the festival reproduces the dialectic of sacrifice. [Author's note]
2. "*Quieta non movere*", don't rock the boat.
3. The "verdant paradise of childhood loves" from Baudelaire's "Moesta et Errabunda" in *Les Fleurs du Mal*.
4. Gaspard de Coligini, French Huguenot, 1519-1572. [Trans.]
5. A festival like the Roman Saturnalia, in which a

slave took the king's role, and later was scourged and then executed. [Trans.] Cf. Frazer, pp.251-253.
6. "*Chaos, rudis indigestaque moles*", Chaos, a rough, unordered mass, from Ovid's *Metamorphoses*.

**Chronology VIII (pp.409-412)**

1. OC5, p.272.
2. Armel, p.393.
3. Galletti (a), p.143.
4. See also Galletti (a), especially pp.144, 153-158.
5. Cited in Galletti (k), p.131.
6. OC5, p.494.
7. OC5, p.245.
8. OC5, p.498.
9. OC5, p.247.
10. OC5, p.500; re Laure's grave: Galletti, phone conversation with Jérôme Peignot, June 2016.
11. OC5, p.253.
12. OC5, pp.509, 515.
13. OC5, p.509.
14. OC5, p.268; cf. also Galletti (e), p.c. These photographs appeared in Bataille's last book, *Les Larmes d'Éros* (Pauvert, 1961), as a part of his demonstration of the close connection between religious ecstasy and eroticism.
15. OC5, p.269.
16. Typewritten note by Andler.
17. OC5, pp.513-514.
18. OC6, p.373.

**Commentaries VIII (pp.413-420)**

1. CdeS3, p.730.
2. Bataille (d), pp.107-108.
3. Cdes3, p.462
4. OC2, pp.242-243.
5. Bataille (h), p.122.
6. Bataille (d), p.103.
7. CdeS3, pp.813-816.
8. Lévy, p.203.
9. Bataille (d), p.109.
10. Bataille (g), p.129.
11. Bataille (h), p.130.
12. Cf. letters between Ambrosino and Waldberg in AS, pp.547-560.
13. OCl, p.682, note 2.
14. *The Marriage of Heaven and Hell*, 77; the French translation has "*fou*" (mad) for "foolish".
15. Klossowski (b), pp.176-177.
16. Caillois (g), p.69.
17. Bruno (b), p.719.
18. OC5, p.269.
19. Bruno (b), p.709.
20. Bruno (b), p.713.
21. Bruno (b), p.714.
22. Bruno (b), p.710.
23. OC1, p.683.
24. Claudine Frank archives.
25. OC1, pp.517-518.
26. OC5, p.514.
27. AS, p.568.
28. OC7, p.462.
29. Waldberg (a); the entire original letter is in Waldberg (e), pp.84-89.
30. Koch (a), pp.38-39, 30 and 29. For the influence of sacrifice in Bataille's thought, see Nancy (b).
31. Koch (a), p.29.

***Acéphale* 5 (pp.423-437)**

1. *Thus Spake Zarathustra*, XXXIV.

**The College of Sociology: "The College of Sociology" (pp.442-450)**

1. After the previous lecture.
2. Atom derives from the Greek *atomos*, meaning "what cannot be cut".
3. Here and below, Bataille throws Caillois something of an olive branch, by calling into question the meaning and potential of the festival.
4. She being impatient to meet God.
5. Bataille presumably read Caillois's letter at this point, but it has not survived.

**The Secret Society of Acéphale, ●97–104 (pp.451-458)**

1. According to two people with knowledge of the group this was: "Enjoy yourselves!" (typed note by Pierre Andler).
2. The pneumatic post was a system for sending letters around the city within a few hours using compressed air in a network of tubes. Once a letter arrived at the recipient's nearest post office it would be delivered by bicycle. [Trans.]

## APPENDIX I. BIOGRAPHIES [MG]

These biographies give an account of the less well-known figures associated with Acéphale and the College, and thus omit the following: Georges Bataille, Walter Benjamin, Roger Caillois, Pierre Klossowski, Alexandre Kojève, Jacques Lacan, Michel Leiris, Sylvia Maklès, André Masson and Jean Paulhan.

**Ambrosino, Georges (1912-1984).** Born in Paris to Italian emigrants, at the end of his schooling he gained admission to the prestigious École Polytechnique, but declined since this course was aimed at a military career. Ambrosino joined the CCD (Democratic Communist Circle) in the early Thirties with two ex-schoolfriends, Barell and Chenon, where he met Esther Tabacman (1908-2002), the daughter of Russian *émigrés* of Jewish origin. A political activist from an early age, she joined the CCD in 1929-30, and became the group's treasurer. They became a couple (and married in 1940), and moved to Strasbourg, then Grenoble where Ambrosino studied physics at the university. He joined Contre-Attaque in 1935 and his friendship with Bataille led to Ambrosino playing a central role in both the Society and the College. In 1938 he was made professor of physics and began his military service. Demobilised in the summer of 1940, after Germany had invaded France, he returned to civilian life and taught in Nantes and then Lyon, where he joined the Resistance under Henri Frenay. In 1946 he was appointed director of Maurice de Broglie's laboratory for nuclear physics where he oversaw research in the field of radioactive isotopes. He contributed to the *Da Costa Encyclopédique* (*Da Costa Encyclopædia*), edited by Robert Lebel and Patrick Waldberg, and to *Critique*, the journal founded by Bataille. He also collaborated with Bataille on his book on "general economy", *The Accursed Share*, which appeared under Bataille's name alone in 1948 after Ambrosino declined to co-sign it. Despite this disagreement, Bataille wrote in the preface: "This book is to a great extent the work of Ambrosino". From 1955 to 1972, with various ex-members of Acéphale, he organised regular informal meetings known as the "Saturdays" (see p.49).

**Andler, Pierre, formerly Henri (Harrick) Obstfeld (1913-1996).** Born in Antwerp to a Jewish family of Polish origin, he grew up in England, Germany and France. He joined the CCD and contributed to *La Critique sociale* while working as an editor at the press agency Opera Mundi, and then joined Contre-Attaque under the pseudonym of Pierre Dugan; he was one of the founding members of Acéphale. In 1937 he became a naturalised French citizen and took the name of Pierre Andler. He volunteered for the French army in 1939 and was demobilised in June 1940. He travelled to New York, where he joined the US army as a liaison officer for the Office of War Information (OWI). After the war he studied philosophy in Montreal, New York and Paris, and translated various works from English on political history. He took part in the "Saturdays" until 1966, when he broke with Ambrosino.

**Atlan, Jean-Michel (1913-1960).** A left political activist with an interest in combining philosophy and drugs, after the war he became an increasingly successful artist. Atlan is mentioned in texts of the Society in July 1938, but according to Koch, he did not actually join.

**Bakhtin, Nicolai (1894-1950).** Brother of the more celebrated Mikhail, he was a passionate student of Greek mythology and a poet, translator and specialist in the philosophy of language. He studied in Paris at the Sorbonne and the École Nationale des Langues Orientales Vivantes, and then did his PhD at Cambridge, where he became a lifelong friend of Wittgenstein, and later taught at the Universities of Birmingham and Southampton.

**Barell, André (1912-2009).** Born in Paris to a family of Russian origin. A fellow pupil of Ambrosino and Chenon, with whom he formed the group ABC within the CCD, Barell was also associated with *Esprit*; a reader of *Acéphale*, he attended some of the meetings of both the Society and the College.

**Bernier, Jean (1894-1975).** A writer and journalist who moved from Stalinism to anarchism. In the early Thirties, Bernier edited the magazine *Clarté* and led the Communist group of the same name, both of which had been sympathetic to Surrealism. In 1926 he had been in a relationship with Colette Peignot. In later life he wrote journalism exposing the harsh realities of Stalinist Russia.

**Carrouges, Michel, pseudonym of Louis Couturier (1910-1988).** A Catholic essayist later linked to the philosopher Jacques Maritain, in the Thirties he was closer to Breton and Bataille. In 1950 he wrote a book on the work of Breton, whose collaboration with an avowed Catholic caused many members of the Surrealist group to leave. He seems to have been at least a "participant" in the Society.

**Chavy, Jacques (1912-2001).** Always fragile of health, Chavy suffered from tuberculosis since the age of ten. He had a passion for the arts and attended classes at the École des Arts Décoratifs. He came into contact with Ambrosino, Chenon, Kelemen and especially Dussat through various leftist groups and then the CCD. A member of Contre-Attaque, and secretary to the first issue of *Acéphale*, he followed Bataille into the Society. After the war Chavy worked as an interior decorator and contributed to the *Da Costa Encyclopædia*, *Critique* and was one of the organisers of the "Saturdays".

**Chenon, René (1912-1993).** A fellow pupil of Ambrosino and Barell, he declined entry into the École Polytechnique in order to devote himself to mathematics. He joined the CCD and wrote for *La Critique sociale*, and was a member of Contre-Attaque then Acéphale. While in a prison-camp during the war he married Reya Garbarg (1909-1980), a Jewish ex-member of Contre-Attaque. Afterwards Chenon taught mathematics in Paris, and actively participated in the "Saturdays".

**Dautry, Jean (1910-1968).** A historian and pupil of Albert Mathiez, Dautry left the Young Communists when Stalin exiled Trotsky to Alma-Ata. He contributed to *La Critique sociale* and *Masses*, and joined Contre-Attaque with Bataille. His name appeared in December 1936 on the "totemic dinner" invitation with other future members of the Society, ●9, but although he did not join (●12), other documents testify to his interest in the group (●14, 39 and 53). In 1941 he rejoined the Communist Party so as to fight in the Resistance. After the war he taught at Vanves and the University of Lille.

**Dubief, Henri (1910-1995).** Also a pupil of the Marxist historian Mathiez. Inspired by the ideas of Rosa Luxemburg, he joined L'Étincelle Socialiste (Socialist Spark) on the extreme left of the SFIO (French Section of the Workers' International) before becoming an anarchist. Active in various ultra-leftist groups in the early Thirties, Dubief was a teacher at the Lycée Dorian. After Contre-Attaque he joined Acéphale (see ●14 §3 and ●15), but left the group when it began to indulge in "dubious activities". This break was not entirely final, as can be seen from ●39 and 52. During the war he was taken prisoner, in May 1940, and on his release he took an active part in the Resistance after joining the Communist party, which he left in 1943. After the war he taught history and was the author of various books on the subject.

**Dussat, Henri (1912-1978).** Raised by his father outside religion after the death of his mother when he was six, Dussat underwent a profound religious crisis around the end of 1927. He joined the theatrical group Art et Action, which had a substantial influence on his early literary and artistic tastes; he also became interested in naturism with a group which, according to Barell, met in Châtenay-Malabry to the south-west of Paris. In late 1929 he met Chavy, and in February 1934 joined the CCD but finding it "devoid of significance" he attended the early meetings of Contre-Attaque, which he found equally disappointing. Dussat joined Acéphale, and wrote several texts, including ●37, 43, 47, 49 and 55. In 1938 he was called up and sent to his former regiment in Metz until October; in the summer of 1939 he left for Brazil but returned to France in May 1943 to rejoin the French army in North Africa. He returned to Paris in 1947, and became editorial secretary for Souvarine's *Contrat sociale* and took an active part in the "Saturdays".

**Duthuit, Georges (1891-1973).** A lecturer to the College on "The Myth of the English Monarchy", 20 June 1939, Duthuit was an art critic and historian close to Masson, with an abiding interest in gnosis. Samuel Beckett's "Three Dialogues with Georges Duthuit" (1949) was the result of their long correspondence on contemporary painters in Paris.

**Farner, Isabelle, later Isabelle Waldberg (1911-1990).** Born in Switzerland, she met Patrick Waldberg in Paris in 1938 and with him attended the lectures of Marcel Mauss at the École Pratique des Hautes Études. The only woman to take part in meetings of the secret society, she was responsible for analysing texts by Nietzsche for its publications, as well as undertaking, with Chavy, a translation of *The Will to Power*. After the death of Laure, she moved with Patrick to Saint-Germain-en-Laye, and continued to participate in meetings of the Society in the forest and at Laure's grave. At the outbreak of war, after the birth of her son Michel, she took refuge in Switzerland before rejoining Patrick in New York, where they married. She became part of the community of intellectuals in exile that included Andler, Breton, Duthuit, Robert and Nina Lebel, Masson and Rollin, and in 1944 had her first solo exhibition. On her return to Paris, she moved into Duchamp's old studio in rue Larrey, and later collaborated on the *Da Costa Encyclopædia*. In 1953 she separated from her husband and devoted herself entirely to sculpture, taking part in numerous exhibitions and receiving the Bourdelle Prize in 1961.

**Folio, Robert, known as Saint-Paul.** A close friend of the Waldbergs, he is mentioned several times in the letters between them (see Waldberg (f)) where he is referred to as "a poet of life", and "majestic and pure". He is also mentioned, along with Atlan, Okamoto and Persenico (or Bersenico), in a letter from Bataille to Patrick Waldberg in connection with a "relatively closed meeting of Acéphale", while on 1 October 1939 Bataille sent him a commentary on the theme of joy in the face of death, ●100. It is not known if he joined the Society.

**Girard, Alain (1914-1996).** While he was close to Koch and Rollin, and a contributor to *L'Agora* and later to *Inquisitions*, he did not join Contre-Attaque nor Acéphale, although his name appears on the agenda for the meeting of 25 July 1938, ●52. According to Rollin he was to have been a member of the Society of the Friends of Acéphale. After the war Girard became a professor at the Sorbonne, where he taught demography, and published several works.

**Kaan, Pierre (1903-1945).** Of Jewish origin on his father's side, active in leftists groups in the Thirties and a co-editor of *La Critique sociale*, Kaan took part in the initial discussions for Contre-Attaque, the Society and the College. A professor of philosophy, during the war he was one of the first organisers of the Resistance and deputy to Jean Moulin. In 1943 he was betrayed by a collaborator, tortured by the Gestapo and sent to Buchenwald, where he died of typhus shortly after it was liberated.

**Kelemen, Imre (1909-1979).** A dissident Marxist of Hungarian origin, he arrived in France in 1933 and made contact with both the anti-Stalinist René Lefeuvre and the CCD. Closely associated with Bataille, he took part in Contre-Attaque under the name of Pierre Aimery, and was to have written one of its *Cahiers* with Dautry. Kelemen joined Bataille in the society of Acéphale, and was called up into the French army (possibly the Foreign Legion); he lived in Paris after being demobilised, and returned to Hungary at the end of the war. Active in the left wing of the Hungarian Socialist Party which was in favour of merging with the Communist Party, he was imprisoned for his part in re-establishing the Hungarian Socialist Party following the events of 1956.

**Koch, Michel (1913-2005).** From a Jewish family in the Lorraine and raised by his maternal grandfather, Koch was a pupil of the philosopher Alain at the Lycée Henri IV. He also attended the lectures of the Catholic philosopher Louis Lavelle and founded the magazine *L'Agora*, whose three issues included texts by Girard and Rollin, his classmates. He was also a fellow pupil of Caillois in the entry class to the École Normale Supérieure. Very active politically, in 1935 he joined the Young Communists, but left after the Laval/Stalin pact. He attended one meeting of Contre-Attaque in Barrault's studio, the Grenier des Grands-Augustins, where Dautry and Bataille spoke, and in 1938 joined Acéphale. He remembered this as a vital experience which, in response to his yearning for an authentic community, led him to take a full part in the meditations at the tree and the meetings at Dussat's apartment. However, according to Rollin, his involvement in the secret society was limited to membership of the Society of the Friends of Acéphale. After the war he worked for the France-Presse agency.

**Laure (Colette Peignot, 1903-1938).** Born into a family of industrialists, she received a Catholic and conservative education, and in 1916 was first affected by the disease that would take her life, tuberculosis. According to her *Story of a Little Girl* she rejected her family's values and faith, in part following attempted abuse by the family priest and also because of his secret relationship with her older sister. In the Twenties she was attracted to Surrealism, while her relationship in 1926 with Bernier was largely responsible for her adherence to Communism. After returning to France in 1931, following prolonged stays in Berlin and Moscow, she and Souvarine became lovers. She joined the CCD and wrote for *La Critique sociale* under the pseudonym Claude Araxe, and also looked after its funding and acted as its secretary. These writings, the only ones published during her lifetime, were later collected as *Écrits retrouvés* in 1987. In the CCD she met Simone Weil and Bataille, who wrote in "Laure's Life" (in Laure (a)): "What dominated her was the need to give herself completely, and directly." Her relationship with Bataille dates from July 1934, as recounted in the *Chronology*. She took no part in meetings of the secret society, but helped finance *Acéphale*, and in July 1938 moved with Bataille to Saint-Germain-en-Laye, where she died on 7 November.

**Lewitsky, Anatole (1901-1942).** A lecturer to the College on shamanism. Born near Moscow, he attended the Sorbonne, studied under Mauss, and became a curator at the Musée de l'Homme. After the defeat of France, he organised the first Resistance cell in the country with members of the staff at the Museum, but was arrested and shot by the Gestapo.

**Libra, Pierre.** Nothing is known of this person except that he signed the "Note", ○31, on the founding of the College and replied to the "Directors of *Conscience*" questionnaire (see p.359). The defence of racism in his reply probably explains his playing no further part in the College.

**Mayer, Hans (1907-2001).** A lecturer to the College and a prolific Jewish and socialist literary critic who was exiled in Paris at the time of the College.

**Monnerot, Jules (1909-1995).** Although involved with the discussions on the founding of the College, Monnerot took no part in it, having fallen out with Bataille. The author of *La Poésie moderne et le sacré* (1945) and *Sociologie du communisme* (1949), he followed a dispiriting political trajectory from militant Communism in the Thirties to Gaullism after the war, and ended up as a candidate for Jean-Marie Le Pen's National Front in the European elections of 1989.

**Moré, Marcel (1887-1969).** A friend of Laure since her childhood, he was close to both Bataille and Leiris. Moré was at once a stockbroker, a literary critic and an editor of the Catholic review *Esprit*. In late 1939, early 1940, he organised various meetings attempting to reanimate the College around Klossowski, Koyré, Landsberg, Queneau and Wahl.

**Okamoto, Taro (1911-1996).** Arrived in Paris in 1929 to study painting, but was also interested in ethnology and sociology. He took part in the International Surrealism Exhibition in 1938, and was close to Max Ernst, Kurt Seligmann, Patrick Waldberg and Atlan, studied with Mauss and Kojève, and attended lectures at the College. His initials appear in ●48. Okamoto returned to Japan in 1940 and in the '70s became perhaps the most famous artist in Japan at the time; there are museums named after him and dedicated to his works in both Kawasaki and Tokyo.

**Puyo, René.** A lawyer and member of Contre-Attaque, and a friend of Dubief, he appears under the name of René Puaux in the papers deposited by Dubief at the Bibliothèque Nationale. He was, at most, only briefly a participant in Acéphale and is mentioned in ●15.

**Rollin, Jean (1912-2000).** A poet and journalist, he published his first poems when he was just eighteen. He was a contributor to Koch's *L'Agora* and an assiduous reader of *La Critique sociale*. Impressed by Breton's *Position politique du surréalisme*, he joined Contre-Attaque in 1936, where he became closer to Bataille. In December that year he went to Spain where he stayed until the end of the Civil War as a foreign correspondent for the news agency Havas. He contributed to *Acéphale* 2, ●4, and during a brief stay in France he joined Acéphale. In August 1939 he went to the USA, also for Havas, and there met up again with Andler, Breton, Duthuit, Rougemont, Souvarine and the Waldbergs. Rollin joined the OWI as a journalist, and did other war work involving journalism and propaganda. After the war he worked at *France-Soir*, and as a foreign-policy journalist on radio as well as a playwright.

**Souvarine, Boris (1895-1984).** A founding member of the French Communist Party, and close to both Lenin and Trotsky with whom he maintained a long correspondence up until their deaths. He left the Party in 1924, and published the first, and uncomplimentary, biography of Stalin in 1935. With Max Eastman he ensured the publication of Lenin's Testament, when he first warned of the dangers posed by Stalin. He was the founder and co-editor with Kaan of *La Critique sociale* and founder of the CCD, where so many of the members of Acéphale first met each other.

**Waldberg, Patrick (1913-1985).** Born in Santa Monica, his family settled in Paris in 1915. In 1932 he made contact with the Surrealists, and also joined the CCD where he was close to Bataille and Queneau. In 1933 he met Okamoto, and with him attended lectures by Mauss and Kojève. Present at the beginning of Contre-Attaque, he was expelled from France in 1936 and travelled to Sweden and then California. In 1937 he returned to France to join Acéphale, and was initiated in ceremonies described in ●63, 67 and 68. After the death of Laure, he and Farner shared Bataille's house in Saint-Germain-en-Laye. He was secretary of the College from 1938 to 1939, and also did administrative work for Mauss. He volunteered for French army service in 1939, and was demobilised in August 1940. In January 1941 he returned to the USA where he often met up with Breton. As a member of the OWI he oversaw the founding of the Voice of America radio station, and took part in the US Army landings in Normandy on D-Day. Early in 1946, while staying with Ernst and Dorothea Tanning in Arizona, he came up with a project that would bring together Bataille, members of Acéphale and the Surrealists: the *Da Costa Encyclopædia*, published in Paris in 1947. In 1951, he left the Surrealist group over the Carrouges affair (*q.v.*). Waldberg was the author of numerous works, including *Le Surréalisme* (1962), the translation of which published by Thames & Hudson, *Surrealism*, was for many decades one of the finest introductions to the subject in English.

## APPENDIX II. BIBLIOGRAPHY

This is a listing of books referred to or consulted, and is not intended as a comprehensive bibliography of Bataille. French books are published in Paris unless stated otherwise.

### I. Primary Sources (abbreviations used in the notes are in brackets)


(AS) Bataille, Georges. *L'Apprenti sorcier*, ed. and presented by Marina Galletti, Éditions de la Différence, 1999.

(CdeS) Hollier, Denis. *Le Collège de Sociologie*, Gallimard, 1995 (CdeS3, republication with additional material of the edition of 1979). Hollier here presents and edits the existing texts of the lectures given at the College by Bataille *et al.* His presentations in the various editions differ. There have been two previous versions: the French edition of 1979 (CdeS1), and the English edition, translated by Betsy Wing and published by the University of Minnesota Press in 1988 (CdeS2).

(OC) Bataille, Georges. *Œuvres complètes*, 12 volumes, Gallimard, 1970-1988.

(*Acéphale*) *Acéphale 1936-1939*, reprint of the journal with an introduction by Michel Camus, Jean-Michel Place, 1980, reprinted 1995.


### II. Secondary Sources


Ambrosino, Georges. "Un inédit de la société secrète Acéphale", Roger Caillois issue of *Europe*, no. 859-860, November-December 2000. (See also Frank (b))

Andler, Pierre. *Je fus un enfant...*, unpublished text, 30 March 1937, Andler archive.

Anonymous. *Guide du touriste en Forêt de Marly*, Ministère de l'Agriculture, n.d. (1930s).

Armel, Aliette. *Michel Leiris*, Fayard, 1997.

Artaud, Antonin. *L'Ombilic des limbes*, Éditions de la NRF, 1925; edition cited: *Œuvres complètes*, I, Gallimard, 1970.

Assouline, Pierre. *L'Homme de l'art. D.-H. Kahnweiler 1884-1979*, Éditions Balland, 1993.

Bachman, Michel. "Le Chêne Joyenval, une célébrité s'est étreint", *Le Char à bœufs*, free newsletter published by Les Amis de Saint-Nom-la-Bretèche, 10, 2009.

Barillé, Élisabeth. *Laure. La sainte de l'abîme*, Flammarion, 1997.

Barrault, Jean-Louis. *Souvenirs pour demain*, Seuil, 1972.

Bataille, Georges; see also Frank (b).
— (a) "Vers une littérature servile?", *Combat*, 30 January 1948.
— (b) "La Rosace, le 'recapitulatif' inédit", in Laure (a), pp.303-310.
— (c) *Visions of Excess, Selected Writings 1927-1939*, edited and translated by Allan Stoekl, Manchester University Press, 1985.
— (d) *Lettres à Roger Caillois*, edited and presented by J.-P. Le Bouler, Éditions Folle Avoine, 1987.
— (e) *Choix des lettres, 1917-1962*, ed. Michel Surya, Gallimard, 1997.
— (f) "La Sociologie sacrée du monde contemporain" (second part), introduced by Simonetta Falaschi Zamponi, in "Bataille au Collège de Sociologie, un inédit", *Lignes* 12, October 2003.
— (g) *Georges Bataille & Michel Leiris, Échanges et correspondances*, ed. Louis Yvert, Gallimard, 2004.
— (h) *Georges Bataille & Michel Leiris, Correspondence*, Seagull Books, 2004.
— (i) *Romans et récits*, ed. Jean-François Louette, Gallimard, 2004, reprinted 2014.
— (j) "Lettres à Joseph Roche (1921-1922)", ed. Marina Galletti & Olivier Meunier, *Cahiers Bataille* 2, 2014.

Baugh, Bruce. *French Hegel: From Surrealism to Postmodernism*, Routledge, London, 2003.

Beaumelle, Agnès de la, Bernadac, Marie-Laure & Hollier, Denis. *Leiris & Co*, Gallimard/Centre Pompidou-Metz, 2015.

Béhar, Henri. "Préface" in *Inquisitions*, facsimile edition, Éditions du CNRS, 1990.

[Benjamin, Walter]. "Walter Benjamin et le Collège de Sociologie", *Critique* 788-789, January-February 2013.

Berthon, Roger. *La Forêt de Marly*, CIDAP, 1958.

Besnier, Jean-Michel. *La Politique de l'impossible. L'intellectuel entre révolte et engagement*, La Découverte, 1988.

Biro, Adam & Passeron, René. *Dictionnaire général du surréalisme et de ses environs*, Presses Universitaires de France, 1982.

Blanchot, Maurice. *La Communauté inavouable*, Minuit, 1983.

Boissonnas, Édith. "Édith Boissonnas au Collège de Sociologie", *Critique* 788-789, January-February 2013.

Bruno, Jean.
— (a) *Papiers Jean Bruno, Dossier biogr. Bataille 1. Vie de Bataille*. Département des Manuscrits de la Bibliothèque Nationale.
— (b) "Les Techniques d'illumination chez Georges Bataille", *Critique* 195-196, August-September 1963.

Caillois, Roger; see also Bataille (d).
— (a) *Roger Caillois*, in Jean José Marchand, Archives du XX$^{e}$Siècle, Radiodiffusion Télévision Française, 12-13 August 1971.
— (b) "Pour une othodoxie militante", in *Inquisitions*, June 1936. Facsimile edition ed. Henri Béhar, Éditions du CNRS, 1990.
— (c) "L'Agressivité comme valeur", *L'Ordre nouveau*, 1 June 1937.
— (d) *L'Homme et le sacré*, Gallimard, 1940 (citations from the edition of 1976).
— (e) *Man and the Sacred*, translation of Caillois (d) by Meyer Barash, University of Illinois Press, 1959.
— (f) Interview with Gilles Lapouge, *La Quinzaine littéraire* 90, 16-30 June 1970 (trans. in Caillois (j)).
— (g) *Approches de l'imaginaire*, Gallimard, 1974.
— (h) "L'Esprit des sectes", in *Instincts et société*, Denoël-Gonthier, 1976.
— (i) *Correspondance Jean Paulhan-Roger Caillois 1934-1967*, ed. Odile Felgine & Claude-Pierre Perez with the assistance of Jacqueline Paulhan, Gallimard, 1991.
— (j) *The Edge of Surrealism, A Roger Caillois Reader*, ed. Claudine Frank, Duke University Press, 2003.

Camus, Michel. "L'Acéphalité ou la religion de la mort", in *Acéphale*.

Cerenza Orlandi, Germana. "Un manuscrit inédit de Bataille: de nouvelles variantes du 'Bleu du ciel'", *Les Lettres romanes*, Université Catholique de Louvain, Louvain-la-Neuve, 1991, XLV, 1-2, pp.77-86.

Charbonnier, Georges. *Entretiens avec André Masson*, Ryoan-ji, 1985.

Clébert, Jean-Paul.
— (a) "Georges Bataille et André Masson", *Les Lettres nouvelles* 3, May 1971.
— (b) *Mythologie d'André Masson*, Pierre Cailler Éditeur, 1971.

Cohen, Gustave. *Histoire de la chevalerie en France au Moyen Age*, Richard-Masse, 1949.

Combalia, Victoria. "Dora Maar, Georges Bataille and Tossa de Mar. New light on Dora Maar and Georges Bataille", *Art Press* 260, September 2000.

Détienne, Marcel. *Dionysos mis à mort*, Gallimard, 1977.

Dubief, Henri.
— (a) *Critique d'une position de Roger Caillois*, unpublished, January 1937, Andler archive.
— (b) "Témoignage sur Contre-Attaque", *Textures* 6, 1970.

Dumézil, Georges.
— (a) *Le Problème des centaures*, Librairie Orientaliste Paul Geuthner, 1929.
— (b) *Ouranos-Varuna*, Adrien-Maisonneuve, 1934.
— (c) *Mythes et dieux des Germains*, Librairie Ernest Leroux, 1939.

Durkheim, Émile.
— (a) "L'Individualisme et les intellectuels" (1898), translation from *On Morality and Society*, University of Chicago Press, 1973.

— (b) "Représentations individuelles et représentations collectives" (1898), translation from *Sociology and Philosophy*, Routledge & Kegan Paul, London, 1974.
— (c) "La Détermination du fait moral" (1906), translation from *Sociology and Philosophy*, Routledge & Kegan Paul, London, 1974.
— (d) *Les Formes élémentaires de la vie religieuse* (1912), translation cited by Carol Cosman, *The Elementary Forms of Religious Life*, Oxford University Press, 2001.
— (e) "Le Dualisme de la nature humaine et ses conditions sociales" (1914), translation from *On Morality and Society*, University of Chicago Press, 1973.

Dussat, Henri.
— (a) *Au plein milieu de la fête foraine...*, unpublished text, March 1937, Michèle Boucheix Bergstrasser archive.
— (b) *Chronologie*, unpublished text, n.d., Michèle Boucheix Bergstrasser archive.

Duthuit, Georges. "For a Sacred Art", in *Vertical: A Yearbook for Romantic-Mystic Ascensions*, ed. Eugene Jolas, Gotham Bookmart Press, New York, 1941.

Eliade, Mircea. *Initiations, rites, sociétés secrètes*, Gallimard, 1959, reprinted 1976.

Felgine, Odile. *Roger Caillois*, Stock, 1994.

Frank, Claudine.
— (a) "Acéphale/Parsifal. Georges Bataille contra Wagner", in *Durkheim, the Durkheimians, and the Arts*, ed. A. Riley, W.S.F. Pickering and W.W. Miller, Durkheim Press/Berghahn Books, New York, 2013.
— (b) *Georges Ambrosino, Georges Bataille, L'expérience à l'épreuve. Correspondance et inédits (1943-1960)*, ed. Claudine Frank, Éditions les Cahiers, 2017.

Frazer, J.G. *The Golden Bough*, various editions between 1890 and 1922. Edition cited ed. Robert Fraser, Oxford University Press, 1994.

Galletti, Marina; see also (AS) in Primary Sources above.
— (a) "Du Collège de Sociologie aux 'debates sobre temas sociológicos'. Roger Caillois en Argentine", in *Roger Caillois, la pensée aventurée*, ed. Laurent Jenny, Belin, 1992.
— (b) "The King of the Woods", *Art Press* 231, January 1998.
— (c) "Une communauté bicéphale? Roger Caillois et la 'parenthèse sociologique'", Roger Caillois issue of *Europe*, ed. Odile Felgine, 859-860, November-December 2000.
— (d) "Sacré et secret chez Leiris et Bataille", in *Bataille-Leiris. L'intenable assentiment au monde*, ed. Francis Marmande, Belin, 1999; English translation in *Economy and Society* XXXII, 1, February 2003.
— (e) "Chronologie", in Bataille (i).
— (f) "Georges Bataille ou la littérature comme 'exercice de cruauté'", in *Le Texte cruel*, ed. Franca Franchi, Bergamo University Press; L'Harmattan, 2006.
— (g) *La comunità impossibile di Georges Bataille. Da "Masses" ai "difensori del male*, Kaplan, Turin, 2008.
— (h) "Georges Bataille e André Masson: dalla 'communauté de coeur' di Acéphale alla comunità ateologica dei 'difensori del male'", in *Georges Bataille o la disciplina dell'irriducibile*, ed. Felice Ciro Papparo & Bruno Moroncini, Il Melangolo, Geneva, 2009.
— (i) "Dai Pieds Nickelés agli dèi messicani,"in *Documents, una rivista eterodossa*, ed. Franca Franchi & Marina Galletti, Bruno Mondadori, Pearson Italia, Turin/Milan, 2010.
— (j) "L'Italia, il capitolo non scritto della biografia di Bataille", in *I pensieri dell'istante, Scritti per Jacqueline Risset*, Editori Internazionali Riuniti, Rome, 2012.
— (k) "Autour de la société secrète Acéphale, Lettres inédites de Bataille à Michel Carrouges", *Revue des deux Mondes*, May 2012.
— (l) "Bataille, Caillois e la dépense (in margine a 'Vers une littérature servile?')", in *Nel nome di Bataille*, ed. Luigi A. Manfreda, *Il Cannocchiale*, May-August 2012.
— (m) "'Esperire tutte le antinomia implacabili' (Bataille e Laure)", in *Georges Bataille, Figure dell'eros*, ed. Fiorella Bassan & Sara Colafranceschi, Mimesis, 2015.

— (n) "Surrealism", in *Georges Bataille: Key Concepts*, ed. Mark Hewson & Marcus Coelen, Routledge, 2016.

Granet, Marcel. "La Droite et la gauche en Chine" (1933), in *Études sociologiques sur la Chine*, Presses Universitaires de France, 1953.

Hertz, Robert. "La Prééminence de la main droite", in *Mélanges de sociologie religieuse et folklore*, Alcan, 1928.

Hollier, Denis; see also (CdeS) in Primary Sources above.
— (a) *La Prise de la Concorde*, Gallimard, 1974.
— (b) "Préface" to Bataille (i).

Jeanmaire, Henri. *Dionysos. Histoire du culte de Bacchus*, Payot, 1951.

Kleiber, Pierre-Henri. *L'Encyclopédie "Da Costa" (1947-1949), d'Acéphale au Collège de 'Pataphysique*, L'Age d'Homme, 2014.

Klossowski, Pierre.
— (a) "Don Juan selon Kierkegaard", *Acéphale* 3/4, July 1937, in *Acéphale.*
— (b) "Le Corps du néant. L'expérience de la mort de Dieu chez Nietzsche et d'une nostalgie d'une expérience authentique chez Bataille", in *Sade mon prochain*, Seuil, 1947.
— (c) "Entre Marx et Fourier", *Le Monde*, 31 May 1969, supplement to number 7,582.
— (d) Preface to *Tarō Okamoto, L'Esthétique et le sacré*, Seghers, 1976.
— (e) "L'A-théologie ou l'église de la mort de Dieu", in *Le Peintre et son démon*, Flammarion, 1985.
— (f) *Sade My Neighbour*, translation of *Sade mon prochain*, Quartet, 1992.

Koch, Michel.
— (a) *Le Sacricide*, Leo Schéer, 2001.
— (b) *Piété pour la chair*, Nouvelles Éditions Lignes, 2008.

Laure (Peignot, Colette).
— (a) *Écrits de Laure*, Jean-Jacques Pauvert, 1985.
— (b) *Une rupture. 1934*, ed. Anne Roche & Jérôme Peignot, Éditions des Cendres, 1999.

Le Bouler, Jean-Pierre. "Trois notes sur Bataille, Brehier, Cues et Hegel (d'après des sources inexploitées)", in *Cahiers Georges Bataille* 1, undated (*c.*1986).

Leiris, Michel; see also Bataille (g) and (h).
— (a) *La Langue secrète des Dogon de Sanga*, 1948, edition cited published by Jean-Michel Place, 1992.
— (b) "... dont on ne sait, à vrai dire, pas grand-chose", in Bernard-Henri Lévy, *Les Aventures de la liberté*, Grasset, 1991.
— (c) *Journal 1922-1989*, Gallimard, 1992.
— (d) *C'est-à-dire*, Jean-Michel Place, 1992.
— (e) *L'Homme sans honneur, Notes pour Le sacré dans la vie quotidienne*, ed. Jean Jamin, Jean-Michel Place, 1994.
— (f) *Miroir de l'Afrique*, Gallimard, 1996.
— (g) "De Bataille l'impossible à l'impossible *Documents*", in Bataille (h).
— (h) *L'Age d'homme précédé de l'Afrique fantôme*, ed. Denis Hollier with Francis Marmande and Catherine Maubon, Gallimard, 2014.

Leperlier, François. *Claude Cahun, l'écart et la métamorphose*, Jean-Michel Place, 1992.

Lévy, Bernard-Henri. *Les Aventures de la liberté*, Grasset, 1991. Citations from the English translation *Adventures on the Freedom Road*, trans. Richard Veasey, The Harvill Press, London, 1995.

Lukes, Steven. *Émile Durkheim*, Penguin, 1975.

Martin, Russell. *Picasso's War*, Dutton, 2003.

Masson, André.
— (a) *Le Rebelle du surréalisme*, ed. Françoise Will-Levaillant, Hermann, 1976.
— (b) "Acéphale ou l'illusion initiatique", interview with Paule Thévenin, *Les Cahiers obliques* I, 1980.
— (c) *Les Années surréalistes. Correspondance 1916-1942*, ed. Françoise Levaillant, La Manufacture, 1990.

Mauss, Marcel. “Essai sur le don”, *L’Année sociologique* II, 1923-1924, edition cited published by PUF, 1950; English translation published as *The Gift*, Cohen & West, 1954.

Mayer, Hans. “Georges Bataille et le fascisme: souvenirs et analyse”, *Cahiers Georges Bataille* 1 (papers from the conference “Georges Bataille et la pensée allemande”, 1986).

Monnerot, Jules.
— (a) “Dionysos philosophe”, *Acéphale* 3/4, July 1937, in *Acéphale*.
— (b) *La Poésie moderne et le sacré*, Gallimard, 1945.
— (c) *Sociologie de la Révolution*, Fayard, 1970.

Morando, Camille. “Le Mythe à l’épreuve chez Taro Okamoto, peintre à la société secrète Acéphale et au Collège de Sociologie (1936-1940)”, in *Art et mythe*, ed. Fabrice Flahutez & Thierry Dufrêne, Presses Universitaires de Paris Ouest, 2011.

Nadeau, Maurice. *Histoire du surréalisme*, Seuil, 1945.

Nancy, Jean-Luc.
— (a) *La Communauté désœuvrée*, Christian Bourgois, 1986.
— (b) “L’insacrifiable”, in *Une pensée finie*, Galilée, 1991.

Panné, Jean-Louis. “Aux origines: le cercle communiste démocratique”, in *Boris Souvarine et La Critique sociale*, La Découverte, 1990.

Peignot, Colette, see Laure.

Pearce, Frank. “Collège de Sociologie and Acéphale”, in *Encyclopedia of Social Theory*, ed. George Ritzer, Sage, London, 2004.

Pic, Muriel. “Penser au moment du danger. Le Collège et l’Institut de recherche sociale de Francfort”, *Critique* 788-789, January-February 2013.

Pierre, José. *Tracts surréalistes et déclarations collectives 1922-1939*, Le Terrain Vague, 1980.

Pintoin, Michel. *Chronique du religieux de Saint-Denys, contenant le règne de Charles VI de 1380 à 1422*, vol. III, trans. M.L. Bellaguet, Crapelet, 1842.

Preuss, Konrad. “Der Ursprung der religion und der Kunst”, *Globus* LXXXVI, 1904 and LXXXVII, 1905.

Queneau, Raymond. *Journaux, 1914-1965*, Gallimard, 1996.

Short, Robert Stuart. “Contre-Attaque”, in *Entretiens sur le surréalisme*, Mouton, 1968.

Silvestre de Sacy, Léon. *Les Arbres historiques de Saint-Germain-en-Laye et de ses forêts*, Les Amis du Vieux Saint-Germain, Saint-Germain-en-Laye, 1932.

Simmel, Georg. *Secret et sociétès secrètes*, Circé, 1991.

Surya, Michel. *Georges Bataille. La mort à l’œuvre*, Gallimard, 1992. (See also Bataille (e))

Tourrès, Marie. *La Critique sociale. Mars 1931-mars 1934*, thesis, Université des Lettres et Sciences Humaines de Besançon, 1982.

[Waldberg, Isabelle]. *Isabelle Waldberg, sculpteur*, Galerie de la Maison de la Culture et des Loisirs de Gauchy, February-March 1988.

Waldberg, Patrick.
— (a) and Waldberg, Isabelle. “Vers un nouveau mythe? Prémonitions et défiances”, in *VVV* 4, February 1944.
— (b) *Une étoile de craie*, Galerie Lucie Weill, 1973.
— (c) *Taro Okamoto. Le Baladin des antipodes*, Éditions de La Différence, 1976.
— (d) and Waldberg, Isabelle. *Un Amour acéphale: Correspondance 1940-1949*, La Différence, 1992.
— (e) “Acéphalogramme”, *Magazine littéraire*, April 1995.
— (f) *La Clé de cendre*, Éditions de La Différence, 1999.

Will-Levaillant, Françoise. “Masson, Bataille, ou De l’incongruité des signes (1928-1937)”, *Cahiers Bataille* 1, October-November 1981.

*The Sacred Conspiracy* is published by Atlas Press, 27 Old Gloucester st., London WC1N 3XX.

Printed in the UK by CPI Ltd.
A CIP record for this book is available from the British Library.
ISBN-13: 978-1-900565-95-0
This book is supported by the Institut Français (Royaume-Uni) as part of the Burgess Programme (www.frenchbooknews.com), and by the Centre National du Livre.



**Distribution.** UK: Turnaround *www.turnaround-uk.com* USA: Artbook/DAP *www.artbook.com*

MAN IS FREE T

BECAUSE T

RUE
GAY-LUSSAC

AND AIML

THAT GAVE HIM LIFE

GRANTED HIM AN